Chapter One

STEVE, MY YOUNGEST BROTHER and I had had a long night. He had arrived from North Dakota and landed in Harare after almost eighteen hours of non-stop travel. I met him at the airport at 2 a.m. and we decided to go to my house next door to his, to catch up, have a bite to eat and have a glass of our favourite Macallan. At about 5 a.m., we decided that Macallan was having the better of us, so maybe it was time to retire to bed.

In the meantime, we had decided to visit our parents near Rusape, about two hours' drive due east of Harare. We planned to surprise our parents, our ageing Dad, who was now wheelchair bound after suffering a stroke, six years earlier, and his wife, our ageing Mum. We were both excited at the prospect of visiting the old folks and spending quality time with them. It was Friday, April 30th.

As I emerged from a lengthy shower and made my way down to the beckoning aroma of a fry up and steaming coffee, my phone suddenly came to life. I reached for it with a curse and demanded to know who dared to call me at such an ungodly hour on May-day holiday. My anger melted when a familiar voice sobbed at the end of the line, "..who is it?" I asked.

"It's me, Liz the nurse, just to let you know your Dad has just died." I sat on the step and felt my wife, Tinao, gently squeezing my shoulder. Her tears gently dripped onto my neck. We sobbed in silence for a few minutes, then decided to walk next door, to find

Steve. As we got to his gate, the door opened. We walked towards each other and embraced in silence for a few good minutes before sitting down in his lounge. We whispered inaudible words of comfort to each other. We were all devastated. Our plans to visit them would not change, but the day had had a somewhat unexpected beginning.

I had to grow up quickly. We all had to. My thoughts went back to that day Dad told me about my unexpected birth at Holy Family School in the Honde Valley. It was Thursday, November 13th, by all accounts a hot day. Dad, then a teacher at the school, was out with a group of school kids collecting wood and specimens for the next Nature Study class. On his return, three hours later, he was greeted, in the school yard, by a small crowd of pupils singing, "Makorokoto Sir, Congratulations Sir, a baby boy has been born in your house."

Dad reportedly dropped a bundle of sticks, plants and a bag containing live specimens which, no doubt, relished the moment. He leapt towards the little house at breakneck speed. Inside, a midwife proudly whispered that mother was resting but the baby was restless, howling non-stop, clearly agitated. Such was my entrance and welcome to this world. Dad cradled me in his huge arms, sat next to Mum and apparently sang lullabies throughout the night. Reports of feeding and interactions between the adults around the time of my birth and the immediate aftermath are sketchy except one, the naming ceremony.

On hearing of the events of the day, the local priest, Fr. Martin Banda, made his way to the house. On seeing the new-born baby's disproportionately large ears, he concluded that the child would, most likely, grow up to be great like Julius Caesar, thus I was named Julius. In deference to the august Padre's prophecy, my parents then named me Tawona meaning 'We realise God's love,' and for good measure, for a future full of glory and daylight, Bright was added to the tally of names by my godfather, a 'Baba Gibson.' This rather obscure collection of names was rearranged at my christening by

Bon Vivant Banker-Bishop
A Life in my Day

RT. REV. DR. JULIUS T. MAKONI

DORRANCE
PUBLISHING CO
EST. 1920
PITTSBURGH, PENNSYLVANIA 15238

Dorrance Publishing Co
585 Alpha Drive
Suite 103
Pittsburgh, PA 15238
Visit our website at *www.dorrancebookstore.com*

ISBN: 979-8-8881-2374-4
eISBN: 979-8-8881-2874-9

Fr. Maurice Bradshaw C.R. to 'Julius Bright Tawona.' To this day, Baba Gibson remains an elusive figure. Fr. Martin Banda and Fr. Bradshaw, I encountered later in life.

That, in a nutshell, is my birth story. The true beginning of my call to life and adventure. Mercifully, it does not contain many confusing details which could cause pain or induce numbness in my inner being like the news I had just received about Dad's passing. Therefore, not much to detox. It is, however, a tale of love and life in an idyllic if different setting.

The day is going fast. I am vaguely aware of the news I received to start the day, but I cannot focus or dwell on that for now. I call my parents' house to speak to Mum, not sure what exactly I would say to her. My niece, Maud, answers the phone and sobs, "Nan is in Grandpa's room with him. She has not left the room since he passed away two hours ago." Tears well-up in my eyes. Increasingly, it dawns on me that I am awake and what I have just heard is indeed real. I will not see my father alive when I get to my parents' house later today.

I sneak into the bathroom off our tiny gym and sob briefly under my breath, wash my face, and re-emerge a few minutes later, to face the day again. Steven calls to inform me that his friend from Medical school, Jerry, has arrived and they are about to set off to arrange for a death certificate, burial order and other official documents that are required. Tinao is there to embrace me. We stand still, locked in silent embrace for some moments, then sigh simultaneously and look out the bedroom window.

The day has a feel like that day when, as a three-year-old, I sat on the floor in the kitchen at St James school Zongoro, just outside Mutare along the Nyanga Road and listened to my Mum narrate the story of her recently deceased father to Fr. Bradshaw C.R. and Fr. Jacob Waddle C.R. Grandpa was a member of the police contingent based at the Rural Camp, in Umtali. He had been out with friends, had dinner, and was found dead by a neighbour in his dining room, around midday the following day. He had not been ill, indeed had survived a stint in Tanganyika with the King's African Rifles, as a soldier and came home with decorations for bravery. Like his colleagues, he had been de-mobbed and reassigned to a special police force comprising ex-military personnel. Nobody ever found out what killed him, but rumours of food poisoning floated about for many years after his death.

It was fortuitous that we were stationed at St James, where my parents had met as young adults and got married. Dad was a teacher at the school, and Mum was a student in her final year before college. Mum went to school there because her family, Mawondo, came from a village of the same name, about 3 kilometres due west of Zongoro. The Mawondos were Methodists, and their church and mission station, Mundenda Church and School, was a further kilometre from their homestead. Grandma lived at Mawondo village with my Mum's brothers, Robin, his wife Alice and their two little children, Jonathan (named after Mum's Dad) and Ellen (named after my maternal Granny). Mum was the eldest of nine children, four girls and five boys.

I used to look forward to Nan's visits or any of my uncles. These were festive occasions, usually with lots of fruits, other goodies like candy and dried meats, my favourite being dried rock rabbits that were casualties of Uncle Robin's hunting trips in the mountains, or the demise of Nan's chickens or occasionally, a billy goat. Mum's youngest sister Mildred or Maddy, as she was affectionately known, lived with us. She helped Mum with household chores. I will spare my readers genethliac detail.

Then, Dad was in the first year of his three years training for the Ministry at St. Peter's College, Rosettenville, an Anglican Seminary in South Africa, answering his calling to serve as a priest. The College was run by C.R. fathers from Mirfield, U.K. In Zimbabwe, the C.R. Fathers were based at St Augustine's Mission, Penhalonga, half an hour outside Mutare, due north. They had outreach posts where they stayed while on pastoral duty in the eastern districts of the diocese. They established schools, churches and clinics to serve the local communities. St James Zongoro was the first such outpost with a large church designed and built by Fr. Waddle. St James Mission station was also a centre where ordinands' wives and children were housed during the years their spouses attended St Peter's College.

The dedication, warmth, and commitment of the C.R. Fathers in their white cassocks and grey monastic scapulars, a sign of their readiness to serve, was forever etched on my mind. They traversed the length and breadth of the diocese on foot. They had three donkeys to carry their belongings. These were usually first aid supplies, religious literature, tuck, mostly dry biscuits, water and sometimes tinned beef and packets of candy. They were assisted by a man, Bessenia, about 20, I thought. He looked after the donkeys, loaded and offloaded supplies. We always ran up the footpath from the main road when we heard shouts of, "Father and Bessenia are coming!" On one such rush to meet my tall hero, Fr. Waddle, I tripped, fell and grazed my left knee which bled in little red spots.

As I howled in pain, Fr. Waddle gently crouched and collected me in his lanky arms, put me on his back and walked towards the kitchen where Mum was preparing tea for the guests. She watched in obvious embarrassment as I sat on Fr. Waddle's knee. He dried my face and washed off the tiny spots of blood from my grazed knee dabbed purple 'g.v.e. ointment' on the wounds. He bribed me with candy to stop sobbing. The pain instantly melted away as I basked in my newfound celebrity status and heavenly candy bliss, much to the envy of my playmates, my sister Emilia, a year and half older than me, my buddy, George Segura and a neighbor's daughter, about my age, Malliet Mandimutsira.

The highlight of the monks' arrival was Compline or evening prayers. Mum's loud singing of the hymn, "Before the ending of the day, Creator of the world we pray…" was always a source of much screeching and suppressed laughter among the children who were there to watch these mighty holy men speak eloquently in impressively nasal tones. We would imitate them as we were frog-marched to bed and told off for being unruly during prayers. Apart from the odd 'discreet' crow peck, or a quickly boxed or cuffed ear, we were never openly manhandled in the presence of the visitors. They were always welcome, as far as we, the children were concerned...after all we did not have to feed them nor did we have to boil water for them to wash their faces in the grey water basins that Mum kept on the veranda, each with a little blue face towel.

It was always a thrill for all the children to have the monks around. We got to eat rice and chicken for the main meal, a welcome break from sadza and beef stew. We were also treated to hot sweet tea with a hunk of brown bread at breakfast, not the usual millet porridge that was the staple otherwise. After meals, we would all sit on the floor while the Fathers read to us in turn. I particularly liked the thin, vatic-looking and avuncular Fr. James Woodrow, who read animatedly. He taught us music, nursery rhymes and how to pronounce English words 'properly.' This entailed how to read fluently, slowly rounding vowels and stressing consonants always. He was the ultimate solitudinarian.

We would imitate their accents, especially the way they sang or recited the Psalms. Great entertainment, we thought! Fr. Waddle's lessons were not so popular: he made us learn how to count, add and spell. He did not always remember to reward us with sweets when we got things right. Later in life, about twenty years later, the C.R. fathers who had taught Dad at St Peter's College would visit us. Mum had to cook for them while they told us stories about Dad's college escapades, especially his two friends, Khotso Makhulu and Desmond Tutu (both great Archbishops in later life!). I still had to read passages from 'Under Western Eyes' for Fr. Godfrey Pawson and Fr. Trevor Huddleston and discuss the significance of Conrad's analysis of the 'Soviet Condition' with them. I was then reading English Literature in High school. How history repeats itself!

The core values of hard work with dedication, a life of prayer and eloquence in speech were thus instilled in us at a very tender age and reinforced periodically during adolescence. I often smile when I look back or when I hear people comment on my unusually staid accent or on my insistence on well-written, thorough reports. I have these monks to thank for that foundation. It got me into trouble with my History teacher in high School. He pronounced 'Jean Jacques Rousseau' as 'Gin Jakwes Russo' during a lesson. I promptly packed up my notepad and textbook, informed him loudly that if he could not pronounce that name properly, he had no right to teach me. The headmaster heard about it and clearly had no idea how to discipline me. I got away with it. Cuthbert, Sir, my then history teacher, apparently still refers to me as *'that pompous shit'* and *'every inch a twerp'*. I felt better for it and strangely, still do.

One bright hot day in October 1959, my sister Emmie ran into the kitchen and yelled at the top of her voice that there was a big fat man lying on Mum's bed! Unmoved, Mum informed her that that man was Dad, her father. He had finally returned home after his studies and would be ordained soon. We were to help pack all our belongings because a removal van would arrive soon to take us to our new home, St. Michael's Parish, Harare, the high-density suburb that is now Mbare.

Uncle Aaron, my aunt Victoria's son, arrived that afternoon to help us pack. He was a jovial man in his early twenties. He brought us green mealies and sweet potatoes which he kept pulling out of his musette. These were presents from his Mum who had planted early crops in her garden near Umtali, now Mutare. Aaron helped Dad carry the lounge furniture which consisted of two dull green sofas and a round coffee table with four little tables under it. They tied everything securely, especially the beds and mattresses, a little pram with a purple cover, mother's 'welcome dover' wood stove and a kitchen cabinet. At about three in the afternoon, they took a break and sat down to a big lunch of sadza, beef stew and biltong that mother had kept specially for Dad.

We did not partake in the biltong because, as we were told, it was not good for us. In any case, there was not enough of it to go round. We were given small cups of sweet Mazoe orange crush drink instead of biltong. We were quite happy with that. As lunch finished, Aaron sprang to his feet, grabbed a hoe that was lying nearby and ran towards the house. A huge rat had emerged from one of the rooms and was scurrying around the house. It was clearly in somewhat unfamiliar territory especially with Aaron and Dad in hot pursuit! The chase was brief as was the rest of the rat's life. He was mashed and beloboured into pulp before being dumped on the rubbish heap where he would be lunch for the crows or eagles that nested in the huge gum tree near the church.

We were all helped aboard the truck and driven away from St James Zongoro as dusk approached. George Segura and his elder brother, Gift, Malliet and Bridgette Mandimutsira and my Aunt Mildred were in tears as they waved goodbye. Aunt Maddy was to join us in Harare a few weeks later. I was to return to St. James Zongoro almost forty years later, as bishop!

Chapter Two

MY MEMORIES OF OUR HOUSE in Mbare, on the circle in front of Sister Barbra's Mansion on Runyararo Crescent, are vivid. It was a small two-bedroomed house with egg-white coloured walls and an asbestos roof. It was in a row of similar township houses, no. 1758 Runyararo Crescent. Next door, number 1759, I discovered shortly after we arrived, was Dad's fellow ordinand, (Fr.) Noel Mutemararo and his family. In 1760, was Fr. Francis Munyavi and his family. These were three houses reserved for the Anglican curates at St. Michael's parish. Access onto our property was through a small wooden croft, onto a grassy pathway leading to a little green front door. This was a massive improvement from our previous accommodation at Zongoro, which had comprised a two-roomed red brick house and a little adjoining round kitchen, all in brown thatch that had seen better days.

The main room in our new house was a lounge cum dining area facing the street, a small master bedroom on the west, with a smaller bedroom, the boys' room, adjoining it. The girls would use the dining/lounge area as their bedroom. They slept on mats on the floor. There was a small kitchen at the back of the house with a door that led into the shower-room cum toilet, which was a hole in the floor with a hanging chain to flush the toilet. In keeping with the rest of the houses in the neighbourhood, there was no hot water geyser.

Just outside the kitchen was a narrow patch of garden, about four square metres, where, without wasting time, Mum planted a row of vegetables, rape, tomatoes and carrots, watered by washing up water from the kitchen and the scullery which consisted of a metal sink and a tap attached to the wall at the back of the house.

Beyond the vegetable patch was a wooden fence partially hiding our neighbours at the back, Baba wa Siriza, they were called. They were migrant workers from Nyasaland, now Malawi. They spoke a mix of Shona and Nyanja, seemingly ceaselessly and always at the top of their voices. Their radio blasted music and news bulletins all day, straight into our backyard and kitchen. This was to be our home for the next two years.

My first task was to explore the neighbourhood, make friends and get familiar with who is who in the zoo. Our clergy family neighbours had children of various ages. Next door was Dennis Mutemararo who was my sister's age, and his Aunt, Catherine or 'Tete Cassy' as we called her. Tete Cassy was a postulant, training to be a nun with the CZR sisters (Chita Che Zita Rinoyera/ Order of the Holy Name), based at St Augustine's, Penhalonga. Then there was Sam Munyavi, who was a journalist, his younger brother Godfrey, who was my sister's age, and their two sisters, Beata and Margret. Margret was tiny, light in complexion and very pretty. We became friends and playmates. Sam, who worked for the newspapers, was said to be very clever. We hardly ever saw him. He always appeared serious.

Dad was a big man, about six foot two, with huge hands and stocky legs. He had been an athlete, a famous boxer in his day and a competent rugby and soccer player. He was blessed with a booming deep voice that he used to good effect in chanting or singing baritone in church. Fr. Noel was also very tall, about six foot four, and very thin. He spoke very softly and gave the appearance of being shy and diffident. Fr. Munyavi was light in complexion, about five foot eight. He had a permanent smile on his face and spoke very softly. The boss, the Rector, Fr. Edward Chipunza, who lived in a detached house across the road from us was short, stocky, noticeably light in complexion and had a gruffy, soft but friendly voice and an extremely dignified air about him.

Mother, at about five foot six or seven, was the tallest of the clergy wives. Always cheerful, talkative and restless, with something to say about every little thing, but above all, an excellent Mother. Mrs. Mutemararo was short, dark and very shy unlike the garrulous Mrs. Munyavi, originally from South Africa. She was light in complexion with bright white eyes, a sing song voice and quite small in stature. Mrs. Chipunza was loud, thin, dark and commanded an imposing figure of authority among the other women, as the Rector's wife.

In the double storey house on the other side of the road lived five white spinsters, volunteer workers, Missionaries from England. They helped run church institutions, nursery schools, clinics, youth groups etc. They were all addressed as 'Sister.' In charge was Sister Barbra Tredgold. Her brother was the then Chief Justice of Southern Rhodesia. She was a stern, large lady with a pair of glasses perched on her nose. Her colleagues were Sister Emma Jane, a short, stocky lady with a motherly disposition, Sister Sybil Lister, always smiling, Sister Gillian, always well perfumed and very pretty, Sister Catharine Dinnis and Sister Shirley Morrel who smoked ceaselessly.

Behind the Sisters' mansion was St Michael's Church. It was an imposing building with extremely high whitewashed walls, large black double doors and a large scary mosaic of the Archangels Michael and Gabriel in a porch where the hearse trolley was kept. Inside, there was always a lingering whiff of incense and a numinous if overpowering, peaceful atmosphere. I always expected to see the figure of Jesus or some other biblical character gaze at me from one of the mosaics on the walls, especially the large colourful one of Father Abraham by the eastern door, complete with a large thurible sensor with smoke billowing from it. Just a few feet inside the church via the western entrance stood a rather high pulpit with narrow steps leading to the podium inside it. I have vivid memories of Dad booming sermons from the tiny pulpit and banging his large hands on its fragile top, to drive home points of theological if eschatological significance. Morning prayers, Holy Mass/ Eucharist and Evensong were held daily except Mondays and Saturdays. All curates were present at these services.

Sunday Mass was always an event I looked forward to. The one service I remember was Dad's ordination to the priesthood. He had been a deacon for three months. Usually deacons had to serve in a parish under a senior priest for a period of no less than twelve months before they were priested. In Dad's case, the rule was waived because the Bishop, Cecil Alderson, felt that Dad had received adequate training under Fr. Trevor Huddleston at Sophia town parish and had good references from his teachers at St Peter's College and current training incumbent, Fr. Chipunza. The Bishop needed a 'strong, reliable and energetic priest' to build up and foster a young congregation at a recently planted church, St. Paul's in the high-density suburb/township of Highfield.

September 21st, 1960, Mum woke us up early in the morning. The service would start at 6.00 a.m. because the Bishop had to be somewhere else after the service. We all dressed up in our Sunday best clothes. I wore grey shorts, a white, short sleeved shirt and a pair of new black shoes. We all had had our heads shaved at the barber shop near the market the day before. We must have looked like baby mice as we huddled in the front pew and woke up to loud singing of the introit hymn, 'Immortal, Invisible God only Wise,' as the servers and clergy processed into the church from the vestry on the eastern side of the church. Bishop Cecil Alderson, preceded by Archdeacon Spencer the Bishop's Chaplain, Fr. Lee, priests including Fr. Noel Borerwe, Fr. Munyavi, Fr. Nyahwa and the Rector, Fr. Chipunza made up the rest of the procession.

The service was long, the singing was very loud. Mother, flanked by Dad's elder brother, Uncle James, a.k.a. Ishe Kamba, was clearly in seventh heaven as people came after the service to shake hands and greet her and congratulate Dad. We had a feast in the church hall adjacent to the church on the Beatrice Cottages side of the church yard, after the service. Large portions of eggs, bacon, toast and rolls were liberally served. This, for all the kids, was the best part of the occasion. I would daydream and imagine me as an ordinand, bishop or just any one of those processing clerics. They all looked so holy in their cassocks and clerical outfits.

I wanted to be dressed like them, sit in those big chairs at the front of the church during services and give people Holy Communion. I would dream about preaching to masses of people as they sat quietly, listening to my message, thoughts and 'words of wisdom.' In a moment of enthusiasm and possessed by an inexplicable sense of holiness and desiring to be of use to the church community, I told Dad about my dreams as a preacher. He smiled, lit a cigarette, then as he exhaled, explained to me that I had to go to school first, read a lot of books, pass many exams before anyone would even consider my little dreams. I was deflated but determined to make a start by going to school. By hook or crook, I was determined, holus-bolus, to make my dream a reality one day.

When Dad announced at dinner, a few days after his ordination, that we had all been enrolled and were to start school in a few days, I could not contain my excitement. My sister, Emmie and Aunt Maddy, were to start primary school at Nharira school, which was a government primary school near the Community centre. I was to go to nursery school, St. Nicholas Preparatory School. It was run by the Missionaries. It was near their mansion. I was in tears as I waved goodbye to Mum and Dad at the school gate. Miss Naomi, my tutor, took me by the hand and led me to a classroom with about fifteen other newcomers. She was fair in complexion, very tall and slim, and had a smile revealing bright white teeth. Her hair was short and brown. She smelt very nicely of exotic perfume, I concluded.

I was introduced to a chubby boy dressed in smart khaki shorts, a blue short-sleeved shirt and grey socks nestled in a pair of comfortable-looking shiny brown shoes. "I am Morrith," he stuttered.

"Maurice," Miss Naomi said helpfully. Not that it made any difference to me. This boy was to be my best friend and partner in crime for many years to come. Maurice was quiet but had a cheeky smile and a naughty glint in his eyes. He was my exact age, only a couple of months older. He always sucked his index and middle fingers determinedly. This looked so cool but after a couple of trials, I concluded that finger suckling was not for me. His mild manner and lisp lent themselves to hypocorism, thus 'Morrith' became his name.

We settled down after a period of shuffling and shoving. We soon got down to the serious business of nursery rhymes, tunes and the all-important alphabet. Thanks to the C.R. Fathers, I had had a head start. By tea break, about an hour later, I was exhausted. My new friend Morrith was fast asleep. We were all shaken up and marched into the little courtyard where we were told to 'visit the toilet,' wash our hands and return quickly for a rock bun and warm milk served in little plastic cups. If school continued like this, I was in seventh heaven, I mused.

At this time, we met the headmistress, Miss Esnath Mlambo. She was dark, stern and appeared unforgiving. My spirits were so dampened I could not wait to retreat to Miss Naomi's class where my buddy Morrith, awaited me with crayons and lots of paper on which we drew colourful masterpieces that by now should be hanging on museum walls somewhere where art lovers go, but maybe were appropriately filed in the dustbin of immediate and now ancient history.

The next highlight of the day was grace, 'Bless Oh Lord the food I take and Bless me too for Jesus sake, Amen,' followed by lunch, almost always stewed beef with at least a ton of diced carrots in the bowl and two slices of brown bread. This was washed down with a small glass of orange Mazoe crush. We were then taken to a large room with pre-assigned little beds and towels. It was nap time. I slept next to Morrith and by now I had figured out that he was Mr. Mutsonziwa, the churchwarden's son. I thought he had looked vaguely familiar! I had met him at Sunday school. He was in Mr. Gibson Keda's group. We sat and either fell asleep listening to Bible stories or looked longingly out the hall windows to see when the parents would appear next as we were starving after the service. Mr. Keda had a nice soft voice that lulled us all into deep sleep as soon as his class began. No wonder I hardly remembered who else was in my little group of seven.

Nap time or siesta went very quickly, an hour never felt so short. Then it was time to learn about counting numbers. I preferred the songs and rhymes of the morning. Numbers were boring and after thirty or so minutes of this, the teachers obviously agreed with us because they gave us more milk with two biscuits each and told us that it was now time to go home because the time was four o'clock. Whatever! School wasn't that bad after all. Just the numbers were out of place. Typical of adults, I concluded, always fun-prevention agents, ready to find a way to ruin a good thing!

That routine established, it remained largely so until the period leading up to Christmas. We were split into little groups and given parts to rehearse for the Christmas pageant which was to be acted out in the courtyard, with admiring parents and relatives in attendance. We took this very seriously because it came with welcome incentives in the form of cookies at intervals and promises of exciting presents on the day, if we were good actors and made the audience happy.

The big day could not have arrived soon enough. I sneaked out from behind Miss Naomi, peeped through the window to make sure that Mum and Dad were in the audience. This meant the difference between having or not having a present! Serious business indeed. I saw them and then calmed down. Morrith did the same. We looked at each other and smiled. Then the play began with sheep dressed in little white dresses led by a shepherd in a striped costume, green and white, with a walking stick. Then a star, my cousin Jessie, dressed in white with a huge star stuck to her chest, worked her way round the giggling flock and their shy shepherd.

So it went until the three wise men, Solomon, Simon and Morrith walked in carrying gifts, looked at the star which by now stood behind a crib in which Eve sat with a doll draped in white cloth placed neatly on her lap. Meanwhile the rest of the boys and girls sang Christmas carols directed by Sister Emma Jane. At the end of what seemed like an endless procession and long hours of waiting, I was nudged as a sign to make the grand entrance.

I was dressed up as a bishop, with a big red mitre on my head and a white cope that dragged on the floor like a bride's gown. In my left hand I carried a wooden staff, which bore a remarkable resemblance to the crozier that Bishop Cecil, who sat in the front row, always carried in church. As I entered the arena to the hymn 'Come O ye Faithful,' I walked, with one eye roving from the bishop to my parents, then the crib. I blessed the baby to loud cheers. Thus, my stardom was established! I did not have to be persuaded to get out of my costume and push my way to the presents' corner where I was handed a book of nursery rhymes, a mechanical butterfly and a chocolate bunny rabbit by the Bishop himself. Instead of Mazoe crush, we were treated to a soft drink, 'hubbly bubbly cola.' What a treat.

That evening, I basked in praise as my sister and aunty Maddy listened and went green with envy. Everything then faded as exhaustion clearly set in. When I woke up, it was Saturday morning, Emmie was pulling me out of bed to help with the chores. This morning, I was to sweep the front yard with a palm branch broom. This was a bit of a come down, especially as I looked up and saw my beautiful playmate, Margret, looking at me and giggling at the sight. I almost melted with embarrassment.

Chapter Three

IT IS NOW 10:00 A.M. The day now seems to be fast forwarding. I am still teary and reeling from the morning news of Dad's passing. I am now trying to remember who else to call. I call my brother, Dominic. After what seemed like a hundred redials, I finally managed to shout the news down a crackly line. Silence. "I'll make a U-turn," he sobbed. "I was on my way to an in-law's funeral in Bindura. Thanks, Nyati." The line went dead. I sat on the bed and took a few deep breaths, then called my other brother, Nathaniel, who, I remembered, was travelling between Tanzania and Kenya at this time. The phone rang. I got a connection straight away.

Natha received the news in silence. "I will come over right away," was all he could muster. I exhaled deeply and looked at Tinao who sat next to me in a daze. I hugged her and forced a little smile.

"I will miss him," she said. She and he were mutual admiration club mates.

Just those few words set off memories of the day we 'graduated' from St. Nicholas. We all hugged each other, cried and wished each other well. It felt like the wonderful world of fun, rhymes, awful numbers, milk and biscuits, beef stew with peas and diced carrots, Miss Naomi and all the friends we had made had suddenly and horribly ended. Will I see Morrith again, I wondered. In typical fashion, my best buddy just looked at me with that cheeky smile playing on his face, then calmly told me that his 'berfdey' was upcoming and we were all going to meet again and share cookies at his Mum's. She was a nurse at the dispensary near the church. This cheered me up no end and made the walk home bearable.

I need not have worried about seeing Morrith again. After his party which was in his garden, with a blue plastic swimming tub, lots of cupcakes, sweet cool drinks and much fun and games, we met again on the first day of school, Shingirayi primary school in Mbare. Some of our friends from St Nicholas were also in our class, Simon Madzime, Derek Manyande, Wendy M'pambawashe, Jessie Mupfekeri, Charles Zvimba, Charles Manyeza, Solomon (who Morrith called 'the terrorist') and Hope Daudi (who we called Hope-Doubt), Livingstone Mutandwa, Joyce, Shakington Golden and Loveridge, who were ' coloured' and lived in Ardbennie, Charles Bassoppo-Moyo, a wholly delightful eccentric with an unerring talent for trouble, sadly destined for an early death. His family had a grocery store near the church and David, who was very dark and had younger twin brothers, Patrick and Patterson.

It was a mini reunion. Morrith and I were inseparable. We sat on little desks next to each other near the back of the class. We had two teachers, Mr. Mashava, whose son Bernard was our classmate, and Mrs. Chieza, whose daughter, Nancy, was also our classmate. The school principal was a very tall white man with a long, neat, red beard, Mr. Chapman. He smoked a pipe. I never saw him smile.

School was enjoyable, especially English, arithmetic and music. We also did a 'general paper' which was a combination of current affairs, history, geography and nature study. Bible studies followed assembly every morning where notices were announced, heard and forgotten instantly. The boys wore brown khakis, short sleeved shirts, orange ties and a pair of shorts, grey socks and black shoes. Girls wore white blouses and red skirts. I think we looked smart in the morning but normal and untidy as the day progressed.

School started at seven in the morning. We had break or recess at nine when we were served rock buns and cold milk. More lessons followed until noon when school was officially over. It was now time for lunch before sports. I hated athletics but enjoyed high jump and rugby. Maurice, as he now was, as opposed to Morrith, loved to play ball bare foot. He loved all sports especially 'head cricket' and was good at it. Afternoon activities included boy scouts, or cubs as we were called. Once a week, we went to the cinema, or bioscope, as we called it, at Stodart Hall, near the market.

At the movies, we never paid attention to the dialogue. We sat and chatted until the critical shout 'fight!' rang through the hall, we then all rose and shouted, "Aah Wuu, Aah Wuu!" whenever the hero landed a punch, "Bootsu!" when he kicked and "Nzveeeeh!" when he ducked. After the fight, we resumed chatting or munching popcorn. When the cowboy film was over, we sprang up, and trotted home imitating the cowboys and Indians. It was either cowboys and Indians or Tarzan films that we enjoyed the most. All cartoons we called 'ma Popeyes,' Tom and Jerry were my favourite Popeye characters.

To complete the routine was the Thursday afternoon meeting of all cub scouts. We wore khaki short sleeved shirts, shorts, grey stockings and black shoes. Around the collar we wore red cotton scarfs with a blue triangle at the back. The scarf was held tougher in front by a hollow bone that we called a 'woggle,' or a leather fastener. The bone was the preferred item. The scout leader, Akela, carried a long staff with a large, plastic wolf head stuck on one end. We would crouch around Akela and shout, 'Akela, we'll do our best! Then spring up, to salute him with 'dip, dip, dip, dip, dop, dop, dop!' whatever that meant, it felt good and grown up too.

The climax of my stint as a scout cub was a trip to Ruwa Scout Camp along the Umtali Road, to meet Lord Baden Powell. There were thousands of scouts of all ages. Morris kept me by him and impressed me by pushing off two white boys, our age, who had rudely shoved their way into the front of the ice-cream queue. When they shouted some racist words at us, Morris bravely stood his ground firmly amidst a sea of little white faces, with the unforgettable 'Mufana, ndinokumamitha" (little boy, I will beat the shit out of you). That was my Morrith, my hero. That was the best ice cream I enjoyed as a boy scout!

Amazingly, this was the same friend Morrith who took great pleasure in watching his boisterous, large Alsatian puppy jump at me and 'harass' me whenever I went to his house to play. He would roar with laughter as I sobbed in obvious discomfort as the wretched dog licked and pounced on me repeatedly. His dad (Giles) almost always had to stick his head out of his study window, near the entrance, by the kitchen, and tell his son to call the dog away. In his dad's absence, his sister, Olivia, or elder brother, Charles, would come to my assistance. His Mum would apologise and inspect my legs for scratches and bruises. There never was any, but the attention at least took me away from the dog who quickly lost interest and crept to sleep under the dad's desk.

Our other close friend, Charles Zvimba, lived at the end of Chinamora Street, in Mbare. We used to love visiting them because they had a television set. We sat and watched Popeyes. Charles had an elder brother, Petros, and a sister, Margret. Their Mum was a teacher and their Dad worked as a head messenger and supervisor at a bank in town. The family car was a little grey Anglia. They came to church every Sunday. Next door to them was The Mangundhla family, who also had a television set which we would ogle from time to time.

We preferred their house because their beautiful daughter, Diana, would give us popcorn and the brothers, Kenneth, Carson and Clifford, sang in the church choir. Cuthbert, the youngest brother, was still at nursery school. They had a stall at the main market, where they sold clothes. They had two cars, a Dodge and a Chevrolet. They were all so cool. I also liked Moses Maisiri, who lived on Rakgajani Street. He had a little brother, Mutsa, and two elder brothers, John, a teacher who sang baritone in the choir and Peter, who was very tall. They also came to church regularly. Moses' Dad worked for Lion Match Company.

In the three years that we lived at Runyararo, my two brothers, Dominic and Nathaniel were born in August 1960 and October 1962, respectively. They were both born at Harare Community Centre near Nharira Government primary school, Emmie's school. The circumstances were remarkably similar in that we were all at school and came home late afternoon to hear the news of the recent additions to the family, from Dad. A day later, in each case, the bundle of joy was carefully carried out of Uncle Murape's car. We would hold the little bundle in turns, as we sat in the lounge. Lots of people came by throughout the day, with presents, mainly baby clothes. It was a time of joy for everyone.

Dad was always cheerful. Mum almost always busy breastfeeding in her room and therefore not issuing instructions to us to run errands such as tidying up the front yard. I was free to visit Morrith, Charles and Moses or go to the grocery stores to watch big boys play table football or listen to loud music over the loudspeakers on the veranda at the shops. I was spoilt for choice without FPOs! (Fun prevention officers).

Returning from one of these free jaunts one afternoon, I bumped into Dad who asked me what I had been up to. Not satisfied with my answer, he asked me if I had read any books, done my homework or offered to help round the house. I could not acquit myself credibly. I was then sentenced to spending my afternoons with Dad, outside his office, reading books, doing my homework while he worked at his desk or talked to his visitors. At this time Dad had been assigned to St Paul's Church, Highfield, to foster and grow a recently planted church, near the new Roman Catholic church. All this had a silver lining to it as I got to ride with Dad on his new scooter that the parish had given him for his pastoral work. The ride from the house in Mbare to Jabavu Drive, Highfield was fun. Dad always made sure I had a tickey (three penny piece) to buy my lunch, a 'dough-cake,' from the lady vendors at the little gate near the churchyard. Life could not be better. I was the envy of every boy in the neighbourhood.

Towards the end of our third year in our little house at Runyararo, we moved into a bigger house near Number One Stadium, now Rufaro Stadium. The house had just been vacated by the new Rector, Fr. Mandihlare, who moved into the new rectory near the church hall. The house had four bedrooms, a lounge, a big kitchen and a large veranda. From the veranda, one could see the Mbare hostels across the road, the stadium, and the sprawling Remembrance Drive cemetery opposite Mupedzanhamo market.

There was a large garden in the front yard, where Mum set to work without delay, growing vegetables and maize near the fruit trees, mangoes, peaches and guavas. The walk to school from here was about twenty minutes and more exciting than before as the winding route took me through the main Musika market, past the nurses' hostel Carter House, past the newly built Evangelical church near Chirodzo school, past Chitsere school, then past our church to Shingirayi school. I loved this walk as there was always something new to see.

Saturdays and Sundays were usually noisy as there was always something going on at the stadium. I had the pleasure of seeing my first football match at the stadium, Number One Ground. I was not really into football, but Dad was a fan, so took me to see a match. I was more interested in the ice cream trolleys and snack vendors who kept advertising their wares noisily as the game progressed. My most memorable visit to the stadium was to a boxing match between Beira Tar Baby and Dhuri, for the heavyweight championship of the country. Dhuri won by a knockout. Visions of a bloodied Tar Baby kept me awake for many days afterwards. I enjoyed the loud crowd rooting for their man.

Dad cheered Dhuri on. Before the main bout we had watched Zaka Madziwa and Jiwa Margarine fight for the light heavyweight crown. The fight was dull. No-one got hurt, but Zaka won. On the way home, Dad told me none of those boxers we saw would last a minute with him in the same ring. I felt a shiver run down my spine. I held firmly onto his hand as we walked through the crowd. I believed him. I had heard stories of his boxing days when he was a student. I felt safe.

Of all the dramas that unfolded in the two years we lived in the curate's house near the Mbare hostels, four have been etched into my mind indelibly. Foremost is the day Dad turned up at our school mid-morning, unannounced, holding my sister firmly. He spoke to the teacher in a low voice and then told me we had to go home immediately. He looked incredibly sad and anxious, I dared not ask why we had to go home in this way. My sister looked confused and stared ahead as we walked briskly through the market, to the house.

As we approached the house, I noticed that Aunt Maddy and Anna Mademutsa were outside the house near the veranda, comforting my younger brothers. We were all led into my parents' bedroom where my Mum's brother, Uncle Nelson and two women clad in Mothers' Union uniform sat and knelt around the bed on which Mum lay breathing through her mouth intermittently in a hoarse guttural sound. Dad looked at us and said, "Mum is dying. Let us pray." We prayed. We were all in tears as the ambulance arrived. Mum was carried away. Dad accompanied Mum in the ambulance.

Late in the evening I asked Uncle Nelson why Mum had died. He told me that she had been bitten by mosquitoes and contracted bad malaria. I declared a war against mosquitoes from then on. I still have a phobia when it comes to the little devils. As we sat silently, the door opened and Dad walked in. He called us all to join him in prayer. He sobbed as he thanked God for sparing Mum's life. He announced that she had regained consciousness and the doctor said she would be well and home in a week. I have re-lived those moments a thousand times in my life. The scenes remain vivid. I hate mosquitoes. I believe in the power of prayer.

Then there was the day I remember as the 'political violence episode day.' There was much political activity and violence especially in the high-density suburbs of Salisbury. On this Friday night, Joshua Nkomo was said to be in town, speaking at political rallies. This was the time ZANU had just split up from ZAPU and the two political groups were at each other's throats, murdering, burning houses and hurling missiles at each other at any available opportunity. Mum and Dad had returned in the early evening from a political party meeting at Stoddart Hall. As we settled down to dinner, we heard a strident screech as a short, dark, well-dressed woman hurled herself into the house seeking shelter from a mob in hot pursuit.

Dad ordered her to lock herself in the little toilet near the kitchen and told her to switch the light off. We were told to retire to our bedroom and sit quietly in darkness. Mum locked all the doors and as she drew the curtains in the main lounge, there was a loud knock on the windows at the front of the house and shouting accompanied by banging on the back door. There were shouts of, "Pastor, she is a sell-out, we want to teach her a lesson." After a scary moment that felt like an eternity, Dad went to the front door and opened it then stood firmly in the doorway. The mob shouted again that they wanted the woman who had sought refuge in our house. In a booming voice Dad addressed them and told them to leave immediately as there was no fugitive in the house. He offered to let one of them to come in and search the house for the fugitive. They all declined the offer. After a few moments of humming and buzzing among themselves, they dispersed slowly.

As they were dispersing, a loud shout rang out to say that another sell-out had been discovered hiding in the hedge along the pathway separating our house and the Dutch Reformed Church. Within seconds we could hear a man screaming as the mob lynched him furiously with loud volleys of sounding thwacks. Dad locked all the doors and called out to the refugee in the loo to come out as the danger had passed. Mum hugged the woman and sobbed, "Victoria, you need to be careful. Herbert is in exile and you need to stay home and look after your kids." Dad echoed Mum's sentiments and later explained to us that the woman was Victoria Chitepo. Her husband was a school friend of Dad's from St. Augustine's, Penhalonga. Later that week, I was asked to remain in Dad's white Vauxhall Velox car and hand over the keys to a big light man who would come and ask for them.

The man turned up. He looked huge to me, gently authoritative but had very kind features on his face. A little smile played on his lips and a well-groomed stubble on his upper lip looked neat. I handed over the keys. He handed me two shillings and six pence and told me not to tell anyone about our meeting. I did not hang about. I headed straight to the shops to spend my well-earned cash. Hebert Chitepo drove away in Dad's car. The next and last time I saw Mr. Chitepo was a fortnight later when he returned Dad's car. He slipped the keys into my hands and vanished behind the Church Hall leaving no trace. He left a huge impression on my little brain. I felt useful and important.

Then there was the Saturday we woke up to find Mum's garden vandalised and all her green vegetables uprooted, cut and stolen. The garden was Mum's pride and joy. Apart from growing fresh vegetables, varieties of spinach, rape, covolo, onions, tomatoes, pumpkins, cucumbers, potatoes and carrots for our use, the garden was a showpiece of Mum's hard work. Auntie Maddy, Sis Anna Mademutsa and Emmie came into the house screaming and sobbing as they told Mum what had happened to her garden. Mum's face dropped. She almost tripped over her lip as she stumbled out of the back door to witness the sight for herself. She was shortly joined by Dad who had slipped into his blue overalls and gumboots. After a short discussion, Dad jumped onto his scooter and rode off to report this heinous crime to the police at Matapi Police Station.

While Dad was at the Police, Mum decided to head for the main market, Mbare Musika, to see if she could identify her vegetables among all the vendors. We stayed at home, distressed and wondered what would happen next. We rushed out when we heard Dad's scooter splutter in the front yard. We wasted no time in telling him what Mum's plan was. Dad jumped back onto his scooter and rode towards Mbare Musika at top speed. The parents returned late afternoon exhausted but cheerful. Success! The thieves had been caught.

Mum confronted two men who were trying to offload an assortment of vegetables to vendors, some of whom were well-known to Mum. Upon hearing Mum's story, the regular vendors helped her to approach two unfamiliar vendors and demanded to know the origin of their vegetables. The police were called in. They interrogated the culprits who eventually confessed to their crime. They were arrested. The money they had collected was given to Mum as were the rest of the vegetables, which were then sold to regular vendors. Various versions of the events and heroics of that day are still told whenever the family gathers. This one is authentic.

The fourth event happened at the time Dad and Mum came back from Uncle Sam Parirenyatwa's funeral, in August 1962. He was Dad's cousin, our family doctor. He had a surgery near the market in Mbare. Uncle Sam had been travelling to Bulawayo when his car collided with a train at Heaney junction just after Shangani. He was then Vice President of ZAPU and therefore a prominent politician. There were reports that he had been murdered by unidentified white assailants, so his death and funeral was a national event. Dad and his cousin, Fr. Noel Borerwe, then based at Rugare chapel as the Railways Chaplain, were the outriders leading the funeral cortege on their motorbikes as the coffin was brought back to his Harare homestead and later, as it snaked down Remembrance Drive to Murehwa.

Mum and Dad returned home that evening exhausted. They described how they had met Joshua Nkomo, Jamela (who was later assaulted and left for dead by the ZAPU Youth), Robert Mugabe and Ndabaningi Sithole. Dad had preached at the service. The whole event was distressing for the entire family as Uncle Sam or Tichafa, as Dad called him since their boyhood days in Rusape was popular with all of us. He was quiet, smartly dressed and always had a slight smile over a very neatly trimmed goatee.

The day after Uncle Sam's, Dr. Parirenyatwa's funeral, Dad was knocked off his motorbike by a white motorist on Remembrance Drive. He was gravely injured especially on his chest and legs. He was admitted at Harare Central Hospital, Ku Gomo, as it was generally known. There was a lot of talk and speculation as to whether Dad's prominent role in Uncle Sam Parirenyatwa's funeral was connected to this incident. There were investigations carried out, a witness had noted the vehicle registration of the motorist who failed to stop, but no arrests were ever made. Bishop Cecil Alderson and later Archdeacon Spencer visited Dad in hospital and when he was discharged, about a fortnight later. Dad vowed never to ride a bike again. A month later, Dad acquired a white Vauxhall Velox car. Shortly after that, he received news from the Diocesan office that in the New Year, he would be transferred from St. Paul's Highfield and St. Michael's Parish to St. Alban's Mission at Glendale in the Mazoe Valley, to be the Priest-in-Charge.

I did not have the chance to say goodbye to all my friends, but there was a farewell party for Mum and Dad in the Church Hall attended by adults only. However, I remained in touch with a few friends, especially Charles Zvimba, Cuthbert Mangundhla, Moses Maisiri and from time to time, Morris Mutsonziwa. These were some of my friends who turned up at the last Christmas party at the missionaries' house at Runyararo, hosted by Ms. Barbra Tredgold. We played games, drank lots of Hubbly Bubbly and ate cupcakes. All the children got presents at the end of the party. Morris got a mechanical butterfly and he looked puzzled as he tried to make it work. I got a chocolate-coloured mechanical bunny rabbit which I licked until it dawned on me that it was made of plastic. At some point at the end of the day, we were quite exhausted and headed home straight to bed. We had to get up early the next morning, to start the next chapter of life.

Chapter Four

"I MISS HIM ALREADY," was my teary response to Tinao's words that she would miss Dad. "Strangely, it is as if this was totally unexpected," I added. I called Steve again and he was at this stage out with his friend Jerry Kadzirange. They were sorting out all the paperwork at the various offices in town so that any arrangements to do with Dad's funeral would be expedited once we got to Rusape. Tinao and I wandered round the house getting my vestments, Bible readings and hymns together. We planned a programme for the funeral. Eventually, we managed to eat a morsel for breakfast. From now on, it would mostly be an agonising wait as we drove slowly to the mortuary in Rusape, where Dad's remains had been taken. The two-hour journey would take hours, it seemed, just like the journey from Harare to Glendale, on the next stage of my life in Mbare. My mind drifted on a paseo down memory lane.

We got up early the next morning and watched as men from Biddulphs Removals loaded all our furniture, beds and other belongings onto a huge truck. They were done by lunch time. We then piled into the Vauxhall Velox and drove through the city centre, northwards along Second Street Extension to the Mazoe Valley. The highlights of the drive were the Mazoe Dam, then a majestic body of water and an imposing dam wall where we stopped to admire the awesome view and sip freshly squeezed or-

ange juice from the little shop at the Travelers' Rest corner overlooking the dam wall. We drove past the dam towards Bindura,
orange groves with neat rows of trees loaded with ripe plump oranges. This scenery stretched all the way to the Glendale turn-off,
where we slowly turned and drove through the village, onto the
dirt road to Centenary. We turned off at Gweshe shops, towards
Kanyemba Salvation Army school. After about thirty minutes, we
arrived at St. Alban's Mission.

Our new home was a shock to the system. The priest's house,
where Dad's predecessor and his family, Fr. Tekere (his son, Edgar,
was a prominent nationalist and politician), had lived, was a large,
thatched edifice. It consisted of four bedrooms, a large sitting cum
dining area and a small kitchen at the back of the house. The ablution facilities consisted of two 'long drop' out buildings labelled
'men' and 'women.' There was no electricity. The house was generally rundown. The roof leaked and the rough clay floors had seen
better days. The windows were all off their hinges. The veranda, on
the east-facing main entrance to the house was full of junk. It had
a musty smell of damp.

About thirty metres in front of the main entrance was a well,
where our water would be drawn. The furniture and all our belongings from Harare were soon offloaded and arranged in our new
house. As soon as we had a roof over our heads, my brothers and I
were soon fighting, claiming our patches in our room adjacent to
our parents' bedroom. Emmy and the other girls would occupy the
two bedrooms on the other side of the sitting room.

Dad oversaw the Mission Station comprising the Church and a
school with an enrolment of 500 students. Mum was set to lead the
Mothers' Union and organize all the Women's activities, feed the
family and assist Dad in his ministry. This would be our home and
base for the next five years. Mum referred to the place by the common demonym, Makorekore. Behindhand folk, she would add, to
Dad's exasperation.

One of our first welcoming parties arrived rather unexpectedly at dusk. Dad was outside in the backyard near the classroom blocks, talking to a group of teachers. Mum sat with the boys, in the living room, trying to work out how to operate two newly acquired paraffin-fuelled tilley lamps. My brother, Maurice, had decided to hang around the kitchen with the girls, clearly drawn by the smells of roasting meat and other food being prepared. For some unclear reason, Maurice decided to leave the comfort of the kitchen and join Mum and the boys in the living room. He had to walk about fifteen yards to get to the living room from the kitchen, which was a separate little thatched building in the backyard. Suddenly the door flew open, and a traumatized Maurice leapt in as if he was performing a Zulu warrior dance. He emitted loud screams as part of the drama.

He hollered in a stuttering fit that there was 'a b-b-bi-ig nyoka (snake) entering the house through the back door, which he had kindly left open, in his flight of terror. Mum, who was mortally scared of any legless creature, leapt up and rushed towards the door with a torch. This instantly revealed a clearly angry and disturbed forest cobra. It displayed an amazing hood as it swayed from side-to-side, hissing menacingly in the doorway. We held on to Mum's dress as she bravely reached for the door and slammed it shut in the face of the intruder.

We clearly created such pandemonium and made more than enough noise to wake up the dead that the group of men bravely discussing politics in the dark, with Dad's loud voice booming away at regular intervals, heard and responded with undoubted urgency. It was only a matter of time before we heard loud voices and massive thuds of hefty blows smashing the terrified, angry, unwelcome guest from head to tail as it caromed from door-to-door between the kitchen and the main house. The snake was pulverized. Afterwards, Dad informed us that the snake was dead. We would see it in the morning as they had hung the repetitive creature on the perimeter fence. He also told us that the teachers had told him that there were colonies of cobras, mambas and vine snakes at the Mission.

This news was not comforting. We hardly slept that night for fear of more intruders looking for rats in the old house. At first light, we all stood and stared in horror and awe at the five-foot fat cobra that was now reduced from a scary hood-swaying monster hissing in fading light to a rather undignified grey and bloodied rope-like specimen hanging on the perimeter fence. 'The eagles will soon see it and feast on it,' Dad told us. He was right. By midday, the snake was gone. Judging by its mangled physical state, it is unlikely that it slithered down that fence.

This was only the beginning of our welcoming drama in the new residence. The following day, the sky was overcast. It drizzled lightly all day. There were several streamlets as water trickled down the grey walls mostly in the living room. Everything was damp. The parents decided to light a fire in the old fireplace in the living room, to warm up the house and dry the room a bit. We huddled round the fire. As the room warmed up, there was a sudden screech as three owls dropped into the fire and fluttered confusedly all over the fire, flapping around the room. We all took off from our positions round the fireplace and headed towards the front door. Someone screamed that there could be snakes out there!

There was general mayhem. Eventually Dad managed to subdue the confused birds and released one surviving bird into the darkening light while the other two partially roasted birds were disposed of in the 'long-drop' Blair toilet to the eastern side of the house. We were all left perplexed and scared wondering what was next in store for us. "It's the damn rats," Dad explained. "They invite snakes, owls and God knows what else." Since then, I have not respected nor had any favourable feelings towards rats.

The visitors to our house in the following days were more conventional. There was the school headmaster, Mr. Nathan Mupfunya, who turned out to be Dad's "homeboy," accompanied by his wife, also a teacher, his niece, Ruby and little daughter, Lillian. Other teachers who came to welcome us included Mr. Kahari, his wife who was also a teacher, and their sons, Chad, Demetrius, Alban and George. Chad was just about to leave for high school. "Bernard Mizeki College," he announced proudly when he was asked where. The rest of the teachers, came in one group. Mother was overwhelmed as she had to prepare snacks for all the visitors. The headmaster announced that he had taken over from a Mr. Cooper, who had been transferred by the bishop to set up a secondary school at St. Mary's, Seke.

Other visitors of note that week were a local Headman and chairman of the school council, Mr. Jeremiah Kafiramutowa Rwanga. He was a tall, distinguished man with little stringy dreadlocks He wore a khaki tunic from his days in the Kings African Rifles and sandals made from old car tyres. He spoke animatedly about his vision for the Mission. He wanted a big secondary school, a new church and a new house for the priest. Mum gave him more cookies as he kept swallowing large amounts of boiling tea while devouring all the bread and biscuits put in front of him. As he left, he emptied the entire contents of the sugar basin into his tunic pocket, then strode confidently and purposefully out of the house in the direction of his village. He lived on the foothills of the majestic Gato mountain, about two miles to the north east of the Mission.

The rest of the visitors that week included, Mr. Alfred Chinhema and his elder brother Lawrence, the churchwarden and subdeacon respectively, Mr. Mupandanyama, Mr. Elijah Kuzvidza, the catechist accompanied by two brothers, students at the school, Aaron and Chocolate Chiureki. (Dad later baptised Chocolate and gave him a new name, Lovemore.) Mr. Chidavaenzi, who brought us a gallon of fresh milk from his small farm near Gweshe village, among others. There was not much drama in these welcoming visits except that we had to buy more butter and sugar after each visit as the guests helped themselves to everything put on the table (on one occasion, the teapot as well) and took it home with them. Mother found this practice quite disturbing, frustrating, rude and 'quite absurd.' Dad just accepted it much to Mum's chagrin. We, the children, found it hilarious.

The next lot of visitors were quite different. First was a white couple, Fr. Basil French and his wife. They came from Umvukwes (Mvurwi) Parish. He was the Rector. They brought with them a tall lanky Jesuit priest who was their neighbour, Fr. Caraman S.J. He had a permanent friendly grin plastered on his face and smelt of pickled onions. They toured the Mission church, classrooms and then had tea with the parents and the headmaster on the veranda. Fr. Basil drove a magnificent brown, Fintail Mercedes vehicle. He had a loud voice and stammered like a hammer, like my brother Maurice. He and his family had just arrived in Southern Rhodesia from Northern Rhodesia where he had been parish priest on the Copperbelt.

Hot on their heels came Fr. Widlake S.J. He was previously based at St George's College in Harare and now looked after Catholic mission stations in the Mazoe Valley. He was a big, burly, colourful man in a white, short-sleeved shirt and khaki shorts, that revealed an old wound down his left thigh. It was rumoured that he had been attacked by a crocodile in the Mazoe river while he was testing the theory that crocodiles only attacked black people but ran away from whites as they resembled fire. Fr. Widlake and Dad would go on trek, pastoral visits, together.They visited and planted churches in the Mazoe Valley from Glendale, Concession, Umvukwes, Chiweshe TTL., through Bindura, Shamva and Mt. Darwin, for the next three years.

We quickly made friends with the Kahari boys. Chad became the leader of the gang, Demetrius, a.k.a. Adrian was a year older than me and became my immediate elder buddy and friend, his younger brothers, Alban (Barnie) and George, teamed up with my brothers Maurice and Tendai. Dominic and Nathaniel, the two youngest members of the boys' gang, now three and two were left to their own devices. They were to be found mostly playing with the girls. The Kahari boys were clearly amazed at these new arrivals who were so ignorant when it came to life in a rural setting. They taught us basic survival skills such as whistling stridently to call for attention or to be heard at least a mile away, climbing trees, the first hill climb, wild fruit, wild mushrooms, wild bees and the dangers of disturbing their habitat, snakes and joys of bush life. They also taught us how to play 'head cricket.' We could not get enough of this newfound knowledge and survival skills.

The Kaharis had a dog called Lucky, a mongrel with some greyhound in its origins. Lucky, according to them, could hunt and bring down a kudu! Not knowing what a kudu was, we decided that this was desirable and were suitably impressed. We were determined to get a dog of our own. On hearing some of the stories we brought home, my parents were always a bit skeptical, and quite amused. Dad said he would teach us how to hunt in the woods, by the krummholz...not for kudu, but for bush hares. Mum laughed.

Dad's next task at the mission station was to rebuild the church, refurbish the classrooms and build more classrooms, houses for the teachers and of course, a new Rectory. He also had five churches which were part of the mission station: St. Peter's at Rosa, Hasfa Homecraft School (Msonedi), St. Denis Mukunyadze, St. Margret at Concession and the Mazoe Citrus Estate chapel. This called for huge fundraise. On a Sunday, after Mass, Dad announced to all gathered that he would negotiate with all the neighbouring white farmers, to employ all the school children from the age of 10 and all fit members of all the churches under the mission station, to harvest their crops and raise money for the project. Dad explained that everyone had to work hard and support the project. He was against going to donors as this was humiliating and unnecessary. Everyone had to play their part. Those with anything to donate were encouraged to do so.

We paid visits to the four farmers bordering the mission: Mr. Brown, Major Robert Bromley, Mr. Wiggle and Mr. Chetwyn. They all agreed to employ people from the mission. They donated a cow each. Major Bromley said in addition, he would donate sheep every Christmas and so he did until he died in a shooting accident at his farm four years later. Word from 'the mealie patch' was that his wife shot him while others said he killed himself after an altercation with his wife. Either way, she had a role in his demise, I guess.

Over the years, Major Bromley became good friends with Dad. When he heard that Mum had given birth to a baby boy at Howard Hospital, he asked that the boy be given his name, Robert, among others. Thus, my brother was named Denis, after my father's elder brother, Stanley, after Fr. Mark, Stanley Wood, later Bishop Mark Wood, the Dean at the Cathedral who baptized him and Robert, after Major Bromley, who attended the baptism service, to everyone's amazement. It was rare then, for white folk, especially farmers, to attend church services with rural black folk in their natural habitat.

The stage was thus set for rebuilding the mission station at St. Alban's, Glendale. As the work began, an announcement was made at the school assembly one morning that Headman Kafuramutowa Rwanga, chairman of the Building Committee and respected elder in the mission, had died. I had never been to a funeral service before. I was apprehensive, scared and uncomfortable on the day as all the school children formed two lines leading from the church and marched to Gato mountain, where the Headman was to be buried in a cave. His body was laid on a flimsy stretcher carried by men from nearby villages. They took turns to hoist it onto their shoulders for the two-mile journey. I closed my eyes as the pall bearers walked past us. Dad, clad in a black cassock, white surplice and purple stole led the procession. I stood next to my new friends, John Zowa and Stuart Gotora. They did not seem bothered as they had seen it all before, I later discovered.

After the funeral, I could not sleep for days. Thoughts about life and death and the meaning of life whirled around my head. I was scared. I wondered why Dad and all the adults were not scared. There was much wailing and screaming especially from the village women. I found this quite disturbing and uncomfortable. I could remember vividly, the dead man, while alive, sitting in our house and drinking tea as he espoused his vision for the mission. I recalled how we giggled when he emptied the sugar into his pocket and strode to his home purposefully. Somehow, I imagined his spirit would come and ask us why we made fun of him. Amazingly, no one else around me seemed to be bothered by all these thoughts or if they did, they did not share them with anybody within my earshot. The funeral was soon forgotten and all the thoughts that had kept me awake at night disappeared as other happenings and life in general came back to its usual course.

Chapter Five

THROUGHOUT TODAY'S EVENTS I have been thinking about the lessons of life that I learnt from Dad. Education was a passion of his and so it was natural and easy for me to drift to those early days back at St. Alban's. Amid the task of rebuilding the mission station, my parents had to deal with raising and educating a young, growing family. By now, the family had grown to eight children, one girl and seven boys. Emilia, the eldest and the only girl was now Thirteen. I was eleven and the rest, Maurice, Tendai, Dominic, Nathaniel, Denis and Steven ranged from ten years to one month. The family was close. We took care of each other and did most tasks and activities together. Emmy was basically one of the boys. We had meals together. After dinner, we would read or do homework together before Compline and then bedtime. If anything unusual had happened during the day to any of us, we would report it to the parents before dinner.

The usual and ordinary school day consisted of early morning chores which included cleaning our bedrooms, making the beds, cleaning the rest of the house inside and sweeping the leaves on the veranda and around the house. By the time we finished cleaning, there was just enough time for a quick bowl of mealie porridge or Tanganda tea with a slice of brown bread, then off to school. The school day started with assembly and morning prayers at seven every morning. There was a tea break at ten then lunch break at one. Juniors went home while seniors came back for sport, music, gardening, sewing etc. at two and finished at four. It was a long day.

As before, I was not good at sports and hated everything except high jump. I enjoyed music and singing but had a terrible singing voice. My favourite subjects were English, Arithmetic, Geography and History. My brothers and I generally excelled at most subjects and we cruised through school without much difficulty. Emmy struggled a bit. After two years the parents decided that we needed to go to boarding school so that we could learn to be 'independent and take school more seriously.' Emmy was the first to be sent off to boarding school at St. Augustine's school.

Dad said no one was educated properly until they had attended St. Augustine's school, his 'alma mater.' We all missed Emmy around the house especially as we now had to do her chores. Every Saturday after dinner, we would write a letter to her and tell her about everything we had been up to. She wrote back without fail and told us how happy she was and how much she missed us all. She seemed to be having lots of fun away from us. We looked forward to receiving her letters and hearing her news.

The parents, especially Dad, were worried that our education in Glendale needed strengthening. They thought we were not pushed or challenged enough and were in danger of not fulfilling our promise. By now I had read Macbeth, Hamlet and Romeo and Juliet, could recite the Mass in Latin, challenged my teachers, to my parents' embarrassment and clearly needed more challenges to keep me calm. Dad then had the idea of engaging private tutors to mentor and teach us various subjects. I had a series of tutors: Dad read with us and got us addicted to Shakespeare, Chinua Achebe, T.M. Aluko, Enid Blyton, Richmal Crompton and poetry, especially Tennyson and Keats. Bishop Cecil Alderson tutored me in English literature, diction and English grammar, as did Miss Faith Rebbeck and Miss Diana Gunn.

Apart from my sister Emmy and the two youngest brothers, Denis and Steven, Maurice, Tendai, Dominic and I had a solid

grounding in English, Maths, literature, history and Geography outside of formal school. We must have been a nightmare for our
teachers at school and they did not hide their mixed feelings of admiration and resentment. We were clearly seen as freaks or
outsiders. We were taunted because we sounded different and behaved like 'creatures from a different world' as one of the teachers,
Mr. Maisiri, put it. Boarding school beckoned. During school holidays, Dad would take us to the Queen Victoria Museum and the
big library near the Kopje in Harare. That was always a treat. We
would stop at El Morocco restaurant near Amato on Kingsway and
have fish and chips and family photographs taken at Studio George.
The pictures and portraits still hang in my parents' house. We enjoyed these family 'educational trips' especially the picnics at Lake
Mcllwaine, Mazoe dam or in the woodlands near Dambo and Nyota
Hills in the Chiweshe Communal Lands.

Dad bought me a guitar after I won the coveted 'top student'
prize. Mum thought the idea of me learning how to play a guitar
was bad as this would distract me from serious study. One day, after
I refused to go to the shops because I was practising my guitar, she
snatched it from me and smashed in into pieces. I was heartbroken.
I vowed that the first thing I would do when I got money was to buy
a guitar and play better than Jimi Hendrix. Shortly after that incident, I left for boarding school. I was twelve when I left home for
St. Augustine's school.

My most enduring memories, at St. Alban's, consist of the time
I spent alone exploring the world around me, my environment,
learning and discovering myself, my fears and aspirations. In these
moments, I learnt to appreciate the attractions of an eremitical existence. Times I spent with my parents and siblings; then the time
I spent with ordinary folks and random people in the community
at St. Alban's were distinctly defining moments.

Dad took me everywhere he went as he pursued his task of rebuilding the mission station, planting churches and being an

attentive father to us. He undertook his roles with zeal and assiduity. Thus, I learnt quickly how to serve at Low Mass, Sung Mass and High Mass. I mustered the thurible and use of incense, which was a feature of worship especially at Sunday Mass, Evensong or Devotions/ Benediction. "We celebrate the Mass in remembrance of Christ's sacrifice on the Cross on our behalf," Dad explained to me when I asked him why we had to celebrate the Mass daily.

This made a great impression on me. It is something I accepted as beyond logic. In quieter moments I would sneak into the church, sit in the side Chapel and ponder on these 'Holy Mysteries' for hours on end. I was in constant search for answers. I listened to and heard Dad's sermons till I could recite them by heart, but the answers to questions in my mind were still elusive. I was determined to find out and wished to have a divine eureka moment and revelation one day. This did not happen.

Periodically, the church organized prayer weekends for all the church members in the wider parish. On our way to one of these events, at St Denis, our land rover, in which about ten MU members were squashed at the back of the open vehicle was suddenly engulfed in flames due to an electrical fault. We scrambled out of the vehicle and, amid screams and shouts, threw sand to dowse the fire. In the melee, I leapt from the back of the truck and fell face down, on the gravelly road. I was badly scarred. Eventually the fire was put out. A mechanic was called to sort out broken wires, while a truck was brought to take us to join the faithful who were gathered at St. Denis. There were prayers of thanksgiving that night. I still bear the scar.

At this gathering, of about a thousand worshippers, I witnessed an encounter with the dark world of demons and possession by 'evil spirits' for the first time. Mass was progressing well, the singing, as usual, was loud and heart-rending. As we started singing the 'Agnus Dei,' there was a strident scream from the midst of the Mothers' Union ranks. I could see Mrs. Chiureki flailing her arms and kicking out wildly as she screamed.

Dad hurried from the altar and ordered the Servers to bring the thurible into which he piled incense, blessed it and directed holy smoke at the struggling woman who was now pinned to the ground by four men. Dad laid hands firmly on her head and prayed in a loud voice, commanding the evil spirit to leave as it had inhabited 'a temple of the Lord.' After a brief struggle, Mrs. Chiureki stopped struggling and laid on the floor motionless, gasping for air. Dad sprinkled Holy Water on her. She sat up, looked exhausted, then demurely joined in the singing, clearly oblivious of the preceding drama in which she was the main attraction.

As if that was not enough, just after Communion, during the same service, the drama was repeated, this time Mrs. Kamubvuri was the main actress. I could hear the demon's voice as Dad quizzed and demanded to know why he had possessed this child of God. Dad held her down with his feet as she shook violently, overpowering the men who were trying to subdue her. Dad urged the people to sing loudly as he prayed over the possessed woman and exorcised her of the evil spirit. After the service I looked at the two ladies as they carried on as if nothing had happened. I did not shake their hands at the end of the service. I conveniently sidestepped and disappeared behind the ranks of the MU as I hurried to empty the ashes in the thurible.

I was terrified and tried not to dwell on what I witnessed that day. Everybody else seemed to take it in their stride. That evening, at dinner, Mum explained that there were lots of possessed people in this part of the country. Christianity was a challenge to a lot of them and this was a form of resistance. Dad said we had to be strong, have faith in God and pray constantly for strength to overcome these powers of darkness. He sounded authoritative, brave and wise until he confessed that the whole episode that morning had left him shattered and exhausted.

He retired to bed earlier than usual. Mum did not say much except to repeat that MU members, as others, were convinced that incense had a lot to do with all these demons erupting. They were provoked by the 'Holy Smoke.' I had a new dimension to think about in my quiet, solitary moments. For now, the demon episode had left me emotionally devastated, drained, confused and scared. I narrated the events to my siblings who listened to me in shocked silence. Dinner was tasteless that evening.

I accompanied Dad to hospital twice in three years when Mum was seriously ill with a particularly virulent malaria cum influenza bout. On the first occasion she was taken to Howard hospital where she remained for two weeks. The second, more serious episode saw her hospitalized at Concession general hospital for three weeks. On both occasions, Mum was unconscious and carried to her hospital bed by the staff. I hung on to Dad as we followed Mum's listless body and watched helplessly as she was laid on the bed and curtains pulled around her. I watched in horror as a needle was inserted into her arm and a drip-stand erected near her bed after a couple of shots were administered on her shoulder.

Dad and I prayed for Mum as we sat in the car outside the hospital in darkness. Dad always told me to be strong and have faith in God and Mum would recover. On one of the hospital visits, Mum opened her eyes as I stood at the foot of her bed. She whispered "please pray for me", then closed her eyes. I left the room in tears and sat in the car with Dad. Each time we got home; we would all pray for Mum. Eventually Mum recovered and we brought her home. I somehow felt responsible for her return. A very strange feeling of extreme if irrational and inexplicable joy welled up in me. I realized, somehow, that I really was close to Mum and loved her. Emmy later told me that this was the case. She said that was fine because she was 'Daddy's girl.'

There were two more trips to Howard hospital. This time, my maternal grandmother accompanied Dad and I to witness the birth of my brothers, first Denis, in 1965 then Steven Neil Chivimbo, the following year. Both were jovial times. My parents had expected girls on both occasions, but they got two healthy, handsome lads instead. Mum had promised to bring home a sister for us each time, but never delivered on her promise. We were not disappointed but delighted. I felt special because I was asked, each time, to carry the little bundles into the house and to rest them on my lap. I was particularly close to Nathaniel, Dennis and Steven. Maurice had Tendai and Dominic under his wing. Emmy was in both camps depending on what she wanted done. Despite the joy of these two hospital visits, I remained very skeptical and apprehensive of all medical facilities. They were sinister places and filled me with a sense of foreboding.

I enjoyed time on my own. Early one Saturday morning, never the anthropocentric one in my family, I called my dogs, of which we now had seven. I carried a black satchel with a bottle of water, two oranges and a hunk of brown bread that Emmie had 'liberated' from the kitchen for me after I told her about my mission. She promised not to let the parents know. I said I would bring back wild fruits, for her. I also had a copy of 'The Silver Sword' by Ian (and Jane) Serraillier in my satchel. I set about to explore the area in the woods on the western end of the mission, towards Nyota Hills.

I had heard stories of abandoned gold mines and bushman paintings. I also carried a small axe that Dad had told us should be carried by all men walking in the forest/woods, as they could come across wild animals like impala, jackals or bush hares. The Kahari boys, especially Aidan, had talked a lot about the wildlife in the woods. I was determined to see for myself. I had visions of being an 'intrepid explorer,' just like the ones I had read about traversing deepest, dark Africa, or the ones we saw in the Tarzan films at Stodart Hall, walking through the jungle with 'native porters.'

It took me about forty minutes to walk up to the top of the first hill, trying hard to keep up with the excited hounds. They chased after anything that stirred in the woods and would rush back to me as if to say, "You are holding us back." As we reached the top, there was a sudden yelp from the dogs as they raced after a bush hare down the western slope towards the little stream that flowed along the foot of the bare rocky outcrop. I just managed to catch sight of the hare as it tore away in leaps and bounds and disappeared into the woods with my pack of yelping hounds in hot pursuit.

The dogs returned about twenty minutes later, panting heavily and promptly slouched in the shade near the rock where I sat watching the view of the Mission below. After wolfing down my tuck, I resumed my trek up the hills towards the higher Nyota hills. I passed through a clear area, a vlei, with heavy soggy ground and a ring of Makute (wild blueberry) on one side. Further along, closer to the hills was another, larger, open space called' Gokoro' by the locals. This area did not have Makute trees but rather lots of Mazhanje trees and a little stream that flowed westwards through very tall Msasa trees. I climbed towards the large rocks until I got to a huge rock overhang that led into a well-lit cave. On the cave walls were rock paintings depicting various animals, hunting scenes and villages. The scenes were amazingly well preserved and clear. I sat in wonder and amazement admiring them.

After a while, I walked further into the cave through a dark passage that led into a slightly smaller, cooler cave. In the corner of the cave was a pile of stones purposefully arranged to form an altar-like structure with an opening at the top. I peered into the enclosure and could make out white objects. I set about dismantling the structure to discover whatever lay hidden inside it. After removing about fifteen stones, I suddenly realized that I had discovered, dismantled and disturbed a grave. Inside lay a skull, leached spinal bones and a few broken leg and thigh bones. I hastily put the heavy stones back where I thought they had been and exited the cave to catch my breath under the Msasa trees.

I felt overwhelmed, stupid and scared all at once. I even felt lost momentarily. Meanwhile the dogs leapt in and out of the caves chasing bats that had been disturbed and fluttered around both caves, confused and clearly agitated.

From the caves, I headed for the highest point in the hills. The dogs sniffed their way as they raced in the woods. About a hundred metres from the caves, the dogs went into a frenzy. They barked furiously and backed towards me then took a few steps forwards towards a grassy anthill with rocks guarding the western edge. Suddenly a large, brown animal emerged from the long grass chasing the dogs as they retreated in my direction. The beast, which I was later told was a resident rogue male hyena screeched to a halt about fifty metres from where I stood transfixed and frozen with fear. It turned around and ran deeper into the woods. The dogs chased after it. This was turning out to be quite an adventure. I was thrilled and frightened but determined to carry on.

By the time I clambered to the summit of the hill, I was exhausted and parched. I had seen a hyena, disturbed flocks of guinea fowls, watched the dogs run after a troop of monkeys and seen a huge snake disappear down a hole under a rock. Near the top, rock hyraxes scurried away and disappeared down burrows. The dogs went berserk in pursuit of the wild animals. I sat down at the summit of the height 'where only wind swept, lichens grew' and watched the sun in the west and the lengthening shadows.

I replayed the day's events in my head. I was exhilarated to be where I was. Somehow, I felt that some force, God maybe, was leading me on a 'voyage of discovery' of my inner self and my surroundings, possibly a test of sorts. I felt an inner peace and joy at being alone in the woods for the first time. I cherished all the events and experiences of the day. It was a strangely edifying feeling. Most of all, I felt grown up. I realized that I really enjoyed being on my own.

Eventually I picked myself up and descended the hill. I closed my eyes as I ran past the graves near the track into the open playing fields near the school. I could hear the dogs chasing whatever in the cemetery. I did not investigate their pursuits. I headed home. Mum was not at all impressed when I narrated my day. She did not like the grave-disturbing incident but was particularly disturbed by the story of the disappearing snake as she had heard of a resident black mamba that fed on rock rabbits in that area.

Dad said I never should go back to the graveyard and never again to disturb the graves in the cave. The consequences of such actions were never clearly spelt out but were unmistakable and hard to miss in Dad's tone of voice. My siblings giggled as I told them tales of 'encounters' that I had had with wild beasts including tigers, bees and horned pythons deep in the woods and dark caves. I must have sounded deranged, but they were evidently quite envious. Maurice and Tendai said they would join me on my next adventure. They both told me that I was brave and was their hero. They named me 'Batman,' after their favourite comic hero. The name stuck. For a long while afterwards, I wondered whether my 'adventures' were really believed or were privately dismissed as the ravings of a mind unable to distinguish fiction from reality, real life from the jejune fantasies of its youth. To me, I had now done it all.

I also spent time on many separate occasions with the school caretakers, Stephen and William. Stephen was fascinated because I could recite long passages from Macbeth, Julius Caesar, Romeo and Juliet and poems by Keats, especially his favourites, 'Ode to Autumn' and 'Ode to a Nightingale.' We would discuss poetry and he would teach me puzzles in Maths and Science. William was more interested in Nature Studies. He showed me how to trap hares, duiker and an impala. Stephen showed me an anthill where an excessively big old spitting cobra lived. We would sit quietly and watch the huge snake bask in the sun until the dogs disturbed it and annoyed it. It would raise its head, stretch out its hood and hiss while it spat jets of saliva a few feet into the air.

I showed off most of these sites to two special guests who were also our family tutors: Diana Gunn, from Bristol. She stayed with us for about six months and coached us on various subjects especially English grammar and church history and Fr. Derek Williams

C.R., from St. Augustine's Penhalonga. Fr. Williams decided to stay with us during his sabbatical. He taught physics and Maths but was extremely interested in the local history especially the rock paintings. On Sundays he took services and generally helped Dad with church duties, preaching, confessions or devotions/benediction.

These visits provided opportunities to revisit the forbidden caves and graves. I took Diana to see the caves, accompanied by my brothers and a few friends. On one of the visits, we dismantled one of the graves in the light cave and had a good look at all the bones and artefacts buried in it before reassembling all the heavy rocks.

Fr. Williams told us about the Bushmen and their way of life depicted on the rock paintings. He also explained all the rock formations, erosion and the granite outcrops and shards exposed by erosion. He challenged some of the theories about creation, mountains and wild animals that William and especially Stephen had told us. We did not tell Mum and Dad what we did during our trips into the woods and hills with the visitors. The visitors were circumspect and only talked about the charm of the rock paintings, the beautiful sites in the hills, the wild fruit and how we all avoided the snake habitats. I do not know how much of this the parents believed but they kept their cool, sometimes with skepticism writ large on their faces.

The two annual highlights in the church calendar were the Bishop's visit for Confirmation, usually in May/June and in August, the St. Alban's Festival. Preparations for both events were always hectic. The candidates for confirmation camped at the mission for two weeks. During that time, they were taught catechism and prepared for Confirmation and their first Communion. The preparation included topics such as Anglicanism, Christian ethics, church history and various aspects of Anglican liturgy. The average age of confirmation candidates was about twenty, which is generally higher than it is currently. This was because of the high rate of conversion to Anglicanism among adults in the area, the preference given by church high schools to members of their own denomination and a result of Dad's ministry in the area.

Apart from these classes/lessons, all of them taken by Dad, candidates were required to do manual work including repairing the road leading to the mission, cleaning up the church and various other buildings and ensuring that there was always enough water for use in the mission. The choir would rehearse various hymns and servers, or altar boys would also rehearse their respective duties. All the teaching was carried out in the numinous St. Alban's Chapel in the eastern wing of the Church.

The Bishop would arrive around three o'clock in the afternoon. Candidates for confirmation, the teachers, students and parishioners would line the road leading to the rectory. As soon as the Bishop's car emerged in the distance, everyone would break into song. The Bishop would make a sign of the cross and bless the gathered faithful as he drove slowly through the admiring crowd at full throated voice as they sang their welcome to their spiritual Father and leader. This was Bishop Cecil Alderson. The Bishop would drive up to the rectory where Mum and Dad would welcome him. We would carry his cases into Emmie's room, which was set aside for the Bishop's use on these occasions.

The Bishop was a thick set, heavy man about five feet ten, a fluent Shona speaker. He was usually dressed in khaki shorts and a purple shirt under his purple cassock. Shortly after his arrival, everyone would assemble in the church. The servers waited outside the house to lead the Bishop, who by now would have had afternoon tea and biscuits. He looked regal, in rich coloured vestments, a flowing cope, tall mitre and a rose gold crozier in his left hand. The Holy Shepherd was ready to bless the incense, utter a few Latin phrases in prayer, then walk at the rear of the procession, into the packed church.

On average, about two hundred candidates were confirmed each year. I was confirmed in 1967. The candidates wore white clothes, a sign of purity. The service would typically last until sunset and first Communion Mass was held early the following morning. The Bishop would be the Celebrant and Preacher at the Mass.

It was considered an honour to have the Bishop stay overnight. We had special meals, especially dinner and including a large, cooked breakfast. After dinner, the Bishop insisted that we show him our schoolbooks. He would test our Maths and English to his exacting standards. We had to speak well and articulate all words to his satisfaction. He even commented on our table manners and complimented Mum on her cooking. Dad and he would discuss church matters then we all gathered for Compline before retiring to bed. We all liked Bishop Cecil. In time, he 'adopted' Emmie and paid for her to go to boarding school. He clearly liked Dad and thought highly of Dad's ministry particularly how he had revived the mission.

So, it was with great horror, shock and sadness that on 12th February 1968, we awoke to the news that the Bishop had died of a heart attack during a visit to South Africa. Emmy and Mum sobbed for a long time. Dad was on the phone to his colleagues. This was hard for the diocese especially since they had lost Canon Edward Chipunza only three months earlier. Canon Edward had been recently appointed Archdeacon and was widely believed to be well-placed to be the next and first black bishop.

Bishop Cecil's funeral service was held in the Cathedral in Harare. It was a big funeral attended by other bishops including bishop Francis Markall S.J. the Catholic bishop of Salisbury and the then Greek Orthodox Bishop in Salisbury, Krillos (Papadopoulos). Bishop Cecil was cremated. His ashes were interred in the cathedral by his successor. In the meantime, the Bishop of Matabeleland, Kenneth Skelton, would be the caretaker bishop of Mashonaland. So it was, that Bishop Skelton came to St. Alban's in May 1968, for the confirmation service.

Dad woke me up early on the day of the Confirmation service and told me he had decided to send me to Glendale and wait by the Glendale turn off on the Salisbury-Bindura Road to meet Bishop

Skelton and guide him back to the Mission. The Bishop had been told that I would be waiting for him at the turn off. Glendale was fifteen miles away. Dad said he had no money for me to take the bus, so I had to walk. I was upset, as was Mum, who we now nick-named 'Minerva,' because she was always right and ran the household. She muttered that I was too young to be alone on that road which passed through the woods, unfamiliar villages and farms. Dad was not persuaded by Mum's protestations.

I got dressed and got myself ready for the long journey to Glendale. I wore grey shorts, a white, short-sleeved shirt, grey stockings and black Bata shoes. I tied my school necktie round my collar. I was so upset I refused to eat breakfast. Dad offered me ten cents to buy a drink at the shops. I refused to take the money and strode off in a huff on the dusty road to Glendale. The Bishop was due at the turn-off at midday. Dad said I was not to return without the Bishop. I left the house at seven o'clock. My siblings and the rest of the folks who had gathered to clean up and prepare for the Bishop's arrival gazed on in disbelief as I strode away towards Glendale in a huff.

I was too upset to cry. I bit my lip and started to trot towards Glendale. I trotted past the village shops. Somehow, the woods that I was now so used to and comfortable in now seemed dark and sinister. I imagined all sorts of wild sounds and kept looking behind me in case anyone or anything followed me. There was no traffic on that track. I only met a man on his bicycle, cycling in the opposite direction. I greeted him politely and once again, broke into a trot towards the next village stores to the main Glendale-Centenary road.

When I got to Gweshe shops, I knew I had now covered five miles. The rest of the journey would be along a wide road, unpaved for six miles, until the bridge over the Murodzi river, onto the Glendale- Makori Range Motel road. As I walked onto the road past the shops towards Glendale, I wished, momentarily, that I had money to buy rock buns and maybe a cold drink. I was hungry. However, each time my mind focused on the task at hand, I felt more determined than ever to accomplish the mission and not succumb to distractions such as pangs of hunger. Dad had always told us that we had to remain focused each time we were given a task to do, then wait patiently for rewards at the end.

Along the way, I entertained myself by singing hymns, reciting poems, parts of the Mass and the Hail Mary, in the way Bishop Cecil had taught us. I imitated his deep voice and clear English accent. I imagined that the deceased bishop and all the Saints were walking alongside me. Strangely, half-expecting the deceased bishop's ectoplasmic appearance gave me strength to walk and trot briskly, through the gate at the fence separating Forda Farm from the Chiweshe communal lands and past Sunrise farm. The next stretch, six miles to Murodzi bridge, is now a blur. It all went quite quickly. The odd car passed me in either direction or disappeared behind clouds of dust. I imagined puzzled faces gawking at me in the vehicles roaring past and disappearing in the distance.

All the time I wondered what Bishop Kenneth Skelton was like. I had heard about him especially whenever he said things against the government's racial policies. Dad said he was a good man, a good bishop. As I closed in on my destination, I got increasingly curious about the man I was going to meet. Somehow all the hunger disappeared. I ran across the bridge, walked briskly up the rise in the road and soon could see the Ecumenical chapel on the curve where the road forked to Howard Institute. The left track led to Glendale post office and carried on to the T-junction on the Salisbury-Bindura Road.

I was obviously an unusual sight judging by the curious looks I got. Two men walking in the direction of the bridge asked me, in a friendly tone of voice, whether I was lost. I did not stop but muttered something of an explanation as I carried on towards my destination. I arrived with an hour to spare. I sat down on the concrete bench near the junction, exhausted, if a little anxious. What would I say to the Bishop? Various thoughts whirled around in my weary head.

Just as I was dozing away on the bench, I vaguely heard a car stop across the road from where I sat. It was Bishop Cecil's green and grey Zephyr Zodiac. I stood up and then smiled as a bespectacled man, quite obviously a bishop, got out of the car and greeted me warmly, 'You must be Julius,' he said. I scurried across the road and shook his hand. He smiled and opened the passenger door for me. I got into the car and sat quietly. There were no seat belts, not that I would have known what to do with one! The Bishop said we would follow the Centenary road; could I point out the correct turn-off to the Mission when we got to it. The Bishop turned out to be a very gentle man with a soft voice. He asked me questions about school, the parish and the family. He told me about his diocese, his love of music and how he thought there would be 'a good man' elected as bishop to succeed Bishop Cecil Alderson.

I directed the Bishop to the Mission feeling a warm sense of pride, joy and importance. We drove slowly through admiring, singing worshippers who lined the road on both sides for about three hundred metres to the rectory. As the bishop parked the car, he stood up sprightly and smiled. Mum and Dad emerged to greet the Bishop. Dad genuflected as he kissed the Bishop's ring. The Bishop blessed the worshippers before we led him, in established tradition, to his room.

There was the confirmation service as usual, but it was mostly in English as, unlike Bishop Cecil, Bishop Kenneth was not a Shona speaker. Dinner that evening was a quiet affair. After dinner we all sat by the fireside at the huge fireplace in the living room. Dad asked the Bishop about his remarks regarding 'Racial Segregation and Discrimination as an abomination...,' as reported widely in recent press reports. I managed to follow most of the Bishop's and Dad's conversation which was deep and full of words I could only guess the meaning of. Basically, the Bishop expressed his displeasure with the government's policy of racial discrimination and segregation. I memorized many of the words that I heard that evening, looked them up in Dad's dictionary and often repeated them to my friends, teachers and others. 'Abomination,' 'too ghastly to contemplate,' 'solipsistic' and 'banal' stuck in my mind. I must have sounded learned, barking mad or simply weird, to those who heard me.

What I understood of the discussion between Bishop Skelton and Dad, with an exchange in soft tones, that evening was etched deeply in my mind. The Church would always play a role in social, political and economic issues whether it was to seek to play that role actively or not because it controls a large and significant share of the country's spiritual market. In Rhodesia, due to historical factors that saw the church operating closely to the state, the church,' ipso facto,' became a strategic actor on issues of national interest and therefore featured prominently in efforts to resolve political unrest by black nationalists and political crises that arose widely in the country. The church, the Bishop stressed that he referred to was his role, beyond prayers. He had to take a fundamental stance against injustice, corruption, cruelty, exploitation and unfairness.

The Church had to take the lead in extolling values of universal solidarity, the common good, respect for life and human dignity. Bishop Skelton's views against the settler, Rhodesia Front regime, earned him the wrath of the authorities. He was often at loggerheads with government policy. The Bishop, with a little wry smile, described the then prime minister of Rhodesia, Ian Smith, as a man with, "The charm of an iceberg sanctimoniously wishing for a place in the Trinity!" Later that year, in his eighth year as the Bishop of Matabeleland, he left Rhodesia for the U.K. under protest, declaring that 'justice is more important than law and order.' He later became the Bishop of Lichfield in England. The Bishop's visit clearly brought much joy in the parish and in our family, not to mention in my own heart, in view of the role I had played in the scheme of things. I expressed my joy in silence, just as a smile holds more meaning than laughter. Whenever I was asked if I had enjoyed meeting Bishop Kenneth Skelton on the roadside in Glendale, I just smiled. (Bishop Skelton recorded his time in Rhodesia in his book, 'Bishop in Smith's Rhodesia: Notes on a turbulent Octave.')

A month later, it was announced that a new bishop had been elected and would take up his post in Harare in July, after his consecration, which was to be at Birmingham Cathedral, just before the Lambeth Conference. The new bishop was John Paul Burrough, an Englishman who served as a priest and chaplain to overseas peoples and a Residentiary Canon in Birmingham. The new bishop's first engagement outside of Salisbury was a visit to St. Alban's, for the annual festival. Dad asked the Bishop to preside at Mass, preach and meet the people. Once again, I was asked to walk to Glendale to meet the new bishop and guide him back to the Mission. This I duly did as I was now quite familiar with the routine.

One of the altar boys, the ever nebbish, John Sibve, at the behest of the head server and other servers, accompanied me on the long walk to Glendale. John was incredibly quiet and rather shy but cheerful. I think he relished the whole experience. We talked as we jogged our way to the appointed place, this time Glendale Post Office. John told me about his family, his twin brother, Joseph, and his atheist parents. The journey was uneventful. We made it to the Post Office with lots of time to spare.

Bishop Paul pulled up at Glendale Post Office in Bishop Cecil's old car. He was accompanied by his charming wife, Elizabeth, or 'Bess,' as he called her. The bishop was a very tall, lanky man with a drawn face. By contrast, his wife was of medium height, smiled a lot exposing well-set dimples. As soon as we got into the car, we talked almost non-stop, all the way back to the mission. The bishop and his wife expressed their shock and admiration when I told them about my epic and intrepid journey to meet Bishop Kenneth. They asked about Bishop Cecil, his visits, and Bishop Kenneth's visit.

Bishop Paul told us about his time as a prisoner of war in Malaya, how he came from an ecclesiastical family: his father was a priest, Canon Burrough, he said. Bess asked about the MU and about the

MU diocesan worker, Ms. Faith Rebbeck, affectionately known as 'Sister Faith.' She laughed when I told her that Sister Faith's mother, Dorothy, who lived at 5, Madeley Road in Ealing, West London, was my pen pal. Mrs. Rebbeck wrote me long letters every fortnight and sent me postcards and books frequently. The Bishop and his wife were clearly fascinated by this unusual relationship.

Invited clergy met the new bishop and his wife for the first time. It was a long day with a long service, celebration of the Eucharist and observance of the feast of St. Alban, the first English martyr. The Bishop preached an exceedingly long sermon in which he outlined his compassionate vision for the diocese. He said he would not rush to judge anyone especially in the political minefield that was Rhodesia then. Dad said the Bishop was a courteous man but disappointed many people by sitting on the fence, unlike Bishop Skelton.

The new Bishop tried to be a friend to all and to please everybody. He, however, had a passion for empowering black clergy and educating their families. Bess talked to Mum about the M.U. and promised to fundraise for them to do more work and attract more members. This went down well with Mum and her colleagues. All in all, the Bishop's visit was low key, especially coming, as it did, on the heels of the fiery Bishop of Matabeleland. There was consensus that the new Bishop was a gentleman, compassionate and courteous but needed time to really get to grips with his new role and take firm leadership of the Anglican Church in the diocese of Mashonaland. Like many others, Dad did not think that the new Bishop would really understand Africans. He had a fond statement: 'The man's ikigai is misplaced.' In time, this proved prophetic and an understatement.

A week after the Bishop's visit, we were awakened late one night to hear that Mum and Dad, who had gone to do the monthly shopping in Salisbury had been involved in a serious traffic accident on the road between Glendale and Concession. They had survived but Mum had to be hospitalized to have glass extracted from her face and head. Her swollen legs were x-rayed for possible fractures. Dad sustained injuries to both legs and chest. He had difficulty walking for about two weeks. They were brought home the following day heavily bandaged. Parishioners came to the house to commiserate.

Dad said if they had both died, their wish was to be buried in the same coffin. All gathered gasped at the thought. Apparently, Dad had driven the land rover off the road onto a side clearing to avoid a dust-churning oncoming Railways truck loaded with cattle. A local (Trelawney) purse-proud farmer, Major Rouse, trying to overtake the cattle carrier, swerved and lost control of his vehicle, smashing head-on into the parked land rover. Both cars were extensively damaged. Months later, the matter went to court. Dad won the case. He was awarded damages including a replacement land rover. The farmer, I believe, said he would donate to the church. Mum and Dad were scarred for life on their faces and legs.

For about two months after the accident, my parents did not do much manual work nor did they travel as often as they usually did. Inanition ruled the days. They had weekly check-ups at Concession hospital where they got good attention from Orderly Zhuwao, who was a member of St. Margret's church in Concession. On one of these 'lazy afternoons' as Dad called them, Mum and Dad sat on the veranda and watched my brothers and I play 'head cricket' with friends. Dad called out loudly, stopping the game, and pointed to a large flock of birds flying in a V-formation.

We all left our positions and went closer to the veranda. He explained that he wanted us to take note and learn a lesson from the flock of birds, which he identified as geese. He said that the flapping of the wings makes an uplift for the bird behind which enabled the birds to fly further easily and faster. As the lead bird tires, he said, it rotates back in the wing and another bird flies point. He said as teams playing head cricket, we needed to take turns in giving direction and strategy if we were to improve and beat the village team. To be united against a shared enemy was a strong binding force, so we had to argue less among ourselves and stay focused on the game, united against the opposing team. We had to be like the flying geese in a V-formation because if we shared a common direction, we would achieve our goal to win more easily and faster. As the birds travel on the trust of one another, so our team, trusting in our abilities as individuals, would effectively be working on the trust of one another. Independent thought and action, in the team, had to take second place to the team's objectives and goals.

I am not sure how much sense this made to the teams battling it out. As soon as we resumed our positions, we went back to our usual game, screaming, arguing, accusing each other of incompetence, cheating and not playing a fair game. It was more fun than Dad's lesson, which made little sense especially as it came after his constant exhortations that independence of mind was a revelation and incitement. It should, he said, promise a counterweight to a supine tendency to follow socially sanctioned practices and ideas. It all sounded arcane to me.

During our stay at St. Alban's, I saw, for the first time, a group of hunters chase and kill an impala with a pack of crazed, yelping dogs. There were not many people about on that Saturday morning. I jumped with a start on hearing loud shouting and dogs barking. About three hundred meters from the veranda, an impala ran towards the vlei in the little thicket between the teachers houses and the road that led down to the village stores. In pursuit of a terrified impala was a motley crew of men from the village in full throttle as they shouted encouragement to the dogs. They wielded knobkerries and axes.

At the bottom of the vlei, in the distance, I saw them gather and beat the life out the impala. I ran towards the scene then stopped as I watched one man slit the animal's throat with a long knife. I was sick to the bottom of my stomach at the sight of blood squirting and spraying over the now demented hounds. The noisy hunters celebrated as the hapless animal bleated and gasped its last breath.

I returned to the veranda where I sat in some distress and confusion for a long time. The word cruelty, to me then, could not describe adequately what I had just witnessed. I felt juberous about walking in the bush after that incident.

Early the following year, about six months after my parents' car accident, Dad was told that he was to be transferred to take over as Rector at Holy Name Mission, near Rusape. He was to oversee about forty-six churches in the chapelry. He would lead a team of three curates. His brief was to transform the Mission into a Parish, with a secondary school and a rural health centre. First, however, he and Mum had to go for further studies at Selly Oak, Birmingham. This was preceded by a holiday in Mozambique and Malawi. We were in various boarding schools and so could not join them. They did, however, visit us to say goodbye. They were away for about a year.

Mazowe Valley had been, for me, an arena of learning and development. It had provided an ideal environment to acquire survival tactics, provide space to explore and develop academic and physical skills combined with an appreciation of the outdoors. I had time to read many books, spend time on my own, involve myself in team sport but above all, I formed and defined remarkably close relationships with my parents and siblings. The time I spent with Dad walking in the woods, reading books sitting on rocks in the hills or assisting him as a server at Mass or running errands for him as he adrenalized the hitherto comatose Mission, forged a strong bond and understanding between us.

This bond would develop in various ways over the next years. It remained strong. The news of his passing shattered this bond. I was devastated. The bond with Mum remains. It had a strong base formed during our sojourn at St. Alban's Mission. Bonds and personal alliances between my siblings and I were strong but varied and developed over time as well.

As we drove into the gates of the Nyaradzo Funeral Home in Rusape just after half past one in the afternoon, I knew my life had changed forever. I was grateful Tinao was there with me. However, I felt a huge empty space within me. A dark cloud hung over us as we dragged our feet into the mortuary. We had mixed feelings and an uneasy sense of fearful apprehension. "My father died earlier today. His body was brought here, I believe," I said to the man behind the desk, not really wanting to hear his answer.

"Yes, we have him here," the man replied, expressionless. Tinao and I sat down in silence, downcast. Dad's passing was now a reality. My spirits were now in my boots. I needed time to digest this new era in my life, just like the time we left St. Alban's, when I left home and encountered boarding school to begin a new chapter of my life.

Chapter Six

I SAT ON THE SCHOOL BUS next to Charles Dutiro. I knew a few students from St. Alban's, including Elias Dekune and Martin Dzvimbo who had been altar boys. They were all 'old boys' returning to St. Augustine's. I was the newcomer. As the bus lumbered up the hill, the impressive church towers soon appeared. They dwarfed the surrounding classrooms, the Priory and the two Convents around it. Things moved fast. We were welcomed by the Principal, Fr. Daniel Pearce, an American, and the Housemaster of Knight-Bruce House, my French tutor, Fr. Keble Prosser. I was shown round by the house prefect, Sam Mhlanga. He also kindly helped me make my bed and unpack the contents of my trunk, toiletries, clothes and a couple of books, into my bedside locker. My bed was nestled between Columbus Kariwo and Meshack Charasika.

While touring the school, I read on the noticeboard that I was enrolled to study Maths, Latin, French, History, Geography, English Literature, English Language, Biology, Physics, Chemistry, Divinity, Art and Music. I could not wait to get started. I soon settled into a routine, Mass in one of the chapels, Holy Name Chapel was my favourite, breakfast, lessons from 0800 hours till 1300 hours, an hour for lunch, back at 1400 hours for more lessons till tea break at 1600 hours, lessons till 1730 hours., free time till dinner at 1900 hours, prep from 2000 hours till bedtime at 2200 hours. On Wednesdays we had sports after lunch, till tea. On Thursdasy, we had Benediction before dinner.

School was a breeze. I enjoyed history and adored Sr. Christine Alison, my tutor. She was in her early twenties and had just come to Rhodesia for the first time, after reading history at London University before joining the Order of the Holy Paraclete Nuns at Whitby. She was friendly. We hit it off and remain friends to this day. Fr. Kingston Erson taught me Divinity. He had no sense of humour and was always shirty. French with Fr. Prosser was enjoyable. I excelled at it. I loved art with Sr. Ruth O.H.P. and music with Sr. Shirley, a perfunctory but delightful musician. Latin was great but my tutor, Mrs. Kuwana, recently arrived from Indiana, was deadly dull.

Mr. Dhladhla, a South African, also taught me Latin. He was delightful, altiloquent and often smelt of alcohol. He was an excellent teacher who loved his subject and passed his enthusiasm for the subject to all his students. We called him 'Chubby.' Geography with Mr. Mitchell, a freegan of note, was scary. Despite a wry smile, he was irascible, prone to fits of angry shouting and was sour at the best of times except to a few of his selected favourite students. He was very clever and intense.

Mr. Henry Darling taught us Physics and Chemistry. He was very English and eccentric but seemed to have a soft spot for me. I was good at and enjoyed his subjects. The biology master, Mr. Innocent Nyamajiwa was cool and immaculately dressed, with impressive sideburns on his face. He spoke softly but deeply. We called him 'Cool Cat.' The English master, Mr. Maurice Tsododo spoke with a broad American accent. He was, along with the Kuwanas, a recent arrival from the U.S. He was a prolific writer and loved to read us some of his works. He was a gadabout who hardly ever smiled. After Mr. Mukoko left for further studies at Durham University, Mr. Joe Vere taught us Maths. Two words only could describe him accurately: excellent, brilliant. I got addicted to his subject.

Most of the C.R. fathers I had already met as a child. Fr. Maurice Bradshaw was still around from the time he baptised me as an infant as were Fr. Jacob Waddle, Fr. James Woodrow and Fr. Derek Williams. I came to know and like Fr. Noel Williams, Fr. Robert Mercer, Fr. Steven Fausset, Brother David Hodge (who had just arrived at the school from Mirfield to run the catering departments at the school. He tragically died after one term) and Fr. Anselm Genders, who would, years later, invite me to his consecration as the bishop of the West Indies, at St. Paul's Cathedral in London. We had met, by chance, at the ice cream van at the market near Christ College, Cambridge.

It was always great to get a break from the whole school routine and re-join family and friends. The only blot on holidays was the dreaded school report which detailed everything from grades in the various subjects, attitude to schoolwork and general behaviour. My first report stated that "He is an enthusiastic, diligent, co-operative pupil but needs to exercise patience and tolerance with colleagues and teachers." This was an overall observation from the Principal, Fr. Pearce. Mum and Dad were not impressed and told me off for not being a model student. I protested, to no avail. I was given countless examples of people who had been through the school, put up with all the conditions and now were leaders in their chosen fields.

I was not impressed. I explained that I really did not like the meals, I thought the conditions of the large dormitories left a lot to be desired. I enjoyed chapel, I got on famously with Fr. Prosser. He took pity on me and supplemented my school meals with tinned meats, crabmeat and fruit. He agreed with me that Mr. Mitchell was racist but discouraged me from confronting him since he was the headmaster and could expel me from the school. All in all, my time at St. Augustine's school was short-lived. I passed all my subjects with distinction and the remark from Mr. Mitchell, the Headmaster, was, "He has done very well in all the academic subjects but is not welcome to further his education at this school."

It was quite apparent that Dad understood my predicament and was determined to get me into another school without delay since I had excellent grades. Mum, on the other hand, said that I had been expelled for being rude and difficult and would not find it easy to get into another school. She was wrong. A week later, Dad came home from a trip to the Diocesan office in Salisbury and announced that his Roman Catholic, Jesuit friends had suggested that he calls St. Ignatius College and explain the situation to the new Principal, Fr. James Berry. Dad had already done this before returning home and had been assured that if I performed well at an interview to be arranged, I would be offered a place at this elite, multi-racial, Jesuit, private boys' college tucked away in the Shawasha hills, northwest of Salisbury.

So it was that I ended up at this peaceful, well-ordered, disciplined institution. The Jesuits were more relaxed and less stuffy than the terribly English Anglican Monks in the eastern highlands. I made friends very quickly and soon settled into a new academic routine. My favourite subjects now were Physics, Maths, Geography, History and French. I enjoyed Physics with Fr. Greg Croft, Maths with Fr. Enright (who was also my Housemaster and Prefect General) and Bro. Wilcott. Geography with Fr. Pat Makaka, Mr. Titus Gororo and Mr. Lovemore Zinyama, French with Mr. Ross Antao, History with Mr. Cuthbert Chiromo and Literature with Fr. John Davies and Mr. Robin Gaylard and his wife, Jane. Biology with Fr. Anthony Watsham. I made friends notably Byron Quarrie, Frank Parker and Stevie Burns, to name a few. In charge of the catering was Fr. Caraman, who I had met as a little boy at St. Alban's Glendale. He visited Dad with the Anglican Rector of Umvukwes, Fr. Basil French. Fr. Brian Porter, the school Treasurer, was Housemaster of Junior House. He became a friend over time. He was a jovial man, enthusiastic patron of the sailing club. I later became Recorder of the swimming team, President of the photographic club and a school prefect.

I worked hard and enjoyed all my subjects. I always looked forward to receiving my school report in the post. Mum and Dad were
pleased. They would visit me often, especially on Parents' Day. I
particularly enjoyed the swimming galas against Peterhouse, St.
George's and Kutama Colleges. Fr. Enright appointed me Recorder
of the swimming team even though I never swam competitively.
This was a great honour and a favour.

I liked Fr. Enright. As Recorder, I assisted Fr. Davies, who was
the College Rector. He was a fine English gentleman who rolled his
own tobacco and spoke with a soft, silky Oxford accent. We became
excellent friends. I would accompany Fr. Davies to serve at Mass
at outstations including Goromonzi School.

In the car, Fr. Davies would recite poems and encourage me to
read G.K. Chesterton, Bernard Shaw and William Blake. He gave
me a collection of poetry books and typed out a copy of 'Lepanto'
for me. I became addicted to English Literature, bordering on bard-
olatry. I would visit Fr. Davies in his rooms at the Community house,
drink coffee, read and listen to Handel, Bach and Mozart. I was
then in Middle House. After prep, before bedtime, I would sneak
into Fr. Enright's room for a cup of hot chocolate and biscuits. He
always had a good story to tell but was down to earth and would
explain anything we did not understand especially things theological. He celebrated Mass every morning in Middle House. I would
serve at Mass.

Sometimes Tony Goodfellow S.J., a Jesuit Scholastic, would join
us as would other scholastics including Roger Riddell and Julian
Hoffman. Tony read history at Sussex University. He tutored me in
English history and encouraged me to read AJP Taylor's and E.P.
Thompson's books on British and European history. I read all there
was to read. With Robin Gaylard's help, I read classics from Caesar's
The Civil War, Virgil, Euripides, Catullus, Odes of Horace to Karl
Marx! His wife, Jane, encouraged me to read Virginia Wolf, Thomas
Hardy, James Joyce, George Elliot, E.M. Forster and a wide range

of novels. By the time I left school I had built a huge library which, added to Dad's library of theology, education and literature, filled two rooms in the house. We were a family of bookworms with mnemonics at the heart of our family creed.

The highlight of the year was the 'Grand Ball.' Girls were invited usually from four or five girls' colleges, the favourites being Dominican Convent, Nagle House, St. John's, Goromonzi and Bonda. A band and disco provided music for the day. We wore smart clothes of our choice and could walk girls around the school grounds and Houses. Special catering arrangements were made for our guests and only a few staff members were around to supervise proceedings. I danced with different girls during my time! I loved music but was never much of a dancer. I was more interested in the band and how the guitar players made their instruments wail. I would play air guitar imitating them.

In time, I would sneak off to the Middle House Recreation Rooms and practice chords and scales on the six string Gibson guitar that was availed for the purpose but hardly ever used. Thus my ambition to be a guitarist of note was nurtured. I loved to play Hey Joe, House of the Rising Sun and Smoke on the Water, among other songs. I often pretended I was Jimi Hendrix. I am not sure those who heard my efforts were convinced of my potential as a musician. I maintained constant contact with my lady friends via the College postal service. Nothing much ever developed nor blossomed as a result, but it was a good way to pass time.

Most Saturdays I would go to Mary Ward House to help Sr. Toma mend library books. She would give me tea and cake afterwards. If I was not with Sr. Toma, I was often with Fr. Greg Croft in the physics lab building gadgets, learning about electricity or other topical subjects or helping him in his nursery. He loved plants and taught me how to graft roses and other different flowers. I became a plant and bird lover. Fr. Croft was famous for his legendary temper. He did not suffer fools easily, but he never shouted at me when I messed up in the lab or in the nursery. He was kind and went to great lengths to explain how things worked. Often, he helped me with my physics homework. He was not as good as Fr. Davies or Fr. Enright at writing letters, but was good company.

The college is nestled in an isolated beauty spot in the Shawasha hills, on the outskirts of Harare. The peace and tranquility at the school was rudely disturbed by the arrival of two police trucks one day. It soon transpired that three sixth form students, Calisto, Christopher Tapfumaneyi and Alois Mlambo had been arrested, allegedly, for being 'terrorist sympathisers.' Within a few minutes, almost all the boys in the college surrounded the two police cars and overturned them. Armed police and the stone-throwing students had running battles around the Administration block. When the police eventually left the college, after reinforcements arrived, the students gathered and decided to walk to the city and stage a demonstration at the main police station, the 'Charge Office.'

The principal, Fr. Berry and a few teachers marched with us. As we approached Chisipite shopping centre, a police roadblock with dozens of armed police officers and dogs halted the march and told us we would be shot if we crossed the line. We all sat down on the tarmac. Fr. Berry addressed us and implored with us to march back to the college. Classes were cancelled for the rest of the week while the situation cooled down. There were daily visits from the police, "To maintain law and order," we were told. Eventually, the detained students came back to the college and peace returned.

One summer holiday, Fr. Greg Croft, Fr. Hugh Ross, Fr. James Channing-Pearce and Mr. Walter Duer took us, eight boys, four each from St. Georges and St. Ignatius, on an 'outward bound expedition' to the Chimanimani mountains. This was an experience of a lifetime for us all, the boys especially. None of the boys, had ever been to Melsetter or Chimanimani mountains. We had all heard about the highest peak, Mt. Kweza, in the Chimanimani range of mountains and had always wondered what it would be like to climb to the summit.

We piled into the college minibus with Fr. Croft at the wheel. It was not long before we broke into song. We stopped for 'a wee break' and sandwiches at Rusape Service Station and at the Roman Catholic Seminary in the Vumba hills, about halfway between Mutare and Chimanimani. The Carmelite Fathers at the seminary gave us hot drinks, delicious sandwiches and cake. They also told us about the sacred mountains we were about to climb. They stressed that we should be careful, stay together, not to pick any plants to bring back as it was illegal and to watch out for little snakes called berg adders. The snakes were small, about a foot long only but delivered a nasty bite around the ankles or crept into warm blankets. This caused some anxiety among the boys.

Almost six hours after we set off from Harare, we arrived at Dead Cow Camp, at the foothills of the imposing mountains. Soon the expedition leaders got to work, packing the food and drink provisions, toiletries and cooking utensils into rucksacks. Fr. Croft then informed us that we had to climb over the first range of mountains to the other side, cross a river, walk along a footpath on the edge of a chasm and ravine that dropped about two hundred feet to a fast-flowing stream at the bottom. We were to spend the night and set up base camp at 'St. George's Cave.'

The walk to our base camp took about four hours, the motley crew assembled and now looking up the mountains as reality began to set in, was informed. This was no walk in the park, as it were, but serious business. I staggered under the weight of my rucksack...'every ounce counts' muttered Fr. Croft close behind me as we walked in single file behind the leader, Fr. Channing-Pearce, who, as was later revealed, was an accomplished, fit and seasoned Aussie mountaineer! He taught us the basics of campcraft.

We stopped by the Bridal Veil waterfall at the foot of the first hill-climb, an impressive quartzite steep climb and looked in amazement at the awe-inspiring sight of water cascading down a cliff. It drops about four hundred feet. A cloud of water dances off the spectacle as the water sloshes into a huge pearl blue pool at the bottom. There, it swirls and gathers before trickling out at the base of the pool in a stream of crystal-clear water. It gathers momentum and becomes a river flowing through the park.

The shock of the sudden physical exertion was numbing. We trudged up the hill slowly in a single file. For the first half hour or so, there was silence, as the reality of the adventure now took hold. At that point, the heavens opened. There was no shelter, we had no umbrellas nor raincoats, so we just kept moving on the slippery track for what seemed and felt like days. The rain eased off after about two hours, by which time we were near the top of the first climb. Shortly thereafter, we left the main track which led to the next imposing ridge, lost in the clouds. We went down a tiny track, off the beaten path, veering right towards base camp and walked for another couple of hours. First, however, was our second rest stop and wee break. We tucked into our rations: two dry biscuits, a slice of bully beef and a small drink of the popular drink, 'Mazoe crush.'

We were soon on our way again. The rain had stopped. We walked slowly along the narrow footpath above the now swollen stream. Suddenly a loud, "Ouch!" came from behind me. At the same time, I felt a strange, itchy, stinging, burning sensation all over my legs as more "Ouches" were emitted by various members of the group.

"Come on boys," shouted Fr. Ross. "It's only stinging nettles!" That was my first encounter with nettles. I hated them.

"Good for soup," added Fr. Croft, grunting under the weight of his load. This adventure was turning out to be a nightmare for me. The whole idea of nettle soup as I walked along a narrow, slippery footpath, soaking wet and shivering high in the mountains did not sit well with me. It was not my idea of a good time.

After about forty minutes on the slippery path, the rain started to fall again and got heavier. I slipped and tripped on some large stones on the path. My rucksack flew violently sideways and pulled me down on the left side, face down, into the chasm. I screamed loud enough to wake the dead as I hurtled downslope. My drop to the bottom was halted by an alert Fr. Channing-Pearce: he quickly dived and caught my feet. Fr. Croft and Christopher Tobaiwa helped Fr. Channing-Pearce to haul me up. I was in shock. We gazed down the chasm in silence. I could only mumble, "Thank you father for saving my life." After a prayer, we were back on track to the next tricky bit: crossing the swollen stream before the final climb to our base camp.

Though small, only about ten feet wide, the stream was flowing fast and furiously. I was still traumatised from my fall, so not yet quite prepared to wade waist deep across the stream. However, my companions realized my state and decided to assist me wade across by grabbing me on either side, supporting me across the swollen stream. I was relieved.

The final climb to St. George's cave was slow and heavy-going but we were now in relatively good spirits. We exchanged jokes and made up funny stories. Tom Zanza, walking in front of me would occasionally turn his head around and surreptitiously hand me sweets. We called it "shaking hands." We chuckled a lot between ourselves, to the suspicion of our mates. They knew we were up to something. The rain had eased off again, a light wind blew in our faces. Finally, we arrived at our base camp. It is a huge overhanging rock with lots of room underneath to accommodate at least fifteen campers. At the back of the cave was a larder of foodstuffs left behind by previous occupants. These comprised mostly canned fruit, meats, flour, cooking oil, sugar, salt and cooking utensils.

We were allocated sleeping- bays in the narrow end of the cave. I would sleep between Tom and Christopher. We unpacked the provisions and set up a kitchen near the entrance of the cave. Fr. Croft had already set up a fireplace with a huge, blazing warm fire from the dry wood stored in the cave. "We must leave the cave in the same condition we found it and leave provisions for the next visitors, as is our tradition," Fr. Hugh Ross told us. We were all too exhausted and overwhelmed by the events of the long day to pay too much attention to the man's exhortations.

Soon Fr. Channing-Pearce was cooking dinner. We had steaming hot Royco vegetable soup that we drank from mugs, followed by boiled cabbage, fried bully beef and boiled rice. We devoured all the food with gusto before sipping hot black coffee. Then it was time for evening prayers, led by Fr. Croft. After prayers, we sat around the fire and talked about our families. We got to know each other well before dozing off and crawling into our respective sleeping-bays in the dust. We squeezed and huddled for warmth in our sleeping bags. We put towels over our walking shoes for pillows. We were too tired to care.

We slept soundly and woke up to golden streaks of dawn, wild birds in full throated song and noisy, curious baboons eyeing us from the rocks on the other side of the stream. Before breakfast, we were shown the ablution area, downstream from the cave, the bathing area, a pool near the cave, and upstream, a small waterfall where we would fetch our drinking water. We did not waste time before making use of the ablution area. It was strange at first, seeing each other squat and squint as we did our business on the wet grass before heading to the bathing pool for a wash. Fr. Croft was already in the cold pool. He encouraged us to join in. We did. The water was freezing cold.

The boys prepared breakfast: hot oatmeal porridge, a slice of brown bread and coffee. After breakfast we washed the dishes, tidied up the cave, said morning prayers and thus set the daily routine. The first day was a day of rest, fun and games near the cave. We explored the surrounds of the cave and got familiar with all the landmarks. The cave is located on the edge of a pass in the rifted quartzite ridges overlooking the majestic wilderness of the Chimanimani mountains. They form the border between Zimbabwe and Mozambique. A stream runs from the top of the ridge and cascades in various stretches of fast flowing and gentler flows as it winds its way through the wilderness. Eventually, it joins the Nyangani river in the rain forest that forms the National Park. The water was clean but brownish, safe to drink, especially after boiling it, said Fr. Croft. Our mission was to climb and scale the highest peak in the Chimanimani mountains, Mt. Kweza. At about 8,000ft above sea level. Mt. Kweza was half a day's walk from our camp.

The plant life was simply breath-taking. The Ross-Croft show was in its element as the two Jesuits who loved plants showed us the different plant species, cycads, strelitzias, wild orchids and tree ferns among others. The two endemic creatures, the Inyanga river frog and the Melsetter/Chimanimani berg adder were also show cased. "A rather handsome fellow," said Fr. Ross as he called us to observe a shiny, brownish puff adder-like eight-inch snake that was sunning itself on the footpath. "Best left alone," he added. We were under strict orders not to touch or destroy any of the plant or animal life.

I learnt to appreciate the beauty of the wilderness, the calm, the sounds, the flowing stream, the mist and the majesty of the rocky ridges including the whole mountain ecosystem. We got a geography lesson about mountain formation from Fr. Channing-Pearce. All rather surreal. He explained in detail, succinctly and convincingly, the origin of the mountains and the topography of the area. He had a full reddish beard that he straightened occasionally as he spoke and chuckled at his own jokes.

After our lunch of tinned sardines, biscuits, an orange and a slice of cheese washed down with Mazoe crush, we all piled into the bathing pool. It was now quite warm, but the water was still cold. We did not mind the cold. The pool was about six feet at the deepest part. Fr. Ross would shout out maths puzzles, we splashed and giggled as we tried to answer. If anyone blurted out the wrong answer, he would shout "Manyupe!" as he tried to remember the Shona for liar, "Munyepi." We had told him the word, the night before. I do not think anyone noticed that we were in our birthday suits. We just had a good time with our teachers. This was a rare experience that bound us together in camaraderie and good spirits. A bond was formed. It persists.

Late afternoon we made a huge fire as the temperature started to drop. Soon it was time for Mass, which the three priests concelebrated. We sang during Mass and somehow I really began to appreciate better than before, as we sat and prayed in the dust, in a cave, around a fire, the meaning of the Holy Mass, prayer and the mystery of God and creation. This was the beginning of a life-time journey and quest for more knowledge and answers. Before bedtime, we discussed the game plan for the following day's business: the assault on Mt. Kweza!

We were up with the lark, to face a misty, drizzly morning. It was too cold to take a plunge after ablutions. We quickly washed our hands and faces, dressed warmly and gobbled a bowl of porridge, a slice of dry bread, "manna" as we called it and hot coffee. Soon we were on our way. We were led by Fr. James, as we trekked our way, partly retracing our route to the cave before turning right towards the first steep climb over the ridge that stood between us, another higher ridge and the awe-inspiring ridge that hid the target peak in the cloudy mists.

We took it on trust that it was there and if anyone could get us there, Fr. James would. We soon broke into song, our favourite chant from the fireside at the cave: "Tipei doro timwe, haaaa ha ha, Tipei doro timwe, Kwangosara chitende." (Give us beer to drink...nothing left but an empty gourd.) Alternatively, we sang "Oh Susannah" and "This land is my land." Soon we had the full force of the Jesuit troika harmonizing and singing along with us. This took the sting out of the strenuous effort exerted as we climbed higher up the mountain into the hazy, misty heights.

It was so misty we could not see very far down below us. Eventually, the misty air thinned and cleared enough for us to see Mount Kweza ahead of us. What a sight! It is a weathered dome in the wind-swept cold wilderness. We stopped and lined up for photographs with the majestic height in the background. After about an hour of more slogging, we reached the summit. We could see the misty clouds below us, but not much of a view except the seemingly endless ridges and mountain passes. Fr. Ross told us that elephants sometimes crossed along these passes and walked from Mozambique into Rhodesia in search of water and food. I did not find this fact very comforting. I did not stray far from the group.

After a little while, we tucked into our bully beef which was expertly put between two hunks of dry bread. As usual, we drank more Mazoe orange crush. This was followed by more photographs and another geography lesson on mountain formation and wildlife. As the wind picked up, we collected our bags, had one more ablution session on the summit, then began the descent back to base. The descent was uneventful except for the weird sensation of legs turning into "jelly." We got back to the cave while it was still light enough to plunge into the pool before building a huge fire, preparing dinner, more bully beef, prayers and wearily zonking out soundly.

After our morning swim the next day, we returned to our cave to witness the resident troop of baboons fleeing up the pass towards the rocks on the ridge. They left a scene of wanton destruction behind them: they had played "hara-kiri" in our cave. They had discovered bits of bread and vegetables on which they feasted. The tinned bully beef was clearly a bit of a challenge. Tins were strewn all over the cave along with cooking utensils, shoes and a few items of clothing. Not funny at all, but we had a laugh as we cleared up the mess. We restored order before settling down to our routine of physical and spiritual nourishment.

This was our final night in the cave. We sat round the fire and listened to our teachers narrate stories about their families. I heard Tom sobbing in his sleeping bag. He was so touched by the Jesuit stories he wanted to be one, he told me later. We were more relaxed in our group and promised to keep in touch. We did. After feasting on bully beef at least twice a day during the time we were in the mountains, I found the sight of meat unbearable. I resolved not to eat beef or chicken or "dead animals" if I could help it. I have not missed meat or chicken since then.

After a good clean-up of the cave we packed our clothes. We stored the unused provisions in buckets which were kept behind a pile of rocks at the back of the cave. There was no time for a plunge in the pool. We were soon on our way as we broke into song walking back towards the Bridal Veil falls. As we walked, Chris whispered to me that he had spotted a "beautiful serpent, a berg adder" just behind him. He convinced me that we should "rescue" the little fella and take it back to the car. It would make a lovely pet, he said. Foolishly, I agreed. I picked up the snake and deposited it at the bottom of my trousers pocket.

I felt the little creature settle down snuggly against my warm body. From time to time, I would press my pocket gently to feel the little bundle inside. When we got to the car, however, the little fella had found its way through a tiny hole in my pocket and had crawled down my leg to freedom. On exit, he left two neat, tiny puncture marks on my left leg, as a souvenir. The little bruise was itchy, warming up and swelling slowly. Chris and I decided to keep this happening, our little secret.

When I arrived home, the 'little secret' was soon spotted by Mum. She noticed the slow walk, and general unease. She demanded to know what had happened. I talked about the area we went to being infested with spiders and a few snakes. That was enough for her. She summoned Dad who wasted no time in whisking me off to the general hospital's emergency room. For the next five days, I got two shots on the buttocks daily, by a nursing sister who resembled a gorgon. Just desserts in the circumstances, I guess. Eventually the swelling subsided. I told my brothers what I had been up to. They were not impressed but promised not to tell Mum.

In response to endless questions from my siblings and friends as to why I put myself through 'ordeals' such as the trip to Chimanimani, I often found myself repeating the new words, indeed a mantra I learnt from Fr. Croft, 'biophilia.'

Chapter Seven

SCHOOL DAYS WERE SOON OVER. I look back at my brief time at St. Ignatius College as some of the most enjoyable learning experience I had growing up. By the time I left the College I was fluent in French, enjoyed Latin literature, loved Maths and Physics, was a keen gardener and budding mountain climber, discovered hidden musical talent: could play several musical instruments including the piano, guitar, bass and the saxophone.

Having been brought up in a strictly, Anglo-Catholic, 'High Churchmanship,' which encouraged a deep personal devotion, I was at home with the Roman Catholic tradition I was now immersed in. A poignant moment, for me, was an occasion on a hot sunny Wednesday afternoon as I stood on the balcony of Middle House watching colleagues play volleyball with Brother Benedict. Fr. Patrick Makaka stood quietly next to me. He spotted a huge ring on my fourth finger on the right hand. Unexpectedly, he genuflected, kissed the ring and spoke very softly as he rose. "You will be a bishop one day."

Years later, that moment remained vivid in my mind. It played repeatedly in my brain the day I was consecrated bishop, almost thirty years later. I have often wondered what on earth made him do that, what he felt, or his thought-process at the time. I have asked him on several occasions. He does not recall the specific moment in question but then always says, like my buddy' Morrith' Arthur Mutsonziwa said nonchalantly, repeatedly, "I always knew you would be ordained one day. You are the only one who did not realize it."

I have many enduring memories of schooldays, from infant school through A-levels. I attended many schools, more than the average pupil because the family moved from place to place due to the nature of Dad's work. Priests were often transferred from Parish-to-Parish at short notice, depending on need and the Bishop's discretion. After a while, boarding school was a possible solution, but sometimes, as in my case, this did not always work for a variety of reasons. We also had our fair share of home-schooling and private tuition to supplement our formal education.

By the time I had been through senior schools in Zimbabwe and the U.K., I had received a fair amount of formal education and been prepared for university education and life in any country in the world. Before going to university, I took a gap year from January till October. I worked as a volunteer and temporary teacher for three months in Manicaland, then read law at the University of Rhodesia from March till May of the same year. If it was my parents' decision, especially in my case, to deracinate us by sending us to boarding schools and thus obliterating our class markings, they succeeded.

In the U.K., I spent time doing odd jobs and getting ready for university. I lived with David Napier Hamilton at 109 Brixton Road in London. He was a kind and generous family friend. David was Head of the Chairman's office at the Greater London Council. Later, he was private secretary to Princess Margaret, I believe. 109 Brixton Road was stately. David introduced me to the world of fine wines and classic cars. He had a vintage Rolls Royce and a Morgan in his collection. His other passion was photography. He had a darkroom in his basement. He spent hours developing pictures especially of models.

David was a great entertainer. He frequently threw lavish dinner parties for his friends, mostly Old Etonians or from Oxford University. He would serve fine wines to accompany gourmet meals till the early hours of the morning. The man was punctilious about English grammar and etiquette. He corrected my grammar frequently as he explained nuances of the English language. He was not really a snob but was clearly proud of his aristocratic heritage. He also had many Ethiopian friends including the exiled family of Emperor Haile Selassie. Previously, he worked for the Ethiopian navy and had also been Secretary to the Governor of the West Indies.

David organized odd jobs for me to help me find my way around London quickly and, get acquainted with the city. I worked as a gardener in Battersea park, as a messenger at Banco do Brazil on King Street in the city and as a 'bricklayer's mate' at Barclays Bank building near Cannon Street Station. Life with David was never boring: going to the theatre, shopping at Harrods, driving classic cars in the countryside.

It was all about sashaying from party to party, meeting old friends and making new ones. In Cambridge, I got to know all the colleges, sports facilities, libraries and most importantly, pubs or 'watering-holes.' Midland Tavern was a hot spot for dancing on Fridays and Saturdays. Sundays, we would ride our bikes to Grantchester for an elaborate English afternoon tea. Occasionally, we would punt down the river to Grantchester.

One of the highlights of my first Summer in Cambridge was meeting and making acquaintance with the novelist Tom Sharpe and his American wife, Nancy. Tom and Nancy were friends of my cousin Tonderai and Scholastica, his wife. Tom was, then, a lecturer at the 'Tech,' (Cambridgeshire College of Arts and Technology), where Scholastica was a student. Tom and Nancy would join us for meals at 5 Croft Gardens, Barton Road. Tom was immensely funny. He had a wicked wit. Nancy was gentle, quiet and reserved but always cheerful.

Tom and I became friends. We would meet at the Eagle pub near the Market for drinks. Tom would talk animatedly about academic dottiness and political satire. He enjoyed slapstick farce and was, sometimes, crude and quite offensive. I enjoyed our meetings and remained in touch with Tom for many years as he spent more time in Spain. His description of the thoughts and background to his novels, *Riotous Assembly, Indecent Exposure* and *Blott on the Landscape* were hilarious and memorable. Tom was then writing his series of novels based on the Tech., the 'Wilt' series.

'Chez Nous,' as we called 109 Brixton Road, had a great collection of books. David was an avid reader, a keen scholar of history and politics. I needed no encouragement to read. By the end of summer, I had read a whole series of African writers notably, Wole Soyinka, Ali Mazrui and Kwame Nkrumah. One afternoon, David took me on a tour of the Houses of Parliament. We went into both houses, guided by Peter Brooke, M.P. for the City of London. We then went to David's favourite place of worship, Westminster Abbey. The Dean, by chance, showed us around. We made a similar tour of St. Paul's Cathedral. That weekend, my sister, Emmie, visited us. She was now a nurse at Newcastle General Hospital. David took us to most of the tourist sites in London and then to The Savoy for dinner.

I had to make up my mind as to what I wanted to read at university. I had an offer to read law at Cambridge, History at London University's Bedford College and an offer and a scholarship to join a select group of eight on a new degree course in International Finance and Banking sponsored by the Bank of England at The City University in London. I was in a quandary. I loved all three courses and would have done them all at once if I could. Tonderai and David advised me as to the pros and cons of each discipline. Tonderai was, at that time, a Ph. D candidate at Cambridge and President of the University's Graduate Society. He was in favour of the new course at City. David was in favour of Cambridge, with Bedford College second. He argued that either of the two were established courses.

The new one, while attractive for a future in the world of banking and finance that I liked so much, was yet untested and therefore risky. Which would you choose?

So, my academic journey began its second phase. I spent the next seven years in university followed by two more years at university after an awfully long break. I left university with degrees in Economics, Finance, Business Administration and finally, Theology. I had attended four universities: Cambridge, Cranfield, London's City. I made many friends during that time and have fond memories of my tutors especially Professors Brian Griffiths, Geoffrey Wood, Gerry Dickinson, John Constable, Ray Vernon, John Stopford, Malcolm Harper, Brian Stanley and David Thompson. John Constable, my supervisor when I was a doctoral candidate became a friend, mentor, role model and confidante.

I visited John and Liz at their home in Bedford often. John taught me how to 'think' and how to play golf. He raised funds for me to go to Harvard Business School as a resident scholar. His Doctoral supervisor, Ray Vernon, tutored me in Multinational Corporate Business Strategy. John also arranged for me to spend time at London Business School where I was tutored by John Stopford in Corporate Strategy. John Stopford and Ray Vernon were the External Examiners for my Ph.D. Malcolm Harper was my Internal Examiner.

My 'viva voce' or oral exam for my Ph. D was, for me, memorable. I had expressed opinions and made conclusions, in my literature review, that were substantially different from the academic work of a Canadian scholar who had been supervised by one of my External examiners. This created an awkward moment. There was a heated exchange between the learned men around the table. I had been warned not to panic as I was 'the expert' in my chosen field. I only had to demonstrate a sufficient grasp of the theory of it, an in-depth understanding of the subject and an ability to defend my findings and analysis adequately. Overall, I had to demonstrate that my work constituted new knowledge and broke new ground in my subject, the economic and financial role of multinational companies.

I must have done all that. After almost three hours, having been asked to clean up typos and rewrite two paragraphs in one chapter, my Examiners congratulated my Supervisor who, in turn, welcomed me into 'the fold of intellectuals.' I was exhausted and numb. The whole exercise felt like a big anti-climax. Fellow doctoral candidates hugged me and offered congratulations. Prof. Constable organized a celebratory dinner party for me. I later realized that three of his other doctoral candidates had been at it for over four years and still had not produced their final theses. No wonder he was overjoyed. I was not particularly clever, but I worked hard.

My colleagues, on the Ph. D programme sponsored drinks and a lunch the next day. It was a week before I recovered fully from the excessive carousing. At that point, I informed my parents, siblings and friends that I was now a 'free spirit'! Two weeks later, I presented a bound, corrected copy of my thesis to Prof. John Stopford at London Business School. We chatted about our clergy fathers, had tea, then after a firm handshake, I left for Kings Cross Station to catch the train back to my rooms. I had wanted to tell him that I dismissed his earlier criticism of my work as hominem nonsense. I kept that to myself.

While I was John's student, he arranged work for me as a lecturer for Troy State University and the University of Maryland on their external campuses at Mildenhall, Lakenheath and Chicksands Airforce (U.S.) in Norfolk and Bedfordshire, respectively. I also assisted him with case studies and tutorials on the M.B.A. course and selected short courses at Cranfield Business School and at Cardington. I enjoyed the experience and made many friends in the U.S. Air Force. My status as an 'Instructor' at the bases gave me access to cheap wines, music and accessories like hi-fi and headphones etc.

I bought myself a fancy hi-fi system and carefully loaded it in my first new car, a Lancia HPE sports car. I had put my salary from all the extra work that I undertook at the various educational institutions to good use. Cases of Pink Chablis, Cherry Vodka and the awful Wild Irish Rose also found their way into the car. In a short time, my rooms in the Postgraduate, Fedden House, was a lively party place. For good measure, I also bought myself several guitars and large speakers. Much noise was made in my rooms over time. Friends, including band members of the reggae group, the Cimarrons, Linton Kwesi Johnson and Dennis Bovell (Black Beard), leader of the reggae group, Matumbi and other musicians such as Wallace Williams and his friend, I-Roy, would come over for jam sessions.

At that time, my friend, Richard Small, decided to get married. His family lived in Cranfield village. Richard's father, Bill, had been a lecturer at the Business School but had recently left to work in industry. Richard was a fine gentleman with a quaint sartorial sense. He knew everything about cars, politics, and any arcane matter. Richard, whose sobriquet was 'James Bond,' asked me to be his best man. A week earlier, I had been best man at another friend's wedding at St. Mark's church, in Cambridge, followed by a lavish reception in Grantchester.

I was the only black person at Richard and Joanna's wedding. Whenever the little flower girls looked up at me, they were visibly terrified and walked into each other. We had not rehearsed the ceremony. Many people found this hilarious. At the wedding in Cambridge, there were only two black people, Luke, the groom and I. This was an 'upmarket' event. The maid of honour was Luke's sister-in-law. She was stunning and friendly. I made jokes which would have been classified as politically incorrect or plain racist today, but everyone found them hilarious. I was the DJ at both weddings, during which time I was sober. After both weddings, we all got together and then had a combined bachelor post-party in Cambridge. I must have been intoxicated for a week after that.

At this time, Emmie has relocated to Northampton General Hospital, which is forty minutes away from Cranfield. I would visit her often. She was a great cook. My brothers, Maurice and Nathaniel, were now at university at Bristol and Leeds, respectively. We would often get together for a 'family gathering.' We enjoyed visiting our friends, Housemaster of G Social at Radley College, the Stoughton-Harris family, our 'elder brother' Tonderai and his family, our cousin James Makoni and his family in Cambridge and London, respectively.

Mum and Dad visited us from time to time and would spend about two months with us, moving from place to place visiting their friends. Diana Gunn, who had lived with us at St. Alban's, now lived in Bristol. She 'kept an eye' on Maurice, a difficult task. Most Christmas holidays Nathaniel and I would go to Radley College to the Stoughton-Harris household. We loved it there. We were friends with their five daughters. I also enjoyed spending holidays, especially Christmas, with Ed Spriggs at their lovely home in Wylam. Ed had two elder sisters and twin younger brothers who also went to Radley College. We had good times in the Northeast! The Spriggs, like the Stoughton-Harris family, were our closest family friends.

During summer, in my undergraduate years, David took a small group of us to France. We drove to Chateau Figeac, Saint-Emilion, in Bordeaux. It was owned by his friends, the Manoncourt family. Figeac is the largest wine estate in Saint-Emilion. It has well known neighbours, Le Pin, Petrus and Cheval Blanc among them. We spent three weeks picking grapes and touring the entire Bordeaux town and districts around Saint-Emilion, Medoc, Haut Medoc, Grave and then onto Provence. We toured St. Tropez, Cannes, Seillans, Nice, then up the French Riviera to Monaco before going to Dijon, Paris and back to London. We did this in three consecutive summers. I got 'addicted' to Bordeaux wines, mussels in Arcachon, cheese, foie gras and the way of life in the south of France. I found myself visiting at every opportunity in subsequent years including a visit to Figeac and Chateau Margaux on honeymoon, many years later.

John Constable had always warned me that at some point, school would be over, and I would have to join the ranks of the unemployed or get a job. I had been to a job interview in the City of London at Manufacturers Hanover, then a leading finance house. I had just completed my Masters' degree in Finance. At that point, after being offered a position as a trainee in the Corporate Finance Division, I talked to one of my tutors, Gerry Dickinson, who advised that it was his observation that I enjoyed research and writing, so why not try to register for a doctorate. So I did.

One afternoon, John summoned me to his office. He told me that he had arranged for me to have lunch at Morgan Grenfell, a top Merchant Bank in the City of London. His friend, Bill Higman, who headed Corporate Finance at Morgan Grenfell would be my host. After a lengthy liquid lunch with Mr. Higman, I caught the train back to college. The following day, John invited me to his office again. He shut the door, shook my hand firmly and told me that I had held my drink impressively during lunch at Greens Restaurant in St. James, London, with his friend Bill. I was therefore 'eligible' to work with his team. Was I ready to start work in a week's time?

And so, my freedom and carefree days as a 'perpetual student' ended. I packed my bags and headed for London to start a new life, my first real job, as a banker. An Investment Banker. A week earlier I had been to NatWest Bank, on campus, seeking, with John's support, a student loan to tide me over a few weeks of unemployment. The manager, a surly Mr. Bristow, literally frog-marched me out of his office telling me that I was a 'good-for-nothing perpetual student' who needs to get a job. As I stumbled out of his office, I blurted out to him that one day I would establish my own bank and he would be a junior clerk in my bank. John Constable reminded me of that incident for many years to come.

On hearing my news about the job at Morgan Grenfell, David arranged for me to visit his tailor on Saville Row. I had two new suits made. He chose a charcoal grey and a pin striped midnight blue cloth. I was duly measured for my first decent business suits. From there we went to Jermyn Street where he bought shirts and socks from his favourite shop, New and Lingwood. Apparently, they were his 'shirt makers' at Eton. I stayed at David's house for a month before I moved into my own 'digs' in the Barbican complex.

The highlight of my little apartment was the collection of musical equipment that I had collected over my seven-year stint as a student: the centre piece was a powerful hi-fi system, guitars and a small library. On my trips to Bordeaux, I would bring back cases of wine. I now had an enviable wine collection. My love of photography persisted. By now I had saved money to buy a Leica camera and video recorder.

I often took time to look back and reflect on my life journey then. From humble beginnings in the depths of the Honde valley, St. James Zongoro with Mum and the C.R. fathers, life with Dad back from College in South Africa and working as a priest, his ministry at various mission stations, early school life, education at various schools in Rhodesia and England and now seven uninterrupted years at universities in England and America and now ready to start work in the City of London.

I had packed a lot into being 24, a friend remarked. I had also been lucky, privileged, worked hard and benefitted from family connections and friends. It had not been easy all the way especially since I did not always seem to have enough funds but somehow managed to pay my way through with help from my sister, scholarships and help from David Hamilton, John Constable and an unexpected but most welcome generous cash donation from Bishop Abel Muzorewa, a relative of Dad's.

I had attended excellent educational establishments, met with influential people in all walks of life, aristocrats, middleclass and other folk. I had established a wide network of friends and contacts that would serve me well in the future and had travelled across Europe and America. I had spent enough time around musicians to know and accept that despite my love of music, I could never make a living as a musician. I had spent time in the studio with I-Roy, Dennis Bovell and Wallace Williams, rubbed shoulders with Joan Armatrading, the Brothers Johnson, George Benson and Harry Belafonte.

I had worked as a gardener, a bricklayer's mate and a bank messenger in the City of London. I had spent time shooting duck, pheasant and grouse on friends' estates in Norfolk and Northumberland and attended lavish dinners, parties and other events. And of course, the trips to France, the whole wine experience was deeply etched in my brain as was the gadzookery that larded ancient scripts and Elizabethan pastiches in David's library. I read them avidly.

Despite my wide and varied experiences, I still felt thirsty for something that I could not define. I felt somehow incomplete. The experience was like I had eaten lots of food, felt full but was unsatisfied. I had escaped the brutalities of a racist regime in Rhodesia and had not encountered much racism directly, growing up. We were deftly shielded from the worst extremes of this evil by parents and to some extent, the Church through various schemes set up to assist the clergy and their families. I would often discuss with David, John, Tonderai and others, but still had a little nag at the back of my mind, that there was something else I wanted to do, something else maybe God had in store for me. On his many visits to his family in the U.K., Fr. Enright would spend time with me. We shared drinks. I enjoyed his family very much. We had extensive discussions around how I felt then.

On one of those visits, as we sat in my rooms, Brian asked me if I would ever consider training for the Ministry. This took me by surprise. I was shocked, answered him firmly in the negative and changed the subject. I had grown up in the church and had seen much that put me off, I explained. I was in denial, I guess. In my lucid moments, alone, I found myself praying to God for direction. I would offer myself for His use according to His wishes. Often, I would spend a quiet moment of reflection whenever I walked past a church. Any church. I noticed that I also felt better and refreshed every time I did.

Mine was not a rags-to-riches story so far. Simply different. I had a relatively opulent though modest upbringing and lifestyle with most 'mod-cons' within reach. In retrospect, I have always wondered what difference the internet, standing as cultural synecdoche nowadays, would have made then. I was relatively privileged, sheltered and yet with access to the wild side of life. My love life was very much undeveloped till much later in life. I had numerous lady friends as a student, but never really fell in love or settled into a serious relationship. Books and music took centre stage. I worked hard, I had to lucubrate to achieve good results in academic endeavors. I had friends who achieved better results effortlessly.

I enjoyed female company very much but was just too self-centered to develop a deep meaningful relationship with any of my female companions. I quite fancied a few of them, but always liked to have more than 'a few' around me at any one time. I think I was also scared of falling in love and the unknown that came with it. Oftentimes George and I would go out together. He would always have a girl on his arm. Not surprising, I thought, he was and still is tall and handsome. Somehow, he could not keep them though: they would sometimes fall for me too! That disturbed me a bit though I never regretted it.

After post graduate studies, George left for Ghana, to run the family business. We stayed in touch. I was very fond of one of his sisters. I got on well with his Dad, JP, we called him (John Prah). He was a fine, true gentleman with a penchant for sports cars, whisky and things Scottish. He had a wicked sense of humour. One day he asked me how much I loved one of his daughters. I 'blushed' and stuttered, 'very much.' He squeezed my hand and said, "I don't see that fire in your eyes!" I almost ran away. I was embarrassed. Thus, my romantic life stayed in the doldrums for years to come.

Chapter Eight

I ENJOYED ALICE COOPER'S music, 'School Time Is Over' was one of my favourite songs. So it was, when I walked into the reception of Morgan Grenfell on Great Winchester Street in the City in October 1982. I was already familiar with the bank as I had visited Bill Higman and had met his colleagues. Bill had previously introduced me to the Chief Executive, Mr. Christopher Reeve. I felt quite at home but was still daunted by what lay ahead for me.

My previous visits had been to discuss aspects of my research and to find out more about the bank's business and financing strategies worldwide, Now I was here as an employee. I had to learn and become part of an esteemed and reputable Investment Banking team. The bank was well known for its aggressive and unsurpassed Mergers and Acquisitions success in the City. Through a combination of good fortune, timing and 'god-fathers,' I had landed this position in an unusual way far removed from the usual graduate recruitment and placement process. This is how I embarked on my banking career.

My first assignment was to understudy and assist one of the directors by gathering and analysing financial information for a capital raise for a large client. They were also planning to list the company on the main stock exchange. I analysed the historical performance, financial projections, market conditions, management strategies and economic outlook, among other factors. I then had to study listing requirements. I sat through numerous meetings with the client's management, accountants and legal team. It was a steep learning curve. The analytical tools I had acquired from school helped, but there was a difference in this real world: I had to learn quickly how to 'use my gut' and ascertain whether an analytic outcome based on figures only was realistic, practical or appropriate in a given setting.

I soon settled into this life and work in the real world of corporate finance. A far cry from the academic cloistered, calm world that I had enjoyed previously. At a lunch to celebrate a successful listing and capital raise, I asked one of my 'bosses' how he had calculated the fee that we had charged the client. He looked at me, sucked his thumb then, with a glint in his eye told me that he settled on a figure that was lower than the earlier one he had quoted, the one at which the client had begun to faint in horror, he then revised it downwards, at which point the client was grateful and just wanted to pay and escape. The important thing was, he said, that we covered all our costs and charged like a wounded buffalo for all the blood, sweat, and tears. I was baffled, but it wasn't long before I also developed the art and confidence to charge an appropriate fee.

The next task involved an acquisition of a series of breweries by one big brewery. Once again, the task of stock valuations, financial analyses, projections and market analyses was the order of the day. As a junior member of staff who had the requisite analytical tools, I was tasked with the initial financial analyses, gathering relevant market data and looking up strategies from similar industries the world over. This was a solid and unsurpassed learning pad. The work came in fast and furious. We all worked long hours in the plexus of high financial dealings. I started early, mostly before 8.am, ate lunch at my workstation when I was snowed under, and generally was one of the last to leave around 7 p.m. I enjoyed my work very much and was eager to learn from the more experienced colleagues. They were always on hand with tips and methods that made the analyst's life easier. Financial analysis became my forte and my pleasure.

I was determined to learn as much as one could. The bookshop at the Bankers' Institute just around the corner from the office, near the Bank of England and the Economist bookshop at the London School of Economics became regular pit stops as I hunted for the latest books in Finance, Economics and other areas of interest. Soon my library outgrew the space in my little apartment. There were books piled on my kitchen table, under my bed and on the hi-fi speakers.

One of the bank's clients, the Anglo-American Group, out of South Africa, had wide-ranging interests in Zimbabwe especially in mining and finance. I worked on advisory and fundraising assignments for various parts of the group. I also met and worked with officers from the various parts of the group, especially those from the banking subsidiaries. The Harare-based one was R.A.L Merchant Bank (Rhodesian Acceptances Limited), a successful Accepting House. After working on a transaction with the then Managing Director, Michael Laws, and visiting other banks including Lazard's and Rothschild's with him, we built respect for each other, We worked well together.

Mike surprised me during lunch back at Winchester Street, when he invited me to visit R.A.L in Zimbabwe, which had just attained independence, and if I liked it, he added, I could join their Corporate Finance team. This would ease me into the system. I would have to spend the first six months as his Personal Assistant and understudy. I was thrilled at Mike's offer but had to consult my colleagues at Morgan Grenfell before I could accept it.

After much consultation, I took up Mike's offer to visit R.A.L. Merchant Bank. I had not been to Zimbabwe in about ten years and was anxious to see the changes that independence had ushered in. I had missed out on the war years. I only heard stories and accounts from those who were in the country during the strife. A lot of people I had known or known of had died during the liberation war. I had watched the Independence Day celebrations as Prince Charles took down the Union Jack and the new Zimbabwe flag raised to music by Bob Marley and his band. It all looked surreal. I wondered what life was really like in households, the workplace and all over the country.

I wondered about the racism and segregation that had prevailed in Rhodesia; how the financial markets, which were mainly white-controlled and owned would react to skilled blacks coming into the sector post-independence. I was anxious but excited. "You don't have to go, old chap," said my boss. "If you think them racist or awkward, come back immediately. There is always a place for you on the team here." With those words of comfort, I got ready for my journey to Zimbabwe.

As I stepped off the stairs of the British Airways Jumbo jet early on a Friday morning in May 1983, I walked sprightly towards the arrivals-hall at the new Harare International Airport. A strange mix of euphoria and doubt whirled in my head. I tried hard to scan the thronged gallery of welcoming, mostly white folks meeting their kith and kin, for familiar faces as I expected at least some family member to meet me. However, the walk into the arrival's hall was too short and the crowd too big for me to scrutinize.

Soon I was through immigration, collected my suitcase and made my way to the exit gate. I emerged from the arrivals hall and walked straight into the arms of a beaming, tearful warm woman with two boys in school uniform behind her: Mum and my two little brothers, Dennis and Steven comprised the 'welcoming committee.' They fought their way through a sea of white people, to meet their 'long lost brother.' I barely recognized my brothers: they were barely five and six when I had seen them last, now they were tall, shy, gangly teenagers. Mum was in fine fettle. Dad was at a meeting at the Cathedral, Mum explained, we would collect him on our way home.

I could not remember much of the suburbs of Hatfield, Arcadia and Hillside as we drove through them to go downtown where we would meet Dad. Everything just appeared new and strange. There were, however, many more black people on the streets than I could remember. We parked in the Cathedral car park along Second Street (Sam Nujoma), near the corner with Baker Avenue (Nelson Mandela) and waited for Dad. I was exhausted but listened to stories about life, which relative had done what, died, joined politics etc., from Mum. My little brothers, especially Dennis, told me about their school and friends. Dennis was just about to go to university to read law and accounting, Steve was doing his A-levels and hoping to get into Medical School to read medicine and later, specialise in Oncology.

In the middle of this vivid discussion and competition to get words in edgeways, the car door flung open and a beaming Dad with outstretched arms and that familiar loud laugh literally dragged me out of the car. He squeezed the breath out of me with a hug akin to attempted murder. We had a laugh as we drove home. My parents had moved away from Rusape as the war got worse and after receiving numerous death threats from both the Rhodesian soldiers and the guerrillas. They bought a house on Ruchengeto Crescent, in one of the suburbs near Hatfield. They worked from home as they awaited the end of the war and the cessation of hostilities at independence.

The weekend was a festive affair. Friends and relatives came by to greet me. Everyone was generally horrified to learn that my eating habits were now strange: I was now a fully-fledged vegetarian. I would not eat beef, poultry or fish. My parents were aware of this as they had experienced my new-found eating habits back in the U.K. My two brothers were fascinated and amused. They thought it was a fad or just a passing phase. They were all wrong. (I did start eating fish, on doctors' recommendations ten years later.) With so much meat and 'braai' parties that weekend, it felt such a waste but

I was happy just to be back and to catch up with events of the previous ten years, especially the war, the voting and the independence celebrations.

Mum gave me her car to drive around with my brothers, familiarizing myself with the town once again, especially the bank where on the following Monday, I was to start my three-month stint. My family were amused but proud that I had left to finish school in the U.K., bootstrapped myself through college and was now addressed as Doctor Makoni. They nick-named me Doc. That stuck. It took me a long time to get used to the title.

On Monday morning, I dressed up in my charcoal grey suit, white shirt with trimmed back collar, wine-coloured tie to match my red socks and black churches' brogues. Mother looked at me and smiled. She gave me a lift to R.A.L. Merchant Bank near the corner of First Street and Jameson Ave. (Samora Machel), across the road from the Reserve Bank. I hugged her and bid her goodday as I reached for my black leather briefcase carrying various papers, Kit-Kat, two cheese and tomato sandwiches and a bottle of still mineral water.

I announced to a perplexed doorman that I was here to see the Managing Director, Mr. Mike Laws. His jaw dropped as a voice on his phone instructed him to direct me to the second floor, the Management floor. I was clearly expected: June, Mike's assistant, met me at the elevator. In a broad Scottish accent, she invited me to an empty office and offered me coffee. "This will be your office. Mr. Laws will be with you shortly. I am June, by the way the other lady, Brenda Armstrong, will assist you." With a little smile and one more look at me, she left the room. Outside I could hear whispers about the new black manager. My heart sank a little.

Just then, a familiar voice sounded outside the door and the little chubby figure of Mike Laws eased its way into the room with an outstretched arm and a handshake. Behind Mike were two men from the Corporate Finance Division, Frank Jackson, the Head, and Mark Scanes, one of the analysts. I had met Frank briefly in London. He was Rhodesian, born and bred, and had just returned from the University of Cape Town where he had spent a year reading for a Diploma in Business Administration. Mark, an Englishman who had been in the country for two years, had recently qualified as a Chartered Accountant.

As Mike introduced me to Frank and Mark, there was a very loud, very English and familiar voice at the door, 'Welcome home my dear Chap! I never thought you would ever come back!,' said Tony Upfill-Brown, Managing Director of Anglo's Sagit Stockbrokers on the third floor of the same building. I had met Tony several times in London. We had mutual friends. He had lost a leg in the Second World War and hobbled on an artificial leg. Tony (Uppers, as he was affectionately known) was very loud but always cheerful. He invited me to join him for lunch at the Salisbury Club later that day.

The rest of the morning I spent touring the bank's divisions, Treasury run by Stewart MacIver, International Banking and Local Banking, headed by the deputy managing director, Dan van Wyk, Economics, under John Robertson assisted by Coleen Willis and Frank Jackson's Corporate Finance. It was a small bank compared to where I had come from, but very well organized. The staff were generally curious but largely courteous and polite. I still felt like I was an object of curiosity. There was a sprinkling of black faces among the skilled staff on the ground floor offices.

Mike Laws briefed me on the reporting lines and management structures of the bank. As a temporary staff member, I would be entitled to use the Executive Dining Suite on the eighth floor as well as the dining hall at Charter House, where the main Anglo-American Corporation's offices were situated. I was encouraged to visit and familiarize myself with the other Anglo subsidiaries in the building, Sagit Stockbrokers and Bard Discount House which was run by one Mike Gibbons who I had met a couple of times in

London. My specially created new position as Assistant to the Managing Director caused a bit of a stir. I was constantly asked as to what my exact role was and whether I was the deputy managing director in disguise. I enjoyed the intrigue.

Lunch at the Salisbury Club as Tony's guest was a colourful affair. We were joined by David Lewis, Senator Sam Whalley (both prominent lawyers), Pieter van der Byl (an ex minister of foreign affairs in the outgoing Rhodesian government and Robert Marple, a shy, Oxbridge-trained educationist. They were all as curious as I was to find out how I found the situation in the country now compared to the time I left for the U.K. I tried to explain that I was too young at the time I left, to be politically aware in the way that I was now, but I thought that if all professional people worked together without regard to racial discrimination, segregation and animosity, there was a good chance that the country would prosper. Balanced economic development and care for the environment should be every Zimbabwean's focus.

Mr. van der Byl (a.k.a. 'The stallion of Salisbury') chuckled as he handed me his card. He spoke about his time at Cambridge, Pembroke College and his love of punting. We discovered that we had three mutual friends in the U.K. We had a jovial conversation. "Let's have lunch in a couple of weeks and let's see if your views still hold," he said. My vegetarianism was another point of debate. David Lewis pointed out that he felt it was not possible for black people to be vegetarian. A heated discussion ensued, 'oiled' by the consumption of generous amounts of the local red wine of choice, 'Mukuyu Cabernet.' It was aptly described by a discerning wine lover as 'a mixture of soda and vinegar.' It evidently did not travel well from the cellars in Marondera to Harare, forty kilometres. Chateau Migraine.

It amazed me how much there was acceptance of the new political order. At the same time, there was a strong undercurrent of racial superiority among my lunch colleagues. Tony would often try hard to make a distinction between me and 'the ordinary African.'

I found this increasingly irksome and rude. Van der Byl, at least, despite his phony English upper class drawl akin to a character in a bad 1960s movie, was unrepentant and blunt in his belief that the ideology, communism, espoused by the new regime, would never work. More skilled and experienced blacks were needed in government and the private sector if there was to be real development and peaceful progress. He was more sanguine than most of the Rhodesians I had conversed with at that point.

I kept asking myself as the day wore on, whether I was imagining the undercurrent of racism all around me, whether I was paranoid or so used to the U.K. environment which was undoubtedly different in its approach to issues of race and colour. It was always my belief that differences help us define who we are. Often, those who are different from us come out on the short end of the comparison. If we think we are doing something the right way, then it is easy to conclude that those who are doing it a different way are wrong. By the time I got back to the office, I was somewhat disturbed and just wanted to go home.

I was relieved to clamber into Dad's car parked in front of the bank just after five. "You look deflated," observed Dad. "Work in the real world is like that. Let us go home and enjoy a cold beer." So, we did. I bottled up my feelings, fears and misapprehensions. At least the Castle beer was cold and refreshing. Dad liked Lion lager and Mum sipped on a glass of local white wine, another product from the cellars of Mukuyu Wineries, 'Mukuyu Colombard.'

Each morning I would meet with Mike for a brief on the day's work. Mike, a keen cricketer and former wicket keeper for Surrey Cricket Club, was a Chartered Accountant. He liked to keep everything in neat boxes. There were projects, advisory work, management issues, lending and treasury matters to attend to, daily. I got immersed in the work but enjoyed corporate finance work and economic reports more. These were distributed twice a week and discussed by management, along with other issues, every Friday morning. I spent a few days in the acceptances and letters of credit sub-divisions of the bank and a couple of weeks helping with analyses of new issues and loan stock among other work, in the corporate finance division.

Mike introduced me to a client I had already met in London, Algy Cluff. He was establishing a gold mine in Filabusi, south of Bulawayo. I went on a three-day field trip with Algy, wrote up the project papers and took the loan application to the board. The loan was approved. I became a hero and a lifelong friend of Algy's especially as the Chairman of Anglo then, Gerry Carey-Smith, was vociferously non-impressed that we had financed 'the opposition.'

I took the fall for the bank. Algy and I still laugh at the whole saga. I also enjoyed the time I spent with Tony Upfill-Brown and his fellow stockbrokers at Sagit and Mike Gisborne at Bard Discount House. I liked the stock market work, especially financial analysis so much I decided to study for the stockbrokers' exams. Just before I left for the U.K., I sat for and passed the Stock Exchange exams. I was admitted as Zimbabwe's first registered black stockbroker.

Three months went by very quickly. I was glad to be back with some family and new friends, especially, but I was restless and wanted to be back in my own space in London. I missed my friends at work and socially. I missed my music, especially my favourite guitar, Wah Wah and my Saxophone, Bluesman. It all felt very strange. One weekend I visited my grandmothers, first my maternal grandmother, Mbuya Ellen Mawondo at her homestead near Manica bridge, on the Mutare-Nyanga road.

I enjoyed her cooking. She prepared dried fish and brown rice with peanut butter, hunks of homemade bread and special herbal 'Makoni tea.' She was curious about my love life and was amused by the fact that I did not have a black girlfriend. "As long as you are happy, I am happy," she would say. My paternal nan, Mbuya Doris was a little different. She lived near Chief Makoni's court in Madziwa, on the Rusape-Nyanga road. She demanded to know when I planned to settle down and insisted that I should look around for a 'home girl' who would 'look after the family in a traditional way.' I was convinced that this is not what I wanted. As I left her place, I was determined to do the opposite or remain single. My parents thought the whole thing was quite amusing. I did not.

I was exhilarated to get back onto a British Airways jumbo jet and fly back to London. My parents were due another four months-visit to the U.K. on church business. My two youngest brothers were back at boarding school and university. My friends at R.A.L gave a farewell party for me and amid the party gibble-gabble, urged me to come back to work with them. This was a sirenic prospect that I would consider seriously, but first, I had to go back to my apartment, decompress and process all the information I had gathered before committing myself to any long-term plans. At least I did not have to worry about a job for now. This was a good place to be.

Chapter Nine

IT FELT GOOD TO BE back in London. A different sort of 'home-coming,' an unusual but happy feeling. It was awkwardly comfortable. Clearly, not an easy feeling to put into words succinctly. The important consideration was that my trip to Zimbabwe had been a 'game changer.' I had to make up my mind which way I wanted my career to go and how. Would I stay in the City, be one of the 'boys' as part of a successful Corporate Finance team, would I like to take up R.A.L's offer for a full-time position, possibly taking over the running of the Corporate Finance Division. Frank Jackson had, apparently, mooted that his new wife was not happy in the country. She wanted to leave Zimbabwe to be close to her parents in the U.K.

"You have to make up your mind in the next six months or you will lose out on good opportunities," advised Bill Higman over lunch at Morgan Grenfell. "You are young enough to take risks at this stage of your career. You can play it safe and stay here. We would be delighted. You can go to R.A.L and try it out for at least a year. Come back if that does not work out. There is also the I.M.F and The World Bank. The world is your oyster, old boy," he continued. Those words echoed in my mind all week especially as I sat alone in my apartment listening to Ronnie Laws' classic, 'Why do you Laugh at Me? 'and Quincy Jones', 'What Good is a Song?'

My life now assumed a certain degree and sense of direction, focus and energy. I was now determined, more than ever, to be a banker, a serious Investment banker. I had worked extensively on various banking projects and now knew my way around the 'Financial Times' and the markets generally. It just felt like I was raring to go. I still felt, however, that I wanted a professional qualification. Accountancy was never my thing, I was now a member of the Institute of Bankers and the British Institute of Management, but financial analysis was where I wanted to be: so I registered for part 1 of the American Chartered Financial Analyst (C.F.A.) programme. Something at the back of my mind had planted the desire to work in the financial sector in America at some future date. My friend, George Prah, had just enrolled on a Management Accountant course in Redditch. He thought I was mad and just enjoyed the cloistered calm of the academic world. We laughed as we teased each other.

George and I spent most of the next six months together. We saw the music groups, War, Brothers Johnson, Earth Wind and Fire, the Commodores, Joan Armatrading, the Blackbyrds and the O'Jays, among others at Wembley and Earls Court Concert Arenas. David Hamilton took us to shows at the Old Vic and other theatres in London. Among the memorable shows we saw were Jesus Christ Super Star and Evita. We became frequent visitors to Ronnie Scott's, Bouncing Ball, Club 100 the Old String fellows and other night clubs and restaurants. The Light of India restaurant near London Business School, Memories of China, on Ebury Street and Mr. Chow, at Knightsbridge, were our favourite restaurants. Sunday lunchtime, we would go to Rosebery Avenue near the Angel tube Station, for the jazz session hosted by one of David's friends who worked for B.B.C, Radio Three, Graeme Tyer.

At work, it was more of the same on Mergers and Acquisitions, listings, new issues and general advisory work for clients in different sectors. I particularly enjoyed working on yet another acquisition of a chain of breweries by a major player in the sector, followed by the merger of two medium-sized merchant banks. The two transactions were hugely different but entailed a great deal of market analysis, pricing issues and management negotiations. Teams of lawyers and accountants worked at the same time on very tight deadlines. Relevant consent from the authorities was sought and had to be in place before anything could be concluded. This was a great learning experience, a rewarding exercise for me. I met lots of other analysts and team members from finance houses that were also involved in the transactions. I made many contacts who became friends or colleagues in the markets as other deals were struck. This laid an excellent foundation for my future involvement in the banking world. I did not realise this at the time.

In my spare time I immersed myself in my C.F.A tutorials at the Institute of Bankers. I was fortunate to be eligible for a few Part 1 exemptions because of qualifications that I already held. The course itself was difficult but not impossible. I needed to work hard and learn a lot of new financial terms, mostly American. The sheer volume of material that one had to cover threw me off a bit initially. In time, I qualified for the Associate level, A.C.F.A and eventually the full C.F.A. This was, to my mind, an achievement that I had not envisaged when I started work. Over the years, I came to appreciate and enjoy the benefits of the qualification much more than I did when I sat for all the coursework and exams.

One Monday morning, about four months after my return from R.A.L. in Harare, I informed my two immediate Heads, Bill Higman and David Suratgar, that I was going to take up Mike Laws' offer to join R.A.L Merchant Bank in Harare. Mike had offered me the position of Head of Corporate Finance, which I had accepted. I would start the following February, five months hence. My last official working day at Morgan Grenfell would be the last day of November. I figured that this arrangement would give me enough time to organize shippers and transporters for my sports car, my musical equipment, books and household utensils and furniture. R.A.L., through their associate company, Knight, Frank and Rutley, would provide me with suitable accommodation and advise me what additional household goods I needed to ship to Harare.

In the event, K.F.R advised me that they had secured a duplex townhouse with two bedrooms, a kitchen, dining room, study and lounge/music room at Claumond, in the Harare suburb of Avondale. This, by all accounts, was a decent location and a good address. I was advised to bring a new electric cooker, a fridge-freezer, a washing machine, dryer and a dishwasher. David helped me buy all the goods I needed including bedding, sheets, towels, cutlery (some of which he donated from his vast collections) and three wine racks. My wine collection and library among other items, were crated, and shipped to Zimbabwe. I went to the depot near Greenwich, to witness my Lancia HPE sports car loaded into the container. The car appeared tiny. David assured me that all would be well, not a single wine bottle would be broken. He was right.

I spent the rest of my time before Christmas visiting friends. I stayed with Ed Spriggs at his parents' palatial home in Wylam. We played squash, went shooting pheasant and ducks. I always looked forward to dinner. We dressed up for dinner every evening, drank fine wines and enjoyed the occasional quodlibet. Christmas saw Nathaniel and I at Radley college, social G., with the generous and ever-lively Stoughton-Harris family. We had a lot to catch up on. Sue had rowed for Cambridge and now worked for the National Trust, Rachel was now married to Andrew, Nina and Tony now lived and taught at a school in New Zealand. Gillian was now married to David Haworth and about to relocate to Scotland. Clare was at Musical College in London. Christmas at Radley with the Stoughton-Harris family was nothing but a treat.

From Radley, Emmie, Maurice and I visited Tonderai and his family in Cambridge. We visited David Hamilton, in London, where we also visited friends and relatives for the New Year. A few days later, the entire 'tribe' drove me to Heathrow Terminal 3, where I boarded my favourite BA flight to Harare.

On the flight, I sat next to an old friend, Christopher Muts-vangwa. Chris had left school with a group of friends including George Chiweshe and Gula Martin Ndebele, to join the ZANLA forces fighting from Mozambique to liberate Rhodesia from colonial rule. I had met Christopher during my three-month sojourn at the University of Rhodesia. He was a law student. Chris narrated his eight-year journey through the war, the battles he was involved in, and who was who in the hierarchy of the ruling party, Z.A.N.U (P.F.). He must have talked almost non-stop for the duration of the flight, ten hours. I was not only a 'captive audience' but was genuinely riveted and interested to hear his take on things.

I learnt a lot about the then cabinet, the president and other civil servants. Chris is a great narrator with a gift of the garb and a fine sartorial sense. His story was very impressive and gave a useful background of some of the officials I would meet in my new position at R.A.L. On the same flight were two more friends, Paddington Garwe and Kevin Terry. They were both in the law faculty at U.Z. in the same year as Chris. Paddington had just been appointed a judge after a few years as a magistrate and Kevin had just joined The Old Mutual, after some time as a lawyer in private practice. We had a friendly chat at the Harare International Airport. We talked about the new political environment, old friends and ac-quaintances. We exchanged contact details.

Back in Harare, I had just under a month to retrieve all the goods that I had shipped, clear customs and set up home in my new apartment, 9 Claumond, Natal Road, Avondale. R.A.L had a small Datsun 120Y ready for me to use as my company car. This came in handy as I rushed from office to office filling in forms as a 'returning resident,' so that I would not pay customs duties on any of the items that I was importing into the country. Essentially my sports car and container with all my goods would not be inspected nor charged any duty. This took a couple of weeks but after a long, tedious process, all my goods were delivered to my apartment.

I went to Manica Travel Depot on Coventry Road in the industrial area near Harare General Hospital and collected my car. I raced back to my apartment where the task of unpacking and arranging furniture took the best part of a week. My brother, Dennis, would come over from the University and help me unpack, arrange furniture and connect all the electric appliances in the kitchen and scullery. In the evenings, we would sit on the balcony overlooking the little rose garden in front of the apartment and drink chilled wine and beers. The Chinese takeaway at the Avondale shopping centre saw many visits from Dennis and I. This was to be my home and base for the next ten months.

I met up with a friend, Nkosana Donald Moyo. He had been my senior and prefect at school. He had finished his studies at Imperial College, London, before taking up a position as a lecturer in the physics department at the University of Zimbabwe. On my earlier visit, I had stayed at his house along the Chase, in Mt. Pleasant. He had many friends, including diplomats and visiting academics. I was introduced into his social circle which was marked by lively parties on weekends, squash, golf and weekend jaunts to holiday resorts including Nyanga, Lake Chivero and Mazvikadei.

There was no shortage of friends, local or foreign, to join us. I got to meet many members of the academic community who had recently returned to Zimbabwe after exile or periods of study abroad. A notable friend was Naison Mutizwa and his wife, Dorothy who were both students in the U.K. at Cambridge where we had met. We spent many happy hours together. They are an excellent, friendly couple who remain great friends of ours. Naison and Dorothy were now part of the university community as lecturers.

At work, I jumped into the deepest end: I was the Head of a competent, well-qualified team of eight Corporate Finance executives. They had worked in the market and established a great reputation for their competence, imaginative solutions and efficient execution of transactions. I was the youngest and only black member of the team. I had met all my new colleagues on my previous visit. I had become friends with Mark Scanes and his wife, Jo. The team were interested in my work experience in London and my academic qualifications, especially my research which fascinated many. From the outset, Mike Laws made it clear who was now in charge. This made settling in relatively easy. Luckily, it was a busy time in the markets, so we tucked into our work without frivolous distractions.

Within four months, we had listed three companies, Rothmans, African Distillers, and Radar and were on track to list Zimplow. Word of a new arrival in the financial market soon went around. I found myself invited to other banks for lunch. Clients were always curious to meet the new Head of the team. After listing Afdis, I heard, through the 'grapevine,' that their outgoing finance director, a Mr. Des Lawler, had expressed surprise that a black person could understand finance and lead a white team. I decided to drive to his office on Lomagundi Road, to talk to him and hear for myself, what the issue could have been. Mr. Lawler received me well. I had called ahead to announce the purpose of my visit.

Over a cup of tea, I told him, robustly, that I was offended and disappointed at his comments. He promptly claimed that he was misquoted and apologised profusely. I made it excruciatingly clear that my team and I had done an excellent job as their own Chairman had acknowledged. If he had complaints, he should approach Mr. Laws directly rather than use 'bar-room gossip' to malign me indirectly on account of his racial bias. Des Lawler 'shrunk' in front of me and turned white as sheet. I slammed the door as I left his office. After that visit, I found attitudes towards me in the bank and in the market at large, significantly different, softer. It was clear that news of my visit to Afdis' offices made the rounds. I just had to focus on being the best professional in my field and delivering excellent service, working well, on good terms with my team. The strategy paid off. We were soon acknowledged as the Corporate Finance team of choice in the market. There was, however, a looming test ahead of me.

One of our Bulawayo-based clients was Super Canners, a beef-canning operation owned by an established Jewish family and run by one of the sons, Mervyn Gonsenhauser. Their main supplier, the government parastatal, Cold Storage Commission, headed by Mr. Eddie Cross, decided to expand their operations by acquiring Super Canners in a hostile take-over bid. Mr. Gonsenhauser was not impressed by the parastatal's advances and he enlisted our help to fend off Mr. Cross. My client was not the best-behaved business-person. He was brash, had a terrible temper and was in bad books with his workers. His mother, who would visit from London, was clearly in charge. She was a tough lady with little patience for bankers or her own son.

On the other side, I was confronted with a soft-spoken white civil servant championing the cause of a new black government in a direction that I considered ideologically misguided and morally wrong. Instead of encouraging private sector growth, government, through operatives like Mr. Cross, sought to expand the parastatal sector and crowd out private sector initiatives. This, to me, was unacceptable. This was a fight I was determined to win. Ideologically, I saw this process as abuse of political power to set up and accumulate an economic base for the new rulers. This was a model used in other parts of the developing world, fueling corruption and abuse of power.

My two meetings with Eddie Cross' team led by him and my team which included our bank Economist, John Robertson, our Bulawayo office manager, Robin Rudd, Mark Scanes and our legal advisor, Dick Turpin, were acrimonious. My client's abusive language was unhelpful as were his unsubstantiated threats of harm to the Cold Storage team. I left Eddie's team in no doubt as to my ideological standpoint when it came to nationalization no matter how furtive. Eddie countered with his idea of government promoting development by taking over private enterprise that they suspected were run inefficiently. The wrangle was protracted. After a court battle which we won and a few more meetings, 'the scales dropped from the eyes' of Eddie and his team. They threw in the towel.

Eddie was removed from his post and sent to head the Dairy Marketing Board. We made good fees. My client eventually sold his company privately, moved to Canada where he lived with his family before committing suicide after a family dispute. A real 'neurot,' Mervyn was. I learnt a lot from the whole exercise and met with a facet of our new government which gave me my first confrontation with that 'unacceptable part of socialism.' I was determined to take up the cudgels for what I considered right and appropriate for our country, in the long run.

Mike Laws invited me to his office, a week later, to congratulate me on the Super Canners transaction and to chat, give me feedback on my work and performance so far. I was relieved to hear that my team thought highly of me and despite earlier threats when my appointment was announced, all except one would stay and work with me. The one who decided to leave, Willie Ford, was going to join and lead a rival team at another merchant bank. The Des Lawler affair, he said, had shaken the market somewhat, but things had settled. Market players now acknowledged that my appointment was on merit rather than to appease politicians and commentators who demanded to see more black faces in management positions, especially in the financial sector.

Apparently, my performance had vindicated Mike's decision to appoint me as Head of Corporate Finance. He told me about the criticism and caution that had been levelled at him as pundits speculated and predicted, erroneously, that my appointment would lead to a run on the bank as all our clients were white businesses. He had dispelled the myth that white Rhodesians especially would prefer to leave the bank to workig under my leadership. It was a sobering conversation, one that made me more confident. It gave me the strength to carry on and strive to excel. I was exhilarated and honoured when Mike informed me that the Chairman of Anglo-American Corporation had asked me to respond on his behalf, to the Minister of Finance's address at the Confederation of Zimbabwe Industries (C.Z.I) and Zimbabwe National Chamber of Commerce (ZNCC) Symposium at Victoria Falls and Nyanga respectively in a fortnight.

This was my first visit to Victoria Falls. I stayed at the ageless Victoria Falls Hotel, where the C.Z.I. Conference would be. I toured the falls with John Robertson. He explained their formation and the whole topography to me. In the evening, we went on the 'booze cruise' on the Zambezi river, above the falls. It was a pleasant Monday evening. The Conference would start on the following day after breakfast. The Plenary session held after departmental reports, would be on the Wednesday morning. The Minister of Finance would give his address, then I would respond.

I returned to my room after dinner on Monday and sat through boring industrial reports and speeches by politicians and captains of industry the next day. As Wednesday approached, I could feel the nerves working through me. The Minister of Finance was to make a statement about the government's chosen development path, 'The Contradictions and Syntheses of Zimbabwe's Developmental Dynamic.' It sounded quite daunting. As I was somewhat familiar with this essentially Marxist form of analysis, 'Dialectical Materialism,' I chose to craft my response in the same framework.

Then it was time to hear the Minister's speech. It was delivered after a lengthy introduction which spelt out his academic, career and war credentials. Impressive. Dr. Bernard Chidzero was an orator of note. He spoke confidently and fluently in a gentle, accent less voice. He outlined government policy in the Marxist-Socialist school of thought by way of background. After laying the foundation thus, he proceeded to predict the path of robust economic growth and equity that would ensue and how the formerly oppressed masses, recently liberated from the colonial yoke would blossom and the fruits of their labour would be distributed equally across the country.

The gathering of businesspeople, politicians, diplomats, reporters and others were wowed and clearly overwhelmed. The Minister got a standing ovation from most of the black participants in the hall. White participants appeared shell-shocked. There was a clear divide between the two groups. We broke for tea and returned for my speech. I was too nervous to leave the hall and mingle with others at teatime, but I went up to the Minister, greeted him and introduced myself before the Chairman reconvened the meeting.

The Chairman, Mr. Eric Bloch, introduced me briefly as a recent graduate from the U.K., now employed by R.A.L. Merchant bank as a manager. I felt deflated and inadequate especially after the Minister's introduction and his big speech. My response was to put into context, the political and socio-economic formations that described Zimbabwe at independence. I then went on to outline, in detail, how the newly liberated masses were highly politicized and had been led to believe that they would simply inherit, as a matter of right, wealth under white control.

I pointed out how the minister's speech omitted everything about investment and production but focused on distribution and 'development' which had been given the status of an ideology now confused with 'socialism' which itself had been qualified to a state of meaninglessness. The masses would be disappointed because the government would not deliver 'development.' Instead, government would be repressive as law and order would be eroded, causing mass economic and social disruption to ensue, over time. I argued that development was a cover for the pursuit of capitalism. The deliberate, intensive propagation of the ideology of development would, I contended, focus expectations on clear criteria of regime performance.

The failure to fulfil these much-advertised expectations would breed disillusion and critical attitudes. This would prepare people's minds for induction into more radical political attitudes. As soon as political independence was achieved, I argued, the ideas which aided the politicization of the masses by the nationalist leadership became a fetter to the purposes of the same leadership, now in government. The demands for equality, self-determination and freedom from poverty and oppression which the new government preached and taught the masses during the liberation struggle against the colonial government would inevitably be directed at them, since they were now at the helm of affairs. For as long as the government failed to promote productive activity to grow the national surplus, its ability to provide the most elementary necessities was limited. The gap between mass demand for the basics and the supply capability of those in power, the ruling class, would only be bridged by repression.

This would happen because ill-advised policies, such as indigenization, would only entail easy opportunities for a small minority to amass wealth at public expense. Favoured entrepreneurs would then receive heavy protection to produce inefficiently and profitably behind protective barriers, aided by all sorts of extravagant and unnecessary incentives. That is the context in which failure of the development effort would have to be seen. We were now at the crossroads as a country and the indications of the path we were favouring, as espoused by the Minister so eloquently was, I feared, the wrong route. A route that would eventually create, for our government, a crisis of legitimacy and revolutionary pressures from below.

I spoke passionately while making my points with conviction. When I went back to my seat, a tense silence overhung a pall of unease in the room. After a 'pregnant' moment, most white participants gave me a standing ovation. Their black counterparts sat in silent confusion, undeniably shell-shocked by my speech. The Minister had a look of horror as he glared at the Chairman. A civil servant from the Ministry of Trade and Commerce, Dr. Dhlembeu, shot to his feet and roared, "Mr. Chairman." I closed my eyes during the last speech. I could hear the colonial master's voice. As he sat down, gasps and murmurs echoed around the hall. I shrank in my seat.

To my dismay, the Chairman announced that there would be no further debate. The delegates would need time to digest the two speeches, he advised. The Conference would be adjourned till after breakfast, the next day. I quickly collected my papers and evacuated myself to my room amid shouts of 'well done!', 'bravo' and 'hey you!' from participants now thronging the exits. Back in my room, I felt 'washed through and cleansed.' I remained indoors till after breakfast the following day. It was such a cathartic event for me. I felt a strangely peaceful inner feeling. Looking at events in and the political-economic scene in Zimbabwe today, I feel vindicated.

I did not wait for the official closing of the conference. I headed back to Harare on Air Zimbabwe, where I sought refuge in my little apartment till the following Monday. I ambled into the office sheepishly, to be greeted by a skeptical-looking Mike Laws and curiously quiet colleagues. It was soon apparent that my analysis of the country's current and future economic prospects had put a cat among the pigeons. I had given them all something to think about. It somehow compounded their fears. Questions from Mike, the Chairman and colleagues at the bank and within the wider corporate structures were basically along the lines: What types of economic measures and orientations was the government likely to adopt in the face of the legitimacy crisis and the latent 'revolutionary pressures' engendered by their failure to deliver 'economic development?'

Eclecticism would be the order of the day, I explained: the government, as others in the developing world had done (and continue to do), would try to combine elements picked out of discredited development strategies tried in the past. This eclecticism of course underlines the fact that they will be running out of ideas. Ideological exhaustion can only further impede the mobilization of the masses for the battle against underdevelopment. Whatever eclectic development strategies the government adopted would entail certain 'tendencies' including an ambivalence towards the struggle for self-reliance and 'capitalism.' Economic stagnation would create and widen the rift between those in power and the rest of the people. The government would try to depoliticize the masses and disenfranchise them politically.

Unable to rely on the energy of the masses, yet under immense pressure to expand the surplus in order to meet urgent demands and to buy legitimacy, they will look abroad for help. They will inevitably resort to thinking of development in terms of the vertical relations between the centre and the periphery – better prices for primary commodities, transfer of technology, soft loans from bi-lateral institutions, friendly governments, 'look east policies' among others and more foreign investment. In short, they would effectively fall back on the factors which underline their own exploitative dependence. This regress would not help the struggle against underdevelopment. The objective necessity of self-reliance will be increasingly obvious, hence the ambivalence.

There would be a similar ambivalence towards capitalism. The government's chosen path of 'development' will necessarily lead to 'statism,' nationalizing enterprises, for example, which, in the economic sphere will become manifest in various degrees of state capitalism which they will call 'socialism.' The government would position itself thus to use political power for surplus appropriation. The impact on the currency or unit of exchange would be inflationary in the extreme and would render the currency worthless in time.

Their policy would be one of 'political, socio-economic containment,' as I chose to call it. Economic stagnation would deepen animosity between various economic and socio-political groupings causing instability but not sparking off revolution in the foreseeable future, I concluded. "Let me read your next speech before you present it," Mike said after my impromptu lunchtime talk to explain my speech to a large group of Anglo-American Corp. employees.

My next speech was in response to the same Minister. I had the same message, but focused more on the country's need to be a competitive foreign investment destination. I entitled my speech, 'Zimbabwe's Foreign Investment Saga: Another One Bites the Dust.' In making the case for more foreign investment, I cautioned that opportunities arising from the relationship with foreign capital from the West or the East would only be converted into economic growth and poverty reduction in Zimbabwe depending not on trade flows alone but also on the quality of the overall commercial relationships underlying as well as shaping these flows. There was need for policymakers to devise appropriate policy responses to improve the quality of these relationships. The main challenge for Zimbabwe would be how to make use of foreign capital spill-over effects by improving the competitiveness of the domestic market. This had to be a priority.

So, too, the creation of sound institutions to assist and facilitate foreign investors in making their investment, the removal of bureaucratic bottlenecks being a case in point, so that when commercial opportunities arose, they can be exploited effectively taking advantage of knowledge and technology transfers and paving the way for job creation. There was need, I argued, for structural and regulatory reform to ensure that the opportunities-challenges nexus becomes favourable in that outcomes are tilted in favour of the opportunity side. Autarky, for Zimbabwe was not an option for the foreseeable future, only a pipedream. Thanks to the euphoria that came with independence, all the visible signs which prognosticated future poor economic performance had altogether lost their significance.

My second speech had a better reception among the private sector participants. Black and white participants gave me a standing ovation, much to the angst and chagrin of the Minister and his entourage of civil servants. I fielded numerous questions, clearly to the satisfaction of most participants. Once again, I stressed that we, as a country, were at a crossroads. We needed to take bold decisions and go down the right path to ensure viable economic growth, development and poverty reduction. Foreign investment had to play a significant part in the equation. We had to manage the political and regulatory framework for it all to work.

Back at the office, I was Mike's hero, once again. I was invited to the Chairman's dining room where all directors and to my surprise, the Minister of Finance, Dr. Chidzero, had gathered for lunch. The Minister was the guest of honour. I sat across the table from him. We discussed a wide-ranging raft of topical issues including our two encounters. The Minister stood firm on his position and I dug my heels in as well. It was an interesting lunch. The Minister pressed me on my predictions for the future, then asked me if I would work with the Government in some capacity, in the Reserve Bank or Ministry of Finance. I told him, firmly, that private sector experience was my goal. I did not have the right temperament for politics. He laughed.

I walked the Minister to his car after lunch. He clearly had some respect for me despite our disagreements. I would later call on the Minister for drinks and general discussions. He loved to narrate his origins and interests in academia and music. We were to become excellent friends over time as we discovered our mutual weakness for claret, cognac and cigars. We also discovered we had many friends in common, David Hamilton was one of them. A bond was thus established.

The new Reserve bank governor, Dr. James Kombo Moyana, was an old family friend who used to babysit us when we lived in Mbare. I had not seen him in a long time. I was delighted when, after the Victoria Falls conference, which he attended, he sent me an invitation to a private lunch in his offices. His memory was amazing. He filled in the gaps about his education, especially his expulsion from Goromonzi school with Tonderai. He recalled how he came to live with us and how our families had been close for many years. He congratulated me on my speech but added a word of caution: "We live in Africa," he stammered. "You must learn how to survive in the system without giving your position away. There is no mercy out there and no second chances." I heeded his sobering advice. I kept in touch with the Governor. We met frequently over meals. He had an incredibly ghoulish sense of humour and adored Chinese cuisine.

Chapter Ten

THE YEAR PASSED QUICKLY. In my annual review, Mike wrote that I had performed beyond all expectations. I should be promoted to the position of General Manager, Corporate Finance. There were two General managers, the other was G.M. Banking, Raymond Feltoe. He had come from Bard Discount House to replace Dan van Wyk. I was thrilled. I also got a new car, an Alfasud, to replace my little Datsun, which was stolen from my carport at the apartment on New Year's Eve but later recovered by police in a high-density suburb two weeks later. I moved into a much larger office next to Mike Laws and recruited two new staff members, Armand Mizan and Peter Chanetsa, both trainee accountants.

I had, during the year, moved from my Avondale apartment to a four-bedroomed house, 10 Farnborough Close in Greystone Park. The house, which had a self-contained four-room cottage at the back, had enough room for my library, my musical instruments, which now included a new upright Steinway and my ever-growing wine collection. My piano teacher, Lynn Bruce, lived nearby on Windmill Lane. There was enough room in the two acres of garden, to accommodate my Rottweiler puppies, Schuman and Lady and a Bull Mastiff, Copper King, a fishpond with assorted coy and a glittering swimming pool. Life was good.

In January of that year, I received an invitation, unsolicited, to attend an interview for a position in the Finance department of the

African Development Bank in Abidjan, Ivory Coast. I had met their local resident representative in Harare. We met for occasional drinks and meals. I suspected he had something to do with it. I accepted the offer and took time off work to attend the interview. On my way to Paris to catch a plane to Abidjan, I sat next to an old friend, Abebe Ambatchew, an Ethiopian diplomat who was UNCTAD's local representative in Zimbabwe. When I told Abebe what my mission was, he remarked that maybe I should apply to the World Bank for the Young Professionals Programme. They hold interviews in the first quarter of the year. When I got to Paris, Abebe and I went to the World Bank's local office on Avenue d'Iena. I filled in application forms for the programme. I then flew on Air Afrique from Paris to Abidjan.

It felt great to be in a bustling African metropolis where, on the surface, things worked well. I knew Basil Muzorewa and Zondo Sakala, who both worked for the ADB, and Eileen Keita, a friend of David Hamilton's, who worked for British Caledonia. My French was a little rusty, but I was comfortable finding my way around the city especially from Hotel Ibis to the ADB offices downtown. After a guided tour of the city, I returned to the hotel early in the evening, to find my cousin, Basil Muzorewa, waiting for me. We had dinner at one of the numerous restaurants on the beach. Basil had invited a Zambian lady, Una Bellingham, who worked in the president's office at the ADB, to tell me about the advertised post of Economic Officer, that I would be interviewed for on the following day.

The interview was in French and English in front of a panel of seven officials. It was chaired by a Director, Mr. Douglas Iheme, from Nigeria. It was a wide-ranging discussion of macro-economic topics. They were all curious and fascinated by my career to date, how I had managed to 'rise so quickly from school to a General Manager in a well-known bank.' I was convinced I would be offered the position. Later that afternoon, I visited Eileen Keita at her office. She informed me that she had spoken with the Bank's

President, Mr. Boubacar Ndiaye, would I go to see him in his office at 5 p.m. I was floored. This was the last thing I expected. Zondo, Basil and Una were equally surprised that I had pulled this off without trying.

I had a cordial, engaging 90 minutes with Mr. Ndiaye in his huge office that afternoon. He was a short man with horn-rimmed glasses and an occasional smile. He preferred to converse in French but would explain things in English from time to time. He explained how the Bank worked and his plans to change the way the Bank ran. He had just replaced Mr. Willa Mungomba, a Zambian national, as President of the Bank. He himself was from Guinea but had grown up in the Ivory Coast and educated in France. He was fascinated by my job at R.A.L. As I left his office, he shook my hand and said,' I hope you will accept our offer to you.' I smiled and left for the hotel Ibis.

This had been a crazy Thursday. I had dinner with Eileen, her husband Ibrahim and their young son, Jamil, in their beautiful mansion overlooking the sea. They told me that I had performed well in the interview and 'Boubacar likes you because you are different.' It was quite clear that there were no secrets in Abidjan. The job was mine if I wanted it! The next day I explored the city on my own. I went to the Roman Catholic Cathedral, the notorious intersection, Carrefour des Mort, where many motorists perished daily due to bad and negligent driving, the golf course, the beach and the suburbs. In the evening, Una and Basil took me to dinner on the beach, then to a night club. We met many of their colleagues from the Bank. They had heard about me.

We caroused till early morning then retired to Una's for a huge greasy breakfast before slouching on the couch. I slept through most of the morning. Una drove me back to the hotel at about midday. I had lunch, a cold shower and went to bed for a couple of hours. Zondo visited me later in the day. We had drinks and a quiet dinner at his favourite watering hole on the beach. I left Abidjan for Harare, via Paris, the next day. I spent a day in Paris shopping and generally goofing around Champs d'Elysee. I love Paris.

It was good to be back in Harare, but I was unsettled. I felt that I had done all I wanted to do in Zimbabwe. I needed to learn more and broaden my knowledge and experience of banking and finance. I enjoyed my work very much. I was successful. I enjoyed seeing more of my parents, siblings and friends but something stirred in me. I needed a bigger challenge. My soul was restless. My experience with the two now famous speeches made me uneasy. I felt a sense of belonging and a simultaneous feeling of being alienated or rejected. I often had long talks with Dad about how I felt. He would say, 'pray about it and follow your heart.' I did. I got sick of being asked whether I was happy to be in Zimbabwe again, whether I missed life abroad, would I join politics one day etc. Fortunately for me, the work was excellent as I gained invaluable experience especially as a manager in a thriving bank.

Barely two weeks after my return from the Ivory Coast, I received an invitation to attend interviews for the Young Professionals Programme in response to my application submitted when I was in Paris three weeks earlier. A week later, I was back in Paris, at Hotel California, on Rue de Berri. There were other candidates for the same Programme staying at the hotel. We met in the bar and tried to guess what the interviews could possibly entail. We need not have bothered: the interviews were spread over two days. They were the toughest test I had ever faced.

The World Bank officers, led by Joseph Wambia, the Young Professionals Administrator, were serious, focused and incisive in their quest for answers on various areas of economics, finance, politics, general knowledge and personal experience. By the end of the second day, I felt washed out. There was no indication at all from these master poker players how the interviews went. I only fell back on the thought that there was always the ADB to fall back on, more time with R.A.L or a return to Morgan Grenfell, in the worst case.

From Paris, I went to London. Richard Small and his wife, Joanna, drove me to their new house in Milton Keynes. We had a week of visiting our favourite pizza restaurant, San Antonello near Bedford and punting in Cambridge. We visited Richard and Joanna's parents in Cranfield Village and had lunch with John and Liz Constable in Bedford. I then realised I had been 'homesick.' I had missed my friends in the U.K. I had grown accustomed to them more than my Zimbabwean colleagues. It felt wonderful to be back in England. I caught up with my siblings and relatives and made numerous visits to David in London and Morgan Grenfell before catching BA back to Harare. By the time I got to Harare, I knew I wanted to be somewhere else, still in banking, but Zimbabwe was simply too 'stifling' for me. There was no room for further professional growth. This was more than just an epiphany. It required active attention and action.

On a Friday afternoon, just a few days after my return from Paris, I received, in the morning post, a letter from the ADB, offering me the job I had been interviewed for. In a fit of excitement, I summoned my P.A., Brenda, to my office and told her my news. Her face dropped as she broke into tears. Mike Laws, who was walking back to his office, decided to put his head around the door, as was his custom whenever he blurted out the cricket score or some market gossip. He could sense something was not quite right. I told him my news. He went to his office without comment. It was an awkward day. Just before I picked myself out of my chair to leave the office at five, there was a knock on the door. Regina, the lady who oversaw the telephones and fax machines on the ground floor walked in, handed me a long fax, then promptly left my office without saying a word. I sat down in my chair and started to read the lengthy message. It was an offer from the World Bank to join the Young Professionals Program.

I sat back in my chair in a daze. Things had now spun into a whirling storm the pace of which I had not anticipated. I must have read both offers at least ten times. I called my parents and gently explained what had happened in the past month. Their response was supportive, but they thought it was too early to leave my new job barely 18 months on. Furthermore, Dad added, we will miss your bank's cottage at Connemara, on the lake, next to 'World's View.' That was the least of my worries then. I left the office just before midnight. By that time, I had called the World Bank office to accept their offer. I told them I would start work in June, about three months later. I wrote to the ADB declining their offer of employment. I had written a letter of resignation to Mike Laws and the Chairman. I had written to David Hamilton, my family, colleagues at Morgan Grenfell, my Piano teacher, Lyn Bruce, and my Karate instructor, Sensei Harunoba Chiba informing them of my decision to leave for Washington D.C. at the end of May.

The next three months were hectic. I had to help choose a successor, John Graham, who spent a month with me visiting clients and getting to know the work. He had recently qualified as an accountant and had worked at another bank. The handover was smooth. I gradually withdrew from all my assignments and focused on mundane issues like selling my two vehicles, arranging for my wine, books and selected personal items to go into storage. Some things I gave away to family and friends. A family friend in Bulawayo, kindly offered to give my dogs a new home. I was grateful, he was pleased. The two Rottweilers apparently threatened to attack his wife, Sheila, on arrival at their new home. Eventually they all settled down and lived well together, I believe.

The bank threw an emotional farewell party. Mike spoke and presented me with a painting by Bone. The Karate Club also had a farewell party for me at Sandro's Club. The party got a little rowdy. As the patrons got more intoxicated, they attacked one of the better karatekas in the dojo. The police were called in to calm things down after fights broke out. It was a lively occasion. We sang rugby songs and swayed to music till the early hours of the morning.

I had to make one last call on some of my favourite clients. Of note were Keith and Clive, at Nottingham estates, on the banks of the Limpopo. Bob Fernandes from our associate company, KFR Real Estate and I often chartered a Cessna from Matabele Air. We would fly ourselves to Francistown, Gaborone, Nottingham Estates and other remote places such as Kariba and Hwange National Park. On this occasion, we decided to fly to Nottingham Estates, say good-bye to Clive, Keith and their families, then fly back via Francistown where we would buy all the groceries that were in short supply in Zimbabwe, including whisky, cheese, tinned fish and wines.

The leg to Nottingham was uneventful. On the way back from Francistown, first we narrowly missed a flock of birds flying in our direction. We were flying at about three thousand feet at that point. Shortly after that, we flew into a violently turbulent storm and lost our bearings. It was hell for about twenty minutes. We eventually re-established contact with the control tower at Bulawayo airport and were guided safely to land at Bulawayo where we cleared customs before flying back to Harare. Despite my hours of flying solo, I was shaken. Mike Laws was livid when we told him what had happened.

When I was not attending farewell parties in Harare, I visited my parents and grandparents for more parties. I managed to let my house to the New Zealand Deputy High Commissioner. She would let me keep the cottage as the house was big enough for her needs. I moved my few belongings into the cottage. This was an ideal arrangement because if I was back in the country at any time, I would have my own accommodation. That was the idea. In the meantime, as time to leave was approaching fast, I decided to give a dinner party for selected friends.

The list of invitees kept growing and I had to change my plans to give drinks and snacks only. I got a caterer, Kevin Meyer, to organize it at my house. There were about forty people in the garden that evening. The drinks flowed and then someone started playing music very loudly on my hi-fi in the main lounge. The party then took off seriously. There were no speeches made. We partied till quite late. There were enough snacks to feed an army, so we all did well.

Three days after my party, I left Harare on the late-night BA flight to London, on the first leg of my journey to Washington D.C. My new employer had organized a G-4 Visa for me and a one-way business class ticket. I had requested a week-long stopover in London, which was granted without fuss. Richard Small met me at Heathrow and drove me to their new house in North Crawley, a lovely village near Newport Pagnell. I used to wander in that neighbourhood around the Aston Martin showrooms and factory when I was bored with writing my doctoral thesis. We had dinner at the Blackhorse Country Pub and Restaurant in Woburn.

After a couple of days with Richard and Joanna, I left for London, 109 Brixton Road, Casa Mia. As usual, David was delighted to have me around. He had many friends in Washington and compiled a small contact list for me. I also visited many friends in London including Algy Cluff and Prof. Geoffrey Wood. Algy took me to lunch at the Stafford in St. James. We had a long lunch in the amazing cellar at the Stafford. We also had lunch at the R.A.C where some of Algy's staff, Alister and Douglas joined us. We discussed their operations in Zimbabwe and their forays into West Africa, Ghana, Burkina Faso and plans for Sierra Leone.

It was great to talk to bullish miners who had great plans, knew all about gold mining and dealing with host governments. I was always fascinated to hear the other side of the story when it came to foreign investment. Geoffrey Wood, who had been one of my tutors in Monetary Economics and Finance at university, and his wife, Lesley, hosted a small dinner party for me at their home on Beauval Road in Dulwich, near Herne Hill Station. It was great to catch up with old friends. I learnt, that evening that one of my former tutors, Jocelyn Horne, now worked for the I.M.F in Washington D.C. I promised to look her up. She is Australian, an excellent economics scholar who was my International Economics tutor after her Ph. D at the London School of Economics. Gold was her favourite subject.

I spent a lot of time shopping for new work clothes. Once again, David took me to his tailors, Chester Barrie's on Saville Row and shirt makers on Jermyn Street. Soon I was well suited and heeled for my new job. I spent a lot of time at the British Museum looking at and reading up on development and other topical issues that the World Bank Group had recently undertaken. Country economic structural adjustment was the hot subject area of the day. I found the whole concept of structural adjustment interesting. However, the area of capital market development, from institution-building to policy, piqued my interest a lot more. This was an area I felt at home with and hoped to work on should the opportunity ever arise. On the Sunday, after the early morning Eucharist service at All Saints, Margaret Street, David drove me to Heathrow. I boarded the early afternoon B.A. flight to Washington D.C.

The flight was pleasant and uneventful. I imagined what lay in store for me workwise and what relationships I would have, socially. Everything faded into a haze as I nodded off into a sound sleep after aperitifs followed by a delicious seafood meal washed down with lots of Chateau Giscours. In between naps, I had time to replay my life so far, how I had come to be thirty-five thousand feet above the Atlantic Ocean heading west, to America at this time. I knew that this is what I wanted to do. This was an opportunity I had not fore-seen but was fortuitously well-prepared for. I always cherished a challenge. Apart from my Doctoral work and my two employment assignments at Morgan Grenfell and R.A.L Merchant Bank, this promised to be the toughest challenge yet. I figured out that, in my new adventure, my experience to date would tilt the risk-reward nexus firmly and favourably to the reward side.

It had been quite an exhilarating life-journey so far. I was lucky to have had a stable, strictly Christian, family background with integrity, hard work, prayer, keeping time, honesty and respect as the creed at the core of our family life. Although we were not always together as siblings, we were close, yet independent. Our parents were our focal point. They held the family together and opened many doors for their children. We, in turn, seized the opportunities successfully. We had all been to good schools and performed well enough to get further and higher education. We had all travelled and were educated abroad. This was quite unusual for the ordinary family in those days.

In the years that I had spent away from home, I had gently drifted away from the church. Whereas I had grown up as an enthusiastic altar boy and attended church services almost daily, I got lazy especially when I got to university. I attended church at Easter and Christmas but very infrequently in-between. I never lost my faith though. I remained steadfast in my belief in the Triune God. My High Church roots run deep. The faith has always flowed in my veins. I found, however, as I got older, that I became more selective about which Church service I would attend and which Priest or Bishop I preferred.

When I was younger, any church, service or church leader would do. I never questioned the establishment. At this stage of my life, I would listen and pay attention to sermons and followed the liturgy. Loud and long sermons I found to be vexatious. I preferred sermons that were short, to the point and drew the theology from the set readings of the day. Since I ceased to be a regular church goer, one would be forgiven to reach the conclusion that I had abandoned the church and my faith and belief in God. Nothing could have been further from the truth.

My love life was like a roller-coaster experience. I had met many girls and befriended several but never really got to the point of losing my head seriously over anyone. In other words, I had dated a few girls over the years. I got very fond of a few, but nothing ever lasted. My maternal grandmother asked me once whether I would ever marry. 'You prefer white women to black ones?' she asked me once.

I had visited her with girlfriends over the years. They were almost all white, she observed. Frankly, I had never noticed, nor did I sit consciously to decide whether to befriend a girl based on colour except that we just clicked. I probably concealed as criminal, any seriously amorous encounters, carnal repasts or other escapades of a similar nature, remarked a friend, one day. I stayed mum.

I valued my freedom and independence and had little time left to socialise after my music, flying lessons, karate and hiking up mountains. Maybe I was just selfish or scared of the unknown. I had not met anyone I felt I could spend more than a week with, let alone a lifetime. Maybe this would change at some point but for now, it was a time of hygge, in matters romantic. I was comfortable and content to be a 'bachelor in paradise,' free to have as many lady friends as I pleased at any one time.

Chapter Eleven

WASHINGTON WAS STIFLING HOT when I got to Dulles Airport at 3pm. I got a taxi downtown to the Concordia Hotel, a block away from the World Bank's main offices, 1818H Street N.W. This was to be my base for the next seven days until I found an apartment. Registration, when I reported for work, took the best part of a day. I signed numerous forms, had to get a picture I.D. for the gates into all World Bank Group and I.M.F. buildings, open a bank account with the Bank's Credit Union, sign up for a new passport, a U.N. Laissez-Passer, then went for a medical. It was a long day, but I finally managed to report to my new boss, Isaac Sam, a Ghanaian national, in the Industry Department, the Fertilizers and Petrochemicals Division. I would work as an Economist/Financial Analyst. This was the first of my two assignments as a Young Professional. Each assignment would last six months. Thereafter, one would be eligible to apply for a permanent position in any of the Group's departments.

The Industry department was headed by a Director, Mr. Amnon Golan. He resigned after two months of my joining the Bank. He was succeeded by Alberto de Capitani. There were two Division Chiefs, Don Brown and Andrew Rogerson, with an assistant each. Isaac Sam was an Assistant Division Chief. On my first full day in the office, Isaac took me to lunch in one of the Bank's cafeterias and 'walked' me through the workings of the Bank, especially the "politics." He impressed on me the importance of working hard and diligently and keeping to deadlines in all assignments. "You will work the hours your boss works," he added with an expressionless visage. "I'm generally in the office by 8 a.m. I never leave before 6 p.m.," he added. "Once you are perceived as good, you will have a 'protective coating' that will shield you against the tendency to stereotype black employees here."

By the end of lunch, I just wanted to stagger back to my office, shut the door and ask myself if I really wanted to be here. Was I good enough, I wondered. Most employees in the Bank had at least the same, if not better, qualifications as I held. My advantage, however, was that I had worked in a commercial banking environment and had already been a manager. Most of my colleagues had joined straight from university.

Later in the day, there was a knock at my door. It was Isaac, accompanied by a Senior Economist in the Division, Anthony Ody, an Englishman. After the introduction, Isaac informed me that I was to accompany Antony (Tony) to Algeria in three days' time. I would work as Tony's assistant on this trip. This would be the first World Bank Mission to Algeria in over thirty years. There would be about twenty-seven Bank officers on this mission. The mission-leader was Hasso Molineux, a Senior Economist. Tony would also enlist the services of a Consultant, Olivier Godron, to accompany us on this Mission. Our focus would be assessing the viability of the Fertilizers and Petro-Chemicals sector.

My brief was to analyse the workings of the parastatals in the sector and ascertain their strategies to assess their efficiency and the extent to which they needed rehabilitation. I would work, under Tony's guidance, to prepare a report on my findings. Tony and I arranged to spend the next couple of days working out how best to approach the task. Tony explained to me how World Bank Missions such as the one we were to go on, worked. This was particularly useful. My personal assistant, Edna, a middle-aged, recently widowed Philippina, showed me how to make bookings, arrange for the necessary visas, apply for travel allowance and how to fill in all the forms on my return. She guided me through the various offices and made sure that all was set for my first trip as a staff member of the Bank.

Tony and I left Dulles airport aboard a Pan Am 747 bound for Heathrow soon after work on Friday evening. As we chatted about our various interests and careers, we discovered that we had friends in common. Tony was educated at St. Edward's School (Teddy's) in Oxford, and Oxford University where he read Economics. He knew my friend George Prah, who was his junior at Teddy's. He had played cricket with another friend, Tsatsu Tsikata, at Oxford. He had friends who went to Radley, including Ed Spriggs, who he also met at Oxford. We talked and enjoyed Macallan and fine wines with our dinner. The flight felt much shorter than the six hours it took.

We headed to Browns Hotel where we were booked for the night, after which we would catch a flight to Paris to board Air Algerie to Algiers. I spent the day preparing for the task ahead. Although I could speak French and had had French lessons at school, I had to brush up on my French as I was warned that not many Algerians were inclined to converse in English. At dinner that evening, I told Tony that he would have to step in and help me out if I got stuck because of language. His own French, he said, was reasonable but not perfect.

Tony and I got on well. He then requested me, with unexpected temerity, I thought, to calculate the opportunity cost of labour in a developing country such as Algeria. I was a little thrown off but quickly pulled myself together. I tried to remember my first-year economics. I remembered the supply price approach under a wider variety of market conditions and types of jobs. After a little discussion he said, 'Not exactly the answer that I wanted but your answer made me think that I had not quite got it right all along. There are several ways to look at it and yours is an excellent one. Well done!' We laughed as we enjoyed Chateau Labegorce 1978, with our dinner. Lesson learnt. There was not going to be a dullsville moment with Tony.

We arrived in Algiers about midday on the Monday. It looked as if the entire World Bank team was on the same Air Algerie flight from Paris. All team members were processed rapidly but when it came to my turn at immigration, there was a 'problem.' In my patchy French, I tried to explain that I was part of the World Bank team. The immigration officers were not impressed even when I produced my U.N. Laissez-Passer like the rest of my colleagues. Since mine was brand new, they had to check to make sure it was not fake and that I was not one of those desperate black Africans trying to sneak into their country to find jobs in the oil sector. I had not heard of any sane person, refugee or not, voluntarily seeking to live and work in Algeria at that time. This was pure racism, in my book, as I was the only black person off that flight. I was livid.

A member of the team, Ivan, a French Professor of Economics and a recent addition to the Bank's team of Economists, finally realized what was going on and intervened on my behalf. Things were eventually resolved. I rejoined the rest of the team in the luggage lobby, but not before a gang of Algerian officers crowded around me gawking at my Laissez-Passer and gesticulating wildly as they conversed among themselves in Arabic. Appalling. I was still seething when we reached the El Aurassi Hotel on the hill overlooking the Mediterranean Sea, downtown Algiers, on the edge of the Casbah.

The Mission leader, Hasso Molineux, called a meeting at five, that evening. We gathered in a large room near the hotel lobby and listened as he outlined our programme. Tony, Olivier and I would be hosted by the Ministry of Petrochemicals and Fertilizers and the rest of the team would be hosted by other Ministries, depending on their focus. Our Mission would cover Ministries including Education, Industry, Finance and Agriculture. That evening, we would be guests at a dinner hosted by the Minister of Finance and the Governor of the Central Bank.

The dinner was lavish. There were many speeches of welcome and niceties were exchanged. All the Civil Servants present were urged to co-operate fully and avail information to the team. We would visit sites, industrial plants and other relevant facilities around the country. Fish, lamb, couscous and roasted vegetables were served. I particularly enjoyed the red snapper, fresh cherries and dried dates. The Algerian wine, a fragrant Rose, was pleasant. By the time we retired after dinner, I was tired of listening to long empty speeches from both sides. Soporific. I was ready to get going with my team and to discover what the sector we had come to investigate consisted of. Information about this sector was naturally sparse and mostly a closely guarded state secret. This was our chance to get to the bottom of it.

I was up early. The sun filtered into my room from across the sea. It was quite warm already. I joined Tony and Olivier for coffee and rolls in the Café off the hotel lobby. Our first port of call would be the Ministry of Energy, responsible for Petrochemicals and Fertilizers. We met with an affable team of four at the Ministry. They gave us a background and history of the sector, how it was largely run down due to lack of investment and maintenance and how it occupied a central position in the economic framework of Algeria. They informed us that we would visit sites in Oran, Skikda and Annaba. Tony then requested if we could also visit the historical sites in Ghardaia in the south of the country and Timgad, near Batna, famous for their ancient Roman-Berber sites and also Constantine, south of Skikda, the birthplace of St. Augustine of Hippo to see the Basilica dedicated to his mother, St. Monica. Permission was granted.

We spent the rest of the day in the Ministry, poring over figures relating to industrial output, expenditures, investments and other areas of interest. We went through voluminous files of outdated and largely incomprehensible data. Tony and I relied heavily on the Consultant, Olivier, to make sense of the data and recompile it into forms that we were familiar with. This was going to be a mammoth task. Our hosts were curious to know, in detail, why we were in their country and the purpose of our Mission. They clearly had not been fully briefed. Algeria was emerging from a dark period of isolation, socialist dictatorship and political instability. The government had decided to open up slowly to foreign assistance especially from the Bretton Woods institutions, hence our fact- finding Mission. This would establish the platform on which future Economic and Policy interventions would be based.

They were fascinated by our explanations, but it took a while for them to relax and really open up to us. Most of the financial information they gave us had not been audited, checked or analysed in over twenty years. There was, understandably, a tangible air of suspicion of foreign involvement especially in the petrochemicals sector, which was the lynchpin of their economy. We also had to explain to them our team composition of an Englishman, a Frenchman and an Anglo-Zimbabwean who to them, sounded 'American,' much to my angst.

The Algerians had reached their own conclusions, which were clearly unfavorable to us and wrong. They were not familiar with the Bretton Woods institutions and how they operated. To them, this was a U.N. delegation and we represented our respective nations in trying to ascertain the current economic situation in Algeria before reporting our findings to the U.N. General Assembly in New York, where their country would be scrutinized.

The frosty atmosphere of our meetings thawed gradually. We made some progress. I decided to ask for permission to talk to the Accountant separately, so that we could focus on the financials of the parastatals in question. This would enable me to start building a picture and framework for my report. It was not an easy meeting; the Accountant did not understand nor speak more than a word or two of English. I struggled to follow his Algerian French accent.

However, we somehow managed to wade through his data. He very kindly offered to make various copies for me to take away. I was grateful for this. I could then ask for Olivier's assistance in unravelling and deciphering the mysteries shrouded in the financials that were availed to us. I was grateful for the lunch break which came at about 3p.m. I was overjoyed when we were informed that there would be no afternoon session. We just had to prepare for our trip to Oran, the following day. I smiled as we left the Ministry's offices.

After the morning meetings, Tony and I decided to walk around the Casbah. The visible signs of shocking degeneration in the walled citadel, were due to neglect and overpopulation, Tony surmised. The Casbah was a hideout for criminals and terrorists in the late 1950s. During the civil insurrection and struggle against French colonial rule, it was a hideout for freedom fighters. We marveled at the ancient edifices, the architecture and how the old and latter, rundown buildings sat next to each other or showed signs of modification and adaptation over time. It was a surreal experience. We were obvious objects of curiosity as we walked about stopping frequently at various points to absorb the impact of the sights, sounds and views of the Casbah. We came across a coffee bar that looked well-patronized and promptly sat for refreshments.

Three men approached us and politely asked if they could join us. We introduced ourselves to each other. The three were local friends, civil servants, who had grown up in this neighbourhood. They offered to buy us drinks. We accepted and chatted to them about our Mission. They, in turn, told us their life stories and life in Algeria. It was all very cordial. The conversation drifted into a dinner of couscous and red snapper for me, lamb for the rest of the party gathered. After dinner, we exchanged contact details. Tony and I thanked them for their hospitality and walked back to the El Aurassi hotel. The views of the sunset colours and lit boulevards lined with trees on the slopes down to the sea, across downtown Algiers were breathtakingly beautiful.

We set off for Oran, about 430 km north west of Algiers, along the coast, around 7.30 a.m. after coffee, French rolls and pastries. The Ministry provided a car and a driver for the trip. Oran is the second largest city in Algeria. The driver cum tour guide told us that the name derives from the Berber word, 'uharan,' meaning two lions. Apparently, lions still roamed the area until 'recently,' the driver went on. 'Recently' here could have meant a hundred years ago, he was not sure. Tony added that the British navy had shelled the French warships in the port, in July 1940, after they refused a British ultimatum to surrender. This was done to ensure the fleet would not fall into German hands as the Nazis had defeated France and occupied Paris. In Oran, we would be hosted by Sonatrach, the country's largest oil and gas company. We would also visit Arzew, the area's oil/gas port.

The drive was scenic. In between conversations about our task, broken French monologues, courtesy of our driver on the history and legends of the route and Oran, we cat-napped. In a light-hearted moment, Tony said to me, 'Jules, when you hear the word 'azote' mentioned, do not take it to mean 'how's your tea?' it is the French word for nitrogen!' We laughed as we called ourselves by our French label, 'La Division des engrais et petrochimiques.' Olivier was not really impressed by what he would later describe as 'English schoolboy humour.' The three and half-hour long journey finally came to an end as we reached the impressive Le Meridien at Oran, where we were booked for two nights. A much welcome relief from the rundown El Aurassi.

Oran had a less 'oppressive ambience.' It was warm and breezy. It just felt good to be there. Our contact, waiting to welcome us at the hotel, was Mr. Ghozali. His younger brother, Rashid, was a financial analyst in our department back in Washington. Raschid had asked Tony to get in touch with his brother who had been briefed to help us find our way. He was employed at Sonatrach. Mr. Ghozali was a pleasant, soft-spoken, affable man, quite unlike a lot of his compatriots especially the ones I had encountered at the airport. Though the onus was on us to be proficient in the country's official and working language, it was nevertheless a relief to meet a local who could converse with us fluently, in English.

After checking into the hotel, we decided to explore the local sites of interest. I had always wanted to visit the Cathedral de Sacre Coeur, which was converted into a public library after Algeria claimed independence from France; the Demaeght Museum. It houses exhibits on prehistoric archaeological findings from throughout the Maghreb. The Great Mosque which was a celebratory symbol of liberation from the Spanish and of course, the Great Synagogue of Oran. The tour lasted all afternoon and by the time we got back to the hotel, we were exhausted and thirsty. We sat on the patio overlooking the sea and dispatched a few glasses of delicious, chilled local beer, Tango, 'La Biere Blonde,' as the locals called it. After drinks we had dinner with four officials from Sonatrach, including Mr. Ghozali. They told us about their duties, the company and their vision for it. It was a long but delightful evening. We agreed to meet at their offices after breakfast, the following morning.

Early next morning, we left the hotel for Sonatrach's offices and main plant. Most of the morning saw us on a guided tour of the complex. It was huge, well-maintained in parts but clearly in need of urgent refurbishment overall. The tour went on for just over three hours. I was relieved and grateful to get my hard hat off as we headed for the cool sanctuary of the company's air-conditioned offices. Once inside, we were treated to ice cold fruit juices and coffee. I asked if I could have a separate meeting with the Accountant. We disappeared to his office while Tony and Olivier met with the C.E.O and other executives to discuss policy and plans for the company.

The Accountant explained that he was new to his job and was not sure where all the records were kept. He would endeavour to gather all the information I needed and deliver it to me before we returned to Algiers. I took him at his word. After compiling a list of the information, I wanted, we talked about our careers and families. He was curious to know how I ended up at the Bank and if it was worth his while to apply for a job at the Bank. I gave him the Bank's contact details and left the rest up to him. We were treated to a long lunch at a fish restaurant by the sea. Once again, we enjoyed grilled fish and vegetables, lots of fruit and the ever-present lovely Algerian wine.

After lunch, we went back to the offices for more meetings. These were quite intense and took up most of the afternoon. The executives were eager to impress on us the urgency and need for reform in management practice and refurbishment of the plant. They wondered if we could make the case, on their behalf, when we had our meetings with government officials at the end of our Mission. We promised to share our findings including our draft reports with them. After the interminable meetings, we were evacuated to the hotel where we discussed the day and all the information we had gathered.

Tony was amused, impressed and envious that I had, once again, managed to corner the Accountant to escape the main meetings and probably get a more accurate picture of corporate affairs. It worked well. The following day we toured the facilities at the port, Arzew. Once again, everything seemed to work but needed refurbishment if efficiency was to be achieved. After the tour, we met to discuss the outline of our report with the Mission leader back in Algiers, and the final report to the Department Director, when we got back to Washington.

Over the weekend, we visited Ghardaia, a hilltop city in the northern central part of the country, in the Sahara Desert. It is a major centre for date production and the manufacture of rugs and cloths. The fortified town is divided into three walled sectors. At the centre is the historic M'zabite area, with a beautiful pyramid-style mosque and an arcaded square. Picturesque and quite distinctive pink, red and white houses made of clay, sand and gypsum, rise in terraces and arcades. The dry heat was unbearable, but the sights were breath taking. All the men wore baggy trousers. The next stop was Constantine, on the banks of the Rhumel river, about 80kms from the Mediterranean coastline. It is the third largest city after Algiers and Oran. It is also known as the 'City of Bridges' because of the numerous spectacular bridges connecting the mountains the city is built on. My main interest was the Cathedral of Our Lady of Seven Sorrows. It was a Basilica dedicated to St. Monica, mother of St. Augustine of Hippo.

Despite its conversion into other uses including Islam worship, it is a beautiful edifice. The city itself has spectacular views of valleys and hills and a web of bridges. The last touristic port of call was Annaba, on the east coast, on the border with Tunisia. This was Hippo, where Augustine was the Bishop from 396 to 430, when he died. I also wanted to see his relics in the Cathedral dedicated to him. His words, 'Our souls are restless until they find rest in you' and 'Audi partem altarem (Hear the other side),' rang in my head. This was the highest point of my time as a tourist during my World Bank Mission to Algeria.

Our sightseeing would not have been 'complete' without a day-long visit to Timgad near the town of Batna. The Roman ruins at Timgad are noteworthy for representing one of the best extant examples of the grid plan as used in Roman City planning, Tony educated me. The site is dominated by the Timgad Arch, a sandstone, Dorian Triumphal Arch of Trajan and a 3,500-seat theatre still used for contemporary productions. While wandering among the ruins, I looked up suddenly to the sound of stampeding feet coming in my direction. It was Tony Ody, in full flight. As he approached me, he panted that he had walked into a big black snake gorging himself on a large lizard. Not being one given to such drama, I took off to see for myself. Indeed, there was a snake, greyish-brown, a house snake, I guessed, duly eating a small lizard. It was lunchtime after all.

As we wandered around the theatre, the taxi driver approached me and inquired which way was East, so he could say his midday prayers. I pointed to a direction that I guessed was East. I watched the man spread his mat and bow in prayer. A few metres away, to my horror, I watched a local man saying his prayers also. He was facing the opposite direction! I knew who was facing the real East. I felt like a tortoise dismounting a helmet. But hey, we all make mistakes. Fortunately, the driver did not discover this little error on my part. It all ended well.

From Annaba, it was back to work, this time, to Skikda. The scenery was beautiful. Forested hills and ridges guarded the western and eastern sides of the city. Sonatrach operates the oil refinery and gas port. The petrochemicals industries are also based here. For the next two days we toured the oil refinery, gas port and three petrochemical plants. One of them makes plastics and fertilizers and the other purifies and bottles de-salinized water. We interviewed company executives and were treated to excellent meals in many restaurants. Thursday, it was time to head back to Algiers and the El Aurassi hotel.

The team met at the hotel that evening and had an hour long de-brief session. Each group presented their findings to the Mission leader. Tony gave our report. After our group meeting, we left for dinner at the Central Bank, hosted by the Minister of Finance and Bank Governor. During dinner speakers from our team read out their findings to the Algerian officials. We then had a frank, robust but cordial exchange of views as we outlined the Bank's plans for their country programme and the possible strategies that the Bank would adopt. Ideally, we would work together in a joint effort to rehabilitate and rebuild industries, transport infrastructure, education programmes, monetary and fiscal policies.

The next day I left for Paris. I expected a tortured exit but rather it was the opposite: hassle free, for which I was grateful. I had been spoiling for a big fight. In Paris, I treated myself to Macallan at my favourite bar at the Hotel California. I had dinner and relaxed to live jazz music till well after midnight. I had plenty of time as my flight to Washington from Paris, Charles de Gaulle, would be at 3.00p.m. on the Saturday. It was a great, relaxed evening without my colleagues from the Bank. I was able to get away from talking fertilizers, oil and gas and economic strategies, at least for two days. I made the most of it. However, in the morning, over scrambled eggs, black coffee and a baguette, I found myself poring over my notes and scribbling the outline of my report back in the office. After writing a couple of pages, I went for a walk on Champs Elysée then checked out of the hotel. I left for the airport after yet another delectable meal at a Chinese restaurant on Rue de Berri.

In the lounge after check-in at Charles de Gaulle airport, I met up with some of my colleagues who had been on the same Mission to Algeria with me. We discussed and compared notes on our respective experiences. I was keen to learn from some of the more experienced colleagues what to expect and how best to prepare the back-to-office Mission report. By the time we boarded our Washington-bound Pan Am flight, I was well-informed and overwhelmed with all the information and advice I had received. On the flight, I revised my outline and draft, in between listening to music, drinking whisky sours and bourbon before tucking into the airline food. By the time we landed, I had my draft report almost done, save for a few points of detail and references, which were in my main notes in a voluminous file safely locked up in my suitcase.

I had time to reflect on my experience and times with the Bank, to date. I had only been in the Bank's employ for just under a month, but I felt at home, like a fish in agreeable waters. I was comfortable with my work and I had already made friends with colleagues in my Division and others in the Bank. This was a far cry from the work I had undertaken at Morgan Grenfell and R.A.L. Merchant Bank. This had a different buzz. The work itself was at a different, in some ways, deeper level. I now had to deal with senior civil servants and tackle strategies and plans that would be relied on by governments in running their countries, ultimately.

My experience in the private sector had prepared me in terms of diligence, client handling, competing and striving to beat the competition at winning mandates and delivering excellent services for handsome rewards in return. By contrast, now, I did not have to compete for mandates, but I still had to be astute, imaginative, up to date with information, widely read, sharp and articulate in making my case before critical peers who, as I had been warned, would not hesitate to stump one at the earliest opportunity. A dreadful prospect and a frightening thought, in the scheme of things. Time would tell.

Chapter Twelve

BEFORE GOING TO ALGERIA, I had secured a small, two-bedroomed apartment in Rosslyn. This was two stops away from Farragut West, which was the Metro stop closest to the office. Located in the north east of Arlington County, Rosslyn is directly across the Potomac River from Georgetown. Characterized as one of several "urban villages" in the county, the numerous skyscrapers in the dense business section of Rosslyn make its appearance in some ways more urban than downtown Washington D.C. My apartment was in a large complex near the U.S. Marine Corps War Memorial. I had good views of the Washington Monument and the Kennedy Centre, among other landmarks.

On a good day, including weekends, I would walk over Key Bridge, through Georgetown and Foggy Bottom, on M-Street, to get to the office, on Pennsylvania Avenue and 18th St., or 1818H street, as it was officially known. The amenities around the apartment complex were simply amazing: 24-hour fitness centres, supermarkets, boutiques and restaurants and an excellent transit system to downtown D.C., National and Dulles airports. An excellent location.

Early Monday morning, I was at my desk. Isaac Sam put his head into my doorway and invited me to join him for coffee in the canteen. He was anxious to hear about the Mission to Algeria particularly how I tackled and approached the work. For almost an hour, we chatted about the Mission. Isaac was eager to help me prepare my first report. He almost fell off his chair when I told him that I had finished the first draft and would be working on technical aspects and other points of detail before handing my report to Tony for his review and comment before submitting it formally to Isaac. He cautioned me against rushing through without paying attention to detail. I assured him that I had been in similar situations in the past and was quite capable of producing a report at the right level.

I spent the next couple of days working on my report and then gave it to Tony for the initial review. Within a few minutes, Tony stood in the doorway of my office and beamed, '"Well done Jules. I knew you had learned something useful at Public School in England! I like the way you write. I have, however, toned down some of the more inflammatory remarks, as you will see. Just tidy it up and prepare copies for Isaac and me."

I was 'over the moon', relieved. Praise from Tony meant a lot to me. He was an ex-Young Professional himself and knew the ropes, as the senior economist in the Division. I was cheerful and chuffed as I finessed my report before handing a copy to a skeptical-looking Isaac. "Too early, my Boy," he said in a gruffly voice.

"Why don't you read it?" I retorted.

After a few minutes, Isaac re-appeared at my door, this time with Tony, with a wide grin plastered on his face; "Well done my boy," he chuckled. "I really like your approach. I can't wait to show this to the Boss, Alberto."

On Friday, we gathered in the departmental conference room to discuss the findings. Tony presented our findings. He praised the 'YP who has produced a superb report.' I felt warm blood rushing into my face and neck. I answered questions on the financial data from Sonatrach and the other companies and relished the meeting. I was co-opted into a small team that would come up with plans and strategies for the next steps for the Department of Industry as they sought to construct a programme for a new member country, Algeria.

I was determined to have more good reviews and an outstanding performance record especially in my first YP-assignment. I set out to read earlier industry reports on petrochemicals, oil, gas and fertilizers and the economics around these industries in various countries. There was no shortage of reports and relevant information on the subject. Above all, there were knowledgeable colleagues who were always ready to share their experiences and guide me in analyses of various aspects of these industries and the 'politics' around the various projects, in the department. I also met with colleagues from Zimbabwe, all of whom had been YPs, Joel Maweni, an analyst in the Energy Department, David Hatendi, a loan officer for Uganda and Callisto Madavo, who was now a Division Chief in one of the Asia Departments. From time to time, we would meet and talk about Zimbabwe over lunch or drinks.

I also had other friends and acquaintances in the Bank including Joe Wambia, the YP administrator, Dunstan Wai, who was assistant to Kim Jaycox, the Director for Africa, my former economics tutor, Jocelyn Horne, who was now a senior economist at the I.M.F and James (Jim) Friedlander, who was in the Legal Department. I had been introduced to Jim a few years earlier by a mutual friend, Lindsay Cook.

My Karate instructor in Harare, Sensei Chiba (then 6th Dan), had given me his colleague, Mr. Jiro Shiroma's number. Mr. Shiroma was a renowned Shorin Ryu karate instructor based in Arizona. He had trained in Okinawa with Sensei Chiba and other instructors now running their own dojos in America. I needed to find a Shorin Ryu Shorinkan Karate dojo near Washington D.C. to carry on with my training. I had now achieved a brown belt and needed to train for and earn my first black belt. Mr. Shiroma was delighted to hear news of his friend, Mr. Chiba. We spoke for about an hour and a half. He narrated stories from his training in Okinawa and news of their famous colleague, Tadashi Yamashita, who was now a stuntman in Hollywood.

Eventually, Mr. Shiroma gave me contact details of their colleague, Frank Hargrove, the highest ranking (at that time, 7th Dan) Shorin Ryu Trainer in America. I immediately called Kyoshi Frank Hargrove and introduced myself. He too was delighted to hear about Chiba Dojo in Zimbabwe. Frank then referred me to Renshi Arnold Mitchell (5th Dan), a student of his, who ran a Shorin Ryu dojo in Baltimore. Arnold had already been briefed by Kyoshi Hargrove. He told me that a senior member of the dojo, Karen Chapman, would pick me up from the office on Friday afternoon and bring me to Arnold Mitchell's Karate Studio in Baltimore for my first training session in America.

On the Friday, I got a call about 1630 hours from the reception desk informing me that I had a visitor. I cleared my desk and rushed to the reception desk where I was met by two beautiful sisters, Karen and Jeavonna (Jea) Chapman. Karen the younger sister, had just finished her engineering degree and Jea, had just completed her postgraduate studies in languages. Karen had recently earned her first- degree black belt. Jea was still struggling at blue belt level, 'whenever she got time to train.' I liked them both right away. We chatted as Karen drove through heavy traffic past Union Station, through South East Washington D.C. past BWI airport.

It was amazing how we chatted like we had known each other for many years. My accent fascinated them. They were ordinary African American folk but had not been in contact with many Africans, if at all. None of the black folk they knew spoke with an English accent. They would imitate my accent and laugh loudly. They knew of my trainer, Sensei Chiba, by reputation. Both were anxious to see my fighting technique. After about an hour and half, we pulled up and parked outside the Arnold Mitchell Karate Studio, on East Street, across the road from the Baltimore cemetery, two blocks west of the train station.

The Dojo was a bright open space on the second floor of an old building. Next to it was a gym full of athletic muscular beings exerting themselves on machines and floor exercises. Around the walls of the Dojo were pictures of various karateka from all over the world including Okinawa and Virginia Beach, the U.S. Headquarters, where Kyoshi Hargrove was based. In the centre was a large portrait of the Grandmaster, Shugoru Nakazato and in one of many group photographs, Sensei Chiba featured with Kyoshi Hargrove, the Grandmaster, Hanshi Nakazato and others. Taking pride of place, next to Hanshi Nakazato's picture, was a huge picture of Arnold Mitchell sparring in the gym with Muhammad Ali. I felt at home immediately.

Renshi Arnold Mitchell, an impressive athletic specimen, tall, light-skinned black man clad in karate Gi walked straight up to me and greeted me. "Hey man, so you are the African Man, Chiba's student? We have been waiting to see you here. Welcome man." Soon I was led into a small adjoining room where I was outfitted with Shureido Gi before joining other karateka performing 'kata' in the dojo. I loved this training space and took to it and the people in it like a fish to water.

After training, Arnold, Karen, Jea and I went to a little restaurant for dinner. Arnold was keen to hear more about Africa, Chiba dojo and how we trained. The three of them were keen to hear about life in Africa and Europe. My personal life-story had them spellbound. We left the restaurant well after eleven and drove back to D.C. Karen and Jea lived in the North-eastern part of D.C. They drove me back to my apartment in Rosslyn. We had more drinks and discussed music, sport and politics. Karen and Jea fell off their chairs with laughter when I jokingly told them that I found them both very attractive and could not choose between the two of them. I asked if they would assist me. This drew even louder peals of laughter. "Africans are just so funny," Karen mumbled, in-between huge gasps and more laughter.

We concluded that we should not date and train in the same dojo where we would spar with each other. Bad ideas do not kosher to philander one's mates. We all agreed and settled down to more drinks. The synastry was good, the attractancy obvious, but the air had now been cleared. Thus, I disentangled myself from the beguiling charms of the Chapman sisters. We left for their house in Silver Springs on the southern edge of D.C. the next morning. We spent the day sight-seeing then drove back to their parents' abode in Baltimore. A huge meal 'to welcome the African,' awaited us. We drove back to Rosslyn on Sunday afternoon after visiting the Aquarium and other places of interest around Baltimore. Thus, we bonded. Our bond remains a strong relationship of mutual respect.

I set up a karate-training routine. After work on Wednesdays and Thursdays, I would take the Metro to Union Station, take the 5.30p.m. train to Baltimore, walk two blocks, past the cemetery, to the dojo. After training, I would catch the 9.30 (Night Owl) train back to D.C., then take the Metro to Rosslyn. This was quite easy and convenient. The rest of the time, I would train in the gym at work. After watching me train, perform kata and fight in the ring (kumite), Renshi Mitchell told me that I would be eligible to grade for the black belt at the next grading session which was scheduled to be held at Frank Hargrove studios in Hampton, near Virginia Beach, in five months.

In that time, I had to perfect all the twelve kata. These are detailed patterns of movements practiced solo, in pairs or in groups. They are executed as a specified series of a variety of moves, with stepping and turning, while attempting to maintain perfect form. It is a display which not only depicts a mock fight but is also a display of transition and flow from one posture and movement to another. Kata are taught and learnt in stages. Previously learned kata are repeated to show better technique or power as one acquires knowledge and experience. Every student, during testing, repeats every kata they have learnt but at an improved level of quality.

I had been training seriously at karate for three years now. I enjoyed karate to the point of being almost fanatical about it. It went beyond physical fitness. Woven into the martial fabric of Shorin

Ryu Karate, Sensei Chiba taught us, are strands of Chan (Zen) Buddhism, bushido (the way of the warrior) and budo (martial way). This school of karate emphasizes courage, honour, duty, respect, benevolence, wisdom, humility, honesty, loyalty, rectitude and self-sacrifice. We were taught to walk away from trouble, lose the ego and fight only as a last resort. To me, this blends well with Christian principles such as 'turning the other cheek', the Golden Rule or principle of altruism, treating others as one would wish to be treated and forgiveness. I enjoyed kumite, freestyle fighting and adhered to the principles and discipline of the dojo with assiduity.

At my dojo in Baltimore, I was soon nick named 'Elephant Blood'. I guess because I tended to punch harder than most people in the gym and never forgot the sequence of my kata moves. I was determined to work as hard as it took to earn a black belt at the next testing station in Hampton. I had heard so many stories about the rigorous testing, the large numbers of karateka from all over the Americas and the championship fights between various dojos. This was indeed something to look forward to. I was prepared to take up this challenge. I had five months to prepare for it.

At work, changes were afoot in the department. A new President, Barber Conable, was appointed to the helm of the World Bank. He appointed six assistants to work in his office. Isaac Sam was one of them. A new Division Chief, V.S. Raghavan, who had been the Bank's resident representative in Nairobi, took over. Mr. Raghavan had interviewed me for the YP programme and had given a strongly supportive recommendation for my recruitment. With a new President at the helm, a reorganization of the bank was on the cards. There were many rumours as to who would end up where. At the same time, I learnt that I was to go on Mission again, this time, for six weeks, to India. The Bank had invested in a fertilizer plant at Hazira, in the Gujarat state, near Mahatma Gandhi's hometown of Surat City. It was time to do a supervision mission and prepare a project completion report (PCR).

I was to work with Vinod Goel, a financial analyst and soi-disant economist, as part of a team of about twelve staff members mostly from the Industry Department. In India, I was to visit the Fertilizer Company, KHRIBCO at their New Delhi headquarters, spend a week with them to understand their operations, then go to Hazira, where the plant was located, to see first-hand how the plant operated. My brief was twofold: to prepare a Project Completion Report (PCR) on Hazira and secondly, start to work on the outline of a Fertilizer Distribution Model for the Gujarat Province. I was now well-acquainted with the Bank's travel arrangements: inoculations, visas for different countries, itineraries and travel allowances.

I left Washington on the Friday aboard the British Airways 'Red Eye,' early flight to Heathrow, checked in at Browns Hotel and spent Saturday wandering from shops to restaurants in the West End of London. I spent the rest of my time reading up on India and nitrogenous fertilizers. The following evening, I boarded a B.A. flight to New Delhi. Monday morning, I found myself at a terribly busy, sweltering and humid New Delhi airport. A driver from KRIBHCO held a placard that read 'Mr. Julious' above his head. I approached him confidently and introduced myself. He shook his head gently, smiled and said, "You're welcome sir." He carried my bags to his well-polished black taxi and took me to the Hyatt Regency Hotel downtown Delhi. The sights and the streets of Delhi were not like anything I had ever imagined.

The colours were vivid and vibrant. The streets were crowded. At least thrice, we had to negotiate our way around cows lying in the middle of a busy street. Nobody seemed concerned, not least the beasts. There were beggars at every traffic light, young boys, girls and some pregnant women. Packs of dogs, clearly feral, were abound. I had not been to India before and this was a lot to take in. Amid all the chaos, somehow things seemed to work. The atmosphere was non-threatening as everyone just went about their business.

The hotel, about half an hour from the Indra Gandhi International Airport, is set in beautifully maintained grounds in Bhikaiji
Cama Place just off the main buzzing traffic and crowds along the
main thoroughfare, the Ring Road. Checking in took an unusually
long time but the staff were courteous and always ready to assist.
Eventually, I got to my room. I promptly filled the bathtub with cold
water, eased myself and wallowed in the calming, salted water. It
felt heavenly after my all-night flight from London's cool temperatures into this exotic inferno. After my dip I was restless and anxious
to explore the hotel surroundings, especially the bustling market
along the road a short distance from the hotel. I was soon mingling
with tourists and curious locals, pushing my way past various stalls
and enjoying the bustle and buzz of it all. Vendors tugged at my
shirt persuading me to bargain and buy their wares, from cheese
cloth to cane juice.

After about an hour or so, I decided to call it quits and returned
to the hotel for a bite of spicy pastries and tea. Soon, I retired to
my room to catch up on lost sleep and prepare for a meeting with
my bank colleagues before dinner that evening. I had already
spotted Vinod Goel with that unmistakable bouncy gait, in dark
glasses as he swanned towards the elevators, when I came back
from the market. Vinod was hard to read and not a natural con-
versationalist. He was, however, not the most modest nor the most
self-effacing of colleagues in the team. Without vilifying the man,
I believed that his presence on this Mission was somewhat otiose.
Time would prove me right.

Dinner was a low-key affair. Don Brown, the Mission leader outlined the programme. Vinod and I would spend a week at
KHRIBCO's offices in Delhi. After that, I would take the train to
Baroda where someone would meet me and drive me to Surat City,
then to Hazira. I would spend two weeks at the fertilizer plant then
come back to Delhi and spend another week at the Head Office.
While in Delhi I would visit Meerut about 70 km north east of Delhi.

I was interested in visiting factories crafting cricket gear and gold processing workshops. At the end of the Mission, back in Washington, I would prepare the Project Completion Report which Vinod would look over and submit to the Division Chief, Mr. Raghavan.

KHRIBCO (Krishak Bharati Cooperative) manufactured fertilizer, mainly urea. Its main plant is in Surat, Gujarat. Oil and gas findings in Bombay High and South Basin triggered the establishment of many new generation fertilizer plants to fulfil the ever-growing food needs of the country. KHRIBCO, established with financial assistance by way of a loan from the World Bank, through the Indian Government, was one of the first projects in the first phase. The company manufactures urea, ammonia, Argon, bio-fertilizers, hybrid seeds and heavy water (deuterium oxide), at Hazira, on the bank of the Tapti River near Kawase village, 15 km from Surat City. The fertilizer complex at Hazira had 2 streams of ammonia plant and 4 streams of urea plant. The establishment of the Cooperative and the Hazira plant especially, was hailed as a developmental success. It would be my job to assess the viability and wider economic impact of the facility then assist in developing an appropriate regional, fertilizer distribution model which would be tabled before and discussed with government officials.

The KHRIBCO offices were in a rather seedy part of town, not far from the hotel. Our first meeting was with the entire board of directors and management. Although our visit was not unexpected, it took all morning to explain the purpose of our visit and request, again, all the information we would need for the PCR and the fertilizer distribution model. We had sent messages to this effect before we set off from Washington. Clearly, nothing had been prepared yet because 'clarification was needed.' Before long, it was clear to me that these were people adept at handling World Bank officers: they knew how to be in charge and in control of visiting Missions on their own terms. They knew the language of the Bank very well. Don Brown explained to me later that our hosts relied on friendly nationals in the Bank to give them tips and a heads-up whenever there were visiting Bank Missions.

By the time we had finished introducing ourselves, our hosts made it clear that they were aware of who we were and where we came from! Amazing. The rest of the day was taken up with rather laboured, pedestrian, almost inane accounts of the genesis of the Cooperative and its place in the agricultural sector and industry generally. By the time we were evacuated back to the hotel for a visit to the gym and dinner, I was thoroughly exhausted. I spent the evening going through information we had been given, a narrative of the Cooperative and its network of operations. Soporific.

The week went by slowly. I laboured away and languished in KHRIBCO's offices daily with welcome breaks when I would sum-mon B.J. Jain, my taxi driver to take me to little food outlets. 'Do not drink the water, even bottled,' Jain advised with a smile, his hand rubbing his stomach. 'I think there is something in our water. It will make you sick if you are drinking it,' he explained. Back in Washington, part of our medical kit for the India visit, apart from at least five inoculations, included chlorine tablets that one would pop into bottled water and let it stand in the fridge for at least an hour before drinking it. At some point, I must have been careless and used untreated water, probably to wash down a particularly spicy hot, delicious vegetable curry purchased in one of the numer-ous food shacks on the dusty roadside.

The consequences were almost immediate and brutal beyond de-scription. 'Spanish tummy' has nothing compared to 'Mumbai tummy' or 'Delhi belly,' I have suffered both. My backside had a cease-less burning sensation and was sore for a few days. I spent many hours in the lavatory seeing blood red in my watery eyes, synesthesia at its best. It was a lesson learnt, an experience never to forget and never to be sought after nor repeated deliberately. I limped around my room, between the bed and the loo, like a Quasimodo imperson-ating a penguin, valiantly managing a gastrointestinal Mt. Vesuvius, constantly focusing on the tiny muscle holding out between me and molten hot lava. I was so disgustingly ill, as I lay on my bed in an acutely catatonic state, with a smell akin to that of elephant dung wafting into the room from the toilet. I hallucinated about who would give the encomium at my memorial service and what they would say about the manner of my demise. There is not a hint of mythomania in this. Long live B.J. Jain.

After a week at KRIBHCO HQ, I was relieved to leave Vinod and the rest of the team behind as I boarded the almost midnight train to Baroda. A sleeper cabin had been reserved for me on the crowded train. It was hot and humid but, all considered, quite comfortable. After a while, I fell asleep and woke up to the sound of a crowd outside my window at a station platform. It was mid-morning, and we were in Baroda. A kindly man walked into my cabin and introduced himself as Veejay, my driver. I followed him to his old but smart little taxi and was instructed to sit in front for a better view. I obeyed. The drive to Surat City and Hazira was hair-raising, to say the least. There were so many cars on the road. It seemed to me like whoever had the largest vehicle had the right of way. Cars seemed to be driving at each other in opposite directions and the number of narrow misses made me quite nauseous.

It was too late to request a change of position. I closed my eyes in the face of oncoming traffic, expecting a crash at any moment. Veejay had clearly done this many times before and evidently survived the experience. He talked non-stop. I paid little attention to his endless palaver. I vaguely remember uttering vituperative phrases under my breath. Eventually we got to Hazira. The beauty of the countryside, along with other sights on the way had been lost on me. I was grateful to be alive. After an enthusiastic welcome from a crowd of about fifty people, I followed my guide to my little room in the guest quarters. Peace and quiet, sanity at last. So, I thought.

I spent the rest of the day with the company's management being briefed on the history of the plant and everything that had transpired from its inception to the present day. Lots of problems had been overcome, notably those to do with distribution of fertilizers. They now used bulk trains to deliver fertilizer since bagged product was constantly raided off the delivery trains and the plastic bags were used for housing and other domestic needs. The company was now very profitable, I was informed. I was promised all the financial statements from the beginning to the present day. This all sounded very impressive.

Every time I showed signs of being awake, attentive or alert, I was introduced to more employees or had more data recounted and thrown at me verbally, at a furious pace. I asked if I could, perhaps, be allowed to spend time alone with the accountant so that I could explain to him exactly what figures I needed and in what form. I then proposed to make time to meet and discuss with the Chairman, Senior management and spend time on a guided tour of the plant. We had to work out a schedule of my movements for the next two weeks. This was finally worked out and agreed. I retreated to my room straight after the marathon session. I turned down dinner invitations pleading, without mendacity, an unsettled digestive system and exhaustion. I was duly spared further torture.

The next few days were much the same. I was up early, did my karate exercises, had breakfast then disappeared into the offices till lunch time. I sometimes took the afternoon off to work quietly on my PCR in my room. Whenever I requested the promised financials, I was told that they were being prepared and I would be offered an excursion to the sea or sightseeing. I had already been taken around the plant twice and knew every corner and aspect of it by heart. I was getting fed up of urea and ammonia. I enjoyed the drives to the beach where I treated myself to fresh coconut water and sometimes, ice-cream. One day I was informed that I would have dinner with the managing director and some members of staff, at his house. Before dinner, however, I was asked to accompany the managing director to Surat City, to buy drinks. 'And just in case of need,' I was told, 'please bring your passport.' This was puzzling advice, but I obliged.

In Surat City we went to the local government administrative office where I was asked to produce my passport so that a permit to purchase alcohol would be issued. My host asked for a permit to purchase three cases of beer and twelve bottles of whisky, Johnnie Walker red label. Apparently, this was what was required for this foreign visitor to sustain him throughout his time at Hazira. Permission was duly granted. The alcohol was purchased. Everywhere I walked, a small crowd would shadow me silently. A man ventured up to me and asked whether I was a student and from whence I hailed. "It's a secret," I joked.

"There are no secrets in India," was the retort. I was duly rescued by my host, who shouted something to the effect that I was an American diplomat, he later explained on the way back. The crowd had not looked impressed at all. Curiously, at dinner that evening, like on any other occasion during my stay, no alcohol was served.

The schmaltz, empty promises and excuses not to deliver the information I wanted and the lengthy responses, void for their vagueness, that I got to my enquiries were exasperating. I found the concatenation of incompetency and mendacity baffling. This seemed to be a way of life. This extended to Veejay who, when I invited him to join me at breakfast always said he would join me in the cafeteria for breakfast but every morning, without apologies, never showed up. By way of excuse, he would shake his head from side-to-side and sheepishly say, "I've already taken it." One day I came back to my room in the afternoon to find a crowd gazing at my door and mumbling to each other.

I had fastened my foot-hook to the door in preparation for my early morning ab crunches and sit-ups as part of my fitness programme. The supervisor explained that when the cleaners saw the device, they thought it might be a camera or a security device, so they decided not to clean my room. I demonstrated how the device was deployed during normal workouts to much laughter and amusement. By now the entire corridor was seething with workers and others who had heard about the device and were driven by curiosity to see this 'dangerous security device' for themselves.

On the penultimate day of my departure for Delhi, I was pleasantly surprised when the Accountant cheerfully told me that his financials were now ready. I followed him to his office and promptly ensconced myself in a battered chair in front of his desk. I was in a state of suspended animation. He politely handed me a sheet of paper with a small column of figures neatly running down the page and added up. "I was expecting a balance sheet and P and L," I gasped. I could feel a stream of sweat flowing down my back.

"Oh yes," came the reply. "You will see and appreciate that we are always in profit and have cash. We pay for everything in cash and we own the plant totally and completely. We have no liabilities," he carried on with a proud grin on his face.

My heart sank to my boots. I could see my career whizzing into freefall on my return to Washington. "Sir, you are not liking it?" came the inevitable question. I managed to utter, barely audibly, words to the effect that I would take the figures away and study them. When I got to the privacy of my room and out of earshot, a stream of colourful language issued out of my mouth, followed by a strident but brief scream. The system had beaten me. I was determined to obtain what I wanted from the Head Office. I had one last chance.

Back in Delhi, I was delighted to meet up with Sanjay Pradhan who was then an intern at the Bank, studying for his Ph.D. in economics at Harvard. He was very bright, always had a toothy smile on his face and told good jokes. Sanjay was in Delhi to collect the data we needed for the fertilizer distribution model, among other things. He was excellent company. We worked well together. Thanks to Sanjay, I eventually obtained the information that I needed for my PCR and did not have to visit the KHRIBCO offices again.

Our meeting at the Ministry of Agriculture was interesting. After outlining our model, the Permanent Secretary told us firmly that our proposed model was inappropriate. They had devised their own fertilizer distribution model, which was better than ours, he told us. We listened in shock as he patiently and skillfully outlined and explained their model. It was identical to ours! We were left dumbfounded but broke into hysterics as soon as we got back to the hotel.

That weekend, I flew to Agra. I had always wanted to see the Taj Mahal. At the domestic terminal at Delhi airport, I caused somewhat of a stir. The x-ray machine revealed a 'weapon' in my bag. Within a few seconds, a group of armed men had surrounded the machine and looked at me as I stood by and witnessed the contents of my bag emptied, unceremoniously, on the floor. The bag contained bottled water, a guidebook, a notebook, sunglasses and a packet of potato chips. Right at the bottom was a small Swiss army penknife. This had attracted the attention. I was frisked and asked to explain what I needed the knife for. I explained that this was an oversight on my part. My pleas for mercy fell on deaf ears until I said, "I don't need the bloody knife. You can keep it." There was an instant smile on the face of the man in charge of the operation. All the time, he wagged his head in that peculiarly Indian way, which is half affirmation, half begging to be believed. He pocketed the knife and promptly proclaimed my innocence. He announced, gleefully, after a violent handshake, that I was free to go.

At that point, a pilot who had witnessed the entire commotion said that he was flying to Agra and would take the knife for safekeeping then hand it back to me on arrival. The security detail chief reluctantly handed the knife back and watched with disdain and obvious chagrin as I strolled to the appropriate gate with a spring in my step. The pilot walked down the aisle and handed my knife back to me before we took off. I was lost for words. He just smiled and went back to the cockpit. I shook his hand warmly as we were alighting. There were no security machines at Agra, and the body search failed to spot the penknife resting in my sunglasses case. My return flight was thus uneventful.

The Taj Mahal was simply stunning. I spent the best part of a day exploring all the buildings and taking pictures of the white and red marble features. There was no shortage of people offering their services as guides. I opted for the official ones taking hordes of tourists around the gardens. It was an excellent visit. The grounds were well kept, all the monuments beautifully cared for. After touring the Taj and surrounding features, I went around the sleepy, tourist infested town. I wandered into a jewelry shop at the behest of a smooth-talking military-looking man at the door. Before I could say "Jack," the man had sold me garnets, tanzanite and a small, ornamental cushion/ rug that I later framed and hung in my study. I was offered hot sweet tea, chai, in every shop. People were generally hospitable and clearly understood the business of tourism.

My next visit was to Meerut, a short drive from New Delhi. I am not sure what the folks there had been told, but I got the reception normally accorded celebrities. I did not complain. I enjoyed walking about weighed down by pretty, colourful garlands around my neck and shoulders. Later that evening, back at the hotel, one of the guides told me that the welcoming crowd had been told that I was a great cricketer! I do not know what name they had been given, Clive Llyod, Viv Richards or Michael Holding. The mind boggles.

Next 'port of call' was Mumbai. The striking feature was the crowded airport. I opted to stay in Juhu as I had heard so much about the beach and celebrity/Bollywood culture which all turned out to be true. A friend from business school, Jimmy Master, who lived in Hong Kong, had given me the contact details for his niece, Tamia, a schoolteacher in Juhu. Tamia was already at the hotel when I arrived. She was of Persian extraction and was charming and beautiful. For the next two days, she would pick me up from the hotel and show me around the city.

I have enduring memories of the foods she introduced me to including Bhelpuri, pani puri and Sevpuri. Simply delicious. There were no episodes of Bombay tummy this time. The joyride on a horse-pulled carriage along the beach was spectacular. Mumbai and Agra were the highlights of my first Mission to India. Soon it was time to return to Washington. It was a roller-coaster six weeks' experience. Between my impending black belt exams, completing the PCR and finalising the fertilizer distribution model, I had my work cut out in Washington. Furthermore, I was nearing the end of my first six months as a Young Professional, I had to look around for a new job in a different department for my second and final assignment. I had ideas of where I wanted to be, but would it work out for me? "Hot girls will never know if they are interesting or not," kept ringing in my head, as did the refrain, "If you need an alarm clock, you need a new job."

Chapter Thirteen

IT WAS GREAT TO BE back in Washington. At the office, the new President had announced his restructuring exercise. The Industry Department, which was a central department servicing the regional departments was to be dismantled. The staff from Industry would have to find jobs in the regional departments. Finding a new assignment was now a priority for me. In this regard, I met with several colleagues and consulted on what departments to avoid. After the India Mission de-brief with the Director, Division Chief and other staff including Vinod Goel, Don Brown, Sanjay Pradhan and a consultant, Mr. Venkatraman, I remained behind to chat with Mr. Raghavan, my Division Chief.

We discussed how I had settled in, my work and reputation in the department, to date, he cut to the chase: "Now you need another job. I suggest you go the banking route since that is your background. I have recently received an enquiry about you from the Capital Markets Department. I promised my friend, Jayant Tata, one of the Division Chiefs there, that once you are back from India, I would arrange for you two to meet. Can I go ahead?" This sounded too good to be true. Raghavan carried on, "If you are not happy after your stint with that department, I promise to take you back in my division, wherever I end up. I like your work." I was left in shock and thanked the man from the bottom of my heart. At the back of mind, though, I wondered how I would get on with Mr. Tata.

I did not have to wait long: that afternoon, I received a call from Jayant Tata (Jay), newly appointed Chief of Division 1 in the Capital Markets Department under the International Finance Corporation (IFC), the private sector arm of the World Bank group. We met in Jay's office in the I-Building on Eye Street, overlooking Farragut West Metro Station. Jay was an ex-Investment banker. We hit it off famously and discussed the various deals we had worked on, where, who with and so on. We discovered that we had many friends and acquaintances in common.

This was a good start. Jay went on to say that on the strength of Mr. Raghavan's recommendation, he would offer me a position in his Division, for my second YP assignment. I did not hesitate to signal my acceptance of the offer. 'If you perform well, I will offer you a permanent position as a regular officer in the department' he whispered. I was thrilled. I pointed out to Jay that I wanted the chance to meet some of his officers and other people in the department, such as the Director, David Gill, the Assistant Director, Antoine van Agtmael and the other Division Chief, Michael Barth.

I still had to finish writing my PCR and finessing the fertilizer distribution model. Fortunately, on the latter, Sanjay had done excellent work and we had already made a lot of progress. The draft report had already been sent to the Director who had given it his nod. When I finished the first chapter of the PCR, I gave a copy to Vinod for his comments. "I want the whole complete document," bleated the man. "My friend," he added. "If you want a good recommendation for your next job, you do what I tell you."

"What a pompous little shit," I thought to myself. The struggle continued until I had written an account of the history, operations, management, market penetration and strategy, financial analyses and a SWOT analysis of the business, including its economic impact in the wider context of the country.

I dropped my opus on Vinod's desk two weeks later. A week or so later, I got my draft back with scant correction and totally devoid of any guidance to enable appropriate finalization. I was deflated but carried on. I had, surreptitiously, given a copy to Tony Ody. That copy came back with useful comments and praise for a 'commendable effort in a difficult setting.' I finalized my Report and gave it straight to Mr. Raghavan. He came back, barely a day after, singing my praises and added, 'I knew your background as a commercial banker would benefit us all. I am sending a copy to Jay Tata so he can appreciate what a favour I have done him.' I was elated. To me, from that point, Vinod was irrelevant. I would walk past his office and whistle. He would scowl and look down.

I enjoyed meeting my new colleagues in Capital Markets Department (CMD). David Gill, the Director, was affable and incisive in his questions about my career to date. He was a Cambridge man, a point of connection for us, and was of South African extraction though now Canadian. David was reputedly on the cutting edge of capital market development especially in emerging countries. He was the ultimate frontiers man. David Gill was famous for the aphorism about the emerging markets, that one cannot emerge from them easily. We had a good meeting, for the best part of an hour. I then met with other colleagues notably Theresa Barger, who was spunky and mettlesome, Farida Khambarta, soft spoken and wisely charming, Laurence Clarke, who was experienced and bullish on all things African (unfortunately destined for an early death), Chung Min Pang, who was fun and focused, Sergio Zappa, cool and experienced and others.

This was my kind of crowd. A big difference from the stuffy department where I had come from. I also met with the other Division Chief, Michael Barth, reserved but friendly and Antoine van Agtmael, who was always in a rush. Cesari Calari and Tei Mante were also in the Department, but in Barth's Division ('Barth's Brigade,' was their sobriquet; we were 'Tata's Terrors.') I also enjoyed meeting with a senior officer in the Department, Rudolf (Rudy) van der Bijl. He was extremely affable but cynical at the same time. I never quite worked out what he did in the Department. He was always present at meetings and departmental gatherings. Everyone just accepted that he was a feature of the Department, a kind of roving consultant. We had cheerful support staff, the formidable Ingrid, David Gill's P.A., Mariatou Morton, Comfort Agyepong, Grace Fonseca and Rani Purushotam.

I had a well-lit 4th floor office next to Jay's, on the north side of the I-Building, appropriately, overlooking Quigley's Wine Bar, adjacent to Farragut West Metro Station. As I was just getting comfortable in my new environment, Jay strolled into my office one morning and told me that I was to go to Cyprus, in a few days, with Theresa, to supervise a struggling merchant bank, Cyprus Investment and Securities Corporation (CISCO), recently established with help from the IFC. Theresa had all the files and information on the company and background. I was to liaise with her. On our return, we were to report on the state of the bank and its management with a view to recommending a sale of IFC's shares in CISCO, or a continued presence, in the hope that the company's prospects would improve. Theresa was bubbling with enthusiasm. She gave me the entire background animatedly and had excellent ideas of how to approach our task. We agreed and set off for Nicosia.

We flew from Washington, had a stopover in London where we boarded British Airways to Larnaca. We caught a taxi to Nicosia as soon as we landed, then checked in to the Nicosia Hilton Hotel. Within a couple of hours of checking into the hotel, we were picked up by one of the Bank's analysts, Maria Achillides. The other analyst, Socrates, received us at the bank. The Managing Director, Mr. Andreas Aloneftis, was warm and courteous. Waiting along with Mr. Aloneftis were John Ioannides, the Chairman of Cyprus Development Bank and Mr. Christofides, Chairman of the Bank of Cyprus.

These banks were IFC's co-founding shareholders in CISCO. After lengthy introductions, we settled down to business. We listened to all the Directors and their versions of what had gone wrong with CISCO and how it could be turned around. We had serious in-depth discussions before adjourning for a long lunch and siesta. It was stifling hot. We reconvened at about 7p.m. when it was cooler, discussed for an hour, then broke for dinner at about ten. We had a delicious hearty mezze at a nearby restaurant, washed down with a couple of glasses of Commandaria, the local dessert wine with un-forgettably distinct, lush, honeyed, dried fruit and toasted toffee flavours. Delectable.

In between long meetings, market studies and discussions, we took time off for brief tourist excursions to a few places. Kourion (Curium), near Limassol, was amazingly beautiful. We looked at ancient Roman and Byzantine ruins, remains of houses, monu-ments, markets, baths and an amazingly intact 3,500-seat theatre. The site thought to have been inhabited in Neolithic times from five millennia BCE. The town is believed to date back to the 13th cen-tury BCE. It was used by Alexander the Great.

The well-preserved mosaic floors were breath-taking. At Kato Paphos Archaeological Park, we looked at monuments from pre-historic times through the middle ages. The mosaics were in excellent condition, as were the colourful stone floors. Remnants of Roman villas and fortresses reminded me of my visit to Timgad, Algeria, as did the second century theatre built entirely out of lime-stone blocks. In Nicosia, we went to see the military zone dividing the Greek side and the Turkish side. We went around quaint little shops and stocked up on Commandaria and halloumi cheese espe-cially, ready for Washington.

After protracted, rather anxious meetings with all stakeholders, Theresa and I agreed that we had gathered enough information about CISCO, the securities and investment environment in Cy-prus, staff, management arrangements and relationships among shareholders including their respective input into the company's operations. After enjoying very generous Cypriot hospitality, including a karate sparring session with a new-found Cypriot karate black belt enthusiast that I met training in the hotel gym and playing table football with fellow revelers in a bar. Theresa turned out to be extraordinarily good at the game ('foosball,' she called it), it was time to pack our bags and leave. It had been a hectic working week in Cyprus.

Back in Washington, we had to prepare our report and recommendations. This took just over a week after which a meeting was convened to discuss and map the way forward regarding the status of our investment. Just before the meeting, I met David Gill loitering outside his office, as was his wont. 'You went for them with a bullet between the eyes,' he said with a wry smile playing on his lips. I escaped, dumbfounded, into the conference room adjacent to his office. About twenty interested staff sat around the conference table in anticipation of the CISCO report. Some, I am sure, were present to see what these two cocky newcomers to the department, an ex-investment banker and an ex-McKinsey analyst, had put together.

I discovered, much later, to my horror, that someone in that room was waiting to hear our report in order to relay the IFC's decision, furtively, back to CISCO. Theresa and I presented our report. We were grilled on our report by all sides. The main criticism was that we had not made strong remedial recommendations after literally 'savaging' our co-investors, management and staff. It was a raucous meeting. I was noticeably unsettled by the end of the meeting. The decision taken was that I would monitor the situation at CISCO and return to Cyprus in six months to see if there had been a perceptible improvement in the bank's performance.

A few minutes after the meeting, I was startled when my phone rang and a vaguely familiar, overseas voice belted a few choice swear words at me and shouted that I had betrayed CISCO after all the hospitality they had laid out for us. Theresa, they could forgive because 'she is white, American and therefore already prejudiced. We were relying on you as a brother from a developing country to support us,' the voice panted. I was lost for words. Eventually, it dawned on me that our report and decisions at the meeting we had just attended had already been kindly relayed to Nicosia by some mole in the department. I stormed out of my office, informed Theresa, then reported the matter to David Gill. David looked at me and smiled dryly, 'Welcome to the World Bank, young Julius,' then sank into his chair. I returned to my office replete with a host of conflicting feelings. I was angry, embarrassed, felt betrayed and abandoned but above all, floored by the fact that no one seemed to bat an eyelid at the incident. Disheartening rude awakening.

Almost six months later, I was back at CISCO. The reception was frosty, to say the least. One of the analysts refused to meet with me. In our report, we had described them as 'unimaginative and not driven and not self-starters.' Clearly, they regarded their role and performance differently. The Managing Director, Andreas, was still affable and polite, as was the chairman. John Ioannides, representing the Cyprus Development Bank, was visibly agitated and looked at me with disdain. I decided I was not going to be intimidated by any of this. After the meetings, I went back to the hotel where I instantly called Jay.

There was a deafening silence after I had told Jay that the situation at CISCO would take forever to turnaround and needed a total revamp of staff and management. "I have decided, Jay, that instead of wasting time here, I am going to find a buyer for our shares. I will not return until I have accomplished my mission."

After a pause, Jay sighed, "I hear you. Get on with it. Keep me posted." Then the phone cut. I was determined to effect a sale of IFC's shares, but where to start?

As I rode in a taxi back to CISCO's offices the next day, I had an idea to try. I talked to Andreas for about two hours and we agreed he would support me in what I was going to propose to Messrs Christofides and Ioannides, respectively. We made an appointment with Mr. Christofides, in his capacity as CISCO's chairman. I explained IFC's position to him and then proposed that Bank of Cyprus and Development Bank of Cyprus buy IFC's shares in CISCO. In exchange, IFC would still support CISCO by arranging a technical expert to work with CISCO staff for a year and advise on a staff training programme as well as new systems and strategic framework for the bank. I knew that our co-shareholders wanted IFC's presence for prestige and reputational purposes only. My idea would suit everyone.

The Chairman was not impressed by my idea, at least initially. I then pointed out that if they did not co-operate, it was possible that IFC's enthusiasm for Cyprus projects would be affected negatively. This got his attention. We left it to him to convince Ioannides to see things my way. The Chairman wasted no time in summoning Ioannides to his office and presented my idea as his own solution to the impasse with IFC at CISCO. Ioannides, after more than an hour of animated discussion in Greek, acquiesced. We shared a small sherry before I left for the hotel.

"I have sold CISCO," I whispered to Jay.

After a characteristic pause, Jay gave me his hearty congratulations and said, "No need to hurry back. You deserve a break. Stop in London, Paris or wherever and chill. It's all facultative, as you know. I'll tell David (Gill)." It was such an anti-climax. I felt a little low as I pondered that maybe I had given up too easily on CISCO. We could have done more to assist but we were more concerned about recouping our investment and walking away. My name would forever be etched in their minds as the 'devil,' I thought. I was not too far off the mark: I met Socrates at a conference in London a few years later and he gave me the cold shoulder. Andreas, on the other hand, invited me to his inauguration as the new Cypriot Minister of Defense, five years later.

Back at my desk, I sat and stared through the window. Theresa came by and we discussed the characters we had met in Cyprus during our earlier mission. We agreed that I had done the right thing for the IFC. Jay sat on my desk and listened as I narrated the negotiations that I had undertaken. Eventually, he said to me, "During your absence, I spoke to David about you. I am offering you a permanent position in my Division. I am not giving you time to think about this. It is a 'fait accompli.' David will come by later to congratulate you and welcome you to the Department, as will your colleagues. Well done. By the way, we have another problem case, a leasing company in Amman, Jordan. I would like you to go there next week, see what you can do. The managing director is a man called Sami Batshon. Find the files, study them carefully and get back on that plane. Congratulations."

I sat at my desk chatting to colleagues who came by during the day. In between meetings I tried to digest the fact that I had been pulled out of the YP programme and was now a fully-fledged Investment Officer. This came with a salary adjustment, among other perks. David shook my hand and that wry smile never left his lips as he warned me that, "This organisation is replete with flagitious beings. You are a brilliant wordier. However, a lot more work is going to be directed towards you because you can deliver. Your immediate boss will claim all the glory, but some benefit will trickle down to you also, in time." With those 'words of wisdom' still ringing in my head, I asked Mariatu Morton, my P.A., to prepare the Jordan Leasing file for me, then make the necessary bookings and travel arrangements for my imminent trip to Amman.

Chapter Fourteen

MY APARTMENT IN ARLINGTON was now too small for purpose, so I moved into a larger, three-bedroomed condominium on McArthur Boulevard, across the road from the water reservoirs near St. Patrick Episcopal Church. It was a ten-minute ride on the number 9 bus to the office. I would alight on K-Street, a block away from the office, the I-Building, which housed the IFC.

In time, I furnished the apartment and bought a comfortable, white, Peugeot 505. My neighbours, including my friend Joe Wambia who lived in the same townhouse complex, must have cringed when they saw me carrying a bass guitar, a tenor saxophone and a twelve-string ovation (semi acoustic guitar) into the apartment. I belted out a few tunes on all three instruments one after the other, to test the neighbours' noise threshold. I did not get any complaints.

Before my imminent mission to Jordan, I had to spend time with Renshi Mitchell at the dojo in Baltimore. I had daily training sessions after work, for my upcoming black-belt grading in Hampton at Kyoshi Hargrove's dojo. Not only was I now even more addicted to karate, I was also determined to excel at it. I was frequently asked by my colleagues, why I was so obsessed and what the value of karate was to me. I had to revert to basics, to explain myself: the nature of karate to me, is three-fold: as athletic training, self-defense and as spiritual training. The nature of karate is that it requires the body to move in all directions, in contrast, for example, to the emphasis on the arms in rowing or the legs in soccer or jumping. Must I teach them everything? I thought to myself.

There is absolutely no need for concern about one-sided development of the body in karate. The fact of uniform development is one of the physical, athletic benefits of karate that appealed to me particularly. As I continued to practice the movements, kata or forms, my speed picked up. I became both quicker and more vigorous. It becomes possible, gradually, to get ample exercise in a relatively short period. This was always ideal to me in view of my other commitments and therefore another major benefit. In addition, kata can be performed anywhere including hotel rooms, gardens and hallways without the need of equipment or a training partner.

"Almost all living creatures have some mechanism for defending themselves, for, where this development is incomplete, the weaker are destroyed and perish in the fierce struggle for survival. The fangs of the tiger and the lion, the talons of the eagle and the hawk, the poisonous sting of the bees and the scorpions, and the thorns of the rose and the Bengal quince: are these not all preparations for defense?" asks Karate Master Gishin Funakoshi. The power of karate is well known for its effectiveness in inflicting severe damage, breaking boards and cracking stones without tools.

Anyone trained in karate can consider their entire body to be a weapon of awesomely effective offensive and defensive power, I explained to my colleagues. No weapons are necessary. Anyone including the young, old and infirm can apply karate techniques effectively to protect themselves with little strength expended. This makes karate a form of natural defense without equal. For me, this was a useful skill to acquire in view of all the travel I was now to undertake all over the world.

As spiritual training, I would point out that karate is no different from the other martial arts in fostering and inculcating the traits of courage, courtesy, integrity, humility and self-control in those who have found its essence. Its flexibility of training is the roborant that makes it sustainable as a pursuit to allow enough time at it to master its techniques, polish its virtues of courage, courtesy, integrity, humility and self-control to make them the inner light to guide one's daily actions. This can only be achieved over many years. It takes a lifetime of devotion to the study of this art, to achieve fulfilment of the need for spiritual training.

I arrived in Amman, Jordan, late afternoon on a Monday and checked in at the Amman Hilton. I called Mr. Sami Batshon, Managing Director of Jordan Leasing, to arrange a meeting as soon as was practicable. A grumpy-sounding Mr. Batshon said he would send a driver to collect me from the hotel at 10 a.m. the following morning. In the meantime, he suggested that, "You may want to go around the shops and see what souvenirs you can pick up in Amman." I called my friends at the Nimbukan karate dojo. They were delighted to hear from me and invited me to train with them that evening. I wasted no time in straightening out my karate Gi, ready for the evening session with Sensei Kareem and Abdallah at Amman's famous karate dojo.

The workout was hard but enjoyable. The emphasis here was Jiu-Jitsu and boy, could they fight. I showed off all my kata and sparring techniques, much to the amusement of the junior section of the class. The sweaty exertion was a welcome break. After training, we sat at Kareem's mother's house sipping orange juice and talking about famous fights especially those involving our mutual trainer, Kyoshi Hargrove. He had an awesome reputation in kumite or free fighting. The famous bouts between him and John Lewis are still the subject of folk lore in karate. It was never resolved as to who was the better fighter, although Kyoshi Hargrove insisted, consistently, that he won both of their fights. After a hearty meal of fresh garden vegetables, cous cous, lamb and fish, I was ready to crash out before my meeting with Sami Batshon on the morrow.

Sami Batshon turned out to be a huge man with exceptionally large hands. His handshake could easily have been mistaken for attempted murder. Sami's corpulent figure was intimidating but not unfriendly. He listened intently to the message from the IFC, a major shareholder in Jordan Leasing. You must show us a turn-around strategy, improve the business, or we are out. We will sell our shares and suspend the line of credit, I explained to him as firmly as I could. After listening and moving his head like a nodding donkey, which I found quite irritating, he picked up his files and invited me to join him for coffee and lunch at his favourite restaurant downtown Amman. I duly obliged.

During lunch, we continued to talk about the leasing business and the role IFC could play in the scheme of things. Mr. Batshon appeared to be tired and at the end of his tether with regards to how else to improve his business performance. We feasted on a large plate-full of the local dish, Mansaf, rice and meat boiled in yoghurt, washed down with generous helpings of Arak. Delicious. Sami Batshon's waistline was testament to the Herculean challenges he set himself at meals, especially lunch. After the lunch-time brainstorming session, Sami dropped me off at the hotel where I did my best to recover from the long lunch and planned an outline of my 'supervision report.'

The rest of the week in Jordan was spent between Sami's offices and the hotel. I did my best to ignore Sami's nodding donkey act as I perused the financial statements. I discussed business plans with management and selected board members. Then there was the training at the dojo and feasting in private homes. I took time off to go on a memorable trip to Aqaba, on the Red Sea. The aquatic life was utterly amazing as was the scenery. The Jordanians were very hospitable. The Al-Maghtas ruins on the Jordanian side of the River Jordan, site of Jesus' baptism and John the Baptist's ministry, were awe-inspiring. At the end of my visit, the dojo presented me with a replica of their shield and other karate memorabilia. Kareem's Mum gave me a beautiful mosaic depiction of The Last Supper, a gift for my Mum. The picture now hangs on my parents' mantelpiece.

I presented my report back in Washington, to Jay, David Gill and a few other interested investment officers including a recent recruit, Anita Priscilla Khan, an English lady. She had expressed a keen interest in working in that region as she and her Pakistani husband had lived in Amman previously. After making my recommendations, I was only too eager to hand over the Jordan portfolio to Anita. There was no escaping the harsh realities of the Jordanian economy and the lack of growth opportunities for financial leasing businesses. However, Jordan remained, in my heart of hearts, an excellent destination with warm, welcoming, orderly, peaceful and educated people. I had played my part.

In the ensuing six months, I travelled to Panama, among other countries. I worked on Banco Latino Americano des Exportaciones (BLADEX), an IFC favourite. Jay accompanied me and made all the necessary introductions. We had a superb 'supervision mission' and a proposal for a $10 million line of credit to the institution. The work was exhilarating especially because the staff and management were well-organized and familiar with the IFC's Capital Markets Department. On one of the visits I worked with Alvaro Quiros, from Fitch in New York, on a credit rating for Bladex.

The routine number-crunching work and supervision assessments were soon completed. Enough time was left for me to explore the louche spots of Panama City and, of course, the Panama Canal, a great engineering feat. My first visit and, coincidentally, my three subsequent visits over the next two years, coincided with mass demonstrations against the then President, Noriega. I joined one of the peaceful, 'candlelight marches' against the dictator one Sunday evening downtown Panama City. It was a moving experience.

When the Americans finally invaded the City to remove Noriega, I was holed up at the Marriot Hotel in the heart of the City. Fortunately, not much violence ensued. This was a unique, moving experience which left an indelible mark on my mind. I wrestled with thoughts ranging from democratic processes in nation states to despotic rule, economic mismanagement and the role and legitimacy of foreign intervention in other countries' internal affairs.

During one of our routine chats in his office late one Friday afternoon, David had explained to me how the Department, CMD, and he himself, were on the 'frontier' of financial market development. The main task was to try and bring emerging financial markets, especially the stock markets, from the 'irrelevant periphery' to the critical mainstream of world economic activity. As a young, inexperienced investment banker, his ideas and schemes pertaining to stock markets had been generally dismissed as 'wild,' David said. Now, at CMD, under the IFC's and World Bank Group umbrella, he had the opportunity to experiment and put some of his ideas into practice.

This was all about re-engineering the financial world in frontier economies. These economies may not seem like promising terrain, explained David, as they are characterized by relatively undeveloped markets generally manipulated politically, weak legal systems and either low per capita income or faltering systems. Listening to David, I felt honoured to be part of this process at this time. He was a passionate and distinguished mentor, a real 'Financial Frontiersman.' This piqued my interest in capital markets development. It set my heart on fire with zeal and determination to excel.

As time passed, I got well-immersed in the workings and internal politics of the World Bank Group especially the IFC. I developed a network of friends and colleagues to navigate through the complex systems of the Group. David Gill invited me to lunch at Primi Piatti Restaurant on EYE Street one afternoon a few days before he announced his imminent intention to relinquish his post as Director of the Capital Markets Department. After a lengthy discussion ranging from what my experience had been so far to what the future could hold in store for me and the Group as a whole, David, sipping on a stirred, dry Martini, whispered, "Only the Church can rival the World Bank Group when it comes to vindictive management, politics, rhubarb and back-stabbing." That was not, in my experience to date, a misplaced observation. I asked David to explain all this to me. I then got a brief history and raison d'etre of CMD in the context of the World Bank Group. In essence, he said this:

The early mission of the World Bank was to finance economic development and to promote domestic capital markets. The objective was to wean these developing countries away from dependence on foreign loans. IFC's mandate was to finance local companies through loans and equity investments and to promote foreign private investments in such companies. The Bank's financing mandate was achieved principally by lending to governments to finance 'projects' that would contribute to development and that could pay their way financially. These projects initially were simply 'brick and mortar stuff': bridges, power stations, government-owned industrial and mining companies.

The Capital Market development mandate was to be achieved through advising governments on developing domestic financial markets in order to increase domestic savings and improve the efficiency of allocation of those savings. To support implementing these policies, both advice and lending, Development Finance Corporations (DFCs) were promoted by the Bank and formed in each country. These financial institutions were usually government-controlled but with some private ownership. IFC was an equity investor in and a lender to, most of those that were not 100% government owned.

Both local and foreign financial institutions were sought as investors in them. DFCs were wholesaling vehicles that could finance projects and companies too small for the Bank or IFC to finance individually. As these DFCs were local entities, they were specifically mandated also to promote their domestic capital markets. Part of the theory was that the DFCs, with domestic government and

Bank backing, were well positioned both to attract foreign capital and to promote development of the local capital market.

The theory, however, was not working well in practice. The Bank's lending activities were growing at a rate faster than the development of local capital markets. Consequently, lending was being constrained in part by a shortage of both local and foreign equity. Much the same was happening with IFC at the time. At the same time, more emphasis was placed on ensuring that recipients of Bank/IFC funds were also examples of sound financial management and good governance. As a new specialized unit, based in IFC, but also working for the Bank, CMD was supposed to address this problem as its 'first and only priority.' As with all investing institutions, IFC also had to have an 'exit' strategy so it could eventually sell out and reinvest the proceeds. The desired exit was to local investors, preferably through the local stock market. At least, that was the original intent.

"As 'white knights,' especially in CMD's developmental role," David explained with relish and a hint of regret and mischief in his voice, "...we had more enemies in the Bank and IFC" than friends, especially among the DFC management group under fire for having failed in one of their missions. CMD was, in their eyes, a group of outsiders, even worse, "Wall Street stockbrokers' parachuted in to solve the problem and thus embarrass them. It was therefore essential to 'learn the ropes' at the Bank and IFC." David estimated that the proportion of the working day spent by IFC and Bank staff on internal politics probably far exceeded that spent in most entities. He recounted a warning given to him by a Professor Sydney Robbins when he joined IFC.

"David, I have worked half my life in government and half in academia and I go to church regularly. They all are hugely bureaucratic. They are consumed by constant infighting. For a long time, I thought the church had the record for the proportion of time spent on turf wars and the like. Then I came to the Bank and discovered quickly it had the record! Be careful." Another long-time professional in the Bank had also warned him, "I'll give you an example of how seriously we take our turf fights. Before I came to the Bank, had I seen someone about to step on a banana peel, my immediate reaction would have been to warn them. Now my first impulse would be to ask myself which would be best for my career: to warn him or let him slip on it and maybe break a leg." Thus, I was well-prepared for life, work and times at the Bank and IFC.

Just before his departure, David promoted me to Senior Investment Officer, "In recognition of his brilliance, admirable work ethic and dedication to duty." I felt honoured and elated. David told me, in confidence then, that he was going to join Dean Le Baron at Batterymarch. He wondered whether I would be interested in working with his new team. I promised to give it my consideration and revert in good time. I valued David's kindness. He clearly had a soft spot for me and I for him.

David's words always played in my mind especially when I found myself in difficult or unusual work situations. His other favourite sayings: "Whenever you are aggrieved, don't get angry, get even," "don't get bitter, get better," and "Never leave till tomorrow what you can do today," became mantras for me as I continued to work on projects in Tunisia, Senegal, Ghana, Pakistan, Nigeria, Namibia, Kenya, the Philippines and Cote d'Ivoire, among others, over the next five years. They guided me as I navigated my way through personnel changes in the wake of institutional and departmental reorganisations in the World Bank Group.

My work focus was varied: Capital market Development. This entailed tailoring new and existing products to enable, induce or trigger and foster financial sector development in emerging markets especially. Sometimes this entailed partnering institutions in developed markets with new or selected ones in emerging markets to strengthen and foster institution-building and transfer of financial sector management and operational expertise.

It was not long after my famous chat with David that I experienced the full force of the brutal politics and exhilaration of IFC/Bank work in full measure. I had put in lots of hours working on putting in place a structured line of credit-cum-medium term loan for Bladex. I had now taken the project past the appraisal stage. Simultaneously, I was working on a venture capital project in Cote d'Ivoire. The Agha Khan Group and Commonwealth Development Corporation (CDC) would co-invest with the IFC to establish a link with the fledgling Abidjan Stock Exchange.

The Agha Khan team was well-organized and always on the ball. We worked well on sharing information for our respective reports. The Agha Khan team flew in largely from Aiglemont, France, they had a strong local presence in Abidjan led by Mr. Siddhi and the FD, Mr. Bhaloo. The CDC team from London and the local West Africa office in Ghana, were not so dynamic but pleasant enough to work with. By now, my French was near the best it had ever been since I had enrolled in French lessons offered by the Bank's languages department.

Jay agreed with David that I should be a 'trail-blazer' and present the two project proposals to the Bank's Board one after the other, at the next board meeting. On average, an officer produced about one project that made it to the board, every eighteen months; two simultaneously, in less than twelve months was, according to David, 'a bit of a record.' Jay did his best to prepare me and calm my nerves. David suggested that I took time to go and look at the Bank Boardroom before the presentation, to get a feel for the atmosphere as the place could be overwhelmingly intimidating.

I felt confident enough to do this since I had done the requisite preparation. I knew about these companies and the projects better than anyone else. I had discussed my reports with the country economists and discussed the issue of the CFA franc with the Cote d'Ivoire country economist, Ben Brahimi, an Algerian national, as this was critical to my financial projections. Panama used the US$

as their currency and so their case was more straight-forward, in the scheme of things.

The morning of the board presentation could not have arrived sooner. The IFC delegation, led by Sir William Ryrie, the CEO, David, as CMD Director, Jay, as my manager and other curious officers who had been following my work progress and were interested to see how history would unfold. David's 'banana peel' analogy was not far from the forefront of my mind as I looked around at familiar faces from the IFC and beyond. We assumed our seats at the table. The room was huge as was the round table with at least fifty executive directors, their staff, assistants and other Bank staff members who were in attendance with their own country programmes and projects for the board to consider.

Board meetings were long , beginning at 0930 hours and usually ending late in the afternoon. Soon it was my turn to present. After clearing my throat nervously, I slowly gained confidence and stopped shaking as I presented my Bladex proposal to the president, Barber Conable, who listened in stony silence. Meanwhile, Sir William, who clearly was not familiar with another English accent, apart from his own, especially from an unfamiliar staff member of a darker hue, cast an occasional wary glance at David, Jay and I.

After what seemed like a lifetime, I invited questions from the board after recommending that they accept my proposal. There was a sprinkling of minor questions, then the president declared that the proposal had passed and should be adopted. I was thrilled, but this was only half of the job done. I then introduced and read my IPS, Cote d'Ivoire board report summary. No sooner had I finished, Mr. Porter, the Canadian Executive Director, challenged my projections and assumptions on the CFA. David interjected to assist, drawing a rather nasty scowl from the president. I then found my voice and told the members that I had consulted with the country economist, who was present at the board meeting and maybe he should answer the question. Barber Conable said he did not see why the bank should answer a question at the board, on a project that was not theirs.

In the ensuing chaos, Ben Brahimi raised his voice and announced that IFC, that is me, had misunderstood his advice! I was floored. David then announced that he was withdrawing the proposal and would resubmit it at the next board meeting. The meeting was adjourned. I was eviscerated. I thought my job had just gone down the tubes. Jay was furious, as was Sir William, but David stuck to his guns. Back in the office, he dictated and sent an explanation to Sir William outlining the politics of the attack and how I had been caught in crossfire.

David could not have been more of a fatherly figure. At the next board meeting, I presented the IPS proposal and cockily announced, much to David's smug pleasure, that nothing in the report had been revised. There were no questions. The proposal sailed through unopposed. It was after this incident that David gave me lunch at Primi Piatti and explained the inner workings of the Bank and how a new member of staff could be affected and devastated by these machinations. This was 'baptism by fire.' Everywhere I went, in the building, I imagined voices discussing this 'debacle' and glee at the stumble of David's chosen rising star.

I had taken to seating in David's chair, in his office, whenever he was away. I announced to all who would listen that I was David's chosen heir and successor and that in his absence, I was the Acting Director. After 'boardgate,' I wound my neck in. I retreated to the sanctuary of my own office. I found comfort in calling my parents from time to time and researching on new work. I had landed with a bump. This was a sobering and humbling experience. I tried to learn lessons from it.

I still had my black belt karate exam to worry about. The exam day started with a five-mile run, barefoot, starting from Hargrove Karate Studios, at six in the morning. We ran through Hampton town, the beach area, a couple of neighbourhoods, then back to the studio. Next was the fitness demonstration. This entailed executing five hundred each of front kicks, sidekicks (mawashi geri), inside, outside, upward and down blocks, push-ups and sit-ups. Senior instructors were on hand to count, correct, punish in the event one displayed signs of exhaustion or poor execution of movements. Sensei Rudolph Barfield, then 4th Dan, was my 'tormentor.' He was gentle-sympathetic but tough. Three hours after the fitness session, it was time for individual kata performance.

For the black belt, one had to perform all fourteen kata, without a single mistake, then perform one kata with the Bo or Staff. After the kata, each candidate had to explain why they deserved to be awarded a black belt and how the practice of karate had impacted them or society at large. In my exhaustion, I tried to be funny. I bleated that I put myself through all this ordeal because I am, "Sick in the head and need my head examined." I was sentenced to fifty push-ups on my bare knuckles, for insolence.

The belt award ceremony was a blur. I could see nothing much through teary eyes. The smell of blood and sweat hung in a heavy pall over the dojo. My body was broken. I was exhausted, hyper-restless and too numb to sit in one place, think or drink fluids. It was a strange feeling that I will never forget. I drove back to D.C. that evening and crashed out on the sofa through the following day. I limped into the office late on the following Monday morning. After listening to the account of my weekend pursuits, David looked at me in horror and out of the side of his mouth uttered, 'You are one mad person.'

Back in the office, there was work to do. I had more exams for my CFA. I was now well into my Part III, having completed all my earlier stages. I was comfortable with the academic side of the course requirements, but the sheer volume of work was overwhelming. I soldiered on. I also attended French classes offered by the Bank. I endeavored to improve my language skills especially negotiating and transacting business in Franco-phone countries. I put my French knowledge to good use in Tunisia, Senegal, Cote d'Ivoire, Togo and France. At the dojo, the focus had now shifted to 'kobudo,' weapons training where I had to muster the bo, nunchaku, eku, sai, kama and tonfa.

Apart from my friend and training partner, Karen Chapman, who was now a second dan black belt, I now had two regular male sparring partners, Mustafa and 'Ghost.' The former had a devastating punch; the latter possessed a fabled high 'butterfly' kick and amazing speed. Bare hand combat was to be my focus for my second-degree black belt. Karen's sister, the charming Jea, stopped training in favour of other pursuits more agreeable with her modelling inclinations. The tough, sweaty ways of the dojo were clearly losing their appeal. I tried to balance work and karate training with the demands of family and social life.

I was now a proficient guitar player. A twelve string Ovation and a Rickenbacker bass had pride of place in my ever-growing collection. My karate friend, Hardy Cash, was also a professional bass player. He would give me bass lessons from time to time. We would jam in my basement on weekends. Hardy suggested that I register at the music studios in Rockville as they were admitting new saxophone students. This was music to my ears. I eagerly enrolled on a course to learn how to play the tenor and alto sax proficiently. I attended classes in the evening, twice a week. It was a lot to take on, especially in the beginning.

I was to be found blowing away at my saxophones early Sunday mornings and Friday evenings. Whenever I got a chance to go to Blues Alley in Georgetown, I would go to see some of the world's greatest jazz and blues musicians. I saw Ronnie Laws, Eddie Harris, Robert Cray, BB King, Taj Mahal, Edgar Winter, KC and JoJo, Johnny Guitar Watson, Stanley Clarke, Gill Scott Heron and Brian Jackson, among others. I got hooked on the saxophone. Occasionally, I played in the office, much to the amusement of my colleagues.

Some work colleagues, including Barbra Wilson, 'Miss Janice,' James Wise, Anne a.k.a. Miss Muffett, Clarence Haynes, Laurence Clarke and Paula Hansen would meet for a meal or drinks on Fridays after work. We were nick-named 'The Black Pack.' We discussed office politics, especially the racial undertones, our careers and most of all, the current entertainment scene. Hip hop was taking root. We all loved Snoop Dogg, Warren G, Montel Jordan, LL Cool J., Dr. Dre and Tupac. James Wise, an accomplished musician and vocalist of note, would hum a tune and we would all sing along. Sometimes we pranced around the tables in full view of amused colleagues.

A sad note was struck when, one afternoon, we received news that our colleague, Bibiana Nerkle, had died in a freak helicopter accident in Colombia while on mission. We remembered her for her mysterious smile and fey manner. We were horrified. At the memorial service, at Georgetown University Chapel, James gave a tear-jerking baritone, memoriter rendition of 'Amazing Grace' to the accompaniment of particularly lugubrious church organ chords. We were all on our feet. As we left the chapel, I felt an arm on my shoulder, it was Sir William Ryrie. In a soft and gentle Scottish voice, he said, 'Upsetting. It will be fine old boy.' We walked, mostly in silence, back to the office. Sir William died shortly after retiring from his post as Executive Vice President of the IFC.

Occasionally the 'Black Pack and 'selected guests' held wild and memorably vivacious, alcohol-fueled events. These were joyous occasions with their dose of mirth and 'incestuous' or in-the- office, inevitable romantic excursions. I hope no one got hurt. Enough said. In my more lucid moments, I have always wondered what drew us together; colour, creed, work, origins maybe all played a part. Amazingly, we all kept in touch for many years as we went on our different life journeys. I will always have fond memories of Laurence Clarke who died in Mozambique while on duty for the I.M.F. Joe Wambia and I still meet and reminisce on those times.

Clarence Haynes, James Wise, Barbra Wilson and Anne, 'Miss Muffett,' still hang out in Washington D.C. We still meet up for drinks and frequently, we break bread.

While I was revising this book, I learnt, from Barbra, of James Wise's death.

Chapter Fifteen

MY WORK ON GHANA'S financial sector structural adjustment programme was exhilarating, challenging and rewarding. Jay returned from a departmental meeting one day and told us that CMD, to save face, had promised to deliver at least one CMD project in Africa quarterly. Accusations of unbalanced focus favouring regions other than Africa, were levelled against the department. Asia and Latin America were regarded as preferred regions to invest and work in. In defense, CMD management, notably Jay, the new Director, Charles (Chuck) Sethness and his new deputy, Nick Noon, promised to deliver projects in Africa. The Bank's VP, Kim Jaycox was due to visit Ghana, which had just launched a Bank-sponsored economic structural adjustment programme. CMD would take the lead on the financial restructuring front.

Reality kicked in as management were informed that CMD had never had a project in Ghana. Jay pulled me aside and told me that if I were to go to Ghana without delay, write a report from Accra or better still, rustle up a project, I would be a hero. In return, I could re-route my flights as I wished. I could visit my parents in Zimbabwe, family in London and friends in Paris, on the same ticket. I accepted the challenge. I had never been to Ghana.

I had two main contacts in Ghana: Afare Donkor, a banker I had met in Harare in my RAL days. We were introduced by a mutual friend, Derek van Heerden. Afare was in town to source technical assistance for a new discount house that he was setting up. It would be the first of its kind in Ghana. Bard discount house were advising him. They offered Nick Vingirayi, one of their managers, to go to Ghana to assist Mr. Donkor in this enterprise.

My other contact, George Prah, who I had met at university in the U.K. George was managing the family business, South Akim, in Accra. He was a client of Afare Donkor's from the latter's days as manager at Barclays Bank, Accra. My final contact was Tsatsu Tsikata, an academic and lawyer who I had met when he was pursuing postgraduate studies in law at Christchurch College, Oxford. We had struck a friendship based on a mutual love of the game of cricket. Tsatsu was a useful left-handed number three batsman for Oxford. He was now a famous politician in Ghana.

George met me at Accra airport on a ridiculously hot and humid Saturday morning. The airport was run-down, the immigration officials were slow and lackadaisical in their duties. Eventually I emerged from the airport exit gate to be greeted by a beaming George. I hugged him for a good twenty seconds. "You are not used to this heat and chaos are you old boy?" said George.

"Damn right you are my old son," I responded, just like we spoke to each other in the good old days. Soon we settled down to a hearty breakfast of hot tea, toast, scrambled eggs and fried yam. After breakfast George took me to see his parents at their palatial residence in the Ridge area of Accra, near the IFC's offices. It was like yet another 'homecoming' for me.

Lunch was a long affair with delicious foods that I had never had the pleasure of eating before. After lunch, George's father, 'JP' or simply 'Dad,' as I called him, took me on a guided tour of Accra. He filled me in on the history of Ghana. He had been a civil servant and was a prominent businessman in his own right. It was surreal to hear about the country from a prominent figure in the nation's history. The highlight of the tour was a stop at his company headquarters and factory where he kept his favourite toy, a vintage Porsche sports car. I was in seventh heaven. He watched me admire and inspect the car. It was a gem. On our return to the house, George said to us, "We all wondered who would lead who astray...." I felt like I was home at last.

The next day, George and his then girlfriend, Marie-Louise, took me on a tour of greater Accra. We drove for about an hour due west, along the coast and passed through their rural home, the scenic, quaint village of Anomabo. We visited many other sites including El Mina Castle, Achimota school and the University at Legon. We stopped at Kokrobite beach, near Winneba junction, for a picnic. As we drove through the village, after the picnic, George stopped to buy 'kenke' from some roadside vendors. Suddenly a throng of vendors surrounded the car selling their wares, including large rodents, grass cutter, cane rat or in the local language, 'akrantsee.'

The roasted rodent was splayed on bits of wood. It was not an appetizing sight especially to this vegetarian. Initially, I mistook the rodent-sellers for protesters who were protecting wildlife from being victims of roadkill. The number of cars driving through bushy areas had increased dramatically as the economy picked up. George corrected my misapprehension and pointed out firmly, that the vendors just wanted to sell their wares including cane rats that they had trapped in the fields. To many locals, he added, this was a delicacy, part of the local diet. It was a cheap and easily accessible source of protein. This did not make the sight of roasted rodent any more appetizing to me, as I explained to George's bemused parents when we got home later that evening.

Early on Monday morning, I went to Consolidated Discount House where I spent the best part of the day with Afare Donkor, then Managing Director. After describing to him what CMD's mission was and the role that we could play in Ghana's financial sector revival, Afare reached for his desk drawer and pulled out a document. "When you go home this evening, read it and let us discuss it tomorrow. I have arranged for you to meet with the Governor of the Central Bank, Dr. Agama. He taught me Economic Theory at University, and the Minister of Finance, Kwesi Botchwey, my old classmate."

I had successful meetings with Dr. Agama and Dr. Botchwey in their respective offices. They were familiar with the World Bank's work in Ghana as they worked closely with various Bank teams on the structural adjustment programme then underway in Ghana. This made my task easier. They both knew Afare Donkor well and were supportive of any projects we may undertake with him. As I left Dr. Botchwey's office, I saw a familiar face with a skull smile plastered on it. It was my friend Tsatsu Tsikata. He had already heard about my arrival in Ghana: 'I hear you are in expansive mood already. Great to have you here,' he said. We shook hands. We chatted briefly and exchanged contact details.

I briefed Afare on my meetings with the two civil servants. The brittle and ephemeral nature of Ghana's economic revival had been brutally exposed by the ongoing structural adjustment programme. There was serious need for institution-building in the financial sector. We agreed. In that regard, Afare had set up the first discount house, Consolidated Discount House. This had been a success. It was now a good time to establish a well-structured merchant bank as a useful addition. Afare had done a preliminary study which I had perused and liked. This would form the basis of my next project for CMD: An Acceptance House/ Merchant Bank, Continental Acceptances Limited (CAL).

The next task was to study the banking market including current players, products, prospects for new players etc. By the time I returned to Washington a fortnight later, I had figured out how I wanted to structure CAL. I had identified opportunities for new institutions to complement existing ones, attract local and foreign investors into the sector and create a show-piece of financial sector development for the benefit of Ghana and the World Bank group.

I had now familiarized myself with the social, business and political environment and met with a wide range of Ghanaians from all walks of life. I assembled a sizeable list of social and business contacts. Afare and his team were to be crucial in my plans. As I did my rounds, meeting people in Accra, I met a friend that I had met in my RAL days, Dr. Kwame Nyantekyi-Owusu. Kwame and I had become friends after he visited RAL, having been referred by a mutual friend. We established an excellent rapport and shared many interests in common. Kwame, I soon learnt, had been at University at the same time as Afare. They both read Economics at the University of Ghana. Kwame now had diverse business interests held through his holding company, Inter-Afrique. We had now re-established contact.

From Accra, I took up Jay's offer to visit Harare on my way back. Ghana Airways had a direct, DC-10, flight from Accra to Harare. In Harare, I had booked myself at the Harare Club. My family congregated there one night for dinner. It was a joyful family gathering. My parents decided to spend an extra night at the Club. I visited various friends in Harare. Merchant Bank of Central Africa now run by Frank Read was my first port of call. David Hatendi and Lazarus Murahwa had just joined them. I told them about my visit to Ghana and suggested that maybe they should consider getting involved as investors or technical assistance partners, in CAL.

I left the same message with Dr. Leonard Tsumba, then managing Director of Zimbank, the then largest commercial bank in Zimbabwe. This was a new concept to all of them but gave them food for thought. I also visited RAL Merchant Bank, my old employer, now led by Ray Feltoe. I told Ray that I had also spoken to a junior member of staff, William Nyemba, who I had earmarked for a job at CAL. Ray grudgingly acquiesced to my request. "William does not even have a passport," he added with a chuckle. "If he is willing to go, we will let him go. It would be good for him to learn something different from letters of credit!" he added with a hint of sarcasm. From Harare I flew to London for a couple of days' decompression stop-over.

"We must tell Chuck about this. Fantastic, Jules," Jay muttered. I outlined how I intended to roll out my work in Ghana. Chuck Sethness and other colleagues from CMD listened to my plans for Ghana with intrigue. They asked lots of questions and offered brilliant suggestions. They were supportive of my efforts. I was quietly relieved and delighted. Over the next two months I worked hard at preparing the necessary reports including the Initial Project Review, the Appraisal and Board Papers.

I made one quick trip to Ghana to secure Government approvals and Local Counsel's opinion. This was followed by negotiations with would-be shareholders including an insurance group, Vanguard Assurance, headed by Nana Awuah-Darko, the Social Security National Investment Trust (SSNIT), and a consortium of family and other groups led by Mr. Afare Donkor. After lining up the Ghanaian side, I flew to Harare to negotiate with the Reserve Bank, MBCA and Zimbank. The negotiations proved futile as the Zimbabwean entities dragged their feet and could not get their minds around doing business outside of Zimbabwe. I thought this was short-sighted and backward-looking. I communicated my views to them robustly. I was disappointed.

In London, I visited Alastair Boyd, who was now the deputy CEO at the Commonwealth Development Corporation. After telling him about my Ghanaian plans, he expressed interest in the CAL project and promised to move quickly on it. Back in Washington, I called on another acquaintance, Geoffrey Dunshee at the Africa Growth Fund. Geoff was excited at the prospect of working with the IFC in Ghana. CAL was a good opportunity.

Finally, I called Malcomn Pryor, who I had met through a mutual friend, Clarence Haynes, 'a truly original native of the District of Columbia,' he called himself. He joined CMD from Bankers Trust's office in Sao Paolo. Malcolmn and Clarence had been classmates at

Wharton Business School. Malcolmn and two friends from Wharton, had since established the first black-owned and led Investment Bank in the U.S., Pryor, Govan and Counts, based in New York. I talked Malcolmn into investing in CAL and playing the role of 'technical partner' in the bank. All my 'ducks' were thus lined up.

It was a personal triumph to make the case at the Bank's Board. IFC would take a 20% stake in CAL and extend a US$5 million line of credit to the company for trade finance. After the board approval, I left for Accra, to finalize all the arrangements for disbursement of funds. The IFC's procedure was that all the other shareholders should disburse before IFC. It was therefore important for me to visit Malcolmn in New York, meet with Geoff Dunshee, stop in London to brief Alastair then visit all the local shareholders to give them a little nudge so that all the funds would be in place to enable the Bank of Ghana to issue CAL's banking license. This would the first license issued since Merchant Bank of Ghana was established, twenty years previously.

As we waited for the various funds to be lodged with the Bank of Ghana, I helped Afare interview prospective staff. Many were known to him from the various financial institutions he had worked with previously. William Nyemba, recently arrived in Accra, and helped set up the office. He would be an assistant manager in the foreign banking department assisted by the indomitable Sackey Mensah. Derek Peacock, a retired English banker, was appointed General Manager. Sammy Adetola would head corporate finance assisted by two analysts, Yofi Grant and Frank Adu. Sam Bannerman Wood would be the Company Secretary, Simon Dornoo was the Accountant while Ebo Quagraine was the IT manager. Comfort Quist-Yeboah headed the MD's office. She had been Afare's PA for many years.

Afare arranged for me to stay at the Company's Guest House in Tesano. It was, coincidentally, near George's house. It was a comfortable, secure, four-bedroomed bungalow with a manicured garden, a cook, Kofi Akrobesi, his 'Sous Chef', Isaac, and a twenty-four-hour guard, Francis. I had a car and chauffer, Kwabena, at my disposal. However, I chose to drive myself since I now knew my way around Accra.

Apart from the CAL project, I took the opportunity, while in Accra, to attend George's wedding to Marie Louise Thompson. George had asked me to be his best man. I had jumped at the opportunity. After all, it was an understanding between us since our student days, that we would be each other's best man. Preparations were underway.

There was a week to go before the wedding. I asked Nick Vingirayi whether we could use his apartment as a venue for George's bachelor party to be held two nights before the wedding. Nick helped me with invitations, alcohol, music and other entertainment. I would oversee the music with help from Fred Apaloo, an accomplished jazz guitar player who worked at CDH. His colleague, Fred Oware, would take care of the rest of the entertainment while a local catering team served food and drinks under Nick's direction. On hand to assist was Robert Mhlanga, a Zimbabwean Airforce pilot on a tour of duty in Ghana.

The party was a boisterous if louche event. There were many familiar faces, many from our student days. George's school mates from Mfantsipim School on Kwabotwe Hill, in the northern part of Cape Coast, were much in evidence. The school had been one of the highlights of my first tour of the countryside during my first visit to Ghana. There was much dancing, singing and carousing till mid-morning the following day, mercifully, a bank holiday. Afare put in a cameo appearance, as did Tsatsu Tsikata and Kwame Owusu.

We had time to gather our senses, visit the local grooming salon and attend a rehearsal. I also had to think of appropriate words to say at the best man's speech slot. We tried out our new wedding attire, charcoal grey morning suits with 'Oxford pop' white shirts and matching mottled neckties to go with our 'crewcut' hairstyles. We were well-heeled in shiny black Bruno Magli shoes. I had a special sleek pouch for the wedding rings. All was set for the wedding, on the following day.

The wedding was a colourful event. About three hundred people attended Ridge Church. Most of the attendees were invited guests. The preacher, Revd. Aryea, was George's school friend. His homily was brief and to the point. The reception in the beautiful grounds of the Ambassador hotel, was organized by George's brother-in-law, Steve Gohoho, a diplomat, married to Mama (Eve), George's elder sister. The décor was superb, as was the food and flowing drinks. The bride was resplendent in her floral gown and pretty crown. The bridesmaids were pretty and angelic in light blue dresses. George and Marie's parents sat with us at the High Table. JP chuckled every time he looked at me. After the reception, the bridal party accompanied the bride and groom to their respective parents' homes to bid farewell, as is the custom, with much fanfare, singing and dancing.

Through the hazy mists of selective memory, I remember dancing closely with George's nubile younger sister, Mimi Abew and newly found friends, Caroline and Sylvia, Marie's friends, in quick succession. At some point, we retired to bed, exhausted. We reconvened for the 'wedding breakfast' and barbecue at Marie's parents' house after a church service. The ladies looked stunning in light blue 'traditional' dresses. George and I wore blue suits. The jackets and ties came off unceremoniously when the dancing started again. My dancing partners from the previous day were noticeably absent.

There was much rejoicing and euphoria at CAL when all the investors' funds were paid in. The banking license was issued. We held the bank's first board meeting, chaired by Mr. E.P.L. Gyampoh, at the new offices on Independence Avenue. I represented IFC on the board but the new Assistant Director, CMD, Bob Graffam, was appointed the substantive director. This suited me fine since Bob enjoyed travelling to Accra with his companion but did not like attending board meetings. So, while he was holed up in his hotel room or at the beach, I would attend the meetings at CAL. By the time I left Accra for Washington, I had planned my next three projects in Ghana's financial sector: re-establishing the Ghana Stock Exchange, establishing a second discount house, 'Securities Discount Company' and establishing Ghana's first leasing company, 'Ghana Leasing.'

Shortly after we finished the CAL project, Jay left CMD to join David Gill at Batterymarch. His successor, Khalid Mirza, a Pakistan national who had worked for the defunct Bank of International Credit and Commerce (BICC), and one of the country departments in IFC, had a vastly different approach. Eventually, we found a way to work together, but it was not an easy beginning. Khalid was scheming. Nothing was ever as it seemed nor straightforward. I did not rate his managerial or technical/financial skills anywhere near Jay's. He was a consummate 'civil servant,' a throttle bottom, which to me, was retrogressive and unexciting, simply boring.

Khalid's focus, unlike Jay's innovative and creative way, was to rake up as many projects as possible to take to senior management and the board, to clear his path up the corporate ladder. He would not hesitate to step on others' heads in his efforts to haul himself towards the top. He dearly wanted to be a departmental director somewhere, anywhere in the organization. Despite these unfortunate quirks, Khalid had a sense of humour, different maybe but amusing, in an irritating sort of way. He had his favourites, They tended to be colleagues from his part of the world or those he found easy to bully, those beholden to him. I was not one of them. We however, agreed that I would stay out of his way and deliver at least two projects annually.

I was not surprised when a Kenyan acquaintance, Vincent Rague (Vince Rag), from one of the Bank's country departments, turned up in CMD one day as Khalid's guest. He had been offered a position in our division, to work on 'African countries.' Khalid's tactics could not have been more nuanced. The more, the merrier, I told myself.

Khalid then came to tell me that he had asked a junior officer, Vijay Advani, a Bangladeshi national, to go to Ghana and see if there are projects that CMD could do. He asked if I could hand over my contacts to him. I gave him Afare Donkor's numbers without fuss, then called Afare to explain and warn him of Khalid's shenanigans.

I believe Vijay made a call to Afare after which he concluded that a visit to Ghana would not be in his best interests. Not one to give up, Khalid informed me that he would join me in Ghana on my next trip. I had now finished work on re-establishing the Ghana Stock Exchange. I had enlisted the help of a bright and enthusiastic consultant, Judith Aidoo, then working at Goldman Sachs in New York. After many turf battles and political 'hide and seek' with vested interests, I won the day. The project was a resounding success. Mr. Yeboah Amoah, who I had got to know and respect, was appointed the CEO. Afare was the Chairman of the board. I then started work to establish Ghana's second discount house, Securities Discount Company (SDC).

Before I left Washington for Accra to appraisse the SDC project, Khalid, once again, this time hiding behind Michael Barth, who was Division Chief of the other CMD division (Barth's Brigade), tried to go behind my back and arrange a project to fund a new bank, Ecobank, based in Lomé, Togo. I had turned the project down after visits to Ecobank's offices to meet the MD-designate, a British national. I concluded that due to 'insufficient, unreliable information and unclear management arrangements,' this was not a good time to invest in the institution. There were, in addition, allegations, unsubstantiated, made against one of the founding shareholders and then Chairman, Chief Lawson, a Nigerian businessman. The designated management, using 'contacts' in CMD, approached Michael and appealed against my recommendation. Seizing the opportunity to show me up, Khalid supported Michael and they decided to send a team to Ghana, to try and assist Ecobank then overturn my recommendation.

I walked into Khalid's office to protest at this irregular conduct which evinced nothing but deceit and lack of respect. After my robust representation to a cowering Khalid seated behind his desk with visible signs of fear and dread, I told him that I knew where he lived. I intended to visit him at home. For now, I carried on, I would not hesitate to attack him physically if he were to leave his chair and venture out of his office before I left for home. I informed him that I dismissed all his comments on my reports as mere comstockery. I slammed his door with considerable force. I marched into the director's office, to report what I had done before he was fed Khalid's version.

On hearing the commotion, apparently, Michael Barth evacuated himself from the office in a hurry. I was informed, later, that Chuck assured and coaxed Khalid to leave his office and go home after six that evening. I had left the office at about 2.30 p.m. Chuck called me to apologize on behalf of Khalid. He urged that we work together harmoniously. Michael's and Khalid's team were not able to meet their intended officials in Accra. Afare refused to meet with them. The team returned to HQ empty handed. That was the kiss of death for Ecobank's efforts to secure IFC's support at that time. There was much egg stuck on Khalid's and Michael's faces, much to the delight of many colleagues in the department.

On another mission to Ghana, I booked Khalid at the Novotel, downtown Accra. I stayed in the CAL guest house in Tesano, a safe distance away. I got a driver to meet Khalid at the airport and take him to his hotel. I had left a message that I would meet him for dinner in the evening. Dinner was a muted event. I filled Khalid in on my programme in Ghana and repeated my commitment to delivering a couple of projects for CMD annually. I had spent the week before he arrived appraising the SDC financial projections and was satisfied that we could now take the proposal to the Board.

After dinner, Khalid gave me a greeting card and a book by Benazir Bhutto before mumbling a lengthy, unconvincing apology. He praised my work in barely audible tones. I accepted his apology and assured him that my training as a karateka would always help me regain composure quickly, dust myself and move on. I drove Khalid round Accra for the next two days. I introduced him to the Governor of the Bank of Ghana, Minister of Finance and selected business contacts including all IFC's investments such as CAL, the Stock Exchange and the board and management designate of SDC. I also told him about my next project, Ghana Leasing.

From Accra, we flew to Harare together. I had two budding projects apart from my duties as a director of UDC. I was arranging a US$20 million trade finance facility, to be drawn down through First Merchant Bank (FMB), MBCA, Syfrets, Standard Merchant Bank (SCMB) and Stanbic. I had to appraise the project proposal and analyze the banks' financials to assess the performance risk and the Estimated Financial Impact of the project. The second project would be IFC's acquisition of a fifteen percent shareholding in FMB. IFC would thereby replace Anglo American Corporation. This would effectively restructure the bank from its RAL format. Khalid was in Zimbabwe for a couple of days. I spent the next ten days working on my two projects. I was based at the Harare Club. The bar offered a comfortable working space.

I met with various officials at the Ministry of Finance including Elisha Mushayakarara, the then Permanent Secretary, Dr. Kombo Moyana, then Governor of the Reserve Bank of Zimbabwe (RBZ) and the CEOs of the merchant banks that would draw down on IFC's line of credit. This gave me first- hand in-depth and invaluable insights into Zimbabwe's financial markets, institutions, personnel and the regulatory environment. I took advantage of this exercise to meet other players in the financial markets. There was only a little time left to catch up with family and friends before returning to Washington.

The Concorde service between Washington and London, sometimes via New York, was now my preferred trans-Atlantic mode of travel as it saved so much time. From Harare, I flew to Geneva on Swiss Air, to meet with Andre Soumah and Benjamin de Rothschild. Andre and I had become friends after meeting in Ghana. His girlfriend, Lauretta Lamptey, was friends with my two friends, Karen Ayodele and Patience Kuruneri. The two ladies worked for Ecobank and the ADB, respectively. We would meet and dine in Accra from time to time. Andre's Mum was Ghanaian, his father was from Guinea. He was a dashing, light skinned, dark haired, tall figure who was extremely popular with the ladies. We nicknamed him 'Errol Flynn,' for his good looks. He had been married to Ms. Boigny, daughter of President Houphouet Boigny of Cote d'Ivoire. He lived in Lausanne and worked for the Rothschilds in Geneva. I often went to stay with Andre and sometimes borrowed his Range Rover to go skiing in Gstaadt.

After meetings in the Rothschild offices in Geneva, we would have sumptuous meals fueled by fine Claret and amazing cognac. I would then take time off work, check out of the President Hotel, downtown Geneva and stay with Andre in Lausanne for a few days. We often danced to soul and jazz tunes on the balcony, overlooking the lake, much to the amusement of neighbours who would peer through windows to witness the sight: two half-naked black men swaying to the sounds of loud music at sunset. The day I left for Washington, I was pleasantly surprised to find that six cases of the finest Rothschild's Chateau Clarke had been delivered to the house, a present for me from Benjamin.

The wine was duly packed and flown to Paris where I boarded the Air France Concorde bound for New York. At JFK airport, after clearing immigration, I collected my bags including my cases of wine to head to La Guardia airport for the shuttle flight to Washington DC. A customs officer stopped me after observing that I had too much wine in my baggage. He motioned me towards a more senior officer who inquired as to why I had been referred to him. I told him that I could not think of any reason why I should have been stopped except that I am a black man who flew on the Concorde. "There's no place for such attitudes anymore," the customs officer declared. He helped me load my loot onto a waiting taxi without further questions. I dined out on this story for many years to come.

At work, my wine story became folklore. There was more travel to New York, Atlanta, Miami and further afield to Dakar, Abidjan, Lima, Tunis, Paris, London and Budapest, among others. Most of the travel within the U.S. was to attend seminars and workshops on topical issues in International Finance and Capital Markets. I also gave papers at conferences. My lectures to Citibank staff in New York, on Emerging Markets, became an annual event, as did those at the ADB in Abidjan. Country Funds, Debt Conversion Funds, securitization, credit, equity and commodity (gold, copper, oil, cotton, cocoa etc.) derivatives, were now becoming widespread tools and products were developing very rapidly.

CMD was at the forefront of this 'revolution' and market evolution so it made sense for us to keep close contact with market players on Wall Street and the City of London. Through these liaisons, I met and developed a wide network of contacts in banks including Bankers' Trust, Goldman Sachs and Morgan Stanley on Wall Street. I still had a wide and ever-growing web of contacts in the City of London.

My last project in Ghana was establishing the first leasing company in the country, Ghana Leasing Company (GLC). IFC would be the main shareholder with CDC, SSNIT, AGF and Inter-Afrique among the line-up of shareholders. This was, perhaps, the most challenging venture to structure because of its nature, complexity and diverse shareholders. My attempts to persuade Blackwood Hodge and a Canadian Leasing Company to be technical partners were unsuccessful. Instead of an institutional technical partner, I opted for a seasoned leasing expert who had worked with CDC on similar ventures, Clive Moir, an Englishman, to be the CEO. I found a helpful local law firm headed by Kojo Bentsi-Enchill to work with

IFC lawyers and eventually produced a shareholders' agreement that took care of the laws of the land and the envisaged business arrangements to the satisfaction of all parties.

As we all waited for the lawyers to finish their task, I took time off, to go deep-sea fishing at Ada, on the Gulf of Guinea, near the border with Togo. Dereck Peacock had introduced me to a friend of his, an English banker, at Barclays Bank in Accra, He owned a cottage on the seafront at Ada. This was an idyllic, double story holiday home overlooking the sea. There was a caretaker, Bibio, who was an accomplished sailor cum fisherman. This was a popular spot for shark spotting and barracuda fishing. I was now a familiar visitor to Ada.

On my first visit to the cottage, I landed a hefty 8kg barracuda, half of which I gave to a smiling Afare Donkor, in Accra. This trip had started off with a loud, music party, on a cruise on Lake Volta. David Chapfika, William Nyemba and Nick Vingirayi, Zimbabwean expatriate bankers based in Accra showed off their dancing skills, much to the joy of Ghanaian ladies on the cruise. We spent the night partying with an unexpected group of revelers that included President Jerry Rawlings, his wife, Nana and my former P.A. at the IFC, Mariatu Morton, at Lake Volta Hotel, Akosombo. Two friends and I decided to go fishing at Ada the following day.

We got to the cottage, just after midday and bought soft-shell crabs for our lunch, on the beach. After a quick lunch, we refueled the boat and were soon in the Gulf, fishing for barracuda. We were out in the heat of the West African sun for about three hours before we decided to take our small catch of one large and two medium-sized barracuda back to the cottage, for Bibio to gut and clean before we returned to Accra. When we got home, I remembered that I had not off-loaded the booze, three bottles of wine and a large bottle of Celebration Cognac.

As I poppled upstairs, carrying two wine bottles in my left hand and the cognac in my right hand, I forgot about the step onto the patio. I twisted my ankle and fell onto my right side. There was a loud explosion as the bottle of cognac shattered. A piece of glass from the broken bottle slashed a gash deep into my right arm from the elbow down for about four inches. There was blood everywhere. My friends came hurtling down the stairs and screaming at the sight of blood and the loss of alcohol. One of them ran to the bathroom and returned with every towel they could get. Bibio was visibly shaken. He explained that the spilt drink was the only disinfectant available. The bleeding just would not stop. We decided to drive to the Military Hospital in Accra before it got dark. This was likely to be the only medical facility that was open at that time.

The drive back to Accra was excruciating. I was dizzy and bleary-eyed. My friends remained mostly quiet. After what felt like a lifetime, we drove through the gates of the Military Hospital in Accra and parked at the Emergency Rooms. It was now about 9 p.m. On seeing my wound and bloody towels around it, the nurse led me to a room and directed me to lie on a metal bed. After about an hour, a forlorn-looking bespectacled figure of a minute, dark man entered the room and announced himself as 'Dr. Owusu.' He looked at my wound while my companions related the story from Akosombo to Ada and now, Military Hospital. Dr. Owusu, fish-eyed, informed me that he was going to clean the wound then 'suture it up.' He needed to put in about nine stitches, he estimated.

There was a 'small problem' however, he cautioned: he had no anaesthetic. The whole procedure was going to be 'quite discomfortable' warned the good doctor. My heart raced at a rate of knots at the news. Soon I was screaming in agony as Dr. Owusu persisted in jabbing away and pulling a thread through my arm. He put in ten stitches before whispering that I was free to go but should not wash the wound for about a week. I did not need encouragement to leave Military Hospital. I retreated to the comfort of the guest house where we consumed at least a bottle of Chivas Regal Royal Salute whisky.

As soon as the Agreements were signed, I left Accra for Dakar. My arm was numb. I hurried through my supervision of Banque de l'Habitat in Dakar with a lot of help from a junior manager, Ibrahim Sal. He had just finished his MBA at Wharton. I had dinner one evening at Ibrahim's family home. His Mum prepared delicious Cebu jen: a flavourful, seasoned rice with pieces of chargrilled fish (grouper) stuffed with a garlicky paste, an assortment of vegetables including cabbage, carrots, turnips and cassava and a mouth-puckering sweet-sour tamarind.

We licked our fingers as we wolfed down our dinner washed down with ataya and palm wine. Ibrahim's twelve-year-old sister, Sade, was fascinated by this black 'American,' who could not speak Wolof. She sat next to me during dinner and gazed at me like an Eskimo would gaze at the Eiffel Tower. Her Mum asked her if she wanted to marry the American, at which point the 'blushing,' giggling lass got up and leapt out of the room, to roars of laughter.

After four days in Dakar, I flew to Paris where I boarded the Air France Concorde to New York. Back in Washington I did not waste any time before going to the Bank's medical rooms in the main A Building. The doctor looked at my wound in horror and inquired, "Which butcher did this to you?", before removing the stiches and cleaning up and dressing wound. This had been a frightening experience. The wound healed without complications. Soon I was back in the dojo exercising and punching the sandbags. It took a little longer to spar seriously and compete in the ring. I focused on my kicks and my kata. Later at the annual karate gathering in Okinawa, when I graded for my third degree black belt, I won the kumite in my division. I knocked out my opponent, Tadashi Yoshinari, in the final round, with a 'flying' sidekick (mawashi geri) to the head. We became and remained excellent training partners despite that contest.

I did not explain my injury picked up in Ghana, to anyone except to say it was a 'fishing accident,' until years later when it really did not matter. I had now been with the Bank for just over three years.

It was time to go on vacation. By this time, I had a family. Two daughters aged three and twelve months, respectively. We boarded the early morning flight from Ronald Reagan National Airport to San Francisco on the first leg of our round-the-world trip. After enjoying the sights and gastronomical delights, we headed north to Seattle for a couple of days. Vancouver was our next stop. We spent four days at my brother, Nathaniel's apartment. We went skiing on Whistler, visited Vancouver Island and the hot springs at Lussier and Liard River. From Vancouver we flew to Hong Kong where we stayed with my friend from Business School, Jimmy Master and his family.

The girls were severely disoriented by jetlag and would be wide awake from midnight to the early hours of the morning. Jim and Nil must have been delighted to see the back of us as we left for Phuket where we spent a week on the pristine, irenic beaches. We went fishing and swimming in the sea, visited Bond Island, a truly beat nest location where we enjoyed Thai cuisine. We then flew north to Bangkok for three days. We visited the famed snake temple. We cradled live snakes in the incense-filled edifice. At the snake arena, snake handlers showed off their skills at playing games with the deadly reptiles. They invited the audience to participate by stroking a very irritated young python.

As the handlers prized open the snake's jaws to reveal its awesome fangs, my younger daughter pounced on the defenseless animal and sank her little teeth into its body. The snake wriggled violently as four men pinned it down to subdue it. It was obviously offended and clearly insulted by this unusual and unexpected assault. "I thought the snake was about to bite you," my daughter explained later, with disarming charm.

Mumbai was our next stop. I knew the city well from my work visits. Despite the debilitating heat and humidity, we spent time sight-seeing and sampling the local cuisine before setting off for Ethiopia, with an unscheduled stopover in Djibouti. We were in

Addis overnight. I have fond memories of delicious spicy foods and fantastic tej, honey wine. We managed a quick trip to the huge open market where we bought woolen rugs and paintings before jetting off to Nairobi for a week. A friend had arranged accommodation for us at a private, gated housing complex near the Serena hotel. We stayed in a luxurious duplex condominium and had a car at our disposal. In no time, we had toured most of the tourist sites including Nairobi National Park, Bomas of Kenya and Uhuru Gardens and the Kibera Market. A day out with friends to the foot of Mt Kenya and a visit to tea plantations in Limuru were among the highlights of the visit.

It was exhilarating to be back in Harare. My elder daughter remarked that she never knew there were so many black people in the world. She was fascinated to see people walking barefoot. This was their first trip to Africa. On this trip, they were to meet other members of the clan for the first time. We visited friends and family in Harare, Rusape and Mutare including grandparents in Mutasa and Nyanga.

It felt a little strange being back as a tourist in a place I knew to be home. Increasingly, I felt a certain distance between me and my country of birth, where I had spent some of my childhood. Despite having the wider family still in the country, my immediate family and siblings had emigrated abroad as did many friends that I had made in the time I lived in the country. A feeling and sense of being alien lingered at the back of my mind.

After a big 'family party,' and an alcohol fueled feeding frenzy, we left Harare for Accra. We stayed at the CAL guest house in Tesano for three days. In Accra, Afare asked me to help him out with some business matters at CAL, regarding expansion plans and a possible restructuring and recapitalization proposal. The family visited sites including El Mina Castle, Achimota School and other places in and around Accra. We spent time with George and Marie and enjoyed a 'banquet' at the Donkor household.

The family were fascinated by Ghanaian cuisine. They feasted on delicacies including cane rat. As I watched morsels of roasted cane rat gorged in this novel culinary experience for them, I thanked God for being vegetarian. After the enjoyable Ghanaian experience, Washington was beckoning. We flew back to Washington via London. After a few days of visiting friends, we boarded the Concorde flight from Heathrow Terminal Four and landed, three hours later, at Dulles International Airport. It felt good to be back 'home,' in a peculiarly reassuring and relaxed sort of way. I had enjoyed time away from work but missed the buzz of Washington D.C.

Chapter Sixteen

DISCONCERTINGLY, IT WAS soon apparent to me that no one had noticed that I had been away from the office for about a month. That was the nature of the organization. It made me realize how, despite all the contribution I perceived to have made for the general good of the institution, I was only a minute cog in the scheme of things. I was dispensable and not always readily recognizable. More changes came to CMD: Chuck Sethness relinquished his job as Director and left for greener pastures at the Inter-American Development Bank. Bob Graffam left the department to join a private sector financial institution.

A former Vice President, Dan Adams, returned as Director of CMD. Jay Tata, who had left for Batterymarch, returned to the newly restructured CMD, where a new Division, International Securities Group (ISG), had been created. Jay would be Chief of the new Division. I was Jay's first recruit. I did not hesitate, equivocate or have any mental reservation whatsoever about joining ISG especially since my close associates, Farida and Teresa were leaving to assume new posts in Treasury and CMD Africa division, respectively. I cannot recall Khalid's fate, but Vince Rague and Sheila Hogan, remained in CMD Africa Division.

The global movement towards financial restructuring of private firms at this time in emerging markets or Less Developed Countries

(LDCs) which had become overburdened from excessive debt levels and rampant privatization in some of the countries, especially in Eastern Europe, had to be eased and facilitated somehow. IFC, led by CMD, came up with the idea of mobilizing funds through a new instrument, 'country investment funds', pooling together billions of dollars of global funds. The ISG would operate on a competitive basis with Wall Street firms in finding international capital markets for securities issued by firms in LDCs that had been assisted by IFC. A new Division, Corporate Finance Services, would be set up, also in CMD, to offer fee-based advisory services. Another admirer of Jay's from my old division, Chung Min Pang, joined me in the ISG.

After spending time working on establishing financial institutions in LDCs and supervising them, I now changed focus to structuring and selling financial instruments. The objective was to assist debt-distressed corporates in LDCs, structure and market country funds to mobilize resources to invest in emerging stock markets and their securities offerings. This entailed spending more time on Wall Street and other financial centres worldwide to work closely with Investment Banks and other institutions. I relished the opportunity and challenge.

Barbra E. Robinson (later Barbra Wilson), my P.A., organized my office move to a new office, on the western side of the I-building, far from the main CMD buzzing area. In this corner, Jay, Chung Min and I had our first strategy meeting as the ISG. After the meeting, Jay, in a matter-of-fact way, informed me that David Gill had requested that I join him, Dean Le Baron, his 'boss' at Battery-march, an unnamed emerging markets investor and three fund managers, on a fortnight's round-the-world emerging markets tour. Furthermore, would I assist and facilitate meetings in Nairobi, Harare, Port St. Louis and Delhi.

"Today is Friday," added Jay. "I have booked you to join David on a flight leaving Dulles airport at 3 p.m. on Sunday, to join the rest of the members in New York that evening. You will fly out in Dean's private jet to London, on the first leg of the trip. By the way, I told David that you are free to join him on the tour. Thank you, Jules, I owe you one," he added as he gave me a pat on my left shoulder.

So it was that I sat next to David Gill, who I had not seen nor been in contact with for about three years, on a flight bound for La Guardia airport on the Sunday afternoon. David sported the same wry smile and welcomed me warmly. "Let us just have fun on this trip," he whispered. I greeted him and nodded in appreciation. Inwardly I felt honoured and elated, despite Jay's less than ceremonial announcement of the news. Not quite the 'Magnificat,' but a similar sort of feeling, if possible, ran through my pulsating heart and veins. I was determined to do my best to showcase my financial skills and knowledge of the markets on this tour. The fact that David had invited me to work with the team at Batterymarch was not lost on me.

The offer was attractive and always at the back of my mind. That would be a good break from the World Bank Group, I thought. We chatted about Cambridge, CMD and Emerging Market developments including our current tour. David was particularly fascinated by the Zimbabwe Stock Exchange. It had been performing spectacularly, relative to other African stock exchanges despite the restrictive regulatory environment. In New York, we checked into the Marriott where we would meet the rest of the party consisting of Chuck Duchampian from GM and from AT&T, Teri Goodale and David Feldman. We enjoyed dry martinis and talked about the trip. We would meet Dean Le Baron in London.

We left New York aboard Dean Le Baron's Citation jet the next morning. We stopped briefly to refuel at Gander International Airport and landed at Heathrow Airport six hours later. In London, we had meetings with Doug Gustafson, the IFC's Resident Representative, some Investment banker friends and acquaintances of David's and Dean's. We stayed at Brown's Hotel for the night. We boarded Dean's larger private jet, a Grumman Gulfstream (GII), bound for Africa the next morning. Cairo would be our next stop.

The five-hour flight to Cairo was smooth and comfortable. We all sat and read quietly or chatted while we helped ourselves to delicious snacks and fresh fruits. "I could get used to this," I said to Dean as he sat next to me, his head buried in a copy of the Financial Times. Dean looked up and with a broad smile muttered, "I suggest you start working even harder and get lucky while you're at it!" We both chuckled. Dean was easy to get along with. He had many searching questions and clearly was well read. He thought very highly of David and had a deep belief in and commitment to emerging market development and investment. The conversation with Dean was so engaging I did not notice that we were descending to refuel in Cairo.

As the jet refueled, we wandered round the airport buildings. I was amazed at how lax the security was. We toured the airport buildings without obstruction and eventually went back aboard our jet. The pilots had obtained permission for us to conduct an aerial tour of the pyramids. We flew three times round the pyramids at low altitude before climbing to our cruising altitude. In Nairobi, we were met by the IFC resident representative, Ernie Kepper. Laurence Clarke, who was now based in Nairobi's IFC office, worked with Ernie to arrange our meetings, to ensure a successful visit.

The Aga Khan Foundation also helped arrange an interesting meeting at a timber and newsprint company near Kisumu. We flew to the factory in two chartered Cessna aircraft as the GII needed a much longer landing strip than the one available. The visit, in the middle of nowhere, as we jokingly referred to it, was run by Indian staff seconded from a similar plant in India. The equipment, sent from India, was second hand, salvaged from a facility that was being upgraded. "We send our old equipment to emerging markets," boasted the managing director. Nevertheless, they ran a very impressive operation.

From the factory, we flew to Maasai Mara for the night. We were housed in elegant tents with bathrooms attached and showers that came from canvas buckets hanging from the tent pole. We had a fantastic dinner in the tent dining hall with an amazing bar. After dinner, the staff treated us to music. They sang 'Malaika' in tuneful tones. We all danced around a campfire. Afterwards, Dean made a short speech expressing his appreciation to David for arranging the tour. Ernie Kepper, in response, praised Dean for his acumen and leadership in emerging market investments. Ernie noted that Dean was indeed always unconventional: at dinner that evening, he had consumed his dessert before the main course.

We retired to our individual tents happy and tipsy. As I zipped up my tent entrance, there was the sudden noise of someone trying to gain entrance into my tent. It turned out to be David, who had been looking for his own tent in the dark. I laughed out loud and invited him into my tent. He refused, very firmly. He 'grunted' indignantly, as he stumbled back to his tent. Everyone heard my story at breakfast. David kept quiet with that familiar wry smile still on his lips. Back in Nairobi, I spent some time chatting to Laurence Clarke about his work and life in East Africa. He was enjoying himself and preferred this to Washington life and the World Bank offices. That evening, at a reception hosted by Ernie and Wattie Kepper, we mingled with the local movers and shakers during a particularly good buffet dinner.

From Nairobi, we flew to Harare. I had arranged for MBCA bank to host us. They provided cars to ferry us from the airport to the Sheraton. We were just in time for lunch at the Meikles hotel. Our host was Peter Dorward, a local industrialist renowned for his habit of wiredrawing debates, to the point of obscuring his point. There was a lively discussion about the future of Zimbabwe as an investment destination. Peter believed, as evidenced by his vociferous and animated gestures, that Zimbabwe's better days were numbered.

He would rather pack his bags and leave the country. David was fascinated by Peter's approach, which belied his Harvard Business School and Cambridge University background. Dean was not so taken in. The Zimbabwe Stock Market though small, had performed very strongly in recent years on the back of a strong economy and sound financial infrastructure. Political rhetoric, however, was turning more socialist, nationalist and worryingly negative in tenor with deleterious effects on foreign investment.

Our visit coincided with polling day for the national elections. Dean insisted on visiting a polling station on Samora Machel Avenue after which he pronounced the conduct he had witnessed as 'normal.' We later paid a courtesy call to the Reserve Bank of Zimbabwe Governor, Dr. Moyana. The Governor kept us waiting for over an hour, then he invited David only into his office. An official seconded from the Bank of England, Mr. Bully, was in attendance. Dean was furious at this shoddy, disrespectful treatment. He and David Feldman stormed out in a huff and went to the Meikles hotel where we all met up later for a low-key dinner hosted by the Chairman of the Zimbabwe Stock Exchange. Despite the abortive visit to Dr. Moyana's offices at RBZ, we remained in high spirits and did our best to enjoy the beautiful weather and all else that the great metropolis of Harare had to offer.

Later that evening, I took Dean to the airport to catch the 10pm British Airways flight to London on his way back to the USA. Our next stop was the Seychelles. We stayed at the beautiful MAIA beach resort. The pilots, David explained, were not keen to fly us to Mauritius then Malaysia, hence the detour for a closer rest stop. However, while we were in the Seychelles, doing all the tourist things, David informed us that the routing had been changed due to unforeseen calendar and scheduling difficulties. We would not go to Malaysia but to Seoul instead. David agreed with me that I should head back to Washington from the Seychelles. So, I did. This had been a momentous experience for me, forever embedded in my mind.

Back in Washington, I regaled my colleagues with a colourful account of the whole trip. Jay, who was supposed to have joined us, was relieved that all had gone swimmingly. He hated flying in small planes, he explained. I 'dined out' on accounts of the trip at the slightest excuse and at any given opportunity. I promised myself that I would, one day, take the time to sit and write a detailed account of the trip including the conversations and an analysis of what it takes to invest in emerging markets. It takes nerve, hope and demands carefully formulated decision-making. This would be a great case study.

Just after my 'Sandan,' third degree black belt exam, I applied to the Shorin-Ryu Association to open a dojo at the World Bank. I would be the instructor under supervision from Renshi Mitchell in Baltimore and Kyoshi Hargrove. The bank gave us a large room, an old gymnasium, first in the main A-building basement, then later, a better-equipped and larger facility in the basement of the I-Building. After a few adverts, I soon had a class of twenty-five keen Bank employees training with me.

I called on Karen Chapman to assist me twice a week. We trained on Mondays, Wednesdays and Fridays after work. Notable among my first trainees/students were Olawale Edun and his wife, Aduwa, Barbra Kaminska, Connie and Shaila, who worked at the IMF, Hardy Cash, a bass guitarist from Hampton, Lt. Paul from the Pentagon, Debbie Young and Mariatu from CMD, Banelle Ba from the Bank's Africa department and Nzuwah from Annapolis. Farida, Chung Ming and Sergio Zappa, all from CMD, made cameo appearances at training but gave up after one or two workouts.

The highlights for our World Bank Shorin Ryu Club were a visit to our dojo by Kyoshi Hargrove accompanied by karateka from the Baltimore, Arnold Mitchell Karate Studio, including my sparring partner, 'Ghost,' Mustafa, 'Mr. Bill' and an assortment of black belts and brown belts. The junior members, green and orange belts, included Mark Andrews (Sisqó), Larry Anthony (Jazz), Tamir Ruffin

(Nokio), and James Green (Woody Rock). They were future members of the R&B / hip hop/Gospel group, Dru Hill. We had a day of training in the dojo. The senior groups trained at kata, ko-budo and kumite assisted by Mustafa, Karen Chapman, and Parnell Jones, all 4th degree black belts.

This was a real treat for our nascent karate club. After training, I treated the entire group to snacks and drinks at my house, 1403 Nevis Road, in Bethesda. We joked and partied in the garden. The younger members were asked to clear up the dishes. They gathered all the chicken bones and other leftovers then duly flushed the lot down the guest toilet. This blocked the loo, spewing out the offend-ing leftovers. We all got on our knees and mopped up the mess. Mustafa knelt by the toilet bowl and fished out the blocking objects with his hands. This was quite a sight and a bizarre end to a day of martial arts training.

The second highlight was a visit to Kyoshi's dojo in Hampton. This would be our first grading for junior members of the dojo, including the first ever competitive kumite for our members. We arrived in Hampton late on Friday afternoon and checked into the Embassy Suites, near the Hampton Convention Centre. We promptly made our way to Frank Hargrove Karate Studio to meet with Kyoshi, fa-miliarise our members with the dojo and prepare for events of the following day. Our team was understandably anxious and nervous even though they had met the giant of a man that is Kyoshi Hargrove, 'Tetsu Cho, the Iron Butterfly, now Hanshi.' He cuts a lumbering six-foot five inches muscular black figure with wavy, combed-back curly hair greying around the ears and a firm, commanding voice.

Kyoshi gave us warm words of welcome and made us feel at home. We were joined by Sensei Theo Bell from Canada, who had brought his team of about thirty to the event. I had met Theo at a Shorin Ryu summer camp where Hanshi Shugoro Nakazato and a team of instructors notably Messrs Ifoku, Gibu and Yonemine had trained us in kata and weapons, especially bo, sai and nunchaku.

After training, we had a light supper and retired to bed early. We were up with the lark and joined the rest of the gathered karateka from all over the Americas. Our first task was to run on the familiar five-mile circuit round Hampton, the beach, suburbs and back to the dojo where grading for the various groups began. This took almost four hours. After lunch, we had the inter-dojo kata competitions then kumite. It was a long day. Our World Bank team got to meet and train with karate enthusiasts from all over the country. Above all, they were promoted to higher grades, including two black belts.

We had lively celebrations that evening and drank at the bar until the wee small hours of the morning. My team bought me drinks and gave me presents including a brand-new Yamaha saxophone, a German Horner harmonica and a new Shureido karate suit. I was deeply touched. Our team grew from strength to strength. Karen became a full-time instructor so that there was always an instructor available when I was away on mission for the Bank. Over time, our dojo was increasingly decorated with various trophies and awards that we earned in competitions in the USA and in Japan. From time to time, we trained with the World Bank Shorinji Kempo Club.

Most members, including the instructors, notably Karen and I, registered for kata and kumite in the annual karate tournament held at the Convention Centre in Washington DC. In the summer. We had six weeks to train for the event. In the final two weeks, we trained hard, daily. It was grueling but fun. The tournament was over a weekend. We were at the centre early and got our registration papers completed before warming up in a quiet corner of the huge floor. There were over fifteen hundred karate enthusiasts in various styles including Shorin Ryu, Shotokan, Shukokai etc., from the Americas, Europe, Canada and Australia. We competed through the knock-out stages and won awards in kata especially, both open hand and weapons.

Karen won the ladies open black belt bo kata, the Chinto kata and freestyle kumite in her weight class. I competed in the bo, sai and nunchaku kata, then on the following day, the light heavy weight kumite. In what turned out to be my last competitive karate bout, I faced a tall Shotokan style member from a dojo in Los Angeles. The skookum specimen had a devastating side kick, I soon discovered. I had to maneuver him into a zugzwang, or I would be dead meat. With patience, trailing by two points, I spotted a momentary lapse in concentration evidenced by his rebarbative stance, as he swooped in for the kill.

I side-stepped and knocked him out cold with a stiff uppercut. There were loud cheers of euphoric relief from my team and other Shorin Ryu members as my opponent whittled to the floor ungracefully. This was a triumph for our style of Okinawan karate. We were exhausted but took time to celebrate our haul of medals and trophies. Our team, The World Bank Shorin Ryu Karate Club were exhilarated to receive messages of congratulations from Kyoshi Hargove, Jiro Shiroma and Arnold Mitchell, among other distinguished karate instructors.

There were cheers as I limped into the office on Monday morning. Various versions of my now legendary bout made the rounds. I received many lunch invitations and applications to join our club. Later I learnt, from my friend, Paula Panton, who was PA to one of the VPs, that word had reached the VPs. My reputation as a pugnacious employee now preceded me. I already had a reputation as a golf fanatic having bumped into Jud Parmar and Azam Alizai, IFC VP and country director respectively, on the Bretton Woods golf course in Potomac during regular working hours. They had, wickedly, waved me on at the par three over the lake. Guilt-ridden, I struck two balls into the lake before hitting a third ball close to the pin. That story also made the rounds in IFC, much to the amusement of colleagues, no doubt. Instead of playing hooky from work to play golf at Bretton Woods, I played at Rock Creek Park golf course, outside work hours.

On one of these 'hooky days,' I decided to sleep in for a couple of hours before going to play golf then go to the office after lunch. As I dozed off, the phone rang. My brother, Dennis, informed me that our brother, Tendai, who had been ill for many months, had died early that morning. I was devastated. It had been only three months since I had last visited him and witnessed his emaciated condition. He was in good spirits then and bravely bore his pain as he, between fits of disturbingly noisy, chesty coughs, assured me that he would be fine. "It's only T.B.," he said. "People have had worse...." He was twenty-six and had a young family. By the time I got to the office, my colleagues had heard. They rallied round and bought me a First Class return ticket Washington-Harare. I was deeply touched. I was in tears at my desk. Clarence whisked me to Dulles Airport later in the day.

During the drive to the airport, Clarence then informed me that Malcolmn Pryor, had made a huge contribution including cash to assist with funeral expenses. The journey to Harare was somber. Seeing my grieving parents was heart-breaking. The sight of my brother's lifeless body artfully arranged in a brown casket was harrowing. Even though his death was not totally unexpected, in view of the nature of his illness, it was still hard to swallow. The funeral went off as well as these things go. "It was a success," remarked Dad. "We went to the cemetery to bury him, and we did not bring him back home. We achieved our goal, to bury him."

Unfortunately for our family, only eighteen months later, when I was on a Capital Markets lecture tour in Nairobi, with Álvaro Quirós from Fitch, New York, I came back to the hotel to see a little note under my door. It simply said, "Your brother, Dennis, died this morning." I made frantic calls to Zimbabwe without success. I jumped onto a Kenya Airways flight bound for Harare via Lilongwe the following afternoon. All was fine until we reached Lilongwe and were informed by a grumpy Captain that due to a mechanical fault, we would be stuck in Lilongwe, on the ground for the next four hours or so. Six hours later, we took off for Harare. We arrived around midnight.

In the morning, I was informed that Dennis' funeral would be at midday. I spent the next two hours trying to hire a suitable vehicle. At about half past ten, I managed to hire an ageing Peugeot 505 from some obscure car-hire firm. I was in a rush to make the two-and half-hour drive to Rusape. As I turned the ignition key, it snapped. I was left holding the key-butt with the rest of the key stuck deep in the keyhole. My heart sank. There was no other vehicle available.

I called Peter Grint, Managing Director of UDC, and narrated my woes. Peter took pity on me and offered me one of his company vehicles. I got to Tandi just after sunset. People had dispersed. I listened to Dad as he described Dennis' funeral. Early the next morning, I went to the cemetery, accompanied by my uncle Dennis, Dad's elder brother. We stood in silence at Dennis' and Tendai's graves. This was an emotional time for the family. We prayed for many hours and shared stories from our childhood as we drank copious amounts of whisky and wine. We smoked Partagas cigars in memory of our departed brothers. After doing what we could to console our parents, we all left and went back to our respective abodes. The memories still linger.

The Art Collection of the NMB Bank

Chapter Seventeen

IT WAS NOT LONG BEFORE the ISG, with Jay Tata at the helm, became a powerful force in CMD, the World Bank Group and the financial markets at large. As Senior Investment Officer, then, I was immersed in work which ranged from Chile's second debt-conversion fund, country funds for Poland, Hungary and Brazil, telecoms infrastructure funds for Pakistan and the Philippines. I worked closely with Chung Ming on a memorable trip/ roadshow to London and New York where we interviewed prospective co-leaders and canvassed investors for our proposed Funds in Pakistan and the Philippines. We had lively discussions after a presentation at Citibank, whose brilliant team, led by one Ilyas Khan, extolled the virtues and strengths of their market reach. It was an impressive presentation until I picked on a point that a member of their team had erroneously made, concerning communications and pigeons at the battle of Waterloo. Lunch, after that, was a low-key affair.

Next in the 'beauty parade' line-up was Daiwa Securities. After a lengthy and nebulous, somewhat pedestrian presentation, they treated us to a sumptuous dinner in their ornate dining room. We met the entire hierarchy of the bank. We had lively, robust discussions about emerging markets and the role of various financial institutions. When we got back to the Hyde Park Hotel (now the Oriental) at Knightsbridge, we were pleasantly surprised to find very expensive shirts and matching ties on our respective beds. This was an amazing and unexpected gesture from Daiwa. We awarded Daiwa the lead role in our Philippines deal (unrelated to the kind gesture, of course), but the Pakistan deal we gave to Rothschilds. They had made a superb pitch and treated us to excellent meals and entertainment in Mayfair. We invited Citibank to play a role as one of the Advisors in all the Funds including the Call Option Fund and Gold Fund that were co-led by the IFC and Flemings.

The roadshow for the Philippines Infrastructure Fund started with briefings at the Rothschild offices near Cannon Street with a sumptuous lunch at Sweetings, the Victorian lunchtime-only fish restaurant at 38 Queen Victoria Street. The oysters were delicious, as was the scrambled egg and smoked salmon starter followed by grilled, lightly seasoned sole and buttered spinach. This was a treat. Chung Min had the burger and lobster with fries. By the time we made it back to the offices to talk strategy and discuss the London-Hong Kong-Manila trip, we were in high spirits and 'raring to go.' On an earlier trip to Manila, I had flown from Washington DC to Tokyo, where I stopped for two nights before proceeding to Manila. Both routes were equally exhausting but stopping in Tokyo was always special. I would shop for karate items especially Shureido Gi (uniforms) and belts.

In Manila, we stayed at the Shangri-La, which was a lot more central and somehow more comfortable than its counterpart and namesake on Edsa plaza, on the other side of Manila. The Manila, IFC staff, joined by the Bank resident representative, Ohene Owusu, a contemporary on the YP Programme, with no intention to malign, the ultimate ultracrepidarian, entertained us after lengthy meetings in the World Bank offices. We also met with two staff members from the Asia Development Bank's CMD-equivalent. They wanted to participate in our proposed funds. We disagreed on who should lead and should occupy top left spot on the tombstone. We left them out of our deals after heated discussions.

Manila was always an exciting place. We had great meals, delectable cuttle fish in thick, sweet and sour brown sauce and 'puto.' The 'Mogambo Bar' was a favourite 'watering hole' not far from the hotel. We even danced and sang along to lively karaoke numbers. The service in the bar/night club and the hotels was outstanding. One evening, as we sat at the bar chatting, a scantily-dressed Filipina with a beguiling smile, beauty and charm to go with it walked up to me, rested her hand gently on my lap and asked me if I was her father. She told us her name was 'Shaun Falls.'

She later explained that her father was an African-American soldier who had met her mother while he was stationed in the Philippines during the Vietnam war. After the war, he had returned to Florida and abandoned his progeny, three daughters and their mother. From the pictures, she had seen of him, I, apparently bore an uncanny resemblance to her father! I denied all knowledge of her father and his escapades. I bought her a drink for her efforts. I have often wondered what became of Shaun. Months later, Ohene told me that he had seen her a couple of times at Mogambo after we had left for Washington. By then, however, my forgettery had set in.

I enjoyed the ISG work and wanted to be more creative in our efforts. Jay, Chung Ming and I discussed, from time to time, how to enhance the group's role within CMD, the Bank and the financial markets. The net result was that I spent increasingly more of my time giving papers, attending seminars and workshops or networking on Wall Street, the City of London, Paris, Frankfurt and Brussels. In Africa, I spent time in Abidjan, Accra, Lagos, Tunis, Nairobi and later, Johannesburg, marketing the ISG and promoting emerging market investment opportunities and developments.

On one of these trips I met Ted Gilletti, an inveterate, latitudinarian Africafile, who was a Vice President at Bankers Trust, in the emerging markets, Africa and Latin America section. Conversing with Ted put paid to the canard that Americans did not understand

Africa. I had been introduced to Ted by Clarence Haynes at one of the World bank annual meetings in Washington D.C. Ted and Clarence had worked together at Bankers Trust, New York before Clarence left for Brazil and Ted left for London.

We discussed various transactions, mainly oil, gold, cotton, cocoa and copper derivatives and currency derivatives. We remained in touch. On subsequent visits to New York, I would visit Bankers Trust's offices at 45 Park Avenue. I was introduced to Ted's colleagues, notably Neil Allen, Mike Don Diego, John B. Harris and Stan Cohen, a brilliant lawyer and self-confessed luddite.

I had now been with the World Bank Group for almost seven years. I felt I needed to take a break. I was getting restless. Fortuitously, Ted Gilletti visited Washington at that time. We met for lunch at Primi Piatti and discussed, at length, various market issues especially his specialty, trade finance in Africa and the opportunities for derivative products in those markets. Ted then informed me that he would be leaving his current position to head the Russia division as managing director. He wondered if I would be interested in joining Bankers Trust to replace him. He then revealed that a head-hunter, John- Eric Bigbie, had suggested to him that he sound me out on the matter.

I told Ted that I had spoken with John Eric, but he had not disclosed his client's identity. We laughed. We then arranged for me to spend a day at 45 Park Avenue, New York, with the Group head, Neil Allen, to see if we would be able to work together. I had a good meeting with Neil. During my meeting with Neil, he revealed that my name had been mentioned several times by a recent graduate recruit, Cephas Takavarasha. He had made strong 'noises' in favour of my joining BT. Cephas had previously visited me in Washington after graduating from Wharton. During his visit, we chatted about Zimbabwe, the Bank, BT and financial markets in general. We clicked.

I told Jay about my visit to New York. He looked at me in shock. After a pregnant pause, he told me that he had my interests and career at heart and would not stand in my way. "However," he added. "I see an opportunity here for both of us: why don't you take leave of absence for two years, learn about derivatives from the best in the market, then come back, maybe to head ISG. I can arrange that with IFC's HR Department easily." I agreed straightaway. I informed Jay that BT had made me a six-figure incentive offer, to join them. I would be Vice President and Head of the Africa and Latin America Unit. The section was housed in the London office at 1 Appold Street.

Jay kindly agreed that I could spend a couple of days in London, to visit BT, on my upcoming trip to Paris and Karachi on ISG business. During that visit, I met with my future colleagues and team including Moyo Kamgaing, Emmanuelle, Alex Knaster, Chris, Cephas, Jeffrey, Peter Chew, Rian Dartnell and Amanda, among others. They treated me to a nice lunch at L'Abat Jour restaurant at 14 City Road.

Jay wasted no time in getting the IFC to second me to Bankers Trust for two years. I was to learn more about derivatives and return to ISG. When he told me that all was set for my two-year leave of absence, I felt like I wanted to fanfaronade round the department shaking hands, hugging or kissing every colleague in sight. I did not. Instead I sat at my desk and allowed reality to set in. There was a lot to be done. Fortunately, I would spend the first three months of my new job in the New York office. This entailed renting a small apartment downtown Manhattan, where I would stay from Monday to Friday. I spent weekends in Washington. I would also use my frequent visits to the London office, from New York, to find suitable accommodation.

Bankers Trust was a leader in the nascent derivatives business. Charles Steadman Sanford ('Mr. Charlie,' as we called him), was the CEO. Mr. Charlie was credited with implementing the first 'value at risk' (VaR) model. Prior to this quantitative measurement, credit and market risk were defined through ad hoc measures. Having de-emphasized traditional loans in favour of trading, BT became an acknowledged leader in risk management. Lacking the boardroom contacts of its larger rivals, notably J.P. Morgan, BT attempted to make a virtue of necessity by specializing in trading and product innovation. This was a defining period in the development and proliferation of financial derivatives.

The highlight of the epoch was being introduced to Mr. Charlie by Neil Allen as, "The British- sounding African who has just joined us from the World Bank. He will lead the Africa and Latin America team." On learning that I was born in Zimbabwe, Mr. Charlie told me he had been to my 'neck of the woods' as he sailed in the Mediterranean Sea on his honeymoon. He had been to Morocco on a day trip. To him, Africa was one country and Zimbabwe could be next door to Morocco.

"We have good people at BT, and we continue to recruit 'em," added Mr. Charlie in his legendary, much imitated, quaintly squeaky southern accent reminiscent of an actor from a forties movie. I smiled attentively and sipped at my dry martini. It was momentous to meet and chat with Mr. Charlie. A rare, if jammy, moment to cherish forever.

The work environment, while like I had left behind at the World Bank, CMD in particular, could not have been more different: both organizations were intense and pressurized, but BT was not characterized by excessive red tape and routine. There was more latitude for innovative, entrepreneurial initiative, deal structuring and risk-taking at BT. It was easy to see how BT management were generally motivated by profit. Staff were pushed and expected to maintain a bottom line or a minimum level of profitability. At the World Bank, there was not always, necessarily, an obvious bottom line to maintain. Instead, management were generally task-oriented or driven by other motivating forces endemic to the World Bank Group such as projects in certain economic sectors or achieving successful development targets in certain countries.

Another fundamental difference between the two organizations was the context in which they operated. A classic difference between the public and private sectors: while the profit-driven BT manager generally had the leeway to get done what was needed to maintain the bottom line, the manager at the World Bank was generally constrained by the relatively more bureaucratic and 'political' framework of the Bank's environment which tended to inhibit autonomous action. For example, the 'political' framework of the Bank would often pit bureaucratic management against Executive Directors (EDs) who are essentially political appointees from competing regions. This created significant limitations in getting the job done since all major decisions needed the imprimatur of E.Ds.

In decision-making at BT, decisions made at the top, in New York, were generally filtered down through the hierarchy of the bank as management handed down orders or directions to subordinates on the corporate food chain. Whereas at the World Bank/IFC, management had to work with 'political' constituencies and navigated between competing interest groups. Decisions were often rendered by creating coalitions and support. Typically, decisions would not be handed down and passed off to the next in command without some type of sanction or approval. I enjoyed the World Bank experience but soon realized that I was more at home in the BT work environment.

In New York, as part of the orientation, I attended a three-week course on derivative products directed by a Math professor from Columbia University, Prof. Ron. Wippern. This was refreshingly different from report writing. I immersed myself totally into the world of derivative products and their place in financial transactions. Exchange-traded and over-the-counter derivatives were already altering the practice of borrowing, investment and risk management. These changes, over time, would affect the fundamental nature of financial activities and the manner in which financial transactions are undertaken. The availability of derivative products provided benefits to market participants. These benefits include the ability to manage the price exposure and create exposure to assets synthetically. There are additional benefits in terms of enhancing the liquidity of the underlying asset markets and in reducing the volatility of asset prices.

The availability of these types of instruments enhanced the attractiveness of investment (both direct and portfolio) in asset markets. The range of market participants is broad. This includes financial institutions, corporations, investors (both institutional and retail), supra-national entities and governments. Several dealers (primarily banks and securities dealers) were getting increasingly active in trading in derivative products, providing liquidity. Derivative elements were frequently embedded in structured investment products for a wide range of investors in developed and emerging markets alike.

The open plan office environment was also different. The camaraderie was similar but different in that now it was based on an underlying loyalty to one's section, area of operation and the targets to be achieved. This was real teamwork. I was to lead a team of enthusiastic, bright, highly educated and keen professionals who wanted to achieve excellent results, get a good bonus based on performance, while maintaining our team's 'pole position' in the market. New York was more enjoyable than Washington DC. My passion for sartorial elegance was satisfied at Dino Baldini, 485 Madison Avenue. The tuna and foie-gras at Le Bernadin restaurant was 'a slice of heaven.'

I became a worshipper at St. Patrick Cathedral and a frequent visitor to the Museum of Modern Art. My favourite entertainment place was Birdland, live jazz. The Cajun foods were simply amazing. I watched many artists including Robert Cray, Stanley Turrentine, Sonny Rollins, B.B. King, the amazing Aretha Franklin and the brilliant Modern Jazz Quartet, among others. John Harris and the hirsute, Mike Don Diego and Stan Cohen from Legal, became regular companions on visits to various louche entertainment venues.

In London, BT rented a three-bedroomed serviced apartment in Monarch House, situated in a luxurious, secluded hideaway off Kensington High Street. The journey to BT's offices was about forty minutes on the tube or slightly longer by bus. I soon settled back into the daily rush-hour routine in London. My office space was the corner cubicle on the fourth floor. I had good views of Broadgate and the footpath on the east side of the station complex.

The team was jovial, lively, motivated and worked diligently. We soon settled down into our respective roles of identifying opportunities, staying close to clients to advise on strategies and sometimes introduce new products to assist them in their businesses. At departmental meetings held every Monday morning we would share updates on deals and their progress or lack thereof, new transactions, review ongoing ones and measure performance against set targets. These discussions were relayed to senior management in New York.

We soon got to work on bidding for the lead role to raise $80 million for Zimbabwe's Agricultural Marketing Authority (A.M.A). This was a familiar annual transaction in the Euro-markets. Our main competition in this deal were UBS, led by Bruce Jewel. He was not quite meretricious but almost there, in my view, and Paul Starling, his assistant, Credit Suisse, Deutsche Bank and Rabobank. Cephas and I flew to Harare to meet with A.M.A staff, notably the Chief Operating Officer, Mr. Rusa Mbiriri, the Chairman, Cephas Msipa, an egregious choleric, (a friend of his, Dr. Ariston Chambati, referred to him as a 'cantankerous geriatric!'). More about him later. The Governor of the Reserve Bank, Dr. Tsumba who I had met in his Zimbank days allowed us a short call. I recalled his tendency to divagate whenever we discussed the possible involvement of Zimbank as a shareholder in the Ghanaian bank that I set up in Accra.

We met with various members of the A.M.A including the Grain Marketing Board, Cold Storage Commission, Cotton Marketing Board and their local bankers. The Tobacco Marketing Board had their own financing arrangements in place, which also presented another opportunity for us. Cephas and I visited the National Oil Company of Zimbabwe (NOCZIM), to discuss derivative-based oil procurement structures. At the same time, Moyo Kamgaing was negotiating with Cocobod to fund their exports while negotiating with GNPC, to raise funds for their oil business. Indy Bedi and Herve Assah were in Tanzania exploring opportunities to fund pyrethrum, cashew nuts and cotton exports, aircraft purchases by the Government's airline, Air Tanzania. They also discussed a possible gold monetization programme with the Central Bank. There was a buzz in this Promethean team.

I left Cephas in Harare following up on unfinished business, while I flew to Washington D.C. to join the rest of BT's senior management including the Vice Chairman, George Vojta, Martha Sanniford, Neil Allen, Ted Gilleti and Mike Don Diego at the IMF-World Bank joint annual meetings. After all the long speeches and lobbying, we hosted a reception for all and sundry at the Four Seasons Hotel in Georgetown. Champagne flowed readily. Smartly dressed catering staff fed the gathered bankers and other businesspeople including politicians, civil servants and IMF/World bank staff.

I thought our reception was grand until I went to two receptions hosted by Morgan Stanley. They hired Union Station for theirs and Salomon Brothers, who threw their party in the vast NASA museum. There were live bands and free-flowing Cristal Champagne. Capitalistic joie de vivre par excellence. I have vivid recollections of Martha dancing wildly with Justin Chinyanta, a Zambian banker, while George Vojta and I sat and swayed to the music, champagne in hand, and talked, sotto voce, about the state of our African business. I do not remember much else about this annual event.

It felt strange to be back in Washington and staying at the Park Hyatt on M Street, rather than my own home. I soon got used to it. At breakfast one morning, I met and introduced myself to Secretary of State, Warren Christopher, then joined Vernon Jordan and Jim Friedlander at their table. I stayed in touch with Warren Christopher till his death in March 2011. He was, humble and wise, a true gentleman.

After the hassle and bustle of each day, in the still depths of the Autumn nights, light rain falling gently on the huge hotel windows and the chestnut trees silhouetted against the George Washington Circle and monuments, I would look back at my life journey. I rejoiced and thanked God for the good, kind parents who had sacrificed all to give their children a chance in life, excellent education and work experience. Life had had ups and some downs, but all considered, it had gone swimmingly to date. Nevertheless, I felt a 'thirst,' indeed a niggling, persistent sense that I was being prepared for greater tasks ahead.

It was during one of these dreamy moments, at about three in the morning, that the phone rang. An excited Cephas, calling from the London office, pulled me back to reality with the words, "We got the A.M.A. deal."

"Do you know what time this is?" I inquired of him.

"Yes, I do," came the reply. "It is ten after three in the morning, your time, but I know you well enough to know that this news would reduce some anxiety on your part. In any case, I refuse to believe that you were asleep. So there."

"What a perceptive prick, sibylline to boot," I mused as I muttered words of encouragement followed by a congratulatory message to the team, complete with the customary keys mash to emphasize my excitement. Cephas' parents, it was clear, had not taught him the art of dissimulation.

I always thought that Cephas could have been the little boy in the story about the emperor's clothes, except the veracity of his outburst would have been more bluntly expressed, "The damn fool is butt naked." Meanwhile, my heart got into an elevator and asked for the top floor.

The next few weeks saw the team in full swing, structuring, negotiating, marketing and advising on various transactions. We sat at our
desks for long hours and often had al desko lunches delivered to us
by a petite blonde with a shrill voice, akin to a demented parrot. We
nick-named her 'Tweetie bird.' The work was backbreaking but exhilarating and rewarding. I enjoyed the competitive aspects of banking.
Each Investment Bank had a team with a reputation in the market.
We strove for something better than mere excellence: there were good
bankers and excellent ones, but we had to be 'outstanding.' Interdig-
itation was the key to our success as a team. We achieved that status
within the first six months of our team getting together. The Bank had
excellent year-end results. We received good bonuses that year.

From the Monarch House accommodation, we moved into a
large four-bedroomed house on The Avenue, in Kew, near the main
gate to Kew Gardens. The two girls were enrolled into Broomfield
House Prep School, fifteen minutes from the house. The house was
conveniently located for schools, shops and the underground station
on the District Line. It was a forty-minute ride to Cannon Street or
Mansion House Stations, which were a short fifteen-minute walk
or a short bus-ride to Liverpool Street. On the odd day, I would
drive to the office, leaving home early, to avoid traffic through central London and would park in the Finsbury Square car park,
opposite L'Abbat Jour restaurant.

During this time, my thoughts always wandered back to my days
and times in the emerging markets, establishing financial institutions. I played a part in advising on and drafting appropriate
regulations to govern capital markets. I admired the 'entrepreneurial spirit' in a lot of my clients. I got to appreciate what they went
through: the pains of setting up institutions, the pitfalls, the joys of
success and the recovery from challenges. In Ghana, Afare Donkor
asked me when I would stop setting up for clients and do something
for myself. He struck a hidden chord. Some food for thought for a
restless soul.

The question haunted me and drove me, eventually, to draft a project proposal to establish my own financial institution. It had to be a bank, a merchant bank, specializing in corporate finance, trade finance and treasury dealings. I had decided that the bank had to be established in Zimbabwe. This was a market I had come to know well from all angles including government and Reserve Bank policies and regulations. I had, for a long time, perceived a need for a new, fresh, innovative, catalytic form of banking approach in Zimbabwe. That entrepreneurial zeal was now tormenting me relentlessly. I knew something would have to give sooner rather than later.

St. Augustine's prayer always came to mind: *Thou maddest us for thyself and our heart is restless until it rests in thee. Grant me Lord to know and understand which is first-to call on thee or to praise thee. And again, to know thee or to call on thee. For who can call on thee, not knowing thee? For he, that knoweth thee may not call on thee as other than thou art. Or is it better that we call on thee that we may know thee?* Often, during my lunch hour, or sometimes whenever I felt the need, I would slip, ophidian style, into St. Mary's Church, on Eldon Street, between Moorgate and Liverpool Street stations, and meditate. I prayed for guidance. Sometimes, recalling Dad's advice, I would just stare at the Crucifix hanging above the altar.

During one of these moments in the church, despite the brumal seasonal blasts outside, I felt a warmth and a sense of approval and encouragement as I dreamt about how I really wanted to be an entrepreneurial banker. I wanted to establish my very own institution. Afare Donkor's words rang in my head disturbingly. When I got back to my desk, I was determined to work hard and have as my objective, my own bank. I mentioned earlier, that, in a sibylline fit, I had hissed at an uncooperative NatWest Bank manager at Cranfield Business School, Mr. Bristow. I told him that one day I would set up my own bank and he would be my employee.

I felt good at the thought of employing Mr. Bristow. Not that I ever believed that it was any student's unalienable right to get money from a bank, but my Supervisor, Prof. John Constable had recommended to Mr. Bristow that I be lent the money. Mr. Bristow uncooperatively passed away before he got my offer.

Things were somehow beginning to 'come together as they should,' was the feeling I had. The idea of a global banking outfit in Zimbabwe appealed to me. I had started working on this idea when I was still working with Jay Tata at the IFC's ISG. I had drafted several project papers and looked through them from time to time to improve the presentation and content of my papers. A seed had been planted in my mind and I wished, in my heart of hearts, that it may soon fructify and the harvest follow.

I had visited South Africa during my time at the World Bank. It was widely anticipated then that the first democratic election would be held and the ANC, led by Nelson Mandela, would be propelled to power. This time I was asked to attend the annual meeting organized for businesspeople and prospective investors by Sidney Frankel, a stockbroker and member of the Johannesburg Stock Exchange. Like most large international banks, we, at Bankers Trust decided to familiarize ourselves with the South African financial sector, public sector and political environment so that we could position ourselves for any fund raising that the new government would be certain to embark on. Our strategy was to get closer to and ally ourselves with suitable local financial institutions including investment banks, stockbrokers, Reserve Bank and Ministry of Finance officials.

The then Minister of Finance, Chris Liebenberg, a former Bankers Trust employee and Trevor Manuel, the then Minister of Industry, were well-known to us. Through a facilitator and renowned timeserver, Kusum Kalyan, who worked for Shell in Cape Town, we were introduced to Malcolm Stewart, a senior stockbroker. My past contacts also included the team at Rand Merchant Bank, especially Laurie Dippenaar and G.T. Ferreira, the Managing

Director and Chairman, respectively. They had previously entertained me to many excellent lunches and gave me brilliant insights into the South African political and economic scenarios in their offices on Fredman Drive, Johannesburg.

The week was eventful, with many well-organized presentations by politicians, corporate executives and academics. There were factory visits, cultural events featuring colourful local tribal dances and food-fares. It was interesting to note the absence of local black professionals at any level. White and Asian businessmen were well-represented. There were only a handful of 'Coloureds,' while Black professionals were mostly ANC representatives, except one or two budding entrepreneurs including Patrice Motsepe and Professor Mohale Mahanyele. The latter was one of the founders of National Sorghum Breweries. He later became one of our clients. We toured a feedlot and abattoir operated by Karan Beef. This was a distressing eye-opener. My vegetarian inclinations kicked in from the beginning of the tour and overwhelming at the end of the three-hour witnessing of the slaughter of the brown-eyed beasts.

The climax of the conference was at the end of the week. After an extensive tour of the vineyards in Stellenbosch and Franschhoek, punctuated by wine-tasting and local gourmet gastronomical delights, there was a formal dinner at Kirstenbosch National Botanical Gardens. This was an idyllic setting at the eastern foot of the majestic Table Mountain in Cape Town. The guest of honour was Archbishop Desmond Tutu. He said a prayer before speaking eloquently and imparting words of wisdom regarding the upcoming first inclusive national elections. Next was the Minister of Finance, who also spoke eloquently. During the Minister's speech, Sidney Frankel crouched next to my seat and asked me to speak on behalf of the foreign visitors. I was floored but determined to think on my feet. I approached the podium slowly.

My recollection of the speech is hazy, at best, but I remember the standing ovation. Accolades of praise were relayed to my

London office by attendees, including a perfect gentleman, a Senior Executive at Credit Suisse, Zurich, Jean Jacques Guinand, before I got back. I sat at the 'High Table,' ensconced between the Minister of Finance and the Archbishop. They were both gracious with their appreciation of my speech. The archbishop said, "For a moment you sounded like your father, Alban. I hope you will have the good sense never to be a politician. You will make an excellent leader in God's Church one day."

I was stunned as I gulped another glass of Meerlust Rubicon. "But then, Uncle Desmond has always been cryptic in his obscure remarks," I mused. Sidney Frankel's colleague, Geoffrey Rothschild, harrumphed his way through a highfalutin vote of thanks. We worked our way through dessert to the accompaniment of loud Zulu and Xhosa drums and vocals from gyrating dark bodies, scantily clad. They were swaying in front of a huge, atavistic blaze fueled by huge logs of local wood.

From Johannesburg, I flew to Gaborone, Botswana, ostensibly to investigate the possibility of funding the muted gas drilling and exploration projects that were being sponsored by a large German company. I hooked up, that night, with a friend, who had settled in Botswana and joined a firm of architects. She and her sister were my contemporaries at university. We had a delightful dinner and reunion and caught up on old friends and acquaintances. My next stop was the Central Bank, where my ex-colleague from Capital Markets, Laurence Clarke, had been seconded as the Deputy Governor of the Bank. Another friend, the effervescent Liyanda Lekalake, also worked at the Central Bank.

From the Central Bank, I visited my uncle, Dr. Simba Makoni. He was the Chief Executive of SADC. Over dinner, I outlined to him how I intended to leave my job, resign from the World Bank, after my leave of absence, establish my own merchant bank in Zimbabwe. Uncle Simba almost fell out of his seat, much to his wife, Aunt Chipo's amusement. They both listened to my plans before hugging me anxiously, mumbling words of caution and encouragement. As I left for the airport, bound for Harare, a new bank, in my mind, had been born.

I spent a frantic week in Harare, ensconced at the Harare Club. I updated my project proposal, ready for submission to the Reserve Bank Governor, Dr. Moyana, the Registrar of Banks, Mrs. M'pofu and her assistant, Mr. Rwenhamo, at the Ministry of Finance. I had compiled a list of possible investors including Local Authorities Pension Fund, The Old Mutual, Mining Industry Pension Fund, Catering Industry Pension Fund, ZESA pension Fund, TA Holdings through ZIMNAT Insurance, Zimbabwe development Bank and The Venture Capital Company of Zimbabwe.

My first port of call was MIPF, where I was welcomed by the Chairman, Sam Sipepa Nkomo. After listening to my proposal, Mr. Nkomo looked at me in silence for a good two minutes. "This is amazing," he finally uttered, as one would address an ectoplasmic presence. "Certainly not what I expected to hear," he carried on through pursed lips betraying a faint grin. Two hours later, I emerged from Mr. Nkomo's office with a bear-hug and a firm hand-shake. I was to return the following day to meet with Mr. Nkomo, some members of his board and representatives of the targeted investors on my list. Mr. Nkomo knew them all and offered to 'round them up' to hear my story.

The meeting was well-attended. Everyone on my list was represented. Several analysts invited by Mr. Nkomo were also in attendance. The meeting was held in the huge MIPF boardroom, which was well-equipped for the presentation at hand. I presented my proposal to establish a new bank in Zimbabwe. The first indigenous-owned and entrepreneurially led bank in the country and beyond. The bank would be a Merchant Bank initially since the capital requirements, at that time, were U.S. $10 million for merchant banks and U.S. $30 million for commercial banks. The idea was to establish the institution and make a mark in its chosen niche markets. We would target blue chip corporate clients in all sectors of the economy and high net-worth families and individuals.

The Bank, to be called National Merchant Bank, NMB, would seek to challenge the existing foreign-owned and white-controlled clubby, complacent banks. We would introduce innovative solutions and products to revolutionize and make a difference in the country's financial markets. I reserved forty percent of the shareholding for the promoters, while the rest would be offered to local and foreign investors. Any investor holding at least a ten percent shareholding would be entitled to appoint a director to the Board of the Bank. All this was, of course, subject to the necessary approvals and licenses being granted by all the relevant authorities.

The immediate reaction to my soigne presentation was a brief pregnant pause, a scatter of handclapping then a barrage of questions. The gist of the questions was what made me believe that what I was proposing was possible. No financial institution, let alone a bank, had been established by indigenous entrepreneurs nor had there been a bank managed by indigenous, black staff, in the history of the country. Furthermore, how realistic were my rich projected returns? Would the Government support this kind of venture?

I outlined my background from education, training and work experience in banking and financial markets in the City of London, Washington DC, New York, Harare and other financial centres across the world in countries spanning Latin America, Europe, Asia and Africa. I highlighted the transactions I had put together including management teams that went on to lead highly rated financial institutions. After a grueling three hours, the meeting ended. Charles Mandizvidza of LAPF, Sam Nkomo and Zimnat pledged their support right away.

This made my meetings with Dr. Moyana at RBZ, the Minister of Finance, Dr. Chidzero and the Registrar of banks, Mrs. Mpofu, much easier. They were all supportive. They pledged to grant licenses subject to capital requirements being met, a suitably qualified management team and an acceptable board of directors being appointed. Before flying back to London, I had dinner with Dr. Chidzero. He was a fine gentleman, a member of my 'mutual admiration circle.' He was supportive of the project and promised to brief the country's president at the next cabinet meeting.

My encounter with Dr. Chidzero, after meeting his staff and the Reserve Bank, in the context of my establishing the first black-led bank in Zimbabwe, the first one to be registered since the early 1960s when no one was quite familiar with the due process for licensing and registering a bank, evoked memories of Theodore C. Sorenson. His thoughts were expressed in his book, *Decision-Making in the White House.* Sorenson concluded that the only way to assure good presidential decisions is to elect and support good Presidents. For in mixing the challenges and forces those presidents must deal with, their style and standard, values and vitality, insights and outlook, will make the crucial difference. A great presidential decision, he concluded, defies the laws of mathematics and exceeds the sum of all parts. A great President is not the product of his staff but a master of his house. That summed up Dr. Bernard Chidzero. He was haloed with that invincible cloud of mystery, the most sagacious President the country never had.

My presentations to would-be shareholders and civil servants had clearly been perlocutionary. The stage was set for me to prepare and submit formal applications to all the relevant authorities. I managed to do this before I left for London. Word had already spread. I could feel eyes gazing at me as I walked down the corridors of power or waited outside offices to be interviewed by incredulous officials, admirers and sceptics alike. I was an object of curiosity in the Ministries. I was viewed with suspicion and faintly disguised derision by the established banking fraternity, both black and white.

I was determined to see my mission through and persisted until I had submitted all my papers. I left no stone unturned in surveying the banking landscape. The more I looked, the more the opportunities for an institution like NMB became apparent. Charles Mandizvidza's prophetic utterance, to the effect that established banks are in for a rude awakening, followed me everywhere. It was up to me to fulfil it. I was on a mission. I smiled as I boarded the next BA 747 bound for London.

With the benefit of hazy, if subjective hindsight, I have often wondered what, at this stage, was driving me and spurring me towards my goal. This is something I will seek to shed light on and possibly clarify at a later stage during this narrative. For now, it suffices to say that historically, the idea that has defined the boundary between modern times and the past is the mastery of risk: the notion that the future is more than 'a whim of the gods' and that human beings are not passive before nature. Until human beings somehow worked out and found a way across that boundary, the future was but a mirror of the past or the murky domain of oracles and soothsayers who held a monopoly over knowledge of anticipated events.

My vision in creating NMB was an amazing serendipity in the fact that it was an exercise in putting the future at the service of the present, converting risk-taking into a catalyst that would help drive the new Zimbabwe as envisaged by the recently instituted Structural Adjustment Programme underwritten by the I.M.F and the World Bank. Managing the risks involved in my undertaking this task became synonymous with challenge and opportunity. The vision had its genesis and deep roots in the cloistered calm of paludal academic environments, the open fields of Bedfordshire, the City of London, Wall Street, the bustling Bretton Woods enclave in Washington D.C. and the louche environs of Ghana's inspiring towns and beaches.

Chapter Eighteen

AS I SET ABOUT assembling a management team and board of directors, back in London, I often mused at the words muttered by
Charles Mandizvidza of LAPF, after my presentation to the would-
be- investors in MIPF's boardroom: "Those complacent white
bankers are now in a little spot of bother and a bit of a rude awakening." The master of litotes chuckled naughtily as he shook my
hand after pledging instant support for the project. No pressure
then.

As David Hamilton used to tell me, "No place for a bumfuzzle,
you need to perform." I had to be mindful to assemble a credible
team that would deliver the promised services and quickly make a
mark in the financial sector.

While I nurtured the idea of setting up a bank in Zimbabwe, I
arranged for William Nyemba, to be part of the new team in CAL
Bank under Afare Donkor. William had now grown into a manager.
He was good at foreign banking, which he made his special focus. I
felt that since he had worked under Afare's guidance in a start-up
banking operation in the environment of a World Bank Structural
Adjustment Programme, he would be a good member of the team.
I appointed him Executive Director, Banking Operations.

I then appointed James Mushore as the Executive Director, Corporate Finance. James was, at that time, a managing partner at

Coopers and Lybrand Lusaka. His background as an accountant, his experience, exposure and market knowledge, would be handy. They would both be assisted by a General Manager, Francis Zimuto. He had extensive knowledge of local banking and the Zimbabwe markets. Francis had previously worked for Barclays Bank and RAL Merchant Bank. I would be the Managing Director. The four of us would be the promoters and founding shareholders. We held 40% of the bank's shares through a vehicle we called NMB Investments.

The next task was to choose a suitable Chairman. My first choice was Dr. Ariston Chambati, then Chairman of TA Holdings, a local conglomerate. I had met Ariston during the World Bank annual meetings in Washington. We had become well-acquainted, over the years. He was 'well-polished,' spoke well and had a sound, Oxford education. He was a political science lecturer at some point in his past. After an exceedingly long telephone conversation, Ariston told me he would be delighted to be the new bank's chairman, but he was already chairman of another merchant bank, MBCA. He would, however, talk to a close friend of his, Cephas Msipa, to see if he could take up the post.

On my next trip to Harare, I would visit Mr. Msipa to discuss the matter. Non-executive directors would be my childhood friend, Arthur 'Morrith' Mutsonziwa, who was now a partner at the law firm, Atherstone and Cook, Afare Donkor, managing Director of CAL Merchant Bank, Accra and Malcolmn Pryor from Philadelphia. Malcolm's firm, firm, Pryor, McClendon and Counts had invested in Afare's bank in Accra. Malcolmn took up 10% of the shares in NMB. The IFC, who had been invited to take up 20% of the shares in NMB would nominate their own director, as would the local institutional shareholders, ZESA Pension Fund, MIPF, LAPF, First Mutual Life, The Old Mutual and ZIMNAT Insurance.

While James Mushore and Francis Zimuto were disengaging themselves from PWC and First Merchant Bank respectively, I tasked William with securing suitable premises where the bank would operate from. Next, he would identify staff for our Treasury operations. As soon as they could, James and Francis would join William and work as a team to set up the bank's offices and recruit more staff. I encouraged William and Francis to nobble good, competent staff from FMB and MBCA. James would look at other firms for Accountants and Corporate Finance staff. Within a short time, we had secured the entire sixth floor of Farnum House, the AA Building next to Pearl House on Samora Machel Avenue, downtown Harare. We were now well-staffed.

I called the team in Harare from London daily to get updates. I also pushed my colleagues at the IFC to expedite their approval process so that their share capital would be paid up without delay. IFC, however, insisted that the promoters and the local institutional shareholders should pay up first before they did. I called on Sam Nkomo to assist us in urging his fellow pension fund would-be-investors to pay up as soon as an audit report on the assets and evaluation of the promoters' contribution had been tabled. In the meantime, the team on the ground had opened bank accounts, submitted the formal applications to the Ministry of Finance, Reserve Bank of Zimbabwe. Amazingly, the president's office had to be copied in on our activities. It was frantic work as the momentum gathered and the project was up and running.

I had now been at BT for just over two years. The IFC had granted me a two-year leave of absence to learn more about derivatives before I re-joined ISG to spearhead their operations. Now I had started this venture in Harare. I was still at BT, enjoying my work and rising on the corporate totem pole. I was in a quandary, torn between the three opportunities. I had to make up my mind sooner rather than later. I decided to fly to New York, to discuss my dilemma with my Head of Division, Neil Allen and Mike Don Diego. I got the Concorde from Heathrow at about noon on a Monday and was in New York three hours later, just in time for breakfast with Neil at the Waldorf Astoria.

We had a hearty chat. Neil was relaxed as he listened to my arrangements. Finally, he said, "Follow your heart. You have had your time at the IFC. Why do you still want to work for someone else? I have been thinking of doing something similar myself. Should you leave BT, we would simply wind up the Division or integrate it into some other unit. And so, life goes on. NMB sounds like a good bet. We would be happy to have BT extend lines of credit to help you get going." I was relieved and delighted. That evening, Mike Don Diego joined me for a boozy dinner. Through a haze of cigar smoke, we chatted about the opportunities that lay ahead for both of us.

Washington was a different affair. I struggled to drag myself into the office as I dreaded my meeting with the Director of Personnel, a rather unpleasant South African, Christopher Baum. A colleague described him as having a brash and undeniably ugly accent from the depths of some Afrikaner kraal in the backstreets of 'beyond.' I outlined to him and his Irish assistant, Michael O'Farrell, my time at BT. I loved my job there. I would, however, consider coming back to the IFC if they would at least match my current salary and benefits as they were significantly higher than my package at the World Bank. "You want to earn more than I and you are threatening to break your contract if we do not accede to your demands?" snarled Christopher.

"Let me warn you, we will get you blacklisted, and you will not be allowed to work for the World Bank Group again, ever. This is dishonourable," he barked.

I got really incensed, stood up and stretched out my hands and said, "Right, you go on and crucify me. It comes naturally to you, I am sure. Go on." Christopher glared at me, deep hatred radiating from his eyes, deeply set in a distorted visage. It is difficult not to banalize the man's attitude into entertainment. Michael O'Farrell intervened and tried to calm us down. At this point I made it clear that they could blacklist me all they want. I was only asking for terms that my white colleagues who had been in my situation, including Jay, had been offered to return to the Bank's employ. Why was I being treated differently? Later that afternoon, I handed in my resignation letter and waved good-bye as I gave instructions on where I wanted my pension money sent.

I went to a Jeep dealership in Arlington and bought a brand-new jet-black Grand Cherokee. I shipped it to Zimbabwe with the rest of household goods that had been in storage for the past two and half years.

That evening, I narrated my story to a motley crew of the black gang as we shared drinks at Quigley's wine bar. They were generally horrified but not surprised at the turn of events. As in the old days, we reminisced about racism and issues of colour as we shared meals. Later, I disappeared to my suite at the Park Hyatt. In my alcoholic daze, I imagined that the suite had the fragrance of exotic ginseng perfume and tea blends with the odorous freshness of water babbling under moonlight. I drifted away with the passion, the effervescence, the fugitive mood of a virgin faun amorously distracted by the sight of nymphs. Next day, the hangover was legendary.

A few days later, I was back in London at my desk. I called William to get updates on NMB. Previously, the calls had been long. I could feel and sense enthusiasm. Something had changed. Frequently I was now put on hold for long minutes and informed that William was too busy to talk to me. When we did speak, the tone was different. After a couple of weeks of this treatment, I decided to take time off and see what was really going on.

On arrival, I was met by Tabitha, our Arcadian 'Girl Friday' in the new office. She recounted how William was unhappy because James was part of the team. He thought that James and I had more in common and were close friends. In the event of a dispute, he concluded, we could vote him out of the partnership. Francis was on the fence. He had worked with William closely in the past, but now, reading the tea leaves, was leaning on whichever side I would be. I called James, William and Francis for a strategy meeting the next morning. We ironed out matters between us then resolved to work together in harmony.

While in Harare I arranged to meet with Ariston Chambati. He introduced me to Cephas Msipa, the new chairman designate. I had met Mr. Msipa briefly, on AMA matters when BT were awarded the mandate to fund-raise for the AMA. He was then the chairman of AMA. I thought that he was an affable old man, highly recommended. After a brief chat, Mr. Msipa, who had been well briefed by Ariston, agreed to be our chairman. As I left Mr. Msipa's office, I met an old acquaintance, Enock Kamushinda, a local businessman.

After listening to my NMB plan, Enock offered to introduce me to a man called 'the Professor,' for his ability to solve problems and navigate the system. The man turned up to be none other than my indomitable, intrepid relative, Roger Boka, a renowned, somewhat pinguid ergate and 'Mr. Fix it.' I had not seen him for a long time. It was inevitable that Roger, Enock and I would collogue. We talked about NMB. After hearing my story, Roger said, "Sekuru, I will introduce you to two people who will be useful as time passes. They are your uncle, Didymus Mutasa, Administrator of ZANU PF, who is known to tergiversate as the situation suits him and Emmerson Mnangagwa, the Minister for Justice."

Within two hours, I had met with the two politicians in their respective offices and briefed them on NMB. Before I left for London, I called on James' uncle, General Solomon Mujuru, who had become a pillar of support for us. I enjoyed the occasional drink of his favourite single malt whisky with the kind, shy, humble, polite, astute and well-informed man.

From Harare, I flew to Cape Town. At the Mount Nelson Hotel one evening, I joined the England Rugby team's Victor Ubogu at the bar after their win over the Springboks that afternoon. I had watched the match at Newlands Rugby Stadium, courtesy of Malcolm Stewart and Kusum Kalyan. Victor was soft-spoken and had a shy smile. This was the first time England had played the Springboks since the country had held democratic elections. We were soon joined by Mr. Thabo Mbeki and Allen Boesak, all friends of Kusum's. We had a wide-ranging discussion covering the new political dispensation, the country's post-independence economic prospects and the impact of recent political developments on regional economic and political formations.

The next morning, the rest of my BT team arrived: Cephas, Avarina Miller, Mike Don Diego, John Harris, Peter Getsinger and Yves de Balmain. We had to compete with several international banks, to issue the first bond for the new RSA government and to arrange for the country's first credit rating. We spent the morning rehearsing our presentations and listened to analyses of the South African socio-political-economic environment from Malcolm Stewart. His colleague Gary, a political scientist talked at length about 'Nelson of a hundred days.' Rudy Gouws, the senior economist at Rand Merchant Bank briefed us also.

In the afternoon, we went on a sightseeing tour of Cape Town including Table Mountain. We were somewhat distracted by a pair of meerkats trying to mate while a crowd of bankers curiously focused on their noisy attempts at consummating their love act. Eventually the meerkats took a dislike to this unwarranted attention and slickered off into the thick bush to carry on their endeavours in privacy.

We were the first team to make our pitch to the Minister of Finance, Chris Liebenberg, his team, the Reserve Bank and a sprinkling of officials from other government departments. Peter Getsinger, possessed of an excellent brain, made the main pitch while Yves de Balmain talked about Bankers Trust and our capabilities. Mike don Diego and I talked about the transactions we had worked on in Africa and Latin America. The meeting lasted for about an hour. At the end of the meeting, Mr. Liebenberg revealed to us that he had worked for BT at some point in the past, in New York. He added, with a glint in his eye, that BT had not treated him well. They still owed him money. We did not waste time in leaving his office. I am sure, in our heart of hearts, we all longed for a black hole or the closest door to crawl into and hide. We did not know how our bid would be affected by BT's past actions.

From Cape Town, we went to Pretoria to pay our respects to the Governor of the Reserve Bank and his two Deputies. We repeated our pitch before heading for Sandton. We were happy to rest our weary heads at the Michelangelo Hotel. We had dinner at the Butcher's Shop and Grill restaurant on Mandela Square. Large steaks and a huge seafood platter were consumed as we discussed our meetings so far. Yves and Peter left the following day. The rest of the team visited ESKOM, Transnet, ABSA and Rand Merchant Bank for more talks.

On Friday afternoon, we took time off to play a game of golf at the Royal Johannesburg and Kensington Golf Club, a superb course. In my four ball were Malcolm, Pieter Louw, erstwhile ABSA banker with fine lineaments reminiscent of George Clooney and Laetitia, an attractive young Afrikaner blonde from Transnet. She was quite a distraction with her beguiling looks. After the game, Malcolm said, "I bet that's the closest you've ever been to a pair of Afrikaner tits then?" I smiled.

I flew back to London over the weekend. It was not easy to focus on anything in the office as we awaited news of our bid in South Africa. I also worried about events at the nascent NMB in Harare. Telephone conversations with James and Tabitha in Harare informed that William was really aiming to be top dog. If he could prevent my coming to NMB as the managing director, he would. This was a coup in the making.

In his shenanigans, William had enlisted the help of the new chairman, Cephas Msipa, including two of the non-executive directors appointed by LAPF and NRZ Pension Funds, Israel Ndhlovu and Sam Zumbika, respectively. They were both based in Bulawayo. From their scurrilous conduct, I often thought they were both, or should have been married to pinguid harridans. There was something unsympathetic about them both. I believe the two directors were beneficiaries of William's largesse. The chairman was the recipient of a huge 'loan' through his near-defunct milling company, Hydra Milling.

Another non-executive director, Norman Sachikonye, from First Mutual Life, was a close family friend of William's. Clearly, William's sojourn in West Africa, though brief, had awakened a hidden sense of venality and turpitude in him. Timothy Chiganze and Simba Mangwengwende of ZIMNAT and ZESA Pension Fund, respectively, were watching from the side-lines. I sent updates on developments to Malcolmn Pryor in New York and Afare Donkor in Ghana. Months later, I received a mealy-mouthed non-apologetic rhetoric from Timothy Chiganze explaining his reticence to assert himself in my corner.

In time, we learnt that Deutsche Bank were awarded the South African mandate ahead of BT and Morgan Stanley. We were gutted but hardly surprised. Coincidentally, in early 1994, despite BT's prowess in managing the risks in the trading room, the bank suffered irreparable reputational damage when some complex derivative transactions caused large losses for some major corporate clients including Proctor and Gamble and Gibson Greetings. These two clients sued BT successfully asserting that they had not been informed of or had been unable to understand the risks involved.

The same week, we were informed that Deutsche Bank were interested in taking over BT. Since they had their own Africa team, we would be reassigned to other functions. We took the view that their past performance and record showed their approach to banking in the emerging markets and derivatives more banausic than inspired, compared to BT's. Most of us opted to take the exit package on offer. I was tasked with winding up the Division's affairs. This included a whirlwind valedictory trip to our clients in West Africa, East Africa, Southern Africa and the Americas. The timing could not have been better.

On previous visits to Harare, I had engaged a realtor, Margot Lavelle, to identify suitable accommodation for me. She had found a beautiful, three-bedroomed townhouse, 'El Paso,' near Fife Avenue Shopping Centre. I moved out of the comfortable home-away-from-home, Harare Club. I had slowly furnished El Paso and moved in bit by bit on my various visits to Harare. This became my full-time abode while I awaited containers with my household effects.

In Accra, Afare Donkor had a surprise farewell cocktail and dinner for me at Flair's, an idyllic, roof top restaurant. There were about thirty guests, mutual friends and colleagues from Ghana's private and public sectors alike. The Minister of Finance, Kwesi Botchwey, spoke kind words with regards to my work in Ghana, as did my old friend and fellow bibliophile, Tsatsu Tsikata. Afare, Johnny Quashie, a prominent lawyer cum ultimate kibitzer and the erudite Yeboah Amoah, chief executive of the Ghana Stock Exchange also spoke favourably. Ken Ofori Atta was then a budding entrepreneur, deontologist of note, setting up his own financial institution, Data Bank.

Ken drew cheers and laughter as he outlined, with wit and humour, how we had met in New York. As 'yuppies,' we conspired to awaken the financial markets of Ghana and Zimbabwe. Our visions were ablaze with innovative ideas, new institutions and a new way of doing business. He noted that electricity was not invented by candle makers. Fresh blood and a new approach were needed in these markets. I had designed a key which then became part of NMB's logo, with the moniker, "In pursuit of excellence, we open doors for you...don't be left behind." That dream was getting all too real.

A highlight of the trip to Accra was meeting with President Robert Mugabe. He was visiting his in-laws after the demise of his wife, Sally. A man of notable arete, I thought to myself. The president read through a copy of my project proposal and then informed me that he would be in London on a state visit in the coming two weeks. He invited me to be his guest at a state dinner hosted by Queen Elizabeth II at Claridge's. The Zimbabwean High Commissioner would be in touch with me. All arrangements would be put in place for the occasion. I was in shock. I accepted the invitation and stumbled out of the president's suite to join Afare for drinks and a sumptuous meal, courtesy of his adorable wife Cecilia.

I had met with the president thrice, previously. Our first meeting was in Washington DC, when he was hosted by all Zimbabweans at the World bank group and IMF during a visit to the USA, for an event at the United Nations in New York. After a brief introduction by Dr. Chidzero and Dr. Moyana, Minister of Finance and Governor of the Reserve Bank respectively, the president and I had a chat about my work, the state of the world's financial markets and life in Washington D.C. He showed a lot of interest and was well-informed when it came to the markets. Derivative products and interest rates seemed to fascinate him a lot.

Our second meeting was in Hong Kong. He had requested that I join his business delegation, which included Algy Cluff, Ariston Chambati, then CEO of TA Holdings, Enos Chiura, thimblerigger of note, apparently, and CEO of Delta, Enock Kamushinda and other captains of industry. I spoke briefly about BT, derivatives and aircraft leasing. In the evening, Algy Cluff called me and informed me that the president had requested that Algy and I join him for dinner at the Hong Kong Club. This was hosted by the local law society, chaired by Bernard Whalley, an ex-Zimbabwean legal practitioner now based in Hong Kong.

The dinner was a relaxed event. The president spoke softly but eloquently about the liberation struggle, his economic vision for the country and the role foreign investment could play in the scheme of things. At the end of dinner, he invited me to join him for breakfast in his hotel suite the following morning. I duly turned up for breakfast with the president on the morrow. We talked at length about what role BT could play in leasing aircraft for the national airline, among other matters. Towards the end of our meeting, he motioned towards a door where his companion, a young lady, who he introduced as Grace, came in with a small baby in her arms. It was an awkward moment for me, at first, but I soon adjusted to the circumstances and just enjoyed the moment before retiring for a post prandial nap.

The president's only State visit to the U.K. would be our fourth meeting. The High Commissioner, in London, Dr. Ngoni Chideya, organized a meeting of UK-based Zimbabweans from all walks of life. He chose a small team to brief the president during a luncheon hosted by the High Commissioner at his residence on the day before the State Banquet at Claridge's. Lunch was a subdued affair with reports on various issues presented by designated speakers, mostly staff from the High Commission. I spoke about the state of the financial markets, interest rates and banking in Europe and the U.K. After my report, the president asked the reportedly agoraphobic Governor of the Reserve Bank, Dr. Tsumba, why interest rates in Zimbabwe were so high compared to rates elsewhere, including the U.K.

The Governor had no clear answer. To my horror, the president then turned to me and asked pointedly, whether I thought the Governor's answer to his question on interest rates made any sense at all. I responded that I did not quite understand the Governor's answer, but I thought the state of the Zimbabwean economy and the competition between the public sector and private sector for scarce capital had a part to play in the long-term structure of rates in Zimbabwe. The silence around the room was deafening. The Governor glared at me as the president thanked me profusely for my 'candid response.' Yet another awkward moment.

The State Banquet, the following evening, was a lively, colourful event. I joined the president at high table. I sat between Prince

Charles and Prince Michael of Kent, a royal sober side. The conversation ranged from three friends that Prince Charles and I had in common, his recent trip to Moscow and his visit to Zimbabwe. There was an almost monologue on moths and butterflies from Prince Michael. After dinner, we adjourned for coffee in an anteroom. The president introduced me to the Queen and informed her that I would be establishing the first indigenous bank in Zimbabwe. "Isn't that risky?" inquired the Queen.

"With support from the president, it should all work out," I replied. The president smiled and squeezed my shoulder. I moved on to greet and chat with other guests.

Fortuitously, I was to meet the president again, a fortnight later at the World Economic Forum gathering at the Mount Nelson hotel in Cape town. I updated the president on NMB and informed him I would be moving to Harare to join my staff at the bank in the following two weeks or so. Once again, he invited me to a reception which was to be held at State House at the time. Meanwhile, in Cape Town, the president introduced me to his Vice President, Mr. Simon Muzenda. The latter gazed at me with a look that was heavy as a feather. I also met the Minister of Mines, Dr. Eddison Zvobgo, a master of catachresis, more in error, I think, rather than for deliberate rhetorical effect.

The highlight of the occasion was President Nelson Mandela. I had seen Mr. Mandela at the Mayflower Hotel in Washington D.C. previously, but had not had the opportunity to shake hands or chat. This was a momentous occasion for me. It was made even more memorable as I had to deliver a speech on the state of the Capital Markets in Africa and the developmental challenges that confronted financial institutions in those markets. I gave copies of my speech to Presidents Mandela and Mugabe. I have often wondered if either of them ever read my paper.

As part of winding up of the Division's operations at BT, I had to help with exit interviews. In addition, I had to clarify, hand over or terminate ongoing transactions. I worked with the Managing Director, Personnel Department, New York, to tie up and close all staff issues satisfactorily. In the middle of carrying out these duties, I received a frantic call from my polyhistor former boss, Jayant Tata in Washington DC, asking me to speak, at short notice, at an Emerging Markets Conference at the Mayflower Hotel. Our history of logrolling compelled me to accept Jay's invitation.

My focus would be African Markets in particular. Zimbabwe was a favourite destination for investment Funds and other potential investors. This was thanks to a strongly performing stock market and well-run Stock Exchange. Jay felt that I knew this market better than most people. My inclusion on the line-up of speakers would probably attract a lot of curious potential investors. He was proved right.

The conference was well-attended. At my session, it was standing room only. At the end of my presentation, there was a lively debate about the issues that I had discussed, including the Zimbabwean corporate sector. I seized the opportunity to announce to a stunned audience that I had just established a new bank, an entrepreneurially led merchant bank. I would soon be in the markets arranging lines of credit for trade finance and treasury activities. In a moment of 'madness,' I told the audience that it was my intention to list the bank once we had established a trading record of at least three years. My thinking and wish were to list the bank in London and Harare at the same time. There was a thunderous applause when I took to my seat. Jay stared at me. He shook his head before taking the mike, thanking me profusely and taking all the credit for being my mentor.

I have always wondered what made me 'ad lib' and talk about NMB and my vision at that conference. It was a gut feeling, a hunch: that feeling of knowing something without any idea why, I guess. This is an example of that presence of unconscious reasoning that has always been in my thoughts throughout my life. I had, by that time, grown used to listening to and being guided, to a large extent, by my intuition and gut feelings much more than I ignored them. It felt as if the words just issued out of my mouth without warning, thought nor plan.

An inner voice told me the time and place were right. I felt comfortable making my predictions and voicing my inner thoughts and wishes. It was akin to a foretaste of Elysium. I guess all those endless hours of meditation and other mindful practices, solitude in empty churches, woods and hotel rooms over the time of my existence had helped me to connect to my deepest inner wisdom and creative thinking. Over time, as if by earthlight, I am somehow able to decipher shapes and structures in the inner recesses of my mind.

This reminds me of Patricia May's words, '*Many of our actions are performed mechanically, following the instincts or habits present in our brain. But the conscious actions are generated by our desires and needs. That is why there are actions done with understandable and clear reasons, and simply unconscious acts that cannot be explained.*' I have often mused that maybe the speech was almost vigorous, if not quite Clevelandish with some enjambment and the absence of extravagant conceit.

Before leaving for London, I used the opportunity to talk to Jay and John Niepold, a newcomer, fund-manager associated with the IFC and the former director in CMD, Antoine van Agtmael. They both gave me useful insights regarding future fund-raising plans for the new bank. After a few more calls on old friends and colleagues, I flew to New York where I met up with Malcolmn Pryor and Allen Counts. We discussed Malcomn's upcoming visit to Africa, which trip would include Ghana, Zimbabwe and South Africa.

We were joined for lunch at the Astoria, by Robin Brooks, James Brown, a Washington-based lawyer and his erstwhile law-firm partner, Willie Leftwich. Lunch turned into an animated, three-hour event where experiences in business and African exploits, were shared. After lunch, the parties dispersed, leaving Robin, Malcomn and I to shoot the breeze and develop our friendship over dinner, after-dinner drinks and recreation. It was an evening of impromptu mellow madness. We listened to Grover Washington's 'And then there is You' and caroused until we dropped.

Robin and I agreed to work together on projects in South Africa. She would assist with raising lines of credit and other support for NMB's trade finance business. Over the years, we had many occasions to work together on deals. Whenever we got a chance, we would play golf. I cannot remember who won at golf. One day I called Robin from London, to chat. She was in Chicago. I got a start when her husband, Frank, answered Robin's phone. Frank was gentle, cool and calm. We chatted like long-lost friends before Frank apologized for keeping me on the phone for so long. "Robin went out and left her phone. Please call her back, she is always so happy to hear from you. You make her happy. I am delighted to have spoken with you at long last and heard, for myself, that cool voice she talks about ceaselessly." Frank died a few months after that call. A rare, black gentleman.

I often pinched myself to make sure I was not dreaming. Life had now assumed a dramatic turn. I had to get a grip and cope with a host of emotions including euphoria and doubt. In my lucid moments, I thought about my life and journey to date, the path I had now elected to follow and all the events, new people, friends, acquaintances, expectations and reactions from various people. Victor Hugo's 'there's nothing like a dream to create the future', rang clearly in my mind. I learnt that having my mind made up had diminished any fears I had. I had now crossed the bridge of my fears and insecurities. I braced myself to face the possibilities. I had also come to appreciate and believe firmly that turpitude and venality played no part in my psyche and were to be treated with the disdain that they deserve, always.

However, I still had to complete the mundane and banal if nebulous tasks of buying household utensils, furniture and other appliances for a fresh start in Zimbabwe. I had to plan for the girls' schooling and sort out all the paperwork for shipping household goods from Washington and London in two containers destined for one warehouse storage facility in Harare. After a good, hectic, three weeks, all was done. The London chapter was closed. Harare was to be the next stop on my journey.

Chapter Nineteen

THE BANK WAS REGISTERED as an accepting house, National Merchant Bank, under the Banking Act, in June 1993. I settled into my new office, an aerie with spectacular views of the city, housed in Unity Court, on the corner of First Street and Kwame Nkrumah Avenue. Amid the various internal disturbances and disagreements within the team, I recalled a paper by Shefrin and Thaler, titled "An Economic Theory of Self Control." The paper made the point that people who have trouble exercising self-control deliberately limit their options. People with weight problems, for example, avoid having a cake ready at hand. After re-reading the paper, I was off and running in pursuit of the purposeful direction and natural, if guided, evolution of NMB. I was now 'in situ,' in charge. I was able to determine who had what options available to them.

My first task would be to make sure we had a competent, cohesive team in place. This meant addressing the differences between James and William in addition to clarifying the role of the Chairman and non-executive directors. There was need to address and consign to the midden, the mundane niggles emanating from various 'Messrs Whoosis,' in the scheme of things. It was time to fossick, in the depths and inner recesses of my brain. I had to search my experience in the business world and education, for the most viable and appropriate way forward. Being at the helm of a fledgling bank in an emerging market proved to be no sinecure.

The first staff meeting I called, attended by all heads of department, managers and their assistants, was an eye-opener. Apart from James, William, Francis and the personal assistant, Tabitha, I did not know the staff well, if at all. They hardly knew me except by reputation. This was an opportunity for me to tell them about the bank, NMB, its genesis, my vision and to explain the rationale for the bank's chosen niche in the banking sector. It would also be an opportunity for me to hear views of the staff and to get to know them and have a mental map, at least, of the team's strengths and weaknesses. My main objective was to dispel that bane of fledgling management teams, that subjective state of uncertainty as to the truth or reality of anything, doubt.

I had to instill a sense of purpose, belief and confidence in our undertaking. In doing so, I also had to be mindful of Bertrand Russell's remark, crystallized in the recesses of my sensorium, that zeal was a bad mark for a cause. No one was zealous about the two times table. It has been shown that sometimes, people are zealous about things they are not quite or cannot be quite sure about. Their anxiety leads them to a compensatory exaggeration. The nascent Bank's emotional ecosystem thus had to be managed with care. Private, personal kingdoms and their boundaries had to be acknowledged and respected. There was a clear need to upcycle the motley crew of assembled, variously able and gifted men and women into a cohesive, formidable, bank management team, without the calamity of groupthink. Esprit de corps was to be the order of the day.

The meeting was a success. James took the initiative to salute William for the groundwork that he had put into setting up the Bank's infrastructure while he, James and others, myself included, disengaged ourselves from other commitments. This was well-received and almost reciprocated by William. Francis, ever the shrinking violet, looked decidedly comfortable, for once. The rest of the team warmed up and expressed enthusiasm for the job and professed their ability to conquer the challenges ahead. The team agreed that there was room in the market for a new style of merchant banking offering innovative products and services to high-net-worth individuals and the corporate sector at large, especially blue chips. The banking sector was due for an aggiornamento.

I resolved to visit all the established banks to introduce NMB and seek working relationships especially in treasury and money-market operations. After that exercise, I accompanied various officers from the corporate finance and corporate banking departments to visit selected clients to offer our financial services. We invited targeted CEO and FDs of various institutions, banks and government ministries to luncheons at the bank, hosted by the chairman and or me. After a month, we would have our first board meeting followed by an inaugural dinner hosted by the chairman at the Sheraton Hotel in Harare. Vice President Muzenda was the guest of honour.

Preparations for all these tasks were to be effected and underway without delay. Only a monticule to climb compared to the other tasks that lay ahead, I thought. We had assembled a small army of support staff, ordinary 'daily-breaders' but street-wise personal assistants, messengers and drivers led by Radford Ncube, a rather formidable 1.96 m tall ex-police Chief Superintendent with a fuse in inverse proportion to his height when it came to poor performance on the part of his subordinates. Adding members to the clown car was his pet hate. "It guarantees delays sir," he said.

Back at our abode, El Paso, the townhouse that James and I shared and called home for about four months, we would sit in the tiny garden and discuss strategy. James, a half-hearted cruciverbalist, guzzled Olsson lager at an alarming rate and smoked cigarettes. I drank Macallan and occasionally chomped at a Partagas Serie D cigar. At times James would help himself to some Macallan. Over time, I noticed that he had developed a serious affinity for the whisky and hardly touched beer. Once, we invited William and Francis to come by for a drink.

This was an important way of maintaining the team's cohesion and remaining woke to that, in view of recent developments. Initially, William declared his distaste for whisky. However, after little persuasion, he was downing large mouthfuls of Macallan while drawing at a cigarette furiously, emitting huge smoke-rings. "I hate whisky, but this, I like. What is it?" he asked.

I told him that he was, in fact, drinking whisky, Macallan. "No ordinary stuff." We adopted 18 Year Macallan as NMB's mascot drink.

James' cooking skills were put to the test. They were often found wanting in most aspects except baking. He enjoyed baking and managed to produce respectable desserts as well. Occasionally we would sneak into his parents' house in Chisipite suburb and gobble huge meals of peanut butter rice, gravy and vegetables prepared by James' Mum. This soon became an established routine. James and I shared accommodation at El Paso. My mouth still waters when I think of those meals at the Mushore household. James' Father was often quietly inquisitive about our activities at the bank. He was always very encouraging.

One weekend, James asked me whether I still remembered Mbare, especially the neighbourhood where we lived when Dad was a curate at St. Michael's Parish. I confessed that I had no clue where these places were and did not know my way well enough to drive around the Mbare neighbourhoods alone. After breakfast on a Saturday morning, James informed me that he would take me on a tour of the south-western suburbs, beginning the tour from Mbare Market. In jeans and tee-shirt, I jumped into James' car and prepared myself for a day of intrepid discovery.

I was amazed at James's knowledge of the neighbourhoods as he led me through a crowded Mupedzanhamo market, abubble with shoppers and bargain-hunters. We drove around the dilapidated hostels, past Rufaro Stadium, Number One Ground in my youth, through a seething, heaving mass of bodies constituting Mbare Musika. James was in his element. I was scared and lost.

From Mbare Musika, where we bought ground roots and other 'natural forest pulverised concoctions', purportedly aphrodisiacs, we headed towards the Community Centre, Stodart Hall, past Shingirayi School, then St. Michael's Church. Everything appeared a lot smaller than I remembered. It was an emotional return for me. I just could not imagine how we had lived in those tiny houses. The whole infrastructure was badly in need of maintenance. The roads evoked images of Iraqi neighbourhoods after a night of air raids by the American Airforce.

From Mbare we drove past Beatrice Cottages, past the big cemetery, towards Rothmans corner, then to Highfield high density suburb. Once again, everything looked smaller, more unkempt and crowded than I could remember. We drove past Gwanzura Stadium, Machipisa Shopping centre, St. Paul's Anglican Church, then to Marimba Park and Mufakose. On the way, back to the City Centre, we stopped by James's attractively cucurbitaceous Aunt, Mary Govere in Kambuzuma. She operated a renowned Shebeen from her house, popularly known as 'Number 21.' I had never been to a Shebeen before. Auntie Mary was delighted to see us. She ushered us into her beautifully furnished premises redolent of perfume and alcohol, with a tiny, manicured front lawn.

There were two or three rather beguiling young ladies hovering in the entrance/porchway to the main house. Once inside, Aunt Mary offered us, with the eagerness of a beaver, cold beers, girls, or both! Never having been members of the lonely-hearts club, we both opted for cold beers only, without hesitation, equivocation or mental reservation whatsoever. James prodded me hard in the ribs as he muttered under his breath, "Don't be silly." I had requested pilsner instead of the only beers served in such establishments, lion or castle lager. He later explained that I should have known better as this was not a downtown establishment. The point was well taken.

This was an eye-opener, an epiphany, in many ways. We returned to El Paso, tired. It had been a long but fascinating day for me. It left an indelible mark, an astrobleme, on my mind. It gave me a nostalgic glimpse into a part of my childhood, evoking images and memories of times past. This was well apart from knowledge of current, prevailing, living conditions in Harare's high-density suburbs. I still tasted dust on my tongue. We sat on the tiny balcony overlooking the garden and downed whisky while we watched an overcast, darkening sky.

Streaks of lightning soon shimmered menacingly through a flocculent dark grey of heaped clouds in a blustery African thunderstorm. Tenebrific shadows danced on the walls as brilliant flashes of lightning appeared through the windows in the house. A moment later, a boom of thunder rattled the windows, doors and loose floorboards. Suddenly, the heavens opened. The brackish film that covered the sky began to drop as a watery haze covered the city.

The rain fell incessantly in large drops, sharp and penetrating. It inundated the walkways outside El Paso and covered Fourth Street with its innumerable threads which joined heaven and earth. The livid sky threw a wan leaden light over the city. Large areas were now transformed into pools of mud, pricked by needles of flowing silver water that joined the puddles. Everything was grey in this sudden, tropical desolation of nature. Only the roof tops gleamed against the dead tones of the walls around houses and apartment buildings. A symbolically cathartic if perfect end to an eventful day.

I was jolted into tempestuous disbelief when I read in the 'Pink Paper,' The Financial Gazette, on the following Thursday, an account of the banking industry and how 'newcomers are attempting to make waves' as they sought to establish themselves. The article, which shared front page with the ridiculous headline, 'A Goat with Golden Teeth,' was a depressingly shallow, ill-researched piece of malapropic drivel about how it was not possible for local, young entrepreneurs of any description, to compete with established, white-led businesses, especially in the financial sector. This was the worst case of logomachy that I had ever encountered in any writing seeking to describe events in the financial sector of any country.

I had often thought and mused that the 'Teacher in Organ-Pulling Drama' article that I had read on my first trip to Lagos during my time at the World Bank had occupied pride of place and favourite to win the contest of 'Silliest Article.' I had to change my mind. According to this article in the 'Pink Paper,' William, after setting up a similar operation in Ghana, was "spearheading the establishment of a banking institution in Zimbabwe." This, it was claimed, was his brainchild. In this endeavor, he was being, "Assisted by Dr. Julius Makoni from The World Bank."

Utter codswallop! This was clearly false. Efforts to establish the source and origin of the offending article were fruitless. I had my suspicions, which William mendaciously and feebly denied, shamelessly offering no facepalm. The same week, amazingly, excerpts from the said article complete with quotes from William's puerile lucubration, appeared in a local Commercial Farmers Union (CFU) magazine. It was adorned with a mugshot of William in the top left-hand corner. A lesson was learnt. A basic lack of integrity, eventually, proved to be his hamartia.

My Dad once explained to me that sometimes we set our hearts on too many things, some of which conflict with others. Habitual following of a desire leads to that desire having a stronger hold over us with the audacity of a scorpion seating on a testicle, nonchalantly. It is always and will be easier to do what one has previously done than what one has not done; and it is much easier to do what one has always done than what is contrary to what one has done before. We tend to keep on doing what we have done, be it lying, procrastinating or some other habit. When the will is enslaved to desire through habit, he said, desire will, in turn, enslave the mind. To justify itself in satisfying the desire, the will enlists the intellect to provide rationalizations, no matter how feeble. Thus, Dad had spoken. Boy, was he right or what? Case closed.

Time passed. I established a work-routine: 7 a.m. I would be in the office to get ready for the day. I read all the local and foreign press, especially political commentaries, financial and economic reports and the markets in general. I would then go through all my personal mail before tackling bank-related internal and external communications. I had black coffee or sometimes black tea/green tea at 8 a.m. My personal assistant, Edline, was punctual; she came in at 7:45 every morning. I had spotted her reading the weather forecast on television, ZTV, liked the way she spoke, then called the T.V. Studios and asked her to come in for a job interview. We made a good team. She quickly learnt and adopted my work ethic and strict routine. In time, she would organize my itinerary, meals, travel and sometimes my household and transport needs.

Edline quickly worked out that when I was cheerful and gregarious, I liked to have lunch with a couple of my friends in our newly decorated dining room. When I was feeling curmudgeonly and wished to be alone, she would arrange for me to repair to my hermetically sealed private dining quarters where I would dine alone with a good book, my favourite claret on hand. An excellent waiter, the eponymous Wonder, was on hand. Edline often enlisted the services of renowned Chef and restaurateur, Kevin Meyer, to attend to my unconventional culinary excursions. Her fiancé, Elmon, an ex-soccer star, soon became my 'Man Friday.' He did maintenance work around my home and the office. By virtue of her position, Edline, though the youngest and least experienced of the P.A.s, soon established herself as 'de facto' head of secretarial staff and all support staff and services.

Mornings were generally reserved for strategy reviews with my fellow executive directors, committee meetings especially credit, loans and treasury dealings. When it came to committees, I relied heavily on Algy Cluff's theory, repeatedly drummed into me during long lunches at The Stafford, that the best committees are comprised of two people, one of them absent. (I have often wondered what my old teachers/friends, Peter Drucker and John Constable, would have to say about this!) Wednesday afternoons I would receive clients and would go on client visits on Thursday afternoons. Friday morning was the management meeting. We reviewed all facilities and discussed the bank's financing plans especially the utilization of credit lines.

Periodically, I paid surprise visits to the various departments to chat with staff and inspect their working environments for tidiness and attention to tasks. These soon became known as the doctor's rounds. Sartorial solecism, poor personal hygiene and tardiness were not countenanced at all at NMB, by 'the Doc.' This was soon adopted as part of the training and introduction and induction of new staff. Doc's brown bag lunch for excelling staff and selected departments became a feature of the bank's existence. 'The Doc's schmoozy but magisterial apercus clearly inspires widespread emulation among his staff and the youth, generally.,' Robert Marple, a dear friend, was heard to mumble as he wandered in the corridor in search of ablution facilities after a particularly liquid lunch in our dining rooms.

It was not long before NMB was recognized in the market for its unique culture of tidiness, good manners, innovativeness with attention to detail in dealing with clients and distinct dress elegance. Our 'In Pursuit of Excellence' oriflamme and logo atop a long key with the words, "We open doors for you, don't be left behind," became a mantra in the market. James played his part by staffing all our reception areas with young ladies who had that rare combination of being smooth skinned, with beguiling, stunning beauty and intelligence. They all had strict instructions to be courteous and helpful to all visitors. I am not sure how he arranged it, but the system worked well and made for a pleasant work environment.

Every Friday after work, James would be found ensconced behind the bar adjoining the main dining room, serving drinks to non-executive and executive directors, carefully selected clients or people of influence and one or two senior managers. It was not unusual to meet various notable guests sallying forth and navigating erratic routes out of our bar, late on Friday nights. However, notwithstanding the abbreviation of the length of our working days by hours reserved for lunches and Friday drinks, business was still dispatched.

"You may have to ruin your liver to establish yourself in this business," remarked the late Marc Kirkpatrick, formerly Managing Director of M.B.C.A and now one of our non-executive directors. We almost did! Sadly, Marc succumbed to a physical condition caused largely by an excessive reliance on alcohol combined with incessant smoking. He was an excellent, old school, lateral-thinking merchant banker with an underlying Irish-inspired, engaging sense of humour and justice. Marc was good company. His stories assumed ever grotesque dimensions and variations in direct proportion to how much he had imbibed.

This tendency for mythomania was elegantly articulated by the silver-tongued Jesuit priest, Fr. Jim Berry S.J. in his eulogy at Marc's funeral. Fr. Berry recounted Marc's story about a somewhat familiar-looking lady walking her three corgis alongside a golf course fence somewhere near Windsor castle while he was on the putting green! Marc's input, insights and guidance as we set up our banking operations were invaluable.

Things were going swimmingly, or so I thought, until one day I got a call from William just before a board meeting, to say that a lot of the decisions we made required the board's approval and this had not been sought. Some board members, apparently, were upset and would raise this at the upcoming meeting of the board. I smelt a rat immediately and braced myself for an acrimonious meeting. As soon as the meeting started, Israel Ndhlovu, supported by Sam Zumbika and Norman Sachikonye launched into an attack on management's 'extravagance' on luxury vehicles, salaries and allowances.

A motion that I should step aside to allow investigations into the various issues while William assumed my position during the exercise was discussed. Afare Donkor and Malcolmn Pryor immediately jumped to my defense. There ensued a heated and vociferous exchange during which I produced a letter of support from the Minister of Justice, Hon. E.D. Mnangagwa. There was no room for maladroitness. The long meeting ended with an exhausted and exasperated chairman admitting defeat and confirming my position as the Managing Director and CEO. William's motley, thewless crew beat a hasty retreat to cower and lick their wounds.

After the meeting, I followed the chairman to his office on Julius Nyerere Avenue and asked for his immediate resignation. After initially putting up some resistance, I calmly informed him that I would be prepared to expose his irregular 'Hydra Milling' loan and that would see him shamed off the board. I further advised him to decathect himself from William as I intended to put in place measures to protect the bank from future underhand operations. These could impact on his and William's ability to transact in the market. The power of paralipsis was clearly demonstrated. Within ten minutes, I had the chairman's letter of resignation in my hands. I was then the de facto chairman. Back at the office, William stormed into my office and threatened to resign unless I appointed him as the assistant MD ahead of James.

As soon as he finished making his threats, I summoned the head of security and asked him to escort William off the premises. I shouted, "I accept your resignation," as he was frog-marched out of our offices and disappeared for good, to join the ranks of those in uncongenially banausic employment in upcoming new financial institutions. We had, at that time, received information that he was in the process of forming his own financial institution, Trust Bank, with the now former chairman's help, no less.

That evening, James, Afare and I went met with Paddy Zhanda at his residence on Sugarloaf Hill in Glen Lorne. We invited him to be our new chairman. Paddy came highly recommended. He was a well-known, established farmer and businessman who shared a passion for hunting and fishing with James. Paddy accepted the offer. The following morning, James, Afare, I left for Kariba. We spent four restful and thoroughly enjoyable days on a fabulous houseboat, The Kamba.

It was during that restful time on the houseboat that I reflected on the erstwhile chairman's Z.A.N.U, political articles that I had read previously. Utterly puerile lucubrations. With the gift of hindsight, his writings had filled me with insufferable boredom. They were wretched in every way. They resembled echoes of a tiny chapel where the apparent worshippers mumble their prayers, asking news of one another in low voices. Meanwhile, they repeat, with a deeply mysterious air, the common gossip of sexual escapades, political shenanigans, weather forecasts and the state of the nation. He clearly affected pretensions of profundity in some fawning folk, William being a case in point. They saw in him a fount of knowledge and wisdom, a giant of his age. Perhaps he was a well, but to me, one at whose bottom one could not find a drop of water. His appointment as chairman will forever be a matter of regret.

Chapter Twenty

TIME PASSED. I was firmly at the helm of this avant garde, leading edge, banking operation. Undisputed bossdom for now. "The guiding spirit" had to evince leadership qualities including genius, innovation and drive. I had to assess and understand the unique qualities and challenges of every member of my staff and act accordingly to make for the best team effort and harmonious, effective and successful enterprise. Within three years, we had about four hundred staff in our employ and had opened thriving branches in Harare, Bulawayo, Gweru and Mutare. A strong NMB brand was now well established locally.

We had shown ourselves to be a team of trailblazers who could think out of the box and structure innovative solutions for clients: we shortened the average time that it took for banks to produce letters of credit from thirty days to less than an hour. This could be done while clients waited and enjoyed a cup of tea and our hospitality; we invented and introduced Grain Bills to restructure the Grain marketing Board's balance sheet, allowing it to finance grain purchases while simultaneously providing paper which could be traded in the market; we structured the first financial lease to enable Cluff's Freda Rebecca Mine to purchase equipment including water pumps, drilling tools and special purpose vehicles, among others; we did the first gold loans and currency swaps by a local institution, for the Reserve Bank, advised and listed Econet, now a major operator in telecommunications.

Externally, we had established correspondent banking relationships with international banks including Citibank, Bankers Trust, Merrill Lynch, NatWest, Barclays International, Deutsche Bank, Commerzbank, BHF, BNP Paribas, West LB., Société General, American Express, ABN AMRO, Rabobank, ING. and the South African Banks. Lines of credit at our disposal amounted to about $500 million. Francis and I would visit these banks at least twice a year to apprise them of our operations, plans and application of lines of credit. This also entailed a discussion of the political and regulatory environment in which we operated. This became increasingly difficult as time passed since we found ourselves in the invidious position of defending the country's then 'enfant terrible' macroeconomic policies and RBZ measures that we challenged back home.

We had to make our case and tell our story featly. Issues such as the then government's land reform and indigenization initiatives were particularly difficult to defend, let alone allegations of electoral fraud, amongst others. This was always a Sisyphean task. Some visiting bankers from Zimbabwe, we were often told, had an obsequious deference to the Government and often told a story different to ours. Meetings with analysts, especially in London, provided opportunities for us to discuss the bank's position contextually and enjoy some heartsome lunches organized by our publicist/P.R. advisors, College Hill, in the City.

On one of our trips, Francis and I, after grueling meetings in London, Paris, Frankfurt, Dusseldorf and Amsterdam, decided to take a couple of days break in Zurich before meetings with Credit Bank, Swiss Bank Corporation and UBS, our Swiss correspondent banks. We had, by now established a strong and extensive network of friends in Zurich especially. Instead of our usual accommodation at Zum Storchen Hotel, we decided to stay at Eden au Lac. We checked in and promptly headed for the hotel restaurant for lunch. We were exhausted and famished. From the moment we arrived at the hotel, we noticed that we were very much objects of a certain curiosity and attention. We thought nothing of it until we ordered our lunch at which Francis, making good a promise he had made to me after losing a bet, ordered a bottle of 1973 Chateau Haut Brion.

Soon, the hotel staff were hovering at our table offering services we had not requested and bending over backwards to accommodate our every whim. Only later did we discover that the legendary singer and musician, Tina Turner and her entourage were staying at the hotel. I had been mistaken for her male companion/husband, possibly Ike Turner, while Francis was seen as a member of the band. We were not in a hurry to correct their erroneous belief. We thus managed to meet with the coquettish Ms. Turner and shared afternoon tea with her. She cracked up with laughter when we told her the story of how we had been received at the hotel.

The following day, our friend from Credit Suisse, Jean-Jacques Guinand, his wife and daughter, took us round the market in Zurich and bought Francis and I large boxes of delicious chocolates to take home. We drove to Hohle Gasse to enjoy Swiss hospitality in a fine restaurant in the place where, legend has it, William Tell performed his many exploits, notably, shooting Gessler with an arrow off his crossbow. Jean-Jacques treated us to a day of champagne, Swiss wines, fine seafood and delicious chocolate.

After lunch, we visited The Monastery of Einsiedeln on the Way of St. James. This, despite the constant threat of hyetal precipitation in the region, is a breath-taking baroque monastery with a statue of The Black Madonna in the Chapel. A crowd of tourists and pilgrims stood or knelt in awe and adoration as a group of monks in black habits and scapulae stopped their procession and sang the Salve Regina in front of the Black Madonna, in several voices. A reverie-like, deeply moving, numinous and memorable madeleine moment to end a perfect day in the Swiss countryside.

Later that evening, our local friends, Hilda, Benno, Gabriela, Fernando, a manqué banker and one or two others, took us to dinner at the FIFA Head Quarters' impressive Sonnenberg restaurant. The king crab lobster pannacotta soup and local fish dishes were exquisite, as were the fantastic views of the lake and the city. Fresh, aged Partagas Serie D cigars recently flown in from Havana and delicious champagne brandy were the order of the post-dinner fare. Just after midnight, we adjourned to a lush night club and danced away.

Whilst I was twisting, turning and gyrating to soulful tunes, around three in the morning, a petite blonde came in front of me. A cute, adorable messan, I thought. She rolled her hips sensually, undulating her curvy butt 'ad absurdum' as if performing a skillful glissade in the alps, winked sexily, smiled, then, as quickly as she had appeared, snatched my spectacles off my face and sped out into the darkness. I tried to give chase, but the recent carousing and culinary excursions had taken a decidedly negative toll on my body. I gave up after a few seconds. Neither Francis nor any of our friends noticed anything as they were all otherwise engaged in the noisy club. I hailed a taxi and retired to the hotel. Fortuitously, I had a spare pair in my case. I now carry a spare pair of spectacles wherever I go.

As we bid our fond farewells to a couple of friends at the airport, we realized that Jean-Jacques Guinand, who was a senior Managing Director at Credit Suisse, was watching us. He was accompanied by his wife. With a saucy smile and a twinkle in his eye, he informed us that he had booked himself on our Swiss Air flight to Harare, via Johannesburg. He had meetings in South Africa, he said. We almost died of embarrassment when we discovered that he was booked in Business Class while we were in First Class.

This was all rather too much for Francis who forgot to check in his recent purchases of sharp, Swiss hunting knives. The scanning machines suddenly lit up and came to life with bursts of deafening screeches. An army of athletic, muscular soldiers armed to the teeth rushed and pounced on a bewildered Francis as he made his way through the screeners nonchalantly. Eventually, after listening to Mr. Guinand's explanation, Francis was released, much to our relief. His 'weapons' were confiscated, and a stern warning was all he got. We sheepishly thanked Jean-Jacques, yet again, as we boarded our flight. We promptly disappeared into our cabin and crawled into our beds, tails between our legs. We dined out on this trip for many months.

As we wrote more business, it became clear that we would soon need to increase our capital and grow the balance sheet substantially. This was 1997. We had been open for business as a bank for four years now. James, Francis and I discussed this matter over drinks and decided to advise the Board that we needed to raise more capital by way of issuing more shares and listing the bank. In addition, we would apply for a commercial banking license so that we could take deposits from the public at large, expand our client base and offer a wider range of banking services. As a new idea, I suggested the idea of listing the bank on a European Stock Exchange since we financed trade between Zimbabwe and European countries.

We also had lines of credit with major European and American banks. We discussed the idea of listing on the Johannesburg Stock Exchange as well. The only African bank that was then listed outside of its home country, at that time, was INVESTEC, which had recently reversed into a listed shell company on the London Stock Exchange. We settled for a dual, 'full frontal' listing on the Zimbabwe and London Stock Exchanges. Understandably, the Board received our idea with animated disbelief. Though they did not fall into it like a vat of melted chocolate, they lent it their full support after hearing us out and much discussion. That turned out to be the easy part. I was about to witness epistemic closure in the extreme.

My first stop was New York, where my old friend Robin Brooks had put together a small team comprising herself, Bill Hickman and Craig Keshishian. These were well-connected bankers with experience in the capital markets. They liked my idea. We put to-gether a plan which comprised their British contacts including a prominent corporate finance, merger and acquisitions lawyer, Mi-chael Steinfeld from the law firm, Titmuss, Sainer and Dechert L.L.P and John Durlacher, an independent corporate finance con-sultant with offices near St. Paul's Cathedral in London.

Robin organized a lunch with some Fund managers, including Malcolmn Pryor and representatives from Morgan Stanley and Ci-tibank. The idea of listing NMB was well-received by the would-be investors who liked the idea of a secondary London listing. From New York, I flew to Washington DC where I met with John Niepold, an emerging markets fund manager, Alemayehu Mengistu and Tei Mante from the IFC and several other friends, including David Gill and Jay Tata. They were all supportive of my plans.

In London, I was joined by James and Francis. We stayed at the Langham Hilton, which had now become our 'home from home.' Robin, Craig and Bill joined us a day later as we got down to the business at hand. Our first port of call was to see Michael Steinfeld and his junior partner, Alex Reid. We agreed that Michael and his firm would provide all the corporate financial and legal work re-quired by the London Stock Exchange. John Durlacher helped us by compiling a shortlist of six firms to approach for the role of lead listing banker and agent. Craig, Francis, Robin, Alex Reid and I vis-ited these firms over the next three days to interview their teams, tell our story and rank them in terms of their assessed competence. We would also assess their pitch to us, market savvy and other rel-evant factors.

They all scored highly in terms of entertainment, but the Société General team led by Andrew Dawber and the colourful stockbroker, Tony Mahalski, scored highest marks on all counts. They were ap-pointed as the lead banker. Their first task would be to prepare a prospectus. By this time, James had returned to Harare to supervise the local team in meeting the ZSE requirements, accounting and legal reports and Reserve Bank approvals. Our own Corporate Finance team would oversee all the local work needed to ensure a successful listing. The team was led by James, assisted by Patterson Timba, Tawanda Nyambirai who had recently joined us from the law firm, Kantor and Immerman and Otto 'Kwete Kwete' Chekeche, our Chief Finance Officer.

In Harare, preparations were well underway. One crucial approval, from the Reserve Bank, however, was proving increasingly difficult to obtain. Numerous meetings with RBZ officers did not yield the results we wanted, so I decided to escalate the issue by requesting an urgent meeting with the then new Governor of the RBZ, Dr. Leonard Tsumba. This turned out to be a marathon meeting during which the bespectacled Governor and his cohorts decried my idea to list the bank in London as a ruse, a ploy to transfer funds from Zimbabwe to overseas destinations.

Furthermore, this would open the banking sector to foreigners whose motives were not always in accordance with the country's development plans. "This could even spark a crisis akin to the Peso Crisis," said one of the Governor's men. I gently pointed out, trying hard not to sound deprecating or contemptuous, that the crisis he referred to was a currency crisis. His analysis was, at best, circumferential, far removed from issues surrounding a public share offering on the local Stock Exchange.

For good measure, I added that the RBZ's position was akin to mistaking obesity for pregnancy. This was met with a stony silence. You could cut through the tension with a blunt knife. My heart sank to my boots when the erstwhile Governor asked me to prepare a paper justifying my position since the Ministry of Finance's nod was needed in this matter. I evacuated myself from the Governor's office two hours later, eviscerated and bedraggled. Although I kept it to myself, it was my strong feeling that the Governor and his team were both benighted and stupid. Any discerning person could have read my body language unmistakably. James, Francis and I sat in my office late in the night. We consumed copious amounts of alcoholic beverages. Our world had just collapsed around us. Talk of things falling apart. I would cerebrate on my own to eliminate the conundrum. I had reached my nadir.

First thing in the morning, I found myself striding from my office purposefully, turning into Samora Machel Avenue at Barclays Bank Pearl House, then single-mindedly heading due west for Korner House, a couple of blocks away. I was seething. I remembered what Professor F.M. Scherer wrote about the interface between regulation and competition: "The Supreme Power who conceived gravity, supply and demand, and the double helix must have been absorbed elsewhere when (market) regulation was invented. The system is cumbersome, vulnerable to incompetence, and prone toward becoming ingrown and co-opted. In some respects, it is directly conducive to inefficiency; in others, it may be merely ineffective in altering the behavior of (those) regulated."

He clearly had the RBZ in mind, I mused as I sat outside Justice Minister Emmerson Mnangagwa's office. I needed a shoulder to cry on. I had, by now, developed an excellent relationship and rapport with him. We met for dinner at least once a month. I needed his advice on the situation we found ourselves in.

The Minister listened to me attentively as I explained the ridiculous and erroneous view espoused by the RBZ that listing the bank in London encouraged capital flight from the country and made it possible for foreigners to invest in our banking institutions. I pointed out that the country had embarked on an economic structural adjustment programme which entails liberalization of the economy and encouraged foreign direct investment, among other things. Listing the bank would enable us to bring funds into the country, rather than the opposite. This would enhance the bank's capacity to underwrite more business and improve our product offering. "If the RBZ says that this is a ploy to steal money," he asked, "whose money are they referring to? Imari ya ambuya wa Governor

here?" (Does the money belong to the Governor's grandmother?).
He promptly sprang to his feet, and reached for his phone.

"Is that the Governor?" he asked gently. "NMB wants to list the
bank in London. This is good for our country. They have a tight
timetable. Please assist them." He slammed the phone down. I was
not sure how this would play out. I thanked him profusely and left
for my office, apprehensive.

As soon as I got to my office, a visibly flustered Edline, my P.A.,
informed me breathlessly that the office phone had been ringing off
the hook and the RBZ Governor had demanded that I go to see him
without delay. My heart jumped into my mouth as I sheepishly
headed along First Street, towards the RBZ building which now
looked quite austere and cruel. Should be known as The Reverse
Bank, I muttered under my breath. My shoes crumped heavily on
the gravelly approach to the RBZ's heavily guarded entrance. I fully
expected the Governor to objurgate me. Inside, the Governor ushered me into his office and warned me sternly against "seeking
political assistance to intimidate him."

"Anyways, my friend, your application has just been approved.
It is ready for you to take away with you. I wanted to hand it to you
personally. Good luck," he panted.

With a skull grin, he walked me to the door and slammed it shut
as soon as I left his office. I was gob smacked, as was everyone else
back in the office. A clear case of oblivescence on the Governor's
part, I explained to my colleagues, omitting to mention my early
morning tête-à-tête with Minister Mnangagwa. When it came to
dealing with NMB, I always felt that the RBZ's attitude was nothing
short of intersectionality: an entrepreneurially led indigenous bank,
the first of its kind, created a conundrum for them. The RBZ represented the unacceptable face of beadledom. Enough said.
Nevertheless, we got down to work immediately as we arranged for
Andrew Dawber's team from Société Générale, London, to come to
Zimbabwe and start preparing a prospectus for the listing.

For the next fortnight, we all worked round the clock to prepare for the much anticipated, dreaded, verification meeting. "Ergophobia is not an option," was our mantra. James and I worked closely with Andrew Dawber and his team. We managed to have a draft Prospectus ready within five days. The second week saw the arrival of Michael Steinfeld, whose associate, Alex Reid, had already been working with us and the Soc. Gen. team. Michael's arrival coincided with the arrival of the LSE's appointed representative law firm, Berwin Leighton Paisner LLP. The two London-based law firms would have long meetings with the two local lawyers, Dick Turpin of Turpin and Miller, Tony Eastwood and Tawanda Nyambirayi from Kantor and Immerman.

Teams from KPMG London and Zimbabwe were also hovering, sifting through submitted financial information. The process was hectic. Last to arrive was the American team comprising Robin Brooks, Craig Keshishian and Bill Hickman. We had a full house. The entire fourth floor was taken up by geeky lawyers, accountants and analysts. Our own in-house team never appeared overwhelmed as they came under scrutiny. They were clearly well trained and equipped for the exercise. It was apparent that they certainly were not in need of moxie and dedication.

The verification meeting began at 8:00 a.m. in our boardroom. Before the meeting started, the Chairman informed me that two directors had resigned as they did not want to go through the verification process which entailed the scrutiny of directors' birth and educational certificates, curriculum vitae and other details. This had to be communicated to the august gathering. Thereafter, it was the painstaking process of scrutinizing and verifying the authenticity of all claims, verbal and printed, in the prospectus.

This persisted for the next eight hours without a break. Fortunately, by 6 p.m., all parties had reached agreement. They were satisfied that the information contained in the prospectus was accurate, met all regulatory requirements and would not lead to legal challenges when the document was published. After the meeting, we all repaired to the bar for well-deserved drinks. Generous helpings of beef and seafood sandwiches followed by an amazing gastronomic experience, courtesy of our celebrated chef, Kevin Meyer, who was always at pains to remind us that 'Excess destroys the essence of pleasure,' were the order of the day.

We worked through the weekend to proof-read and finalize the prospectus. We prepared for the road show to launch our prospectus to investors locally, in Harare, followed by New York, Washington and London. Our Marketing department ably managed by Lyn Mortimer-Lutz who, with Liz Oosthuizen, who ran the Human Resources department, organized a gathering of all the fund-managers, analysts and other market players at the Borrowdale racecourse. We launched our prospectus on the Thursday evening with a fanfare. I outlined our future strategy as a bank and explained where we would be after the capital injection. By all accounts and from the subsequent support we received, our story was well-received.

The next evening, I was back on the BA flight to London, then boarded the Concorde to Washington to meet with analysts and fund managers and to deliver our prospectus. In New York, it was the same exercise. Morgan Stanley hosted the gathering of analysts. We had a successful launch before flying back to London for another round of meetings with various funds. The meetings culminated in a dinner organized by College Hill, at the Guildhall. Our prospectus was well-received. It was voted the best on the ZSE. It was set down as a benchmark for future similar endeavours.

Thus, 1997 turned out to be the landmark year when NMB Holdings was listed on the ZSE and was simultaneously admitted to the Official List of the London Stock Exchange. The public offer was 4.5 and twice oversubscribed in Zimbabwe and London, respectively. Eighteen months later, the bank was granted a commercial banking license. The then Chairman of the Zimbabwe

Stock Exchange, Mark Tunmer, described the newly listed bank in inevitably agreeable Aesopian language as, 'The Tiger Woods of banks in Zimbabwe.' The Chairman of the London Stock Exchange was equally gracious in his praise of what we had achieved in listing the bank. He treated our team to an excellent lunch at the LSE to mark this capstone event in the bank's evolution.

The huge success of our public offering put us in a strong position to write more business and to expand our banking operations, but we also wanted to keep ahead of all the other banks. Put simply, we just wanted to be outstanding, second to none. For six years or so since our listing, we won several awards including Euromoney's awards for excellence in various sectors and best bank overall in Africa. These accolades came with demands for more visits to correspondent banks further afield to include the Netherlands, Mauritius, South Africa and Italy to add to the established routine visits to Frankfurt, Mainz and Dusseldorf, Paris, London, New York and Washington D.C.

We were now on 'everyone's' menu for directorships, advisory services and speaking engagements. 'Fiddle foots' became our nickname. We decided to grow our financial leasing business, international money transfers and regional advisory services. We assisted to establish and took a small shareholding in a new bank in Mozambique. We took up advisory services mandates on projects in South Africa, Tunisia, Angola, Zambia, Ghana, Kenya and Nigeria, among others. We worked hard, basked in the glory and adulation, but always were cognizant of the reality that markets have no lenity. We therefore had to stay ahead of the game. Success was no berceuse for us, it spurred us on.

Staff training, development and welfare were paramount. We enlisted the help of a Washington-based consultant, Michael Whelan, who trained World Bank Group staff to improve and standardize report writing and presentations. Like all staff in Washington, I had benefited from a week-long course with him. His courses were mandatory for all staff. Michael did an excellent job with our staff. Our reports, publications and presentations were acclaimed to be different and second to none in the country. Our weekly economic commentary, NMB Notes, published by our economics department, outlined the country's prospects and news from around the bank. It featured my weekly column on various topics such as inflation, the term structure of interest rates, monetary and fiscal policies. "NMB Notes" became a staple in the president's office and the RBZ. I have often wondered how much of what we published was really taken to heart. I enjoyed writing my lead, editorial column.

Our Human Resources Department had arranged ongoing staff training throughout the bank. All staff had to go through an orientation week. I would get to meet them and introduce them to the bank and its culture including our peculiar dress code which entailed uniforms for the ladies, smart suits for all men from Monday to Friday. Friday as a dress-down day for all. The highlight of the year would be the staff Christmas dinner. This was generally in one of the hotels or golf club houses around Harare. Troutbeck, Nyanga and Leopard Rock were favourites.

On one such occasion, we held our year-end party at Chapman Golf Course and danced to the lively music of the Police Band. The saxophonist, Givemore Masinyane, invited me to play the saxophone with him on the song, "I wish I knew how it would feel to be free." I did, much to the amazement of my staff. I then played the electric bass on a version of 'Fever.' This kindly received an ovation which almost brought the roof down.

One bystander said, "They are only dancing because you are the boss.... Admittedly," she carried on, "you do play well." I simply smiled and bowed three times to acknowledge and appreciate the wild applause.

The World Bank's ESAP was well underway but now creaking under the weight of the prescribed measures. The government's resolve was beginning to buckle. New institutions had sprouted in the economy, notably new indigenous banks. NMB was now well established and in its wake, came other small financial institutions including Metropolitan Bank, Genesis Bank, Time Bank, Trust Merchant Bank, Heritage Bank, Royal Bank, Barbican Bank, Inter-Market Discount House, Tetrad, Universal Bank, CFX, ENG Capital, United Merchant Bank, Interfin and Renaissance Merchant Bank, among others.

In a nutshell, the liberalization of the economy entailed significant changes in the structure of the country's banking sector. It also ushered in a credit boom in which loans were issued without proper risk assessment or appropriately valued collateral. As monetary policy tightened to curtail the consequent high bouts of inflation at this time, there was an overall reduction in aggregate demand which caused a slowdown in economic activity.

This was a financial crisis in the making, fueled by gross irregularities in the form of breakdowns in corporate governance practices, abuse of group structures, technical insolvency and widespread misuse of borrowed and depositors' funds. All this played out with weak regulatory arrangements, bureaucratic procrastination and incompetence as the overall environmental framework. Eventually, this resulted in a sector-wide debacle, depletion in the capital base of many banks. NMB and most of the established, well-managed banks, survived this debacle, to this day.

As I write these memoirs, I become increasingly conscious that while we live life looking forward we generally understand it looking back. As we live from day to day, our life can seem like a meaningless sequence of random events, a series of accidents and happenstances that have no shape or inner logic. A traffic jam makes us late for an important meeting. A stray remark we make offends someone in a way we never intended. By a hair's breadth we fail to get the job we so sought. I have come to realize that life as we experience it can sometimes feel like Joseph Heller's definition of history as "a trash bag of random coincidences blown open in a wind."

Yet looking back, it begins to make sense. The opportunities I missed along the way have led to even better ones now. The shame one felt at one's unintentionally offensive remarks from time to time have made one more careful about what one says in the future. Failures, seen in retrospect many years later, have turned out to have been deepest learning experiences. It is now clearer to me that my hindsight has always been more perceptive than my foresight. I have come to accept that we do indeed live life facing the future, but we understand life only when it has become our past.

Chapter Twenty-One

AS THE BANK GREW, issues such as succession planning, future expansion and direction of growth began to loom large in our corporate strategy and planning. I always believed that any good leader had to challenge the assumptions of value creation constantly, for the sake of the shareholders, employees and other stakeholders. With regards to succession planning, I believe, firmly, just like others, that it is a travesty to appoint both the Chairman and CEO from outside. The Chairman and CEO should not only understand the business but also all the senior people in it. A poor signal is necessarily transmitted to staff when it is made clear to them that an existing employee can never aspire to one of the top jobs in the business. Equally, investors, I think, would wonder why a company would need to do something which apparently shows no faith in its own management, such as conducting an external search every time a vacancy occurs. Another lesson from Algy.

Never being one to be limited by other people's imaginations and with the firm belief that I would rather regret any risks that would not work out eventually, than the chances that I did not take at all, I flew to the U.K. to spend time with the master of corporate strategy, my mentor, supervisor and director on the bank's board, Prof. John Constable, at 20 Kimbolton Road, Bedford. John's elegantly beautiful wife, Liz, was always on hand to bring us down to earth especially when John got into a huff after I had won at golf. We sat in their manicured garden behind Bedford School and explored the options available to the bank in our quest for growth. Just as he did when I was his Doctoral candidate, John was succinct in his approach as he took me back to basics.

We had to analyze, try to appreciate and understand a lot of the things that we now took for granted, he advised. This included our competitive opportunities and threats. We then had to assess our own growth capabilities. Secondly, we should then articulate sound strategic growth plans, identify, evaluate and prioritize growth opportunities and craft new high potential business lines. Finally, we would have to improve the connection between our growth strategy and execution by aligning our resources and improving our delivery processes. A combination of organic growth where we would grow by increasing our 'output,' customer base expansion and new product development combined with inorganic growth, especially acquiring selected targets in the financial sector, was the way to go.

Time spent with John and Liz was always extra special to me. Theirs was one household where I could truly relax and be myself. John and Liz left me to 'house sit,' after a week with them. They often went on walking holidays in Devon. I used this time to work on my project in the still depths of the night as light rains fell on the windows overlooking the garden. Bliss. By the time they returned, a week later, my thoughts had crystallized. I had hatched a plan.

I had, in the meantime, recruited my trusted lieutenant from Bankers Trust days, Cephas Takavarasha and a recent acquaintance, Lynn Zhandire. Tawanda Nyambirayi vouched for Lynn. She had been an intern at their previous law firm, Kantor and Immerman. I knew Cephas to be a brilliant analyst. I trusted Tawanda's judgement that Lynn could deliver satisfactorily on the legal review of our processes that I had in mind. Neither of them disappointed. I went through my plans with John. He gave his full support and endeavoured to get the other non-executive directors on board.

By the time I left Bedford, the ball was rolling. Cephas and Lynn were hard at work in our offices in Unity Court. Cephas was attached to my office, Lynn worked in Tawanda's Legal and Corporate Finance Division. While Lynn set about reviewing our legal structures and processes, Cephas set about reviewing, analyzing and prioritizing acquisition targets which included Bard Discount House, Standard Chartered Bank and MBCA. They were both tasked with producing epigrammatic reports 'sine mora.' We considered new product lines and settled for leasing and global money remittances.

Value creation was indeed at the heart of our chosen options: Bard Discount House would enhance our ability to expand our Treasury and especially money market operations; Standard Chartered would avail us an extensive, established branch network and deposit base, not to mention new clients and staff; MBCA would enhance our Corporate financial services delivery, give depth to our team and introduce new clients while giving us a link into some of their external shareholders, notably Nedbank, Rothschilds and Medio Banca.

The new business lines would complement all the mainstream banking business and add a differentiating dimension to set the bank apart from the rest of the pack. The missing link was a London office, preferably with a deposit taking license and ideally a full banking license, to take full advantage of our London listing. That would complete the jig saw and create a formidable financial institution, the first of its kind in Africa and beyond, immortalizing our oriflamme, *'In Pursuit of Excellence.'*

Back in Harare, I sat in my back garden, one Saturday afternoon, working my way through a bottle of Chateau Margaux, strumming tunes on Wah Wah, my electric guitar. Tossing in my head was the whole concept of value creation in the theory of the firm and its place in corporate strategy formulation in the context of the exercise that was now at hand. Since value creation involves both a supply side and a demand side, I reasoned, bringing it into the Theory of the Firm debate surely also explicitly brings in an ethical dimension.

Through their creation of value supply and demand, firms should be and most probably are, to a large extent, responsible for the norm-setting in society. Therefore, I mused further, rather than a peripheral issue, the relationship between economic and ethical values becomes a central issue to account for in any credible theory of the firm. As my mind wandered and meandered, assisted by the 'draught of vintage,' 'the true, the blushful Hippocrene,' which was sending me 'Lethe-wards,' I jumped and came to my senses at the sound of a familiar voice greeting me in rather charming, dulcet tones.

"I knew we'd find you here. Do you have any more of that wine?" This was Ruth Bakare. She was accompanied by her daughter, Tinao and a companion, on vacation from the U.K. Ruth was set to take up the post of Assistant Manager in our Mutare branch. Her husband, Sebastian was to be the next Anglican Bishop of Manicaland. Tinao, who happened to have been a friend of Lynn Zhandire's, had finished her law degree at Leeds University and was going to take up a new job with a wealth management firm in the Channel Islands. Our paths had crossed previously, through mutual friends.

We sat in the garden beneath the Natal mahogany and sipped away at more of the same vintage. I set aside a couple of bottles of Dornfelder Cabernet Sauvignon for the visitors to take away. This would remind them of their German roots. I found it difficult to take my eyes off the charmingly beguiling Tinao as she threw knowing and amused glances in my direction. Beads of sweat trickled down my back as I bade them goodbye after a good hour. I mumbled something about Tinao's stunning looks, obviously inherited from Ruth. She walked like a model, I added, much to the chagrin of her companion, I learnt, years later. I was, probably, visibly smitten. The rest, as they say, is history.

As my visitors left, another, unannounced, but welcome visitor showed up and headed to the garden furniture now replete with empty bottles and well-used wine glasses. Dr. Herbert Murerwa, who had just been appointed the Minister of Finance, made himself comfortable as he selected a suitably luscious cigar from my humidor and sucked away as he quaffed a generous helping of Armagnac.

Pure serendipity it was. This was an ideal moment to narrate my plans to the Minister in an agreeable environment. His support would be vital in what we had decided to put in place especially in view of Leonard Tsumba's impending departure from the RBZ. The word from the mealie patch was that one Gideon Gono, then CEO of CBZ, may be the next Governor.

The erstwhile Minister would not confirm the word from the mealie patch, but listened intently, with all the coolness of an iceberg lettuce. He assured me of his support. I must admit to feeling a little like a Rasputin figure, forever whispering ideas and recommendations into the Minister's ear. Nevertheless, as was now customary, Lazarus Murahwa and Arthur Mutsonziwa dropped in for 'a couple of toots.' This was our impromptu monthly 'hoot.' We called it our 'hootenanny,' our meet to drink, play and sing old tunes.

The gathering turned into a full-blown party that raged on as we carried on till way past midnight. This was fueled by more wine, cognac, whisky, barbecued Mozambique tiger prawns, salmon, steak and pork chops. There was some discussion of our plans which were, inevitably fantasticated as the evening wore on and progressively blurred in the haze of spirituous liquor and the impromptu concert. I strummed the guitar and double bass. Arthur took to the microphone and gave us a rather Goldilocks rendition of 'City Girls,' 'Unchained melody' and 'Hey Joe.' Herbert and I did our best to keep our respective instruments in time with Arthur's vocal exertions. The concert would not have been complete without the gathering belting out a tutti rendition of 'Wild Thing' to add a frisson to the impromptu do. The neighbours were quietly gracious. They raised no complaints, apart from the odd comment, days later.

We had Sunday to recover and face the world again. Monday saw our 'In Pursuit of Excellence' motif back to the fore. I was back at my desk with Cephas seated in front of me. Michael Porter's 'Generic Strategies' and 'Five Forces Analysis' were the order of the day. We analyzed our situation and options available. After much discussion, we concluded that we were on the most viable, optimal path in our choice of strategy. We were joined by the rest of the team led by Tawanda and Lynn. They presented their findings, which were positive and in line with our wishes and expectations.

This exercise necessarily had to go beyond a simple mechanical assessment of action and reaction. At times, I mused that the complex psychology of fringe beliefs, such as ufology, were not far removed from some of the mental gymnastics we often engaged in in the corporate world. Nevertheless, it all almost always added up and proved worthwhile homework and preparation. Clearly, nowhere near an aberration. Certainly, well worth the effort and an excellent discipline to boot.

The next steps, formal and specific Board and regulatory approvals would be a foregone conclusion, or so we all expected. Our plans would lead to a stronger institution, more jobs, larger credit lines to finance exports and other business requirements for our clients, among other positive results. All these were opportunities and developments that the Government was promoting as part of the Economic Structural Adjustment Programme (ESAP.) instituted by the World Bank and embraced by Zimbabwe then. Did we have enough knowledge of the present, based on experience, to predict the future in terms of the Authorities' attitude to our plans? For now, we had partial knowledge of the future, based on present and past facts, but essentially, the future was still shrouded in uncertainty. Daunting though the task was, I decided to lead the team full speed ahead, prepared to overcome any obstacles that we could possibly encounter.

The first port of call was the Reserve Bank, a new Governor, Gideon Gono now at the helm. I had met Gideon in my World Bank days, on a visit to Harare. I visited the Zimbabwe Development Bank's then Managing Director, Rindai Jaravaza. Gideon was the company secretary then before he rose to head the resurgent CBZ, formerly Bank of Credit and Commerce International. In that capacity, I met him very briefly, once or twice but never really connected at any level. He hounded me for a copy of my doctoral thesis as he claimed to be interested in multinational corporate strategies and international finance. I referred him to the university library for assistance. Whenever I could, I phubbed him. Francis told me that he was a budding entrepreneur who had borrowed money from NMB to fund his business ventures. I took him to be an ordinary, innocuous, living monument to ineptitude, trying to earn a crust like all of us. Rough around the edges, I thought.

After hearing of his life story and humble beginnings as a messenger and teaboy, the penny dropped. Nothing to do with rumours off the mealie patch, that he was part of a cabal that were peculating funds from CBZ with the RBZ's connivance. I saw him sitting on the floor in Francis' office, one day. He was begging for an extension of his loan which he was struggling to pay back. I remarked, in jest, and retrospectively, poor judgement, that he would always be the garden boy that he was. We all laughed.

That statement would come back to haunt me. I had stirred, unwittingly, a deep-seated truth that hit a raw nerve sitting on a toxic cocktail of insecurity, vindictiveness and envy in the inner recesses of the man's psyche. This was someone who would happily make a tzimmes over the slightest mistake or at the first opportune moment to his own advantage or in pursuit of vengeance. A real-life, benighted, Machiavellian villain straight out of an awful, West African/ Nollywood, seriocomic satire. My every paseo, down memory lane, of the few encounters I had with the man are always particularly excruciating in the extreme. Just the sort of being whose head I used to love to busticate into a thousand pieces, in my karate days.

The Governor listened to our strategy and expansion plans, with a stupid grin all the while plastered across his face. He leered at me. He promised, as best as he could, to lend his support to our applications when submitted. Curiously, he pointed out rather ominously, that in such cases, 'the junior staff' must be allowed to make independent assessments based on the merits of each application. He himself would try not to influence their decisions unduly. How different from his predecessor, the strangely behindhand yet astute Governor, Kombo Moyana. The latter thought through any proposal, raised awkward questions but always helped come up with a solution. Once he was satisfied that a proposal was sound, he gave his support unequivocally and everyone would know about it. He never hid behind a finger nor took refuge behind 'junior staff'. Every time I entered or left the new Governor's office, I got the creeps. I almost always broke into a cold sweat.

At a bankers' meeting called by the Governor a fortnight later, I sat next to Mthuli Ncube, founder of Barbican Bank. Mthuli and I got on well. We shared many interests and had friends in common, especially at INVESTEC, South Africa where he had spent time working in their corporate finance department. Mthuli and I shared similar views about the new regime at the RBZ. We were also less than diplomatic at airing these views. We sat stone faced as we listened to Mr. Gono outline his 'vision' and programme for his term in office. Absolutely sonorous, prolix nonsense issuing from a totally unsound mind, I mused. The drivel rested comfortably on a toxic bulwark of narcissism and unfamiliarity with the subject. This was the view shared and aired by the gathered bankers. Most were visibly irritated by the Governor's thinly veiled threats which were received with sounds of disbelief and disapproval.

The ensuing question and answer session turned into a circus as we piled into the erstwhile Governor and bombarded him with questions that he could hardly answer. He was clearly clueless about his role, let alone his vision for the economy. The deputy governors had to intervene and called an end to the hostilities as the de-feathered RBZ officials beat a retreat from the meeting room. Mthuli and I walked past little groups of mumbling new bankers who, thanks to the ESAP, had tended to pullulate in a rather disquieting proportion. We headed across Samora Machel Avenue, to the sanctuary of sanity that was the NMB bar.

It was clear after that meeting that the financial sector, if not the whole economy, was approaching turbulent times marked by major disruption and confusion at the RBZ. Misguided, bull-in-China shop policies were likely to be the order of the day for the foreseeable future. We had to gird our loins. As Mthuli and I emerged from behind the RBZ's grand doors facing Samora Machel Avenue, we observed a 'street kid' relieving himself on the Bank's wall. We looked at each other, chuckled and agreed that the boy had selected an appropriate target.

I needed to take a break from the hectic developments. A welcome opportunity knocked at my door as I received an invitation from my friend Zenani Mandela, to be one of her escorts at her father's eightieth birthday party in Johannesburg. I had met Zenani (Zeni) and her family on their two visits in Harare, in the recent past. She was married to a member of the Swazi Royal family. I flew into Johannesburg on a Thursday afternoon and went straight to the Saxon Hotel where a palatial suite had been reserved for me. That afternoon, I pampered myself with a pedicure, facial and body massage which left me fast asleep, reminiscent of the memorable thriller of a massage I got from a blind old lady in Manila years earlier. Zeni picked me up later in the evening for dinner at the Westcliff Hotel's beautiful restaurant. It has breath-taking views of the City of Gold.

Dinner was a cozy affair for five. It was marred slightly by an overly zealous young white waiter who was keen to point out to us that we had chosen an expensive wine and caviar. Zeni was flustered. She called her friend, the restaurant manager for a chat. The waiter was moved away from our table and assigned to other duties, in the kitchen maybe, but out of sight. We soon settled into Sevruga caviar with a chilled vodka wash down followed by lightly marinated Scottish salmon and crispy potato chips and braised red cabbage, with a beautiful Meerlust Rubicon to accompany the meal. The crème caramel and Sauterne followed by a generous helping of cognac on the balcony overlooking the zoo and Sandton in the distance took me back to my halcyon days on vacation in the Caribbean.

On the way back to the Saxon, Zeni informed me that we would visit her Mum, Winnie, for lunch at the famous Soweto abode. It was now almost a museum. Mum would not be at the main event, the dinner, on Saturday night. Among the celebrities already checked into the Saxon for the main event on Saturday evening were Oprah Winfrey and her husband, Bill and Hillary Clinton, Prince Bernard and Princess Beatrice, Richard Branson and Bono.

Lunch and afternoon tea in Mrs. Mandela's household was quite a treat. It was an unforgettable experience. I sat and listened to undocumented accounts of life under apartheid and what the family endured. I was amazed at how she still had charm and a sense of humour far removed from her portrayal by the media. She was a most amazing, generous, welcoming, affectionate mother and grandmother. She was well-informed about Zimbabwean and African politics in general including the polemology of the various political and tribal factions in Zimbabwe.

The icing on the cake was an unexpected visit from my Archbishop Desmond Tutu. He was always game for a craic. We were treated us to a toyi-toyi jig when he saw us. He repeated stories of him and my father as students at St. Peter's College, Rosettenville. We laughed heartily as we devoured home-made ginger cake, strawberry tarts, scones with cream and fruit jam served with hot tea in enamel mugs.

When we got to the Saxon, Zeni informed me that a friend had reserved the presidential suite at the Grace in Rosebank. Privacy for me, would be better and not as much an issue as it had become at the Saxon due to the huge number of celebrities staying there and countless security details. It was an excellent move. In the afternoon before the dinner, we stopped by the Convention Centre to pass a quick dekko at the venue. Zeni, being meticulous to a fault, was a little anxious as the workmen could sometimes bungle some and not pay attention to detail in the preparations. In the event, preparations were progressing well. Zeni's nephew, Mandla and her brother-in-law, Amoah, were on hand to supervise. All was taking shape with breath-taking flower arrangements that would decorate the tables and walkways, a stunningly decorated high table, a stage for the band and a fancy rostrum for the Master of Ceremonies. We repaired to Illovo for afternoon tea before I was dropped off at the Grace.

I emerged from the elevator in my black tie at half past six, to be met by a stunning Princess Zenani, in a crimson, chiffon gown with a short train and stiff shoulders. I went down on one knee before her, then kissed her hand which I promptly tucked under my ribcage as I escorted her to the waiting limousine. This had all the makings of a fairy tale. I was speechless when Zeni told me that we were to join her father, Madiba, accompanied by her stepmother, Graca, for pre-dinner drinks in a private room adjoining the ballroom where the dinner would be served. We posed for photographs before the 'intruders' were ushered out.

I laughed out loud as Mr. Mandela imitated Robert Mugabe's effeminate mannerisms and accent. He wondered why no one had yet chucked a dornick at the famous 'wailers' when they disturbed the peace and wreaked havoc with traffic as they transported their dozing lord and master to various destinations, mainly Harare international Airport and the homestead.

"Forget Mugabe," Graca interjected with a smile. "I just want to say you guys appear to be incredibly happy together in your odd group." It was clear, obviously, that Zeni, beautiful and gifted, was an object of desire on the part of her male companions. I never voluntarily admitted to losing my senses over her.

At dinner, Zeni and I shared a table with Queen Beatrix and Prince Bernard, Oprah Winfrey and her husband, Hillary Clinton and Germaine Jackson, who was devoted to the Mandela family, notably, Zeni. After quick introductions, the table settled down to lively chit-chat and banter. Zeni, addressed by all as 'Princess Zeni,' knew everybody round the table. She stuttered endearingly, as she introduced us as her crew. I was the only non-celebrity at the table. I am sure nobody remembered my name although the banter with Bill Clinton who came by our table and Oprah Winfrey was particularly close to the bone. It elicited raised eyebrows from the Dutch royalty and Hillary Clinton. Germaine Jackson seemed a bit distracted. He spent much time whispering clearly lugubrious tales of woe into Zeni's ears. In turn, Zeni offered an affectionate, motherly ear.

Dinner was a sumptuous, five course affair, with freely flowing champagne and delicious wines. Then it was time for speeches. First, we were treated to a highly charged, emotional, traditional greeting between Mr. Mandela and long-time political opponent and leader of Inkatha, Mangosuthu Gatsha Buthelezi. The two men embraced, to loud cheers and exchanged greetings and fraternal pleasantries. Next was Jacob Zuma, then Thabo Mbeki's deputy in the ruling party, the A.N.C. After exchanging loud fraternal greetings, Zuma reached for a microphone and promptly broke into song, accompanied by the band. He sang with a surprisingly soulful, powerful voice, to everyone's delight. Within a few seconds, we were all up on our feet, singing along. Mr. Mandela gave his famous sway, complete with pumping fists and an infectious broad smile gracing his face. Zeni explained that the song was a popular revolutionary anthem. It set the scene beautifully.

The family, led by Amoah, paid a touching tribute to the adorable Patriarch who was clearly reveling in the accolades and loving every minute of the beautifully choreographed event. Then it was time to hear the 'birthday man' himself. The hall fell silent and listened intently to the brief, humble but powerful words of appreciation and joy from Mr. Nelson Mandela. He gave us a short account of his life's journey, its highs and lows including his regrets that his ex-wife, Winnie, Zeni's Mum, was not able to attend the event. This was echoed by his wife Graca as she gave the vote of thanks. As soon as the couple sat down, the band, including Ray Phiri, with Sibongile Khumalo at the lead vocals backed by Ladysmith Black Mambazo, broke into loud chords of 'Meadowlands' followed by other South African melodies.

Hugh Masekela joined the musicians on stage and blew his horn to wild applause. We were treated to Stimela, Bring Back Nelson Mandela, Halise de Hana and other popular tunes. We danced until it was time to leave. We walked behind Madiba and Graca as they made their exit. We were joined by Zeni's Swazi prince, a perfidious rascal, by all accounts. The prince radiated hostility as we disappeared into a waiting limo and slipped away into the darkness of the early morning. As I wrote this memoir, I learnt, sadly that Hugh Masekela, 'Mummy Winnie' and Ray Phiri had been destined for 'untimely' deaths. Jacob Zuma since had an ignominious exit from the Presidency.

The gathering to honour and celebrate Nelson Mandela's birthday was attended by people as diverse as anyone can contemplate. One can imagine the antagonisms wrapped in layers of codes, sideways feints and deniability. Getting folks to sit together and enjoy, held together by a common thread, admiration for the birthday man, was nothing short of miraculous. It was clear, to me, once again, that differences really help us define who we are. Often, those who are different from us come out on the short end of the comparison as intimated earlier in this narrative. "It follows then, that if we think we are doing something the right way, then it is easy to conclude that those who are doing it a different way are wrong."

I shared these thoughts with my friends as we sat around a table, enjoying sundowners later that day.

As the evening progressed, I am not sure what possessed me to recite poems initially then rap to the rhythm of hand clapping from those sitting around our table. Curious patrons in the bar joined in, a strange hive mind. I have always tried to forget this little ballad-monger episode at the Westcliff. Unfortunately, some of my friends make it a point to remind me of this occasion, much to my embarassment. This is mainly because I have no clear recollection of what transpired afterwards.

Chapter Twenty-Two

IN THE OFFICE, in Harare, preparations for our upcoming tenth anniversary celebrations were underway. James, Marcus Reynolds, Lyn Mortimer and Liz Oosthuizen oversaw organizing the event. I had to prepare a speech outlining the history of the bank and plans such as were now being put in place. In this regard, I had been to Forrester Estates, Mvurwi, to meet with Rudiger von Pezold, who was a shareholder in Bard Discount House and MBCA. Our strategy was to buy significant stakes in our target institutions, to place us at an advantageous position if we either merged with them or acquired them. I also met with my neighbour, Hilary Duckworth and his Financial director, Mario dos Remedios, an NMB board member, to negotiate the purchase of their shares in Bard, held through their Investment Fund, Trans Zambezi.

After grueling negotiations, we acquired most of the shares held by minority shareholders in MBCA. Negotiations with TZ ran into a brick wall, so we gave up on Bard. After several meetings with Standard Chartered Bank in London, we failed to reach agreement on several matters including the ultimate corporate structure, post-merger. We decided to shelve the exercise for the time being and focus on MBCA and London Trust Bank Plc.

On a Thursday afternoon, just over a week after my return from the Mandela birthday celebrations in Johannesburg, I received a call from a London-based friend inviting me to join him in Nairobi, the following day. I have always trusted his judgement, taste, and work ethic. I worked with him successfully on an agricultural enterprise in Zimbabwe and London. We played golf with three other friends from time to time. I was not expecting to hear from him, even less, to get an invitation to join him and a group of friends, in Nairobi, the next day. My brother, Nathaniel, met me at the airport and drove me to the Norfolk Hotel, where my host, accompanied by his son and four school friends, an American Fund Manager based in St Petersburg and a Swedish stockbroker, were on hand to welcome me. Animatedly, with much enthusiasm, they told me that we would leave for Tanzania the following day, to climb Mt. Kilimanjaro.

At dinner that evening, Nathaniel voiced his concern. He warned me that climbing the big mountain would not be 'a walk in the park.' A surprisingly large number of people lost their lives attempting to climb the mountain every year. The main challenge was acute mountain sickness, also known as altitude sickness. This is caused by acute exposure to low amounts of oxygen at high altitude or in low air pressure. It resembles the flu, carbon monoxide poisoning or a bad hangover. Breathlessness is one of the minor symptoms of mountain sickness. Furthermore, my brother pointed out, I was probably not physically fit, relative to my fellow travelers. My friends had told Nathaniel that they had trained for this adventure for the past four months.

By the time Nathaniel finished rattling off the attendant dangers, I was sweating and a little disturbed. After some thought, I informed him and his wife that I was determined to go. My friend, who could not have been totally unaware of these dangers, was going. I trusted his instincts. At that point, my sister-in-law got up and handed me a large package containing walking shoes, gloves, warm mountaineering clothes, a woolly hat and a walking stick. She said these were essentials for the adventure.

Early the next morning, our gang of nine loaded gear onto a minibus. We set off for Tanzania. We drove through the varied Kenyan Savanna landscape of long grass, scattered trees and dry riverbeds. Herdsmen tended to their cattle with purple-headed mountains in the background. The paved road was relatively quiet and well-maintained, in stark contrast to the pothole-riddled roads commonplace in Zimbabwe.

We stopped for tea and a comfort break at a tourist camp on the roadside, about an hour from the border. We wandered round the curio shops, consumed pies and chocolates, listened to a Maasai warrior narrate stories, somewhat far-fetched, of killing lions single-handedly, armed with only a spear. Impressive. We soon left the colourfully decked warrior and his wares behind and proceeded towards a crowded but functioning border post between Kenya and Tanzania.

It took us about forty minutes to clear both sides of the border and head for Arusha past the very impressive Mt. Meru. Arusha was decked in spathodea, fire trees and bougainvillea blooms. We headed east to Moshi, on the edge of the Kilimanjaro National Park. The journey from Nairobi to Moshi took the best part of a day. We arrived at our base camp, a run-down motel in Moshi, just before sunset. My host got down to work immediately. He sorted the gear, gave each of us a rucksack with a torch, glucose in the form of a small supply of chocolates, assorted biscuits, water bottle, first aid kit and a sleeping bag. We would carry these ourselves. Ten or so porters would carry the tents, food and cooking utensils. The organization was military-like in its precision. There was attention to detail and overall care. Nothing was left to chance.

After a somewhat restless night at the motel, we piled into a truck after our disjune (as we referred to breakfast) of eggs, spinach and coffee. We drove towards the northern end of the park, to the foothills of the range of mountains which shielded Mt. Kibu, the summit with the glacier. An hour and half later, we disembarked the truck with some relief and got our final instructions before our march. We walked up the first hill in single file behind the leader, Earnest, a local Chaga man. He guided us and the porters. Earnest told me he had, at that time, done this trip, right up to the top, more than fifty times.

Earnest was built like a proverbial brick shit house. He was strong as a mule and had a rugged, shaggy head resting on broad shoulders. A magnificent belly belied his fitness. His hands were broad and rough. I am sure one could strike a match on the palms. His large feet were like little boats. He was fascinated that a black man would come to climb the mountain with a group of white companions. A rare occurrence, he said. 'As the only black person in that group,' he said, 'I hope you will not embarrass our black race by failing to reach the top.' The words came from a brooding visage bearing down on me. I chuckled nervously.

As we wound our way up the initial climb and left the mealie fields and isolated thatched huts behind us, we could see clouds in the distance below. After about an hour and half of lumbering up the slope, we found a flat patch of green stream bank where we sat and rested on rocks in the shade of the few stunted umbrella trees scattered along the way. This was a welcome break. We tucked into fresh water, mars bars and dried fruit. After twenty minutes, we resumed our slow trudge up the slopes. We were now way behind our thickly muscled, heavily laden porters who just carried on walking as if this were just a breeze, a walk in the park.

We walked up the slope for another hour before stopping for another break, refreshments and glucose fix. The vegetation got gradually sparse, the grass grew shorter and thinner, the trees were much shorter than those lower down the slopes. The temperature dropped markedly as we climbed higher. We reached our rest camp as the sun was setting. The porters had established camp in a sheltered spot at the foot of a rocky outcrop. A stream flowed down the northern end of the site. I made my way to my tiny tent, threw off my rucksack and made my way to the designated ablution area before joining the rest of the gang in the communal tent that served as our refectory.

Dinner was served early. We were exhausted. We gobbled our vegetable soup, spaghetti, rehydrated vegetables and munched dried fruit for dessert. We were warned that we had to be up, washed and ready to eat at six in the morning. I retired to my tent immediately after dinner. As I tossed and turned in my cold sleeping bag, I could hear the schoolboys laughing loudly and shouting as loud farts rang from some tents. Some names were called out more than others, as the responsible villains. I did not hear any 'mea culpa' coming from any tent. I drifted into an restless slumber.

Thoughts of wild animals, snakes and other threats swirled round my head until sheer exhaustion overwhelmed me into a deep sleep. I was up with the lark, in time to watch the porters build a fire to warm up water fetched from the nearby stream. We washed the sleep from our eyes and brushed our teeth. Slowly, the camp came to life as we huddled over bowls of hot porridge. There was a crust of dry bread and a cup of hot chocolate to tee us up for day two of the climb.

We walked up the rugged slope in a light drizzle and sparse mist, winding our way through gullies and scenic, rocky, increasingly barren terrain. We had a couple of rest breaks at about two hourly intervals before finally stopping at another sheltered cove where the porters had set up our camp for the night. There was enough time to play volleyball and splash about in the freezing, fast flowing stream nearby. We had walked for about five and a half hours, had lunch on the hoof and were ready for a break. We relaxed and talked about family, school, financial markets, football etc. before congregating round our boiling pot of minestrone soup, bean patties and more dry bread for dinner. We were treated to chocolate, peanut and granola bars and hot custard. We wolfed down dinner without wasting time.

Back in my tent, I rummaged in my rucksack and pulled out my satellite phone. I was homesick. Only my brother and his wife in Nairobi knew where I was. My little camera had frosted up badly and my little Walkman was dead. Fortunately, I had a miniature copy of the Bible. I fingered my way through the book of Genesis before reading Psalm 35, then dozed off. I woke up at dawn with the Holy Book under my cheek, my little broken camera beside my head, my satellite phone and spent batteries at my feet. I had slept through the night, too tired to be anything but oblivious of the world.

Day three was a relatively leisurely affair. We were four hours away from the foot of Mt. Kibu. The windswept, barren landscape was in stark contrast to the thick forests of green that we had walked through on the first day. Way below, in the distance, we could still see storms and streaks, perseids of lightning through dark clouds. In the distance ahead of us, we could see the rugged peaks guarding Mt. Kibu which, at this stage, was shrouded in low cloud and mist. I had lost my bearings. I was not sure where we were except that we were at the mercy of our guides and the stars. The four hours to our next base camp felt like ten days of climbing slowly up the winding trails in gusty winds. Taking our mark from Earnest, who kept exhorting us in surprisingly ariose tones, 'Polei polei,' meaning slowly but steadily, in local or maybe mountain speak.

Mountain sickness had already started to affect at least two members of the squad. By the time we arrived at our windswept base camp, it was clear that three members would not be able to continue on the final assault. For the first time since we started the climb, we encountered other human beings on the mountain. There were about a dozen scattered tents, set up by aspiring conquerors of the imposing, majestic mountain. By now, I felt like I had shed at least fifteen pounds in body weight. Although I had not trained specifically for this feat, I was generally fit. I had a gym at the office and trained at the karate dojo at least twice a week.

We ate our evening meal at about four in the afternoon, just before sunset. We needed to get as much rest as possible and prepare for the final climb which would commence at midnight. We were scheduled to reach the summit at six in the morning. We therefore had to repair to our tents and try to sleep or at any rate, get lots of rest before the midnight assault on Mt. Kibu. The final climb is only possible in the hours of darkness to avoid UV damage to the skin and direct, harmful, blazing sun's rays.

At this stage, I was questioning my sanity and wondering why I had agreed to do this. I fell asleep wondering. Around midnight, I was awoken by Earnest's strong voice, rounding us up, making sure we were suitably equipped for the freezing, arduous task ahead. We carried a torch and spare batteries in our rucksacks laden with a water bottle, dried fruit, mars bars, granola bars and a basic first aid kit. We were clad in woolly hats, warm mountaineering clothing, thick gloves and rubber-soled boots. We must have looked like beings out of a 1950s, science fiction or horror movie.

Once again, Earnest's ariose voice rang out in the moonlit night, 'Polei polei,' as our dwindling gang puffed, heads down, in single file, up the volcanic ravaged steep slope leading to the summit of the majestic height of Mt. Kilimanjaro. The colleagues who had succumbed to mountain sickness stayed behind at base camp. An hour into our climb, another member collapsed due to mountain sickness. He had to be evacuated off the mountain to the base camp. In the faint moonlight, I stayed as close to Earnest as I could. To my relief, Earnest suggested that we halt and rest for about fifteen minutes to catch our breath. We obeyed instantly and found the nearest suitable perch to sit on before delving into our rucksacks for biscuits, water and glucose. We ate in silence.

There was something spiritual about the whole experience. I felt light-headed but could think clearly. I thought about my relationships, my parents, my life, my work and kept asking myself why I was here. Why was I 'punishing' myself like this? Self-flagellation of sorts? I hardly noticed the surrounding terrain as the light was poor and I was in too much pain to care. This was physically demanding, more so than any other exercise I had ever put myself through. Curiously exhilarating in a sadistic sort of way but excruciating yet bizarrely enjoyable, almost erotic in its bitter-sweet feeling. I have often wondered if I was losing my senses. After listening to my account, my Mum was convinced that I had gone mad. She says this is a condition induced by a phenomenon called '*Chahwihwi.*' The word has onomatopoeic tones of furiously howling winds on a demonic mission. Mum clearly derives onomastic pleasure from assigning nicknames and playing around with names.

Our final rest stop before reaching the summit was about two hundred metres before our destination. The end was tantalizingly close. As I sat, trying to deal with the various thoughts and sounds swirling in my head, I reached into my bag for a bottle containing the last drops of water, enough to wet my parched lips. I was debating within myself, whether to give up or carry on. Unexpectedly, I felt a heavy arm on my shoulder. An unmistakable, ariose voice whispered gently but firmly into my ear, "If you are considering giving up, I suggest you abandon that thought immediately. We have put our money on you getting to that place, the summit. It is within reach and you will get there. You will not let us down." Earnest's voice was menacingly clear.

I truckled to Earnest's exhortation immediately. My thoughts wandered back to stories of unexplained 'accidents and incidents' as people tried to climb the big mountain. I needed no sulfur between Earnest and I at this stage. Without hesitation, I summoned strength somehow and managed to drag myself to the summit to join the surviving rag-tag members of the gang. I was exhausted but delighted. I stood next to a grinning Earnest and hugged the four colleagues who had also achieved the feat. We were on top of the world. Above us was a clear, unblemished blue sky. Below us was a thick cloud cover through which we had climbed for the past six hours in near darkness. Marlow's words in Joseph Conrad's "Youth," rang in my head: "Impalpable and enslaving, like a charm, like a whispered promise of mysterious delight."

To the south, the 'Valley of Death' lay, somewhat demurely. It was so named because of the deadly sulfurous clouds that cover the abyss. Strange thoughts ranging from delirious imaginings of being an angel, to purely suicidal thoughts of having accomplished everything the world has to offer and wanting to hurl myself into the darkness of the Valley of Death, ran through my mind. I felt an imperative to escape from the reality of existence, to leap beyond the confines of thought, to grope towards the mists of an elusive, unattainable existence.

The familiar inner perceptions of my body, including the headache that had oppressed me since we began the climb at midnight, had given way to a vague lightness and exhilaration and a strangely delightful effervescence of thought. For a moment, I wondered if I had died and was entering some wholly unexpected new existence. This banal possibility exasperated me but I soon comforted myself with the thought that I was not dead, but in some sort of trance. My mind was clearly unhinged by the impact of experience beyond its comprehension.

William Langland's words in 'The Vision of Piers Plowman,' came to mind: "As on May morning, on Malvern hills, Me befell a ferly of fairy, methought....." This was the whisper of time bending over the mountain; a susurration of mortality none can escape.

This was truly a 'ferly fare' to my sleepy, fair eyes. "We cannot stay here for more than twenty minutes," Earnest announced emphatically. "It is now sunrise and we need to commence our descent. Congratulations gentlemen. You may collect your certificates of achievement to commemorate this occasion when we get to the main camp."

Whatever else he said was lost on me. I was so lightheaded and near delirious. I was in a world of my own. Before commencing the descent, I joined my colleagues for pictures around the monument marking the summit. I took one more gaze at the glacier and the sulfurous mare, which is the Valley of Death, then muttered The Lord's Prayer. I shuffled down, behind Earnest and got off the mountain. We slid downwards on volcanic ash covering the slopes. There were glimpses of mountain tops and some sparse vegetation in the barren landscape below us. Two hours after leaving the summit, we could see the base camp in the distance below us. I felt that I had been to the mountain top and caught a glimpse of 'beyond.' I thanked Earnest profusely as I staggered into my little tent. I crawled into my sleeping bag and promptly fell asleep. I could have kissed the monster if I had to, I thought to myself. Perish the thought.

About four hours later, we were huddled in the communal tent with bowls of vegetable soup and hunks of dry bread. We ate our meal with gusto before setting off on the three-hour walk on the trail which led to the main camp. The prospect of an end to this grueling episode spurred us on. We chatted and bantered all the way to the well-organized camp. There was a healthy crowd comprised of aspiring big mountain conquerors, failed aspirants and returning, triumphant folks such as we were.

We did not waste time before jumping into the rows of open showers. It felt heavenly to wash off close to a week of dust and grime, brush our teeth with clean water and enjoy the use of private ablution facilities. It is amazing the little things that we take for granted in our daily lives, things that contribute and make for comfortable living beyond mere existence. Spare a thought for those folks the world over, for whom these little creature comforts are non-existent.

We were treated to a hearty, welcome meal of rice and beef stew, (vegetable stew for me), and fresh fruit. I was tired but hyperactive, confused with mixed emotions. What I had done in the past week still had not quite sunk in. One thing was clear to me, my life would not be the same again. I had spent long hours excogitating and meditating, asking myself questions I had always avoided, including what life and death meant to me, how other people perceived me, what I really wanted to achieve in life, what my personal legacy would be, how I could be a better person and what I could and would change about and in my life. Those nights shivering in a sleeping bag under an alien sky in the wastes of the Kilimanjaro National Park had given me time to interrogate my inscape and think things through. This was a situation I never could have presaged. I was thankful I did not bilk. Thrilling, intriguing kismet, I guess.

Honest, no holds barred and deep conversations with my host and friend opened my eyes to alternative ways of looking at my world and my relationships. Something stirred in me. I was deeply convinced that I could do more with my life. Getting to the summit of Mt. Kilimanjaro was only the beginning. After our final camp disjune, before we went back to a life of 'breakfast' and other creature comforts, we were treated to a music concert by our porters, led by Earnest. That ariose voice was now put to good use, bellowing and belting out Kiswahili songs bidding us goodbye, till we meet again. I listened, almost in tears, as we climbed into the back of our truck. Our gang was now safely back at full strength. I slept all the way back to our motel in downtown Moshi.

In Moshi, we visited a local school where two nubile VSO Norwegian ladies were spending their gap year teaching English to the local children while they learnt some of the local languages. It was inspiring to see such dedication and passion for excellence in the volunteers. There was also a passion and thirst for education and knowledge in hundreds of small African children. Most of them were barefoot but full of smiles and enthusiasm coupled with curiosity. Our host donated to the school. We were treated to songs and laughter as we kicked balls around the fields, much to the kids' amusement. After a large helping of piping hot tea and cassava cakes, we left for the downtown market where we did touristy things like inspecting all the wares. We tried to bargain, much to the amusement of friendly, local onlookers. They were clearly used to better performance from tourists.

After dinner, back at the motel, we looked at old and current maps showing where we had been. It slowly dawned on me that I had been to the summit of Mt. Kilimanjaro! I treated myself to a beer before retiring to my room. It felt like I had never slept in a bed so comfortable. A real luxury. The lizards and geckos chasing mosquitoes around the thatched roof beams, the broken windows and the dusty sheets were a non-event to me. I slept well. I was up early, packed and ready to join the gang on our bus. This time to Arusha airport, to board a noisy DC 4 to Nairobi. As we alighted the bus, Earnest tugged at my shirt tail and reminded me that I had promised to give him my climbing shoes, as a souvenir.

There was much amusement as I opened my bags, retrieved the Nikes and handed them to the beaming Chaga man who proceeded to hug me so tight it felt worse than murder by asphyxiation. I was happy to board the plane. I took one last look at Mt. Kibu as we flew to Nairobi. Later years and long acquaintance may have drowned out any echoes of romance, but a certain mystery and sense remains. The exhilarating experience of the entire trip, especially of standing on the mountain top, facing the glacier and the Valley of Death, remains with me. The course of my life seems repeatedly to have insisted that it should. This was certainly my epiphany.

My brother and his family were all ears and full of admiration on my return. I was treated to a huge meal of brown rice meal sadza, fish stew, collard greens and gem squash. Back at the hotel, I sat in a quiet corner in the bar and downed a few beers before retiring to bed. I spent the next couple of days 'decompressing' and chilling in Nairobi with Eunah and Nathaniel. I visited my old business friend, Fadhili Namoya and his family. He took me to Limuru, where we had a game of golf before dinner at an excellent seafood restaurant.

My friends, Naison and Dorothy, also invited me to their newly built mansion where we were joined by their friends and colleagues for a lively barbecue. My uncle, Simba Makoni, who was on a stopover en route to Addis Ababa, joined us. Drinks flowed till almost dawn.

On my return, my body hurt all over. I occasionally used a walking stick when walking long distances. I lost about ten kilograms in weight in the fortnight that I was away. Beyond being an object of curiosity and amusement, my big mountain adventure was met with near total apathy and disinterest. I was gutted but felt good for not bilking the experience. I had to put this behind me without wasting time. I still had the forthcoming tenth anniversary celebrations to worry about. Hot on the heels of the celebrations would be a trip to London, to negotiate the takeover of London Trust Bank and hopefully, finalize it.

As I stood and stared in a daze on the mountain top, I experienced the intimation of a glance into the past that I now take to be a foretelling of the future. For a while, I avoided facing up to this realization for fear of ridicule. Now, in my heart of hearts, my inscape, I remember feeling an increasingly deep hollowness and sense that I really needed to be somewhere else, doing something different. In that ineffable moment, I felt in my mind that my heart was no longer in what I was doing in my daily routine. My personal relationships just were not where I wanted them to be. I desired and wanted change as ardently as an anemic young girl might desire some loutish Hercules whose arms could crush her in a strong embrace.

I was numb emotionally. I sought advice from Fr. Brian Enright, by default, over the years, my spiritual director. 'Maybe you are just burnt out,' said Brian, over a drink. 'I think you need to take a break, go away on holiday and do something different. Try prayer and meditation while you are at it. If that does not work, you can always come back and join me for a drink on my veranda. For now, pull yourself together.' Always down to earth, these Jesuits are.

Meanwhile, the NMB Tenth Anniversary preparations were at an advanced stage. The organizing team were well on top of their game. All that was left for me to do was to make sure that my black tie was dry cleaned and ready for the occasion. My out-of-town guests would be put up in suites at the Meikles Hotel. They included my parents, Bishop and Mrs. Ruth Bakare, Rob and Jenny Smart, family friends and established farmers in Rusape. For now, everything in Harare was under control.

In London, my office organized long term accommodation for me at the Grosvenor Hotel Apartments in Mayfair. This was conveniently located near London Trust Bank's offices at 30 Upper Grosvenor Street. All this activity helped to take my mind off my mental turmoil. My heart was indeed restless and sought to find rest somehow, somewhere, in something, "Our hearts are restless until they find rest in thee....." I felt like the fabled thirsty giant ordering his slaves to bring water to him in sieves.

Over the previous seven months or so, I had occupied myself and exercised my mind, in my spare time, to redesign my house. The original edifice contained a main lounge off the entrance hall, a family entertainment lounge, a bar area, a study, an ornate, treen staircase, the iconic cynosure, leading to the upper floor with five bedrooms en suite, three guest toilets, a music room, dining room and two-car garage. I added two more guest bedrooms, a larger, purpose-designed music room, secluded study cum library area with a lounge and full bathroom, three additional balconies, a large wine cellar and dining room with an adjoining breakfast nook, a larger kitchen, pantry and scullery with an adjoining TV viewing lounge opening up to the swimming pool and tennis court. Two more garages attached to the existing ones and a Porte cochere on the main entrance completed the remodeling of the house.

The garden was also redesigned with new security lights, redesigned flower beds between bacciferous shrubs with cinquefoil blooms. The plants hosted ocellated butterflies and colourful sunbirds along the sabulous edges lining the lateritious outer limits of the garden. This was a total transformation of my habitat, now my very own Shangri-La. I had never exercised my mind at architectural design before. The residence assumed an agreeable air of opulence. This exercise confirmed to me that my mental vagility or ability to roam freely and creatively increased or declined in direct or inverse proportion with authoritarian, supervisory footprints... enough said! I was conscious, always, to avoid Disneyfying the property to impress others.

Chapter Twenty-Three

THE FRIDAY NIGHT OF OUR Tenth's Anniversary dinner finally arrived. A ballroom adjoining The Bagatelle Restaurant had been prepared. It was well decked and decorated with banners, posters, pictures and other images portraying our journey as an institution. Our logo and oriflamme were emblazoned and loomed large on the high screen perched on the front wall. A host of paparazzi clicked cameras as the guests in flowing gowns and black ties, were introduced. They were ushered past a saxophonist who blew jazzy riffs at the top of the staircase. Inside, guests were offered glasses of champagne and shown to their seats. This was a gathering of Who's Who in the business sector in Zimbabwe and beyond.

The presence of our families, notably James Mushore's, my parents and our siblings, was special. Francis's parents were not present but were represented by his siblings. Our Jesuit mentors were represented by Fr. Fidelis Mukonori, the Jesuit Provincial. The former Fr. Socius and Archbishop's assistant, Fr. Brian Enright looked sharp in a neat grey suit. Not to be outdone, four Anglican clergymen including Bishops Bakare and Hatendi, my father, then Vicar General of the Diocese of Manicaland and the Dean of Harare, Very Rev. Mutamangira, renowned for his unerring talent for trouble, were present. My uncle, Simba, now back from Botswana and soon to be Minister of Finance, sat with my parents, Rob Smart's family and British Embassy representatives.

Once guests were seated after cocktails and mingling, the ever-daedal MC, Marcus Reynolds, invited Fr. Mukonori to say Grace and bless the festivities. This was followed by a five-course dinner of smoked salmon and bedeviled eggs, grilled chicken, poached haddock, beef fillets and roasted pork belly. At my request, bread and butter pudding, Welsh rarebit and tiramisu were on offer for dessert. Fine wines and champagne including a selection of South African wines, Chateau Margaux for the top tables, dessert wines and digestifs were also served. There were intermittent jokes and small anecdotes, courtesy of Marcus's English wit, in between courses. James gave a touching speech after dessert. He narrated our corporate journey, including his take on the attendant genethliac influences. After a musical interlude and more of Marcus's witticisms, I took to the podium to deliver the keynote address.

To paraphrase, I outlined that our country was in mostly unsuccessful progression from independence to democracy. At the heart of this situation was the government's unwillingness to respect property rights. Changes of ownership by force were being used as the means by which leadership rewarded their loyal supporters. As was the case in some other countries in Africa, the now ancient and out of touch President, Robert Mugabe, had re-established a feudal society with himself as feudal overlord. He had given himself and his cronies, powers to confiscate assets from whoever had them so that they would have prizes to dole out to their admirers.

This was evident in 'indigenization' and 'land re-distribution' phases. Taking assets from productive people and giving them to unproductive ones had contributed to the high levels of poverty plaguing the country. Zimbabwe was now producing less than half the food needed to feed its own people, thanks to a chaotic 'land reform' programme. Furthermore, the 'redistributed land' remained outside the market. Those who acquired a piece of land are still, as they were then, unable to fund more efficient farming activities.

Zimbabwe's progress in earlier years outpaced that of its neighbours because its formalized property rights and laws of contract were respected. The country was once among the world's most outstanding examples of what could be achieved by a developing country. With a little carefully directed help, I surmised, our country could reclaim that status quickly. Failure to address civil and property rights issues in an environment of increasing corruption, would push and give momentum to the country's descent into poverty, economic and social disruptive activity and chaos.

There was need for political liberalization. History and the experience of other countries showed that economic success was a function of, among other factors, an effective and honest government, the rule of law, an open economy and democratic systems and practice. People need freedom to realize individual and collective potential. There was no room for political mushy headed idealism. In making my remarks, I was aware of the rantings of certain soi-disant economists, a clear oxymoron in their case, who offered their tub-thumbing nostrums, ad nauseum, in the local media. I distanced myself from their nuanced, pleonastic, astroturfing endeavours.

It was now a system, in my view, of, "For my friends, everything, for my enemies, the law." The courts and law had now been transformed into discriminatory weapons against perceived enemies in politics or the economic sectors, with President Mugabe and his lackey, Gideon Gono, leading the charge. They would, meanwhile, look the other way when their friends or allies skirted the law's boundaries. This crippling and weaponizing of the law, was a huge step toward Schmittian sovereignty. In their respective agendas, the two men achieved what other despots before them fantasized about but lacked the will, or hubris to perpetrate.

That illiberal, populist blueprint was much in evidence. The populist programme of colonizing the state with loyalists, reinforcing the party and state leaders' executive capacity, assaulting liberal, democratic institutions or institutional blitz and the use of various forms of state patronage to the benefit of political supporters, wealth transfers and immunity from penalties for breaking the law on the part of favoured groups was now the order of the day. Blatant lying to the citizenry was not the only trick in the political agnomancy playbook. Censorship, secrecy and 'classifying' documents, taking them out of circulation was another weapon employed. The classification of knowledge such as the structure and dimensions of the country's external debt or inflation rates as secret-sensitive is an act of anti-epistemology that does not so much deny knowledge. It fractures and disrupts the topography of knowledge. In this sense, secrecy acts as a spatial epistemic tool in the exercise of power.

I remember vividly the standing ovation at the end. The audience roared their approval and appreciation. This was probably the longest speech I had ever given. It came straight from the heart. I also revealed the genesis of the bank and my personal journey all the way to the mountain top. Finally, I gave hints of our plans. Our parents were visibly touched. Bishop Bakare gave the closing prayer and vote of thanks. To close, the band launched into loud soulful twangs that led to a rush to the dance floor. I have enduring memories of my parents dancing away with their friends. Our wish to mark the occasion with a fireworks display over the city had been turned down by the police, so we settled to dancing wildly on the roof of the Meikles hotel till early in the morning.

There was something dreamlike about the event. It evoked an eschatological mindset. Indeed, it turned out to be an inadvertent velitation with the State. I have often been reminded by some of those present that I did not have many kind words for the politicians and the RBZ in my speech. I did not go out of my way to vilify them but expressed heartfelt concern. However, my remarks and thoughts on the government-sponsored chaos on the farms, deleterious government policies including the lack of the rule of law amid glaring economic mismanagement, corruption and human rights abuses did not escape the attention of the Central Intelligence Officers monitoring the event, as became apparent a short while later.

I am not ascribing super liminal qualities in their abilities to decipher and discern. I shall not comment further on the short supply of imagination and truthful reporting on the political punditocracy represented. I reiterate, however, that the Zimbabwean media's pathologies of disinformation, defamation and fascination with scandal was in evidence as the event was reported in the aftermath. It was clear how the media was caught up in the post-truth culture, where facts mattered much less than impact and narrative was seized to wield power. This was a cathartic moment for me. I felt 'washed and cleansed through,' emotionally relieved, at inner peace with myself as I joined our guests on the dancefloor.

In the euphoric aftermath of the event, I set about preparing the next move. My mission was to restructure the bank and chart a new path to consolidate gains made to date. It was time to introduce new ideas, mores and a new corporate trajectory. This would necessarily entail a lengthy absence from Harare. This presented an opportunity for me to take sabbatical, after achieving what we had set out to achieve for the bank at the outset. As an avid reader, insatiable consumer of history, banking and economic history and mythoclast by constitution, the idea of spending a term or two, reading, at INSEAD Business School in Fontainebleau, held much appeal. This had been offered to me in the past, but I had passed on the opportunity. Now was the right moment.

Through John Constable, this was soon arranged. I would set aside the first three months of the new year to negotiate and effect the takeover of London Trust Bank (LTB) Plc., then go to INSEAD for three months to read and refresh my mind, 'recharge my batteries.' As required by the RBZ regulations, I duly wrote to the Governor and Bank Supervision Department, informing them of my plans. In my absence, James would act as CEO. The RBZ acknowledged my letter and wished me well in my endeavours. The stage was set.

Within a week of writing to the RBZ, I was happily ensconced in my spacious Grosvenor House apartment. My daily routine consisted of an hour in the gym, juice, coffee and breakfast before settling down to work in my office at 30 Upper Grosvenor Street, at London Trust Bank. The directors had offered me hospitality and office accommodation while we negotiated the takeover of their bank by NMB Bank. At this time, the two banks had a correspondent relationship and co-financed several transactions.

The LTB Director working with us, Ted Roberts, was a colourful, Falstaffian character whose capacity for mischief was insuppressibly evident. He declaimed his sex life to anyone who would care to listen and adored Bob Marley. He was an accommodating, progressive businessman. The General Manager, Geoffrey Wells, was an affable Englishman, a keen tennis player. He was well-liked by NMB staff. The staff complement of about twenty professionals including Rosette Shammas, Terry Healy, a booklore fanatic, Christine Burrell, blonde, Karen popularly known as our in-house 'lollapalooza' for her stunning Marilyn Monroe looks and 'garrulous' Richard, among others, were hard working, co-operative and typically, reserved.

The offices were situated on the Grosvenor Hotel's West Wing, facing Hyde Park, on a prime, convenient, idyllic piece of London's Mayfair real estate. This was an appropriate milieu for an upmarket investment bank. LTB thus became, in effect, NMB's London outpost. Every Friday lunchtime, Ted Roberts would invite me to join him at his favourite Sino-French restaurant, Kai, on South Audley Street. Ted always sat at the same table in a cozy corner of the louche establishment. Before long, I got used to joining Ted in attacking, with gusto, the bill of fare, which could content the daintiest palate. The bonbons Ted ordered for dessert always melted in the mouth, inducing misty, infinitely tender memories. The fragrance and essence penetrated the papillae of one's tongue, recalling the very savour of voluptuous kisses. They always evoked the real love aroma, a delicate hint of riotous episodes past.

Over the following three weeks, with Ted's help, I reached an understanding with the Board of LTB. Most of the Directors were based in the Middle East. It took Ted a while to convince them all that the proposal I had put before them was to our mutual advantage. I took full advantage of Ted's knowledge and skill at negotiating with the LTB Directors, especially those from Syria and other Middle east countries. We signed a Memorandum of Understanding, Non-Disclosure Agreements and other bits of paperwork. The next task was to approach the Financial Services Authority (FSA) for their blessing.

By sheer coincidence, the eponymous Mr. Bully, formerly a consultant with the RBZ, would be our contact person at the FSA. Despite his name, past life and role as a regulator marked by distinct civil service phraseology, Mr. Bully turned out to be yet another affable Englishman who had a soft spot for Zimbabwe. He knew the RBZ well and was willing and ready to assist us beyond the call of duty.

The next fortnight saw Geoff Wells, Ted Roberts and I, in long meetings with FSA officials. The FSA was concerned that LTB was currently under-capitalized. They wanted to ensure that the bank was adequately capitalized either by the existing shareholders or by the new shareholder, NMBZ. The correct capitalization levels would have to meet the regulatory requirements. If LTB failed to raise the requisite capital, their license to accept deposits from members of the public, corporate or personal, would be revoked. Furthermore, the FSA sought to establish whether NMB would have the resources needed to capitalize LTB if our application to take over LTB was approved.

In addition to matters of capitalization, the FSA wanted to make sure that the RBZ had been informed of our move and that they were fully supportive. While NMBZ could show that they could afford the cash to take over LTB, delivering RBZ's approval was another thing. We had no control over the RBZ's processes. We had provided the RBZ with all the necessary paperwork outlining our plans, funding sources, economic and financial rationale and the estimated financial and economic impact that this move would have in Zimbabwe.

This was an arduous task. Dealing with the FSA was a joy compared to the RBZ. This was despite that the then Minister of Finance had visited LTB and given us, verbally, his full support. He had accompanied us to the FSA's offices to show his support. After what seemed to be an eternity in meetings and interviews at the FSA, Mr. Bully informed us that our application was successful. This approval, however, was conditional on obtaining RBZ's formal approval and capitalizing LTB to meet the regulatory requirements so that we could retain the license to conduct business as a fully-fledged commercial bank in the U.K.

If the RBZ's approval was not forthcoming, NMB would be allowed to buy a controlling stake in LTB. NMB would then run the company without a deposit-taking license, as a registered corporate finance boutique. LTB would therefore do everything that all commercial banks do except take deposits. The ball was then in RBZ's court. As I was already London-based, effectively, it was up to the team in Harare, James, Francis, Otto and the non-executive directors, including the chairman, Paddy Zhanda, to try to get the RBZ to respond positively to our application to buy LTB. The FSA had given us, graciously, a three-months window to achieve all that was required of us, after which time, the deposit license that LTB held then would lapse and we would have to apply anew for a new license.

I received daily updates from James. Meanwhile, NMB Investments, had decided to go ahead and buy the entire shareholding of LTB in anticipation of getting the RBZ's nod timeously. In that event, NMBI would sell a controlling stake in the company to NMBZ Holdings. As the new Chairman of LTB, I convened a board meeting of the new directors, comprising Prof. John Constable, Afare Donkor, Jim Friedlander, Geoff Wells, James, Francis and myself. At that meeting, we resolved to appoint Jim Friedlander as the CEO. Geoff Wells would remain as the General Manager.

After the meeting, James and Francis returned to Harare to prepare for the NMBZ board meeting scheduled for the end of January. In the meantime, they would continue to push for a favourable response from RBZ as we were running short of time. I would remain at LTB and keep in constant touch with the FSA while running LTB before Jim Friedlander assumed his post in a month.

Two weeks before the NMB Board Meeting, my P.A., Cheron, had called me to report a break-in at our offices. The intruders had broken into James's office, trashed it, then smashed through the wall separating my office and James's and entered my office. They removed my computer hard drive, took all the cash that I kept in my desk drawers, my entire collection of eight Patek Philippe wrist watches and personal items including pictures of Zeni and I with her father and step Mum at her father's recent birthday party. Curiously, they did not remove my two handguns that I kept in my desk drawers.

Our internal security team led by retired Assistant Commissioner of police and Head of the Harare Province Homicide Division, Negion Moyo, tried to establish how the intruders had entered the bank, to no avail. They, however, concluded that all the evidence pointed to a state-sponsored break-in, especially since the police refused to 'get involved.' It was quite apparent that this was no ordinary burglary.

A week later, I received another disquieting call from Cheron, telling me that there had been a series of visits to our offices, by 'shady-looking men in grey suits.' The men had asked about my whereabouts and left when they were told that I was away but would be in the office for the Board meeting scheduled to take place later in the week. I relayed this to Jim who was preparing to fly out to

Harare for the NMB Board meeting. We had planned to travel together. We were booked to arrive in Harare two days before the meeting so that we could attend all the Committee meetings that usually preceded the main meeting of the Board.

Just before we checked in at Heathrow, Cheron called to say that more 'men in grey suits and dark glasses' had visited the bank again. Apparently, they walked around and smiled politely but did not say much except to inquire as to my whereabouts yet again. At that point I called my Dad to get his opinion on the whole saga. He advised that I should let Jim travel alone to Harare for the Board Meeting. Jim would then assess the situation and advise me whether to travel to Harare or remain in London for now, or until the mystery had been cleared up. I acquiesced to Dad's advice. Jim and I hugged good-bye. He was under strict orders not to disclose my travel plans to anybody.

Back in my apartment, nothing was making sense but my hunch was that I had done the right thing by not flying to Harare until the mystery of the men in grey suits and the break-in at our offices which targeted James's and my office only, had been solved. James called me to report that he felt tired and had booked himself and a friend on our houseboat on Kariba for a week, starting the day after the board meeting. In his absence, Francis would oversee the bank as acting CEO. He was worried by the break-in and the presence of shady characters mysteriously if not menacingly strutting up and down the bank's corridors.

Later that evening, Jim called to say that the presence of the men in grey was disturbing. The atmosphere around the bank was uncharacteristically tense. He was convinced that we had made the right decision for me to stay away for now. In any case, I had informed the RBZ that I would be away till the end of April. There was, therefore, no need for me to attend the routine Board Meeting. Furthermore, there were no issues that required my presence urgently at this time.

Despite the presence in the bank's corridors, the Board Meeting went well. All present expressed their concern regarding the break-in, the presence of the men in grey and the standoffish stance adopted by the police. Jim flew out just after the Board Meeting. James left for Kariba the following morning. At about midday, Francis called to inform me that the men in grey had swollen in number. He now felt threatened. I advised him to leave for the airport immediately. He was to drive an unmarked old vehicle from the bank's underground car park and head for the airport. I had already instructed our trusted travel agents to book him on the 2:30 p.m. SAA flight to Johannesburg.

Francis got the message loud and clear. At the airport, he boarded the flight and nervously found his seat. To his horror, the crew announced that there would be a delay in take-off as they had been asked to check on some unexplained details. Francis called me and whispered that he was terrified. He thought that the State Agents would burst onto the plane and whisk him away. To his relief, after an interminable twenty minutes, the pilot announced that the plane had been cleared for take-off. The delay, apparently, had been caused by two Indian men who boarded late after being detained by airport security who never disclosed what they were looking for.

I was relieved. I reached for a gin and tonic. Three hours later, I spoke with a nervous Francis who was now in a hotel on the outskirts of Johannesburg. I told him to 'sit tight' for now as we watched how events would unfold. At dusk, there were reports of an unusual number of men, some on bicycles, loitering in near darkness on the drive leading to my house. When challenged, they withdrew about a hundred metres, to the main road, Steppes Road. There was a small truck parked under the tall pine trees. Apparently, my four rottweilers were barking furiously at the gate. They clearly sensed an unusual presence which upset them.

The edentate gardener from next door, Mr. Marata, a repository of backstairs gossip, was reported to be restless and making loud noises. He hoped to scupper whatever plans were afoot. My brother, Nathaniel, was visiting from Kenya. He reported hearing voices at his gate which is the adjoining property to the western side of my property, next to Steve's house. Nathaniel's Great Dane cross rott-weilers were also barking furiously at his gate. There was clearly something unusual happening in the neighbourhood. Similar occurrences were reported at James's and Otto's homes. Fortuitously, they were both away from home. James was in Kariba and Otto was chilling at a friend's house.

It was now about seven in the evening. I sat at my desk at LTB and listened, with horror, to news reports from Zimbabwe. It was reported that James, Francis, Otto and I were fugitives from justice and must be apprehended at all cost. My heart sank to the floor-boards. I was eviscerated, shocked to the core. I had to act fast to rescue James and Otto. I called a friend at the British Embassy in Harare and explained the situation. He gave me a sympathetic ear and sound advice. After a brief chat with some friends, arrange-ments were made for James's and Otto's evacuation that evening. This was done in true 'James Bond' style involving a select group of people and equipment. It was a nerve-wrecking experience but by three in the morning, my mission had been accomplished. I knew that my colleagues, James, Francis and the schlimazel, Otto Oris Chekeche, were safe.

I repaired to the all-night bar at the Grosvenor House Hotel shortly after three in the morning. As I nursed a glass of Macallan, I felt that maybe I was an object of curiosity to the few bleary-eyed patrons. The East European bar tender's palpebral twitches induced by chronic hypnagogia, were not difficult to mistake for concupis-cent flirtation. I headed for my apartment, lest deviant proclivities set the pace. In the corridor, an entrepreneurial 'love monkey' was soliciting just as she left some patron's room. The 'hot pocket' was never my thing. I entered my apartment feeling like I was joining a funeral service for someone I had just murdered

Later that morning, I was at Heathrow Terminal Four to meet James and Francis off the overnight BA flight from Johannesburg. It was an emotional reunion. I took them to my apartment where they camped for the next fortnight before they moved into their own accommodation.

Chapter Twenty-Four

EVENTS HAD UNFOLDED fast and furiously. We had to take stock and regroup. Our portraits were plastered over the newspapers in Zimbabwe. We were vilified publicly as were other bankers who had left the country in a hurry. We were accused of 'externalisation' and seeking to undermine the authority of the RBZ. It was hard to understand these charges as they related to acts that were non-existent in Zimbabwean laws. Bankers left the country en masse and hurriedly to avoid arbitrary arrest without trial. New laws stating that anyone could be arrested on suspicion of wanting to commit a criminal offence, had just been promulgated. In the event, the victim would languish in prison for a minimum of thirty days while anyone in authority investigated their hunch to their satisfaction.

The appalling and decrepit state of Zimbabwean prisons was legendary, the cruelty to inmates, famously brutal. It was no wonder that the exodus of bankers at an accelerated rate needed no encouragement. The man instigating and directing this reign of terror and havoc in the financial sector, was the mercurial new Governor, Gideon Gono, it was said publicly. He was no stranger to this form of vindictive, narrow-minded, deleterious pursuit perpetrated to eliminate imagined and perceived threats to his position. The man's much-reported, dark triad characteristics combining narcissism, psychopathy and untrammeled Machiavellianism came to the fore.

Apparently, they were nurtured by a doting President and his scheming, perfidious wife. Gono, it was believed, sought to impress and get close to the president at any cost. At least the basic nature and properties of our chief persecutor were not beyond our ken. That would be key to our fight back strategy.

This was the nadir of my professional career as a banker and entrepreneur. Understanding what was going on was not easy. I was grateful that we were safe and had had the foresight to set up LTB as our outpost. We settled into our offices and sought to ensure that NMB Bank's operations were not adversely affected by events. We had to inform Mr. Bully at the FSA in case doctored information reached him before we informed him. Fortunately, Mr. Bully was already aware of our plight and the trumped-up charges that were being levelled against us. He offered us his sympathy and a haven should we require it.

As a precaution, we engaged a law firm to make sure that our position was solid. Reports in state media in Zimbabwe were that we had exported funds from Zimbabwe with the help of foreign security agents. They also accused us of purchasing huge properties in London's Mayfair, including most buildings near the American Embassy. The reports were treated with the contempt they deserved. The British authorities informed us that they were aware of what was going on and we were free to carry on with our work in the U.K. without fear of prosecution on spurious charges, or persecution from errant Zimbabwean authorities.

We would make daily calls to family and friends including our domestic staff to try and ascertain what was going on. The first two weeks were devastatingly difficult to deal with. With the passage of time, we managed to pull ourselves together emotionally and settled down to business. We urgently needed a CEO in Harare as it became clear that we would be in exile for an indeterminate period. Fortuitously, we had just invited David Hatendi, a quondam MD of MBCA, to join our team at NMB. He was an obvious choice to be a caretaker CEO. Surprisingly, he had managed to build a better rapport with Gideon Gono, than we had. I say 'surprisingly' because, on the surface, the two had nothing in common and privately, they were reported to despise each other. While none of that was my concern, I was happy to entrust the role of CEO to David, with whom I had had long association including a distant family connection. David would be assisted by NMB non-executive director, Mario dos Remedios.

This was a harrowing experience. I was devastated, eviscerated and angry. However, I was determined to soldier on and persevere the way I did all the way to the summit of the Big Mountain. I was not going to feel sorry for myself, yield or succumb and give in to evil. I would take it head-on. For me, it was grit in attitude and end game. Defeat was never an option. In my heart of hearts, I knew that I would overcome this adversity, no matter how much time it took.

I had to dig deep within myself and ask myself hard questions about who I truly am, how did I get here, what have I done in my life and accomplished to date, among others. I concluded that I had the fortitude and grit to see myself through this dark period. I saw this as a test of character. This would test me and prepare me for life and times ahead. I accepted the challenge. I knew it would be difficult at times, but the end game would be nothing short of victory.

My friends rallied around me and gave me a lot of encouragement. Archbishop Walter Makhulu, always a paragon of virtue, wisdom and kindness was always on hand to give us advice and wise counsel. Brian and his beautiful, witty, delightfully bluestocking lawyer wife, Maria, who had well-manicured fingernails, nacreous as the inside of an oyster shell, invited me to the Opera at Garsington, as did Nick and his equally astute and beautiful wife, Pamela. Other friends would invite me out for meals or to stay with them at weekends.

I became a frequent diner and member at some wonderful Dining Clubs in London. I enjoyed meals at the Beefsteak, White's, the RAC, Travelers', Buck's, The Athenaeum, Boodles and the Turf Club in addition to the Oxford and Cambridge Club. The cigar evenings at White's were always something to look forward to. I was almost always in the company of trenchermen including Robbie Lyle and Bruce Anderson. Apart from fine dining, I made friends with several fellow 'travelers' at these establishments. I also renewed other 'extra-mural', personal pursuits.

These special moments with friends provided an outlet for me to vent my anger, anxieties and fears. I had to do my best to mask or at least, show no trace of the carking anxiety and deadly uncertainty which filled my head at the thought of what the future may hold for me. I had no peace of mind. I would call my parents and siblings almost daily to give them updates on my life. They were equally devastated. I blamed myself and excoriated myself constantly for making them feel helpless and sad. I knew, just like my family, friends and colleagues did, that I had done nothing wrong. I was innocent and yet I felt responsible for 'letting down' everyone who knew me. Quite a strange feeling.

I spent hours in the Jesuit chapel on Mount Street, and sometimes, at All Saints, Margret Street, meditating, praying and demanding answers from God. This was a form and level of cruelty that I had never experienced nor envisaged. It was a kind of brontide in my life, like thunder on a clear day, the unexplained sounds of artillery when there is no battle. I had to be sanguine about the whole experience and put it into perspective as I looked back at my life.

I had faced temptation and been through ups and downs. I had had good times and not so good times. I had seen bad things happen to good, innocent people. There was nothing new in what I was now going through at this stage of my existence. Not being one to mump or blamestorm, I accepted this as part of life, a section of the journey that is life, part of what every traveler must endure. I just had to get on with it.

I found renewed zest and enthusiasm in playing musical instruments. I acquired yet another double Bass, Billy, a couple of electric bass guitars, a rhythm (Fender) guitar and two Selmer saxophones, tenor and alto. Depending on the mood, I would select and play an instrument for hours on end or jam with two friends, Larry and Ryan, who were professional musicians. On Thursday mornings, at 7 o'clock, I would join three friends, sometimes four, on the golf course in Hampstead. I always looked forward to this event. One morning, as we waited our turns to putt on the green, a fox emerged from the bushes and picked up my golf ball before sauntering away nonchalantly and sitting, with impunity, on a nearby green, while it eyed us calmly. "Racist fox," I remarked, to everyone's laughter. We never retrieved the golf ball as the wretched vermin disappeared with it into the bushes behind the green. I cannot remember how we scored the hole.

After the game, we would drink hot chocolate, discuss topical issues including news from and memories of Zimbabwe, among others, before going back to work. This routine kept me sane and gave me strength to carry on. I was among friends who trusted me, were supportive and would go out of their way to make me feel comfortable and wanted. We have remained a close-knit group and still play golf at the same place, circumstances permitting. From time to time, I also played golf at my old club, Royal Mid-Surrey, near Richmond, Walton Heath and Coombe Hill Golf Clubs.

In the office, James, Francis and I continued to run the bank in Harare by remote control. At the same time, we had to focus on rebuilding and redirecting LTB. We had now acquired LTB but did not have the banking license. We quickly developed and strengthened our corporate finance and advisory services business while expanding the international money transfer function to cover all parts of the globe, with emphasis on Africa, especially Southern

Africa. In no time, we were running a sizeable operation from 30, Upper Grosvenor Street and were transacting with banks and corporate clients in Europe, Africa, the Middle East and Asia.

We kept in touch with the RBZ through some of the Directors. It was strange to be in touch with the people who were pursuing us and vilifying us. From time to time, I would speak to the Minister of Finance who professed ignorance of our persecution and distanced himself from all the hype and persecution that he labelled as 'political and at Gideon Gono's behest.' Gono, according to his Minister of Finance, was the director and lord of the omnishambles in the economy. The Minister clearly had a scunner for Gideon.

After enquiries, I got the details of the Police Chief Detective who was tasked with pursuing us, a Mr. Mhene. I called him after obtaining his private number from a sympathiser in the police. Initially, the detective adopted and evinced the disposition of a consummate pococurante. He would cachinnate nervously periodically. We had a cordial conversation for about an hour. He narrated the background of his brief. He was instructed to detain us while charges were either fabricated or we were tarnished with negative publicity, he confessed.

Our influence and standing in society at large and the financial sector would be irretrievably damaged. He pointed out, further, that I had not been their primary target. Their main targets were James, Francis and maybe, Otto. My colleagues were accused, by police informers, of being implicated in some "unauthorized financial dealings". Total hogwash. 'Externalisation' was the term they used. The whole episode was a pathetic farce.

Finally, Mhene intimated that my name had been removed from the 'wanted' list. I had been 'de-specified.' I had no case to answer. Within two weeks, there was a notice in the Government Gazette stating that I was 'de-specified.' I was no longer considered a fugitive from justice. This was not even cold comfort to me. It was as a ploy to divide us, break us and maybe even lure me back to Zimbabwe.

We were dealing with untrustworthy beings. I would not take chances. In any case, I would stand in solidarity with my colleagues as was our custom.

Induced pococurantism on my part was not an option. We would fight evil and injustice together, on the same platform. I remained at LTB, in London, in solidarity with my colleagues. The spurious charge of 'externalisation' was not one in our statute books. The term itself had become and still is a panchreston as it has become a catch-all phrase that means different things to different people and has no legal standing.

Our location on Upper Grosvenor Street, was not a secret. It was clearly marked by an age-old antigodlin London Trust Bank sign above the main entrance. Soon, we had a tide of visitors including exiled Zimbabweans, politicians, ordinary folk looking to remit funds to their families back home. Clients sought our advice on various banking and other financial matters. Family, friends and other well-wishers visited us. Amazingly, our visitors included senior civil servants from the Ministry of Home Affairs and Ministry of Finance.

I asked the then Home Affairs Minister, when he called for assistance with school fees for his children, whether he saw it proper to seek assistance from people branded as 'fugitives from justice.' All I got in response was a lecture about being realistic, playing the game and knowing how to survive. Sacrificial lambs and all that. I got the message. It was a crazy situation, surreal in many ways. This made me fully grok the messy realities of life and politics. I feel no need to assail the Kafkaesque system in pasquinades, despite the temptation and obvious attractions.

We worked hard and established LTB as a major and innovative player in its sector. Friday evenings, however, were reserved for social drinks and catching up. Wine, Macallan and Partagas cigars were served and consumed with gusto. For us, it was now business as usual. The spectre of 'Mr. Omnishambles' and his shenanigans back in Zimbabwe had receded and almost consigned to experience and the dustbin of history. We often discussed and debated whether we could have done anything differently. We agreed that there was nothing we wished to change or would have done differently. We were victims of circumstances and would face up to it squarely.

Twelve months later, our lease at 30, Upper Grosvenor came up for renewal. We decided to cut costs by moving to smaller, more private premises at 58, Grosvenor Street, near Bond Street Station. The location was easily accessible by bus, tube or taxi. James, Francis and I shared offices and facilities on one floor. The rest of the staff, under the watch of our neatnik General Manager, Geoff Wells, were accommodated in a compact area with a communal kitchen. We shared the boardroom with three other corporate tenants in the building.

The system worked like a charm. From time to time, we held our NMB/LTB Board meetings in our offices. Francis and I found apartments in Kensington, just off the High Street, conveniently located near a gym, tube station and restaurants. I would walk across Hyde Park to the office every morning on most days. Through an acquaintance, Ed Marlow, I accepted an offer to join the newly established Principal Investments, Emerging Markets team at HSBC, Canary Wharf. In time, I invited Cephas Takavarasha to join the team.

There was a sense of Deja-vu in all this as we were set to work in the same markets that we had all worked in previously. For me, it was a huge step from running my own bank, back to being employed by someone else. I took the view that while it was a timely and welcome distraction after the recent madness, this was also a good opportunity to refresh, update and broaden my banking skills and contacts. My gut drove me on this one. There was no immediate apparent windfall in terms of material benefit, but long-term rewards would be invaluable. This required patience and a sanguine perspective. It would serve me well in the end. The agreeable pecuniary and other remunerative arrangements also made the deal attractive.

I had to get used to dressing up for work, jumping onto a crowded train to Waterloo Station then the tube to Canary Wharf every morning. It felt strange to work at a desk in an open office, report to a Departmental Head and to account for my time and travel. I soon settled into the routine and once again enjoyed the camaraderie in the office and the excellent work ethic.

I was invited to meet the Group CEO and Chairman, now Lord Stephen Green. He was a soft-spoken, brilliant man of the cloth.

I had been introduced to Lord Green in my World bank days, by a mutual friend who would later invite me to climb Mt. Kilimanjaro and play golf at his Club with the rest of the 'Ex-Zim Hackers and Bushwhackers' every Thursday morning. We discussed my current undertaking and how my group, only recently established to make direct investments in emerging markets, fitted into the rest of the HSBC group. We chatted for about an hour and half. We talked about matters spanning banking, current affairs and the church, including his Ministry as a priest in the Church of England. His quiet wit was, to me, a clear clue to the quiddity of the man's genius.

The meeting with the estimable banker turned out to be a welcome, 'sub rosa,' mental and emotional watershed for me. Stephen's lucid historical overview of the development of the prevailing financial culture and his incisive analysis of the issues concomitant with that culture, were clearly informed by a deep religious faith. We discussed my recent experience in this context.

The question then became how working in capitalist, profit-driven organizations, we can cope with the pressures of political interference, globalization and existence in an increasingly urban, connected world. Could we combine moral and spiritual values with our everyday work? Was it possible to use our varied experiences to contribute to changes that would enable us all to live in a richer, more dynamic world? I had been wrestling with these issues in my mind over time, especially during solitary moments in places of worship, including when I climbed Mt. Kilimanjaro.

The conversation with Stephen provided me with a fresh, philosophic way of looking at my situation. It felt, at last, like I had found a way to deal with the restlessness within me by adjusting and refocusing my thought-process. In my heart of hearts, it dawned on me that my thoughts, expressed to friends, especially in the recent past, unlike the conversation with Stephen, had been somewhat parochialized into a subcategory seen as a quaint exception to the dominant rhetoric. I was characterized by 'friends' as 'different.' This is essentially 'division' in the understanding of many. I now realized that this is no more a tool of self-defense and conquest akin to depicting someone as an object in a private zoo. I saw myself and my relationships in a revised way, one that was a lot more comfortable than before.

I had to re-confront the question of my own multi-layered self-definition once again. It appears to get more complex with the passage of time. My identity was clearly becoming increasingly multi-layered. I was born and grew up in a mix of settings and environments. These included the mysterious and breath-taking mountainous countryside of Zimbabwe's Eastern Highlands, the rugged, cordillera-like Great Dyke environs of Zimbabwe's Mashonaland Central (spanning the Mazoe Valley, Bindura, Mt. Darwin and Matusadona Mountains), the mixed, urban settings of Salisbury's high-and low-density suburbs, London, the English countryside including Cambridgeshire, Oxfordshire and Northumberland, the South of France, Rhodesian and English boarding schools.

I had a Liberal Anglo-Catholic upbringing. This was nurtured, fostered and mentored by distinguished, estimable C.R. Fathers and Jesuits. I attended popular English and American universities, undertook ground-breaking work in established financial institutions in the City of

London, Wall Street and the Emerging Markets. I had achieved entrepreneurial success in several world financial markets.

I was never shielded from the more routine cruelties of human existence, nor coddled from the inevitable discomforts of life but was relatively protected from the severe, unusual, disastrous ones including seismic occurrences, war, starvation and pestilence. I had the pleasure and privilege of working with brilliant, astute folks with superluminal minds. I also encountered a couple of people who turned out to be as dumb as lobotomized cabbages. None of them have, so far, stopped the sun from rising in the morning and setting when it wants to.

I am, remain and continue to be black, African, hailing from a continent which is not just a geographical entity but a cultural tradition with a uniquely diverse, shared history. This makes for multiple overlapping identities with multiple loyalties embedded in it. These layered, omnifarious identities are all interconnected in me as an individual and with other beings through the different cultures that we share. It is part of my being. It defines who I am.

It has a bearing on the direction my life has assumed and continues to develop, by a combination of accident, design and default. I remain a confirmed and self-styled oenophile and turophile with a strong love of things musical. I have learnt and gained strength from adversity, pain and unfavourable experiences in my life. I have also learnt to accept that life is what it is. I must accept it the way it is and live it the best way I can. This entails focusing on select, realistic goals to guide myself through life.

As an entrepreneur in the banking industry, I had three guiding principles: firstly, the need to adapt to change constantly. While having a good year was good, I always believed that having numerous successful years is, a more desirable and different skill entirely. Technological changes and regulatory changes in a fluid political and economic environment demanded a dynamic strategic response and planning. Rather than stay away from what is new or unknown, I chose and preferred to embrace change and adapted to market conditions.

Secondly, I accepted that I could not possibly know everything. I therefore selected mentors who offered me new perspectives, filled in gaps in my knowledge and used their lifetime of experience to help me stay at the top of my game. Finally, I sought, always, to break down barriers. I had to execute business so well that it had a significant impact on our target markets. This meant directing and leading our business in new directions, entering new markets, developing new products and services and above all, thinking outside the box.

Chapter Twenty-Five

MY WORK AT HSBC was exhilarating, euphoric at times, but had its dull moments and its fair share of frustrations. As a newly established unit, we were left alone and expected to be forgetive or inventive and self-starting within the guidelines, which were, at best, open-ended and sometimes, 'ad hoc.' Richard Cole was the titular head reporting to Stuart Gulliver who deputised Stephen Green. Ed Marlow and I reported to the Bank Advisory Committee. We oversaw origination, structuring and screening all investment opportunities and deals. These were originated by the ten or so Officers (Vice Presidents) and Associates.

Our offices were on the 21st floor of the HSBC Tower, in the eastern quadrant of Canary Wharf. From our office, the houses below looked like congeries of little brown boxes. We were assisted by a team of experienced support staff who had clearly, aside from skills at producing endless supplies of antemeridian coffee, intently listened to bankers around them in their years at HSBC. They had acquired an astonishing hash of investment banking flubdub. To hit the ground running, we had to do our best to produce what could only be called a spagyric banking feat. There were high expectations all round. All eyes were on us. No pressure at all.

When I had last worked in investment banking, so much of the business was increasingly done on e-mail and cellphones. Fixed line phones were almost unnecessary, they were virtually a sort of quaint atavism that ordinarily, nobody thought of to use, if at all. In this department, however, desk phones seemed to ring incessantly. Amazingly, one soon settled down to this reality and buckled down to work. Soon I was getting ready to travel to Johannesburg and Cape Town to investigate investment opportunities that had been put before us.

This would be my first trip to Southern Africa since I had left Zimbabwe almost four years earlier. I had to overcome my initial foreboding about travelling to the region and having to deal with elements of the notorious security details unleashed on the public in general and bankers in particular, by the RBZ governor who was now the de facto chief of police, presidential 'advisor', national scout master and champion of widows, orphans, war vets, guilds of illegal small-scale gold-panners and snake-charmers across the country.

In the event, the trip to South Africa turned out to be timeous and safe. After a week of meetings in Cape Town and Johannesburg, assisted by the local HSBC office, I managed to come away with four viable prospects for our pipeline. I took the opportunity to re-acquaint myself with my old banking contacts, especially at Rand Merchant Bank, ABSA, INVESTEC, Nedbank and First National Bank. I also visited ESKOM, Transnet, Development Bank of Southern Africa, Anglo American Corporation and Goldfields' head offices, to introduce HSBC's interest in working with them and other corporates.

I made a daytrip to Gaborone to meet with a German entrepreneur who was developing a power project based on coal-bed methane. In Johannesburg, I was introduced, through the local HSBC office, to another German entrepreneur, Bernd Schmidt, who was trying to purchase a power plant in Mozambique, while establishing a jatropha plantation. He invited me to fly to Maputo in his smart private jet and booked me into the impressive Polana Hotel overlooking the Indian Ocean, downtown Maputo. I toured his well-run operations in Mozambique and returned to Johannesburg exhilarated and fired up, raring to get on with the task at hand. This was indeed an auspicious start.

Back in London, our small division, was buzzing and poised to expand. The analysts went to work on the pipeline that we had now built and within three weeks of my return from South Africa, we were ready to present the first two proposals to the various Committees. All our proposals were excellent prospects and resources were allocated for final appraisal before finalizing the investment process. This entailed another trip to South Africa, this time with a couple of analysts, to appraise and negotiate the finer points of the transactions with our would-be partners. We worked from HSBC's office on Maude Street in Sandton, conveniently located near the Stock Exchange buildings. The office was headed by Mr. Patel. His glacial disposition won him no friends.

During the visit, we were joined by a team comprising analysts from Morgan Stanley and Credit Suisse. They accompanied us on a site visit to a large beef operation which included feed lots, abattoir, meat processing and distribution centre. I had to put my vegetarian beliefs aside as I, once again, toured the plant and watched cattle being fed, transported, butchered and processed. I felt ill. The visit was over two days. It was grueling for me, but I thought the beasts being processed had it worse than I, so I stomached it to the end.

Over the next two weeks we worked frantically on the three projects that we selected. These comprised a real estate proposition on Maude Street, the Karan Beef Company, (We code-named it 'Project Red') and a project to raise funds for Transnet to build an eighty-kilometre long mass transit railway system in Gauteng Province connecting the main airport, Oliver Tambo and Pretoria in preparation for the Football World Cup. This would relieve transport congestion along the Johannesburg-Pretoria corridor. This would be called 'The Gautrain.' This was also an opportunity to update the Mozambique jatropha project and the Botswana gas and electric power projects.

It was also a good time to catch up with personal relationships. I visited 'Uncle Desmond' Tutu and his family and the Mandela clan. I also had an interesting lunch with Derek Keys, a former minister of finance and Executive Chairman of GenCorp. He was quite an extraordinary character, larger than life, respected by all and always on hand to give tips on who is who in South Africa's business and political circles. On Sundays, I would go to early morning Mass at St. George's Anglican Church, Parktown, where the then Rector, Charles May, later Dean of Johannesburg and Bishop of Highveld, was always welcoming and available for a chat and coffee after the service.

On our way back to London, I met General Solomon Mujuru, unexpectedly, at O.R. Tambo Airport. He invited me to join him for a drink at the airport hotel. We had a wide-ranging, cheerful chat as I watched him work his way through a bottle of Chivas Regal Whisky. Very impressive. His ideas and accounts of his military exploits during the war of liberation became increasingly gonzo, inversely proportional to the amount of whisky left in the bottle. He assured me that James, Francis and I, could return to Zimbabwe anytime. He would be at the airport to meet us and ensure our safety.

Ever the gentleman, he walked me back to the terminal building where I checked in for my flight to London. We did not take him up on his offer. I had had a long association with the General and his family, going back to the early days of NMB, when Cephas Msipa and William Nyemba were attempting to wrestle away control of the bank from us. The General, always friendly, polite and full of self-deprecating humour belying his political clout and reputation as a fierce combatant and soldier, played a critical, behind-the-scenes part in ensuring that we did not lose the bank. The same goes for his quieter, seemingly farouche, ever-alert, cunning, political rival, Emmerson Mnangagwa.

At HQ, we worked on all the gathered information. Richard Cole, Ed and I had a lunch to de-brief and consider the next steps.

It was an excellent lunch. We all expressed satisfaction at the pace of work and how the pipeline was showing great promise so early in the life of the department. During lunch, the conversation ranged from our current projects, banking and African political economic prospects to religion. I knew that Ed had read theology for his first degree. Richard read history at Cambridge.

On a recent visit to Sydney, Australia, I had walked into a bookshop and bought a couple of theological books that caught my eye. A friend, who accompanied me, bought me a copy of The Minister's Manual 2006, edited by James Cox. 'This should keep you quietly amused,' she said with a smile as she handed it to me.

It was a fascinating read. It kept me occupied on the flight from Sydney to Hong Kong. I stayed with my college friend, Jimmie Master, and his wonderful family. By the time I got back to London, I had read the book. It was a commentary on selected lectionary readings and sermons based on selected biblical texts. When I narrated this to Ed and Richard, they were both intrigued. The conversation at lunch had somehow sparked a flame within me. It got me thinking more about what more I could do with my life.

For the next twelve months or so, we worked assiduously as the projects now poured in. It was a case of 'cacoethes scribendi' as I churned out reports at a furious pace. I travelled to Accra, Nairobi, Maputo, Johannesburg, Dubai, Washington D.C. and Zurich. I attended conferences, meeting with clients and explored investment opportunities. In Zurich, we reserved an office at the Baur au Lac to meet with clients

Jean-Jacques Guinand, my gourmand flexitarian friend, would always invite me for lunch at Casa Aurelio, the ornate Spanish restaurant on Langstrasse. Fine foods and the best wines had given my friend's jowls a butyraceous sheen in retirement. We feasted on broiled baby eel, octopus and prawn curry washed down with fine wines and mellifluous chocolate mousse for dessert. Lunch was followed by a brisk walk along the riverbank to festinate digestion.

On one occasion, Jean-Jacques listened to my Nigerian-sponsored aviation proposal with some concern and discomfort. After a short while he uncharacteristically motioned me to stop talking and advised that I abandon the project forthwith. His gut was right. In short, the project never took off. The sponsors turned out to be conmen of note.

Soon we were well into our second year of operation. Business was flowing swimmingly. Work was a great success, but my heart was still restless. I was a member of the celebrated team of Altar Servers at All Saints, Margret Street and enjoyed the Anglo-Catholic services especially High Mass and Benediction every Sunday. The clergy were excellent. There was an endless supply of brilliant visiting scholars and preachers including bishops from the Anglican Communion and occasionally, Roman Catholic clergy. Cardinal Hume was my favourite preacher. Succinct, heartfelt sermons delivered in gentle tones were his hallmark.

I enjoyed the annual visits to the shrine at Walsingham. I befriended a local Catholic nun, Sister Joyce. She always had a hearty meal, an appositely sweet smile and coffee when I visited the Shrine. I would take her chocolates from Fortnum and Mason. I would offer her the latest jazz music from my collection. She adored Hugh Masekela, George Benson and The Crusaders. We often discussed matters spiritual. She encouraged me to pray, fast and meditate. I found this life attractive and amazingly peaceful. It gave me joy and comfort. She became and remains a friend and confidante.

Later in the year, I decided to spend Holy Week and Easter at Mirfield, with the Community of the Resurrection, who I had had a long association with. I had visited them from time to time, to see friends including Fr. Nicolas Stebbing, Bp. Anselm Genders, Fr. Aidan Mayoss and Fr. Aelred Stubbs. I was a regular visitor to the monastery. I enjoyed the peace and quiet. I used the time to read, go on walks, play golf and enjoy the vast library. Meals in silence, the prayer routine and great debates were also a major attraction.

I volunteered to assist the Community with financial advice in dealings with their main financial advisors, Dolphin Capital Investors, in the City. I felt that this was a good time to reflect on my life and what I really wanted to do and maybe get a grip on why my soul was so restless even though I had achieved much and was financially relatively more comfortable than my peers.

At Mirfield, the organist was clearly in love with Bach. We celebrated Mass by Palestrina and Orlando Lasso, Psalms by Marcello, Oratories by Handel and Motets by Bach. I enjoyed and was bewitched by Fr. Lambillote's sixteenth century "Laudi Spirituali." I extracted ineffable pleasure while listening to the plain Chant. I was thrilled under the spell of the "Christus Factus Est" of the Gregorian chant as it rose from the nave whose pillars seemed to tremble among the rolling clouds of incense. When the "De Profundis" was sung, sad and mournful as a suppressed sob, it was so poignant it was like a despairing invocation of humanity bewailing its mortal destiny. It seemed to implore the tender forgiveness of our Saviour! I sat and listened to the Choir rehearsing cherubim hymns that likened the singers to angels. They rehearsed their music with a pattern of repeated undulating motifs which built up rippling momentum until the sound essentially achieved lift-off.

Coincidentally, there was another visitor at that time, David Neaum. His grandfather had been a priest and worked with my father in the diocese of Mashonaland, in Rhodesia. His father, a colleague and peer of Fr. Nicolas, was ordained priest at St. Mary's Church, Highlands, now my local church. I was a schoolboy then. I attended the service with my parents. Dad was the only black priest at that service. He processed side-by-side with Fr. Andrew Neaum, David's grandfather.

David and I struck up a friendship. We attended Morning Prayers, Mass, Mid-day and Evening Prayers together. After Compline, we would meet near the cemetery and consume large amounts of malt whisky, always in fits of 'spirit'-induced laughter which grew in direct proportion to the increasing ullage in consecutive bottles of spirituous liquor. On Maundy Thursday, more visitors checked in. Accompanying the ordinands from the Theological College were at least a hundred visitors preparing for Easter in the College and monastery. It was a liturgical festival of prayer and worship. There was excellent music courtesy of the College Choir and rousing sermons. Fr. Benjamin Gordon-Taylor quoted extensively, with an air of bravura, from Virginia Woolf's 'To the Lighthouse,' among others.

On the Saturday before Easter, Jenny Totney, David Neaum and two new friends, a parish priest from the diocese of Oxford, Fr. Richard Cole and a self-confessed 'gay activist,' garrulous, Oriental, Durham University theology student whose face was constantly adorned with a buttery smile, took time off to go to Holmfirth in the Holme Valley where the T.V. series 'Last of the Summer Wine' was set and filmed. We walked around the scenic sites and had tea at the magnificent 'The Old Bridge Inn' on Market Walk. This was an excellent break from the glorious but exhausting worshipping at the monastery.

The Easter Vigil was sombre and prayerful. This was followed by an explosion of Easter joy and celebration of the Resurrection in the early hours of Sunday morning. By this time, I was exhausted by exertions in matters trans mundane. I managed to sneak in a quick nine holes of golf at the nearby Dewsbury Golf Club on the rolling hills with a copse on the southern edges. I used the ablution facilities with yellow and black floor patterns. This evoked the squamous covering of certain snakes. Shortly thereafter, I joined the southbound traffic on the M1 motorway. This was a befitting end to an emotional and spiritual week.

It was good to be back at my desk in Canary Wharf. Despite regular doxology mind-pops, I did not talk much about my Easter adventures into the trans mundane realm and matters ecclesiastical. I felt rested and at peace within myself. I had, however, opened myself to something that, in my quiet moments, I found delightfully satisfying. I longed for more of it. I had always enjoyed my role as an 'altar boy' or server at All Saints, Margret Street. My pilgrimages to Walsingham were even more enjoyable. This was now a different level, in the scheme of things.

Occasionally, I spent some time in LTB's offices, catching up on NMB and Zimbabwe matters with James and Francis. The volume of business traffic between our London office and NMB had diminished considerably due to RBZ interference and witch-hunts. The new management regime in Harare, in a bid for self-preservation and apparent opportunism, began to be increasingly less co-operative, culminating in a period of froideur between the London team and the Harare squad.

We disagreed on how to handle the ubiquitous and voracious RBZ pressure. They felt life would be easier for the Bank in Zimbabwe if the management danced to the whimsical tunes of the RBZ. We, in London, took a different point of view. This created froideur between my successor as MD and us. His advisor and right-hand man-cum-company secretary was Munesh Narotam. Munesh was allegedly a Viagra-addicted makebate. I had no evidence of this allegation. I agreed with those who considered him a dreadful epigone, a panjandrum of all matters vaguely legal.

After a series of meetings and discussions, we decided that changes had to be made to the board and senior management team in Harare. The first step, replacing the Chairman, Paddy Zhanda, with one of the directors, Dr. Gibson Mandishona, proved to be the easier task. The next step was to invite the then CEO, to London, to discuss the way forward. After a lengthy meeting with him at 58 Grosvenor Street, I was tasked with the uncomfortable task of conveying the news to my friend, that he was fired with immediate effect. We offered him a severance fee. The rest he would have to sort out with the office in Harare in line with his contract. I broke the news to him as we walked along Davies Street, towards Claridge's. Thereafter, we sat down for afternoon tea.

It was a tense encounter between us as friends with a family connection. However, this had to be done. We parted on good terms. Inevitably, there was froideur and a brief exchange of thersitical e-mails between us. That redefined our relationship. A calculated, evil and malicious 'family' influence was also at play on his side. This was the last time we conversed. He was destined for a sudden, early death, a few months later.

As a replacement, James arranged for our former head of risk, a faux-friendly thespian blessed with the contradictory, if inappropriate name of Benefit Washaya. He was considered a safe pair of hands, or so we thought. I did not object to this arrangement although my gut was inclined to oppose it outright. I believed that a few of his coevals were better qualified for the position. I would be proved right, in time.

Meanwhile, HSBC work progressed well. We had now built a healthy portfolio of projects. Soon I was back in Accra with Ed Marlow, to investigate opportunities in the oil sector. There was, in addition, a horticultural project championed by my old friend, Kwame Nyantekyi-Owusu, Chairman and Founder of Inter-Afrique Holdings. Ever generous, Kwame, who had recently shed off his pretty wife, Sylvia, invited Ed and I to his cosy residence in Legon.

We were treated to an excellent meal with delicious wines, cognac and cigars on the veranda. The scenic views of Kotoka International airport and planes taking off and landing were impressive. Around midnight, Kwame's driver helped us to navigate our way into his plush vehicle before depositing us at the Novotel Hotel, downtown Accra. We set up base for the duration of our visit at the hotel. It had been seven years or so since I was in Accra.

The infrastructural improvements were breath-taking. The potholes had disappeared. New buildings had sprung up everywhere. There was a new business verve and buzz about. If it were possible to dig into the landfill of poor economic decisions and political upheavals of fourscore decades past, one would be singing odes to garbology. It was good to catch up with my old friends, Afare Donkor, who was home on leave from his duties as Ghana's ambassador to China, George Prah, who was running a successful export-import business and Ken Ofori-Attah, destined to be a future Minister of Finance. I made a nostalgic visit to CAL Bank to see more friends.

Before leaving for Ghana, I had followed up on Stephen Green's suggestion to try reading theology books and articles to relax and get away from economics and finance. This was essentially eschewing corpocracy for the cloistered calm of an academic environment. Not being one ever to be knowingly 'underdressed,' intellectually, I decided to go a step further: I applied to read theology at Cambridge University. Yes, something 'different,' a subject new to me. On my return from Ghana, there was an invitation to go up to Cambridge for an interview at the Graduate Centre. A friend had also arranged for me to visit Westcott House for another interview. It felt great to be back in familiar territory where I had spent time as a verdant student.

Over the years, I had often found myself on the Cambridge Express or on the M11, driving to Cambridge. I would wander through my favourite spots especially Christ's College, Queens, the University Library and Little St. Mary's Church. I spent many hours at the Graduate Centre and often enjoyed meals and drinks by the large windows overlooking the river. I enjoyed my interviews, especially with Canon Angela Tilby, Michael Beasley and the new principal, Canon Martin Seeley. Michael and Martin were destined for bishoprics of Hertford in the diocese of St. Alban's and St. Edmundsbury and Ipswich, respectively. I spent the day wandering around Westcott House and the Divinity Faculty in the University. In the evening, I attended Candle Mass in the College Chapel. After dinner I joined Michael Beasley and others for drinks at the college bar before joining some friends for port at the Queens College bar.

A week later, I received news that I had been accepted to read theology and would have accommodation in Westcott House.

Although I was not officially enrolled to train for the priesthood, I would be free to attend classes with the ordinands. I agreed to undertake chapel duties. At the same time, I would pursue my degree in theology in the Divinity Faculty at the University. I was in denial about the strong sense of vocation to ordained ministry that plagued me constantly. However, I settled in my rooms at Westcott House, above the college library on D corridor. I was a member of Queens' College and the Divinity Faculty. Soon, I immersed myself in the routine of lectures, seminars, tutorials and the Westcott House routine of worship.

This was now all about lectures regarding the philosophy, realities, spiritual aspects and work in a parish among real, ordinary people, 'Life and Service.' Canon Martin Seeley, Church History by Dr. Margaret Tolstoy and Rev'd Dr. Angela Tilbury led this. Theology and The New Testament studies were taught by Dr. Andrew Mein, Mission and Homiletics by Rev'd Dr. Michael Beasley, Liturgy by Rev'd Dr. Vicky Raymer, Doctrine by Dr. Anna Rowland. Professor David Ford, my Director of Studies in Queens College, Rev'd Dr. Fraser Watts and Rev'd Dr. Jeremy Morris also lectured in the College in addition to their duties on the College Council.

There was a steady and constant stream of visiting lecturers and scholars including Archbishops Rowan Williams and John Sentamu of Canterbury and York, respectively. As part of the Cambridge Theological Federation, we joined with ordinands and scholars from other colleges including Ridley Hall, Wesley College, the Orthodox Church and the Roman Catholics, Reformed Church, Islamic Mission and the Jewish Foundation, for joint sessions and services.

The College Chapel is a special place for me. Its stark austerity is dominated by its famous icon of Christ with an inscription of John 15:16: "You did not choose me, but I chose you." In the words of Rowan Williams in his magisterial book, at the risk of contextomy, "Dwelling with the Light: Praying with the Icons of Christ (Canterbury Press,2003),the icon of the Pantocrator in the chapel of Westcott House, Cambridge, is a profoundly significant image. The point is simple: face to face with Jesus, there and only there do we find who we are...when we look at him looking at us, we see both what we want to be, bearers of the divine image and likeness, and what we have made of ourselves."

For the next three years of studying theology and training for ordained ministry, the chapel at Westcott House was my spiritual home. There, I found peace of mind and rest for my soul. My guiding principle or rule of life came from Brooke Foss Westcott's 'A Disciplined Life' (1868): "*We want a rule which shall answer to the complexity of our own age. We want a discipline which shall combine the sovereignty of soul of Antony, the social devotion of Benedict, the humble love of Francis, and the matchless energy of the Jesuits....*" A rule of life works on the principle that we are all creatures of habit and it would be best if we cultivated good habits. In all this I had a tutor, a supervisor and a spiritual director to discuss and share my thoughts with.

In Queens' College, I had tutorials with my Director of Studies and tutor, Dr. Fraser Watts, a quiet, avuncular professor type and self-proclaimed locavore with an endearing stutter. I also kept my mailbox at the porter's lodge and attended most college functions, especially the feasts. The Divinity Faculty, on Sidgwick site, on the western side of the Cambridge City centre, near the college backs, was a short fifteen-minute walk through King's College, whenever I had to attend lectures, or use the faculty library. I had a personal tutor for every subject.

I enjoyed all the lectures. Works of St. Augustine, Karl Barth, Thomas Aquinas and Schleimacher were especially enthralling. New Testament studies were a special treat, particularly the intriguing Gospel of St. John, which I later specialized in, with a concomitant crush-course in Greek. World Christianity was refreshingly new and an eye-opener, as was Black Theology, Political and Philosophical Theology, Liberation Theology and Contextual Oriental Theologies.

Professor Ford's lectures on the modern theologians and Christian Thought in Hermeneutics and Dr. Graham Stanton's lectures on the Gospels were always thought-provoking. The Subject Specialist lecturers were always on hand to assist and discuss various topics. The faculty was a hive of academic activity. The personal, individual tutorials, though demanding more work, were always outstandingly enjoyable and took me back to yesteryears.

At the beginning of the Lent Term, I decided to negotiate my way out of my contract with HSBC. We agreed to have a gradual disengagement culminating in my leaving the bank completely at the end of the year. Simultaneously, I would do an attachment at Little St. Mary's Parish in Cambridge. The parish was under the erstwhile Vicar, the leonine Fr. Andrew Greany. I had taken a lot onto my plate. I juggled my life and time between Cambridge University, Westcott House, Queens College, HSBC, NMB, LTB and still retained a sense of sanity. I had to shed off LTB, NMB and HSBC, in that order.

My mind was now made up as to what I wanted to do with and in my life. "Doubt is the subjective state of uncertainty as to the truth or reality of anything." I had no doubt in my mind, without being over-zealous about my new undertaking. A serendipitous luncheon with a relative, Canon Chad Gandiya, who was employed by the USPG in London and destined to be the next Bishop of Harare, convinced me I was on the right path. Chad not only encouraged me to persist with my degrees in theology but also to embrace training for the priesthood. Furthermore, he would enlist the assistance of his employer by availing a grant for me to assist with University fees and books.

Things were falling into place swimmingly. I owe Chad and the US (former USPG), a huge debt of gratitude as they assisted me financially, over the next three years of my study and training for the Ordained Ministry. Furthermore, Chad informed the then caretaker Bishop of Harare, Bishop Bakare, of my undertaking. In time, over afternoon tea in Northamptonshire with Bishop Bakare and his wife, Ruth, I agreed, in principle, to join his staff as Principal of Bishop Gaul College in Harare or joining the staff at Harare's St. Mary's Cathedral. Back in my rooms in Westcott House I could not recognize myself as I gazed into the mirror. I shuddered at the pace and direction that my life was taking.

Every Monday morning in Westcott House, tutorial groups would meet to share thoughts, discuss themes or reflect on selected readings from the Bible, theological articles or other trending ideas. I was in Anna Rowland's group, which included Neil Walsh, Andrew Hammond, Angela, a rather attractive American lass on an exchange programme from Yale University Divinity School, the ever-kyoodling Nick Davies, Simon Tibbs, almost always raffish, Chris Thompson and one or two others. Whenever the group met, the members took it in turns to provide breakfast. We had excellent feasts. On my turn, I invited the group to meet at the Copper Kettle restaurant, for our breakfast. It was a costly affair, but one welcomed by all, in view of my unknown cooking skills.

My year had the largest intake of black students ever. They were Neil Walsh, Louise Codrington- Marshall and Meymans Sala, a recently converted Roman Catholic postulant and me. This was a record for the College. It clearly unnerved some people. Eventually, this blew over into a scrap in the bar between Neil and a fellow ordinand, Bob, an interloper of note. Bob accosted Neil and accused him of being one of 'too many blacks in this College.' I flipped when Neil called me in shock and disbelief, to report the incident. I stormed into the Principal's office, sat down heavily and did my best to contain myself. Through clenched teeth, I threatened to unleash violence yet unseen, in the College, in response to Bob's racially motivated attack on our group.

We named ourselves 'Simon de Cyrene,' for obvious reasons. The Principal listened calmly but clearly horrified. He promised to take appropriate remedial action. For the next week, we all had to attend race awareness courses. Bob was suspended briefly from College. We all prayed together and eventually held a healing and reconciliation session. In time, all was forgiven though not necessarily forgotten. Bob has since been ordained priest. I have often wondered how many others really thought and felt the way he did about us but never had the courage to say it like Bob did. Just as well that I do not know.

I would often lie awake at night and ask myself why I was putting myself through all this. At times I would go through periods of doubt whereby I was directionless and really did not appreciate my presence in College nor the need to pray. I would chat with the Principal, Martin Seeley, who explained to me the 'dry patch' syndrome and how it was quite common. He was an excellent listener and really did a lot to help me think things through.

My life had galloped away at a furious pace and I was now trying to catch up. I persevered through the dry patches and always emerged stronger, calmer and more tolerant. I would read my Bible with a new sense of purpose and appreciated, increasingly, the homiletics sessions that we had in the Chapel. Just as well, because all ordinands had to preach, at least once, in the Chapel, to one's colleagues. A frightening prospect.

I would listen to my colleagues preach impressive homilies with ease. Then it was my turn. My first script was a Promethean opus about ten pages long. I intended to deliver it with passion and pathos, to touch the very soul of any human within earshot. It was complete with quotations from Aquinas, Augustine, Barth and Schleiermacher. The script was returned to me by my Tutor, with a red line through it. In place of my opening lines of, "In another three weeks, it will be Advent...," he had scribbled, "In three minutes, you will all be fast asleep."

I had little choice but to embosk myself in the College library and pen a glanceable script. My rather sudoriferous homily received comic reviews in the College magazine. I resolved never to preach for more than twelve minutes. Thanks to my dreamboat Tutor, many who have sat through my sermons have been spared the misery of aural assault. This is my hope and belief.

I have enduring memories of the three weeks I spent on attachment at Mahram Royal Airforce Base near King's Lynn, Norfolk. This is the home to No. 138 Expeditionary Air Wing, making it one of the RAF's main operating bases where two squadrons of Pan avia Tornado GR4s and other multi-role fast jet ground attack aircraft are based. I was attached to the Chaplaincy at the base when the attack on Libya was launched from there. We would often meet for prayers and counselling with the families of those involved in the war. We also visited and spent time with Chaplains and RAF crews from two other military bases nearby. It was interesting to get a glimpse into the military establishment and how well-organized it is, including the support services for staff and their families.

Every morning, we would join the staff at Mahram for physical exercises in the gym before Mass. This was followed by meals in the Officers' Mess. One afternoon we were joined for lunch by the then Bishop of Norwich. As we applied ourselves to the port after lunch, it was observed that the Bishop, unlike one of his predecessors, was not so fond of port as to apply himself to it with zeal to the exclusion of fellow diners. There was much laughter around the table. In time, the erstwhile Bishop sent an excellent, favourable, 'tongue of good report' to our College Principal who duly praised us for work well done.

The Divinity Faculty had brilliant lecturers and personal tutors. The work was demanding. The volume of reading was heavy. The endless essays and preparations for the individual tutorials were nebulous. I wrote a dissertation comparing the role that the church had played in colonial Rhodesia and its post-independence impact. This was followed by a thesis which compared three Latin American Liberation Theologians with three Southern African proponents of Southern African Black Theology. I was guided and supervised by

Dr. Brian Stanley and by Professor David Thompson, respectively. They were both thorough and fair. It was always a joy and a pleasure to discuss the subjects and listen to their thoughts on various theological, historical and philosophical issues. I had to work hard. I passed all my degrees theses without revision.

After graduation, ordination was the next step. First there was the small matter of dinner and drinks at the Diocesan Bishop's residence. All fifteen ordinands, some accompanied by their spouses, attended the festive event. This was the prelude to six days in retreat at Witchcroft, remotely nestled in the fields in Kent. The erstwhile Diocesan Bishop, Tom Butler, joined us on the first evening. He exhorted us to spend our week at Witchcroft in silent retreat. Prayer and reflection were the order of the exercise. A fellow ordinand, Chris Thompson, informed the Bishop, who had a reputation for being a disciplinarian, that he had a problem with the silence aspect of the retreat. Chris thought the practice was outdated and not practical.

The Bishop checked himself visibly before repeating the order sternly, adding that it was unbecoming to disturb others. The reticulated wrinkles on his face said it all. We were all required to attend the services in the chapel four times each day. We would be led and guided by a retreat conductor, a retired priest. The conductor would give us two addresses daily, following a theme of prayer and service. Three days into this Trappist regime, we all found ourselves repairing to the pub in a nearby village after dinner. We returned to our rooms loudly talkative and clearly inebriated. I believe the Bishop never found out. The 'Bishop's Charge,' on the Saturday, marked the end of the retreat.

The following day was Ordination at Southwark Cathedral. We were up early, despite the excesses of the previous night. We looked an unfamiliar sight in dog collars. I donned a light blue clerical shirt while everyone else wore the traditional black. I thought blue was sharper! On a recent trip to Rome, I had visited the clerical outfitters, Barbiconi and Gamarelli. I purchased what appealed to my taste and choice in ecclesiastical apparel. This was quite obviously beyond a different sartorial sense, as became apparent when we got off the bus at Southwark Cathedral. We streamed into the Vestry to prepare for the service. Probably as a result of a bad hangover and nerves, I walked straight past an unusually familiar figure of a corpulent black member of the clergy. The smartly robed figure bent over the centre console in the Vestry, deep in prayer.

It took me more than a split second to recognize my Dad. I had not expected to see him at the service. I hugged him firmly. He whispered, 'Lord, now I can depart in peace, my eyes have now seen thy salvation,' before pointing towards the pews where my Mum sat demurely. I walked over and hugged her. She giggled and appeared to be proudly nervous but happy. Brian and Maria Fitzpatrick waved and smiled, as did all the other people in the pews. Friends, family and work colleagues came to witness this hitherto seemingly nugacious, unimaginable event.

The service remains a bit of a blur. The sermon was not particularly memorable. As I walked back to my seat after taking Holy Communion, there was a scrap of paper on my seat, with the message, 'I refuse to believe my eyes.' It was not signed. After the service, through the throng of ululating well-wishers I saw a familiar face. It was my old friend Yeshiwas. He was accompanied by his lovely wife, Jill. They pushed their way towards me through Zimbabweans in diapasonic song. We hugged emotionally. I had not seen them in over a decade. They had come to support my colleague, Louise, who was destined to be their new Vicar. The coincidence was breath-taking.

At the same time, yet another previously gnathonic friend, Christine Smith, who I had lost contact with since my Cranfield days, approached to congratulate me. She had come to support her friend, Sally, my next-door neighbour in Westcott House. Sally was seconded by St. Mary's, Rotherhithe, to train for the priesthood. This was truly bizarre. The contingent of servers from All Saints, Margaret Street, led by the only black gentlemen, Ian and Joe, was present. I was overwhelmed. My friend, Richard Small and his parents, remained in the background. However, they made their presence felt at the ensuing party organized by my sister at Steve and Julie McNally's house, in Godalming. I remember bits of the festive occasion. I was confused, exhausted and overwhelmed. A new era had dawned. A cyclopean adventure in my life had begun.

Before launching myself headlong into my new incarnation of clergyman, banker and private consultant cum amateur golfing musician, I felt in need of a vacation to let off steam and decompress. As G.K Chesterton put it, I needed to, "Engage myself in that rich and intricate mess of pleasures, duties and discoveries which, for the keeping off of the profane, we disguise by the exoteric name of Nothing." (Tremendous Trifles,1909) I accepted an invitation from a friend to join his family at their palatial stately home in Hertfordshire.

I spent the next week amusing myself in the unthreatening warren of pathways in the historic maze. An amazing feature of the stately garden. I went for long walks in the woods and across the fields and watched deer in the park. The vibrant birdlife, pheasant roaming freely along with other exotic species including seemingly psittacine varieties were refreshing. Nothing to discommode nature here. Discovering secrets of the stately abode and extended periods of prayerful meditation in the private chapel were precious. This was a piacular period for me. It was intended to preserve my spiritual life against the inroads of upcoming challenges. It was a time to rewild my body and soul.

The lord of the Manor had warned me the family would not hear sermons in the chapel. They would, instead, be glad to hear them in the village church, should the need arise. This suited me simply fine. I had the chapel all to myself. Dinners were sumptuous, elaborate affairs with port, cigars and coffee in the huge lounge. There was a constant retinue of friends including public figures and royalty, guests at various meals or just available for wide-ranging conversations with my hosts. The hosts were gracious. They remain my rock. I took full advantage of their hospitality, which knew no bounds. In a relaxed, private moment, my host leant over towards me and asked if I was set on 'abandoning mammon' and 'curtailing my voluptuary inclinations.' I mumbled something in the affirmative. We laughed as we shared delicious port. Truly the most acceptable face of aristocratic living. I was destined to return to this refuge a few months down the road, to make more life-changing decisions.

Chapter Twenty-Seven

THE FOLLOWING WEEK saw me back at HSBC, sitting at my desk and wondering what had happened. Time had passed. I had been to University and back. I was now a deacon in the Church of England and still a banker. I was counting down my time at HSBC. In the evenings, I would stop by LTB's offices to chat with whoever was available, be it James, Francis, Jim Friedlander, Terry Healey, Rosette Shammas or Geoff Wells. They had witnessed my ordination to the diaconate at Southwark Cathedral. I often wondered what they made of all this. One day, I had occasion to explain to my erstwhile colleagues, at LTB and HSBC, what it is that I had gone through. It was not easy. I summarized that being ordained as a deacon confers on one the Sacrament of holy Orders. However, deacons are not yet priests.

Deacons have three main functions: the proclamation of the Gospel, the service of the liturgy and the administration of charitable works. In particular, the deacon may assist the bishop and priests in a variety of liturgical functions: Deacons may baptize, witness the exchange of vows and bless marriages, distribute Holy Communion, impart Benediction with the Blessed Sacrament, bring Viaticum to the dying, read sacred Scripture to the faithful and especially proclaim the Gospel, preach, officiate at funerals and burials and administer the sacramentals. They are also expected to dedicate themselves to other charitable works, particularly in the parish community.

Unlike priests, however, deacons cannot absolve sins in the Sacrament of Penance, offer the Mass or confect the Holy Eucharist, administer the Sacrament of the Anointing of the Sick, or administer the Sacrament of Confirmation. The diaconate is a transitional period prior to ordination to the Priesthood. It is like an internship whereby one continues final studies for the priesthood and serves in a parish for practical experience, usually twelve months, until the time of ordination to the Priesthood.

As I lived in Hampton Court, I approached the local Vicar at St. Mary the Virgin, Fr. Dereck Winterburn, to ask if I could serve my term as deacon in his parish. He graciously welcomed me in the parish, to assist him. On completion of all the Church's paperwork and formalities, I joined the parish, as the deacon. Dereck Winterburn would be my training incumbent. I was in good hands. There were two assistant priests, Clenwyg Squire and Geoffrey Clarkson. Both were old school priests in the high church tradition, warm and welcoming. They were assisted by a sub-deacon, Pat Felstead.

Dereck is liberal Catholic, comfortable with high church as well as evangelical liturgy. The parish offered a traditional Communion service at 8am on Sundays, a traditional main service with a choir, at 930am and a second main service at 11 a.m., more informal, with a band leading contemporary worship. A traditional, Book of Common Prayer evensong was offered on Sundays. Having two main services which are different in style enabled people to express their worship in a way which resonates with them. The styles may be different, but the content is generally similar across the services. Such were the ineluctable realities of my chosen life-pathway, my 'road less travelled.'

Dereck put me through my paces straight-away. I had to prepare for my first sermon at both Sunday services, assist him at the three Holy Communion Services on Sundays, speak at the monthly Men's

Breakfast and conduct my first baptism. I was relieved when a parishioner followed me into the vestry after my first sermon and told me that she was deeply moved as were her family. She invited me to the first of numerous meals and house calls in the parish. On Sundays, I would also take the Blessed Sacrament to the sick and house-bound parishioners. In addition to my duties in the parish, I had to attend the Diocese of London's Post Ordination Training (P.O.T) with other curates, at St. Michael's Church, Turnham Green. P.O.T was under the guidance of Fr. Kevin Morris.

My parish work was mostly from Friday to Sunday. The rest of the week I was at HSBC in Canary Wharf or at LTB's offices at 58 Grosvenor Street. I got used to this routine and settled in well. Increasingly, Dereck gave me more responsibilities outside the parish as he was also the Area Dean. He had to look after churches in the Deanery where they had inter-regnum situations. I would lead services and preach at St. Augustine's Church, All Saints, Hampton and St. Stephen's Church, Twickenham. I was lucky in so far as I never encountered problems in my church work.

Dereck was a good example of the proverbial good, appreciative, supporting and attentive boss who had a rare gift of listening and the ability to counsel, guide and open my eyes to the work of a parish priest. Clenwyg Squire and Geoffrey Clarkson, the two assistant priests, were also incredibly supportive and occasionally invited me to dinner at their homes. Unfortunately, Clenwyg succumbed to a rare cancer and died after a few months. Clenwyg's family donated his substantial theology library to me.

From time to time I would meet Archbishop Walter Makhulu to break bread. Our favourite meeting places were Boudin Blanc and Fino's, restaurants in Mayfair. On one of these occasions, Arch. told me that his ailing wife was quite poorly and had taken a turn for the worse. A few days later, I received a call from his daughter to say that her Mum had passed away in her sleep. I went around to their house to offer my condolences and get information on the funeral arrangements. We were joined by the erstwhile Bishop of Pretoria, Joe Seoka, at Memories of China restaurant on High Street Kensington for lunch and finalization of Rosemary's funeral service at St. Mary's Church, Fulham.

The solemn funeral service was befitting of an amazing, brilliant and motherly lady. The then Bishop of Botswana, Trevor Mwamba, gave a rousing homily with amusing anecdotes from Rosemary's life and times. He referred to her affectionately as, 'The queen of laughter.' After the private burial at Fulham cemetery, Trevor and I agreed to meet for lunch at Fino's, later in the week. Chad Gandiya would join us.

The lunch at Fino's turned out to be an exceptionally long event. Trevor had invited a recent acquaintance of his, a news anchor on Sky Television, to join us. On her way to the restaurant, Trevor's guest stopped to ask for directions, fortuitously, from James Mushore, who was on his way to join us. James assumed the lady was joining me for lunch. He decided to accompany the lady, Miss Lukwesa Burak, to our table. There was near pandemonium at the unplanned gathering, much to the amusement of other diners and restaurant staff. Eventually, James left, as did Lukwesa, allowing Chad, Trevor and I a chance to discuss the ongoing crisis in the Anglican Church in Zimbabwe.

Two renegade bishops in the dioceses of Harare and Manicaland had recently been dismissed and ex-communicated. They had tried to withdraw their dioceses from the Province illegally, contrary to the wishes of the faithful in those dioceses. They had both been replaced, in the interregnum, by two retired bishops. The action of the two renegade bishops had caused much suffering. The two had managed to enlist political support from the ruling ZANU PF party through connections in the president's office and Central Intelligence Organization, CIO.

The Church was torn. Christians were barred from worshipping in their churches as the two renegade bishops and their followers, supported by the police, would keep them out of their churches. At times they were brutally assaulted and imprisoned on spurious charges. High Court Orders to share church properties during the dispute were totally ignored by followers of the renegade bishops. They terrorized and attacked members who remained loyal to the Anglican Church of the Province of Central Africa (CPCA). The victims wisely eschewed the new church recently established by the two renegade bishops, the ill-fated 'Anglican church of Zimbabwe.'

The two renegade bishops played on the then President's (Robert Mugabe) expressed hatred of homosexuality. They alleged, mischievously, that the mainstream Anglican Church was in favour of same sex relationships. For that reason, they were breaking away from the established church to distance themselves from this doctrine. This found favour with the senile President. He did not waste time in committing the police and state agents to support those persecuting Anglicans who chose to remain steadfast in the established, Anglican Church.

The dispute received world-wide coverage. Canterbury took measures to support the C.P.C.A. The Church made it clear that the renegade bishops, Kunonga and Jakazi, were no longer members of the Anglican Church. The world-wide Anglican Communion united against the two reprobates who sought to wreak havoc in the Anglican Church.

Lunch extended into an early dinner at Fino's, fueled by alcohol. Towards the end of dinner, Trevor asked what role Chad and I could play in this matter. Through his work at the U.S.P.G, Chad was already involved in various ways to assist afflicted and persecuted clergy and their families including other Anglicans who suffered at the hands of state-sponsored agents. Trevor wondered whether having us in some capacity in the Church in Zimbabwe, would make the difference. "Perish the thought of being back in Zimbabwe at this time," I responded.

"All depends on The Holy Spirit, my brother," said a smiling Bishop Trevor. I put it down to spiritous liquor and thought nothing of it any more. The idea did not appeal to me.

A few days later, at the same venue, I had a similar discussion with Bishop Bakare. He was, then, the caretaker Bishop of Harare. He was on a visit to London with his wife, Ruth. We had met at a service at Southwark Cathedral. Bishop Bakare gave graphic accounts of police brutality in the diocese. He had come 'face-to-face' with evil as the two factions continued to fight over church property in the war-torn dioceses of Harare and Manicaland. He narrated the faithful's notionate resistance to the wicked endeavours of the disgraced bishops and their backers.

My father then worked in the diocese of Manicaland. He had also given me similar accounts of police brutality and 'state-sponsored terrorism against the church.' I was shell-shocked by these reports. I gave the erstwhile caretaker Bishop of Harare an account of my own ministry and my personal journey of faith. Apart from a few questions, the Bishop focused on his meal with gusto. He inquired about my personal life and work. His wife unexpectedly asked if and when I would be dining with her daughter. I was fidgeted by her hunch. I felt that she knew or at least suspected that I was besotted with her daughter. Motherly instinct, perhaps.

Lunch with Tinao at Fino's the next day was a memorable, delightful affair. We must have looked like two long-lost lovers. We laughed and discussed our personal lives. We worked our way through Dom Perignon, claret and a generous helping of fine cognac during the alcohol-fuelled luncheon. It was quite apparent that we enjoyed each other's company. We agreed to meet up more frequently. Our next get-together would be at Balls Brothers Wine Bar in three days. At the wine bar, later that week, we had dinner and toasted our blossoming friendship. We had a drink at waterloo before catching the last trains to our respective abodes. This became our favourite weekly routine. She now had my heart in a headlock. No complaints.

It was now a year since I was ordained deacon. Time for my ordination to the priesthood was fast approaching. I was soon back in Rome at my favourite hideout near the Pantheon, the Grand Hotel de la Minerve. This was now my Roman base. I visited my friends at Barbiconi for all the accoutrements for my ordination to the priesthood. I wasted no time before inviting my Roman Catholic cousin, Fr. John Makoni, to meet me at our favourite eating place, the Osteria Pizzeria di Agrippa where Marco and Anna had our white, tasty bresaola pizzas ready, with the house white as the ticket.

This followed a morning of shopping for clerical clobber including a new black cassock, clerical shirts with dog collars, a lovely, lacy Alb (present from Fr. John), a set of chasubles with matching stoles and a Mass Set. After a sumptuous meal, John and I retired to the nearby Basilica of St. Catherine of Sienna, as was now our custom. We knelt in prayer before John blessed the vestments. We deposited our shopping in my room before heading for an ice-cream and 'bird-watching' at the Gellateria Della Palma, the lavish ice-cream parlour on via Della Maddalena. It boasts 150 flavours of their famous ice-cream. This crowned another satisfying visit to Rome.

Derek and I had to jump through all the hoops of ordination preparation. The ordination would be conducted by the new Bishop of Kensington, Paul Williams (now Bishop of Southwell and Nottingham) at St. Mary Abbott, Kensington. This would be Paul William's first episcopal engagement since his ordination and consecration as Bishop. The ordination would be preceded by a week-long silent retreat conducted by Bishop Williams at the idyllic Kairos Retreat Centre in Roehampton, South West London.

The centre, an urban oasis, run by Catholic Nuns. It is situated within three acres of landscaped gardens overlooking Richmond Park. The tranquil setting of peaceful, secluded gardens provide space to think and space to be. The Nuns provide exceptional, wonderful hospitality which includes hearty home-cooked meals a beautiful chapel and comfortable accommodation. In the group of nine deacons to be ordained, two had been my contemporaries at Cambridge. The rest had trained at other colleges, including Oxford and Mirfield.

It was a jovial, all-male group of deacons occupying various places on the Evangelical spectrum of Anglican tradition. Guy Treweek, a contemporary from Westcott House, a former banker, and myself, were firmly planted on the Anglo-Catholic, High Church end of the Spectrum. We all got on famously. One evening after dinner, I walked past the TV lounge and observed the Bishop watching a comedy programme as he feasted on potato chips and a drink. I went into the lounge, sat next to him, helped myself to a whisky and proceeded to engage him on matters ecclesiastical. The Bishop responded graciously. We had a robust but most enjoyable discussion. I told him about the situation in Zimbabwe and the turmoil of the church in the dioceses of Harare and Manicaland. The Bishop advised me to stay put and focus on Parish ministry in the UK.

After the morning service, the Bishop announced that we could break silence after breakfast and were free to watch the ladies Wimbledon final on TV. This was welcomed by all present. Serena won that match between the Williams sisters. The retreat developed into a wide-ranging, wine-fueled event punctuated by lengthy, loud and joyous prayer sessions. The Bishop played tuneful gospel sounds on his guitar with brio, to the accompaniment of a fully diapasonic choir comprising near delirious, spiritually charged ordinands. Some had outstretched arms liberating as one in a trance. This was a befitting preparation for the service of ordination the next afternoon.

About ordination, in response to many questions, I will explain: Ordination is the sacramental ceremony in which one becomes a deacon (diaconate), priest (priesthood) or bishop (episcopal) and is enabled to minister in Christ's name and that of the Church. Ordination itself is in the sacrament of Holy Orders. The ceremony of ordination includes various rituals rich in meaning, symbolism and history. Some of the symbolism includes prostration, laying of hands, giving of chalice and patten and the sign of peace. Only the bishop can ordain priests because he shares in the ministry of Jesus passed down through the Apostles. By the laying of hands, The Holy Spirit is invoked to come down upon the ordinand giving him a sacred character and setting him apart for the designated ministry. Prostration symbolizes the ordinand's unworthiness for the office to be assumed and his dependence upon God and the Christian Community. The anointing of hands, which stems from the Old Testament, indicates being set apart for a sacred task or duty.

Ordination marks the formal end of the initial stages of formation, a process which takes a lifetime. Formation itself is a human, spiritual, academic (intellectual) and pastoral process. In addition to academic coursework, there is a requirement and expectation for one to participate fully in a schedule of spiritual activities such as morning and evening prayer, daily Mass, spiritual direction and retreats. This remains the case throughout one's life and ministry. Formation also includes preparation for future pastoral ministry in schools, prisons, hospitals, parishes, preaching, presiding at Mass and pastoral counselling.

Sunday afternoon found us gathered at St. Mary Abbotts, robed in diaconate apparel, awaiting the arrival of Bishop Williams. Archbishop Walter and another retired bishop were present. They were decked in regal episcopal robes complete with white mitres and golden copes. The Archdeacon of Northolt, the Venerable Revd. Treweek, Guy's wife (now the Bishop of Gloucester), marshalled us into the requisite order for procession into the church to our designated sitting area. The Bishop arrived to much fanfare as the service began.

It was a long service on a sweltering, late June, Sunday afternoon. The Bishop preached about responsibility and reliance on

God. Finally, prostration, the laying of hands and the rest of the ceremony happened. As newly ordained priests, we were asked, by family members, colleagues and others, for a blessing. Arch, Fr. Kevin Morris, Fr. Adam Boulter, Fr. Derek Winterburn, supporting congregants from my parish, St. Mary the Virgin, Hampton, my sister Emmie and her accompanying MU colleagues were present. I laid hands on their bowed heads and invoked God's blessing on them for the first time as a fully-fledged priest. It was surreal. The service was followed by a photo shoot with the Bishop, then high tea at the vicarage.

I celebrated my First Mass at St. Mary the Virgin, Hampton Court on the following Sunday. Archbishop Walter preached on that special occasion. Although I was familiar with the Eucharistic ceremony, I had never presided. I was a bag of nerves. I spent the week rehearsing the liturgy of the Mass. Derek was on hand to help with useful tips on what to do when, how to remain calm and collected while being firmly in control and how to appear relaxed. Sunday could not have arrived sooner. My sister Emmie, her children, Mara and Tino and other well-wishers, decked the Church with flowers. At that Mass, I would bless a rose for my Mum. She would be interred, according to tradition, with this rose whenever she passed on.

My nerves disappeared as soon as the service began. The Choir was marvelous as were Arch's words of encouragement in his homily. There was yet another photo shoot after Mass as the congregation gathered round to offer their congratulations. I received presents including a copy of the King James Bible, signed by the Bishop. We spent the rest of the afternoon at Sou' Sou' West, on Hampton Court Road, on the River Thames. We feasted on gastronomical delights provided by my sister and friends. We reveled in the merry, unrestrained consumption of food and drink.

The following Sunday I celebrated the Mass and preached at St. Augustine's Parish, Twickenham and All Saints, Hampton. I was now in my comfort zone at the service. I enjoyed my ministry immensely. I would look forward to my daily office of morning and evening prayer, sometimes joined by Derek, in the beautiful, peacefully numinous Parish Church. My soul had found rest. 'Our souls are restless until they find rest in Him.' Arch's message exhorting the inculcation into our moral considerations of beneficence as an internal good rather than an ethical calculation resonated with me. Simply put, 'Be good, for goodness sake.'

Chapter Twenty-Eight

TEN DAYS AFTER MY ordination to the priesthood, as I left the house to walk to the station at 7.30 a.m., my phone rang. An unfamiliar voice asked if I was Dr. Makoni. I answered in the affirmative. "I am calling to let you know that you have just been elected as the next Bishop of Manicaland." This somehow sounded far-fetched, like a bad joke. I told the caller that I was late for my train and was not in a particularly good place, time nor frame of mind to entertain frivolous calls. I cut off the call and continued on my way. Within a few seconds, the phone rang again. Before I could hurl abuse at the caller, a familiar voice addressed me as 'Jules,' then informed me that I had just cut off and insulted the Archbishop.

He put the Archbishop back online. I apologized and explained that his was an unexpected voice. Furthermore, the news he had tried to impart was ridiculous since I was only recently ordained priest. The Archbishop repeated his earlier message and asked if I would accept the invitation. I searched for an answer but could only ask for time to consider the offer. I slumped onto a sofa as my briefcase dropped onto the hard floor with a thud. Not for the first time in my life, my world had been shattered and disrupted without warning.

At about midday, I came to my senses. I called Bishop Christopher Chessun, then Bishop of Woolwich. After a brief conversation, Christopher, who was on pilgrimage in the Holy Land, asked me to pray and accept the offer. I called two Jesuit friends, Fr. Brian En-right and Fr. Patrick Makaka. They both rejoiced at my news and did not hesitate to urge me to accept the offer. Finally, I called my parents. They were on vacation in Minot, North Dakota. Dad sighed and said, "We've heard. Our commiserations. I would not take it if I were you. I know the place and the people very well. However, if it is God's will, which we believe it is, there is nothing you are going to be able to do about it except to accept gracefully."

"God has His own plans. He will make it all happen before you can blink. So please rejoice and thank God. Pull yourself together and get on with life. We need to get some sleep. It's late." I was not surprised at Dad's response. Typical of the man. After speaking with my Vicar and training incumbent, Derrick Winterburn, we prayed tearfully then went out for lunch and an exceedingly long drink. I was still in a daze. I did not go to the office. I spent the day working on the brightwork of my cars and mended the rusty bars on the postern.

The next day, I was back with my friends at their country home near Hatfield, in Hertfordshire. I spent the next four days praying and discussing all maters under the earth with them and other guests. Eventually, with their support and good wishes, I left the calm of their hospitality to face the realities of my world on my own. After two weeks, I sent a message to the Archbishop accepting the offer to be the next Bishop of the Diocese of Manicaland in the Anglican Province of Central Africa. By now, word had gone around.

I received news that Chad Gandiya had accepted the bishopric of the Diocese of Harare. I called him to offer my 'commiserations.' We laughed at the unexpected turn of events and agreed to meet up for a drink at the earliest opportunity. Chad was already in Harare. He was preparing for his ordination and consecration as the new Bishop of Harare. My colleagues at HSBC and LTB were confused and dumbfounded as were all who heard my news. They were supportive. The congregation at St. Mary the Virgin were ecstatic but sad. They resolved to contribute funds to purchase a bishop's purple cassock at J. Wippell & Co. in London.

I made a quick trip to Rome. Fr. John, never knowingly a fuss-budget, was on hand to pray with me at the Basilica of St. Catherine of Sienna on Piazza de la Minerve. Afterwards, we visited Gamarelli and Barbiconi for episcopal garments. John bought me a gold and a white simplex mitre with golden lappets. To complete the set, we purchased a silver pectoral cross and a ring. John blessed my vestments. We went to 'Chez Agrippa' for a wine-fueled, late afternoon meal. Two days later, back in London, I went to Arch.'s for dinner. He asked me to select three mitres, a crozier, a cope and a Mass set from his collection. I was overwhelmed.

We dined at his favourite Portuguese restaurant in Fulham. At dinner, Arch informed me that he would conduct my episcopal retreat at the Kairos Centre, Roehampton. I had just had my retreat there before ordination to the priesthood. What a coincidence, I mused. It was at the same place that Bishop Williams had told me that he felt I was destined for the episcopacy. He had advised me to reject any such offer since, he thought, it would be too soon in my ministry. It could, therefore, be too tough an undertaking. Clearly his advice had fallen on deaf ears. Time would tell.

The episcopal retreat with Arch was special. There was no room for hebetude. Five days of silence, punctuated with morning prayers, Mass, daily address and reflection. Angelus and afternoon prayers, lunch in silence, afternoon address and meditation before tea, evening prayers, dinner followed by compline was the routine. Arch's addresses comprised paragraphs of theology, philosophy and life experience which seamlessly moved into pages. This kept me or any linguaphile in spasms of dazzle. Arch proved to be quite a sennachie in his own right. I learnt a lot about our mutual family friends and his own roots.

After five days, exhausted but refreshed, I felt ready to face the world and take on new challenges. I no longer felt apprehensive nor anxious. I was delighted when Arch told me he would preach at my ordination and consecration on Sunday, the 22nd of November 2008, feast of Christ the King. I had eight days to pack my bags and get to Zimbabwe for the first time in six years. I then realized that 'mal du pays' was in effect.

My return to Zimbabwe was uneventful. At the Harare International Airport, the officers from Immigration and State Security welcomed me back with big smiles and words of congratulations and well-wishes. They kindly carried my cases to the waiting car, the same Lexus SUV I had left behind to the care of my trusted and long-time driver, Roderick Choruwa. The ecstatic driver broke into a run towards me before jumping into my arms. He sobbed like an overgrown baby. Everything around me appeared run down. Times had been tough, explained Roderick. In a short half hour, we had arrived home to cheers, laughter and tears as the workers, led by Anna, my housekeeper of twenty years, the two gardeners and the neighbourhood domestic workers crowded around me. They broke into song as they carried my cases into the house.

We prayed and burnt incense in the entrance hall before I inspected the house. Everything was the way I remembered it to be. It felt like I never left. Buddy the parrot screeched her welcome as the four rottweilers yelped on the main entrance. I gave them a bone each and watched them disappear into the garden. Buddy danced as she tore open her seedy present. The welcoming party was treated to beer and chocolates. It was a highly emotional re-union and home coming. I listened to harrowing stories of dire economic circumstances, unemployment, food shortages, raging inflation and a recently introduced new currency, the U.S. dollar. It was a lot to take in and digest in a short time.

Once settled, I called my parents and had a long chat with Mum and Dad. My maternal Nan, Mbuya Ellen Mawondo, had recently passed on at the ripe old age of 104. We shared fond memories of Nan. We recounted her stories about seeing white people for the first time, how people lived in the early part of the 20th century, the two wars, especially the second world war. Her husband fought the Germans in Tanganyika as part of the King's African Rifles. She often narrated how she brought up and educated her nine children, all of whom survived her. Dad filled me in on church politics and recent developments including preparations for my big day, now underway.

Guests including most of the Anglican bishops in the Province of Central Africa, Bishops Albert Chama, Northern Zambia and Dean of the Province, destined to be the next Archbishop of Central Africa, William Mchombo, Eastern Zambia, Brighton Malasa, Central Malawi, David Njovu, Lusaka, Trevor Mwamba, Botswana, Godfrey Tawonezvi, Masvingo, Chad Gandiya, Harare, Christopher Chessun, Southwark and Archbishop Walter Makhulu were now trickling into Harare. Revd. Louise Codrington-Marshall, her husband, Mark Gregory and three priests from Southwark Diocese joined us as our convoy left the Bronte Hotel in the Avenues of Harare, bound for Mutare. Arch, Christopher Chessun, Trevor and I checked into the Mutare Club.

We had an early dinner after our evening office/prayers then turned in for an early night. I had not been to Mutare in over eight years. I had a sleepless night. I decided to jump out of bed and walk about around five in the morning. I was overcome with fear and trepidation. I sat down in the Mutare Club lounge and cried my eyes out. I, for some inexplicable reason, did not want to go ahead with the consecration. I had had a change of mind. The task ahead was now real. It loomed large, daunting and impossible. I felt inadequate and unworthy of the task I had been asked to undertake.

As I sobbed, I felt a hand on my shoulder, a soft voice said, 'You will be fine. God will do all the work, but He must work through you. Please allow me to pray with you.' This was Peter, the Head Waiter at the Mutare Club. He put his hands on my shoulders and prayed in a very loud voice, asking for God's protection, help and guidance. He entreated with God to eliminate futilitarian thoughts in undertaking my assignment as Bishop. When he finished, he smiled at me with the gentlest of faces and asked me to get ready. I promptly went to my room, showered and dressed up in my bishop's apparel for the first time.

Downstairs, Peter was waiting with coffee and biscuits. 'You were born to be a Bishop,' he said softly. In a short while, the club was a sea of purple as Bishops piled in to wait for transport to the Show Grounds. The venue was on the foothill of Mt. Murahwa, at Christmas Pass, believed to be littered with thunderstones. We joined the procession at St. Agnes Church, then snaked our way to a thronged Show Grounds. Reportedly, in excess of ten thousand people had gathered for the occasion.

It was a long service, well over three hours. My parents, siblings, relatives and friends sat on reserved chairs next to the altar. I glanced at them as they all waved and sang hymns along with the cathedral choir. I noticed Tinao sitting next to her Mum, just behind my Mum. My heart pumped and almost missed a beat. During the service, I would cast a longing glance at her from time to time. My old friend from kindergarten, Maurice Arthur Mutsonziwa and my sister in law, Felistas, read the Old Testament and New Testament lessons, respectively. Louise Codrington-Marshall read the Gospel. Arch's sermon was well-received. The ordination and consecration followed the sermon. I lay prostrate in front of the High Altar for a seemingly interminable period. Eventually, after the laying of hands by all bishops and anointing with holy oil, I was enthroned and given authority over the Diocese of Manicaland.

I gave my first blessing as a Bishop then sat in the Cathedra to read out my address to my diocese. I laid out my plans and strategies to achieve them. The main task would be to fight in the courts to regain control of our properties that had been expropriated or occupied by the renegade bishop, Elson Jakazi, and his followers. Next would be the rebuilding of our diocese. We had to unify the faithful who had been unsettled by the havoc wreaked by Kunonga and Jakazi. We would then train more priests to run our parishes. There were about twenty priests left after about thirty followed Jakazi. Those who had left with Jakazi had effectively expelled themselves from our church. We needed urgent and serious fundraising to carry out all the necessary tasks. After my address, I blessed the City.

As soon as the service ended, the heavens opened, an almighty downpour rained on the congregation. This did not stop the people from rejoicing in song and dance as they queued to shake my hand, kiss my episcopal ring and lay gifts at my feet. An old lady awaited her turn patiently as she pulled her reluctant present behind her, a live goat! This was clearly, her treasured possession. I was touched deeply by this generosity. At that point, I felt inner strength and a determination to minister to my flock. We repaired to The Wise Owl Motel for lunch.

At lunch, I reunited with old friends, family and met my priests. My dad, Arch and Bishop Bakare, laughed loudly as they shared stories at their table. I was introduced to and chatted with other Bishops and well-wishers. I thanked them all for their support. At the end of lunch, Louise asked me why I kept glancing across into the congregation. She smiled and winked wickedly as she watched Tinao walk in front of us to join her Mum who was in deep conversation with my Mum. We both smiled. It had been a long day. At evenfall, we were back at the Mutare Club. The Bishops gathered to polish off a bottle of Macallan before settling down to a hearty dinner. A beaming Peter, the headwaiter, was on hand to dish out his prodigal generosity. He poured copious amounts of wine for the thirsty Bishops.

The day after my consecration, I woke up to the sound of my bedside alarm. I felt strangely rested, reset, a tabula rasa, until I was informed that I had to drive to St. Anne's School near Wedza, two hours' drive from Mutare, for a confirmation service. I had never presided nor preached at Mass in Shona, nor had I ever conferred the Sacrament of Confirmation. Fortunately for me, the estimable

Arch was around to accompany me and 'hand hold' me through the service. He whispered instructions from behind the altar.

The parish priest, Taurai Mavhezha, who was also the school chaplain, was also handy in assisting me through the service. There were sixty candidates for confirmation. It was a backbreaking but exhilarating 'baptism by fire.' We held the service in the school refectory which was hastily converted into our halidom or sanctuary since a renegade priest, a follower of Elson Jakazi, had locked the church and disappeared with the keys. The local police stood guard in case we tried to force our way into the church. It was a tense and bizarre situation.

In Mutare, I had to find somewhere to live and an office to work from. I was a guest at the Mutare Club, but I needed permanent, more suitable accommodation. All the diocesan properties including the bishop's house and offices were either occupied or had been sold or desecrated by the renegade Jakazi regime. I met my office staff for the first time. Mrs. Cecilia Chinguwo would be my P.A., her husband, Jonathan, would be my driver. I appointed Fr. Luke Chigwanda as the Diocesan Secretary, Mr. Lazarus Nyatsanza as the Education Secretary, Canon Kingston Nyazika as the Vicar General, Canon Joseph Chipudhla as the acting Dean.

I asked them to appoint the rest of the junior staff. We found an old house that had previously been a nursery school. It was located near the eastern suburb of Murambi, on Herbert Chitepo Avenue. This was refurbished and set up as our diocesan offices. While work was going on the new offices, I arranged for a week-long diocesan clergy retreat. This was for me to meet all my priests and get an account of the situation in the parishes before I barnstormed round the diocese to meet my flock.

Just before leaving for the clergy retreat, we received news that one of our prominent church wardens from St. Agnes parish had died suddenly during a football match while away on business. We prepared for a big funeral. The funeral service was held at the deceased man's house where a huge crowd of mourners was in attendance. I took charge of the service and officiated at the requiem mass. We then processed to the Mutare Cemetery for the burial. At the graveside, there was no public address system, so I had to read out the prayers at the top of my voice. I said the prayers of commendation then waited for the coffin to be lowered into the grave.

There was a deafening silence, nothing happened. Canon Chipudhla announced that the Bishop had read the wrong prayers deliberately, in preparation for the correct ones which he has just been given. I was horrified and embarrassed. I had performed an infant's funeral service, which is hugely different from an adult's! The service seemed endless as I said the correct prayers. I am told many people, especially clergy, dined out on this faux pas for a long time. I did not.

We held the clergy retreat at Anglers' Rest, Nyanga. The centre is run by a Franciscan order of monks. The prior, Brother Peter, a Zambian, turned out to be a good, reliable man. He was a behemoth who ruled his novices with an iron rod. He kept the centre in good order. I had invited Fr. Nicolas Stebbing C.R. to conduct the retreat, but he could not make it in time. Consequently, I had to prepare a theme, readings, a series of motivational addresses, homilies and prayers for the week. We prayed through the first three days then broke silence to discuss our strategy and way forward as a diocese. According to Dad, they were all relieved at this stage as they could hardly understand my theological addresses which contained lengthy tracts from Barth, Schleiermacher and Aquinas.

Dad pointed out that they found my homilies torporific, 'replete with rococo flourishes' and just too difficult to follow, the ultimate soporific. No surprises there. The priests were more worried about immediate needs such as when they would get paid, where the funds would come from, their families, the state of our churches and schools which were being wrecked by the Jakazi followers. In addition, they were worried by the police, who terrorised congregations, arrested them and barred them from their church buildings. The situation was dire. At this point, I realized that Dad had prescient visions that were accurate, penetrating and defied four-dimensional explanation.

The entire organizational ossature and fabric of the church, right down to its foundations was weakened to the point of collapsing in an ignominious heap. The courts were taking their time to make a definitive ruling on the matter. They had made hocus-pocus, opaque, judgements based on technicalities rather than facts. This was unhelpful. Our church suffered as many Christians decided to join other denominations. The Roman Catholic Church, who were our pillar of support and Pentecostal churches, were beneficiaries of our chaos.

I needed to motivate and lead our team. We had to fight and retake our properties, then rebuild the diocese. My take on hermeneutics, biblical interpretation and western, Augustinian style theology were clearly not the answer. I needed a humdinger of a motivational push on my priests and diocesan flock at large. This was easily the biggest challenge that I had ever faced. Business school and many years of university education had not prepared me directly for an undertaking of this nature.

My task was to pull together an estimated three hundred thousand Christians in dis-array. They were harangued and harassed by state security agents for their faith. They were bereft of their church buildings, schools, hospitals and other facilities. Leading them was a group of priests, also persecuted by the police. They had not been paid in over two years and survived on handouts from their congregations. Despite this, they soldiered on assiduously. They were solidly combative and did their best to resist or overcome the evil confronting them. At the same time, they had to take care of young families.

My priests were brave and relatively dirigible. The timorous ones, I was informed, had left for easier posts in quieter dioceses or had left the church altogether. The misguided ones had followed the renegade bishop. All very understandable of course. I was the new face, a complete outsider that was now their Bishop and leader. Tabula rasa indeed! This was clearly a source and sign of fresh hope in so far as I had not been aligned to any faction in the diocese, previously. My reign, it was hoped, would usher in new ideas and possibly new sources of funds to meet diocesan needs, especially for the clergy and for lay staff stipends. My work was cut out for me. No pressure at all. For all that, the Gospel has always required an institutional apparatus without which it simply will not be able to perdure throughout history. I could not be cheeseparing in my efforts to succeed in my mission.

My first task was to assemble a team of able, competent and determined people to assist me. I decided to call a diocesan synod where I could meet delegates from across the diocese including clergy and professional laity. This would be the time to hold elections for the various organs including the Standing Committee, Finance Committee, Education Committee, Senate, Chapter, Elective Assembly, Trustees and Mothers' Union Leadership. After three weeks of preparations, the Synod finally happened in a huge tent pitched in my office grounds.

There were about eighty delegates and a dozen or so observers from the four other Zimbabwean dioceses. The debates were robust and protracted. I had to take the daring move to decipher and clearly highlight the penumbra of abuse perpetrated across the shattered collective psyche of Manicaland Anglicans by my predecessor. My tactic was to be firm and univocal in outlining my strategy and asserting my authority. The zeugma emblazoned on the main refectory at St. Augustine's School, 'Time and Tide Wait For No Man,' was to be our guiding motif.

We were not operating in normal conditions, therefore appropriate measures had to be adopted or we would perish as a diocese. I outlined my war-strategy to 'fight fire with fire' to a stunned audience.

The message was well received. At the end of the day, I managed to surround myself with competent, determined, reliable and brave individuals in all the diocesan organs. I led the opening and closing prayers, thanked them all profusely and gave the final blessing as the gathering dispersed. Dominick La Capra's sentiment echoed in my head: 'For any given element – event, character, development – is never simply univocal or one-sided but generally has two or more valences: it is serious and ironic, pathos-charged and parodic, apocalyptic and farcical, critical and self-critical.'

Shortly thereafter, I took over the chairmanship of the Anglican Council of Zimbabwe from Bishop Godfrey Tawonezvi of Masvingo. The hand-over ceremony was at Masvingo Cathedral. Bishop Gandiya and I travelled together from Harare. We met the erstwhile Bishop of Central Zimbabwe, Ishmael Mukuwanda at the entrance to the church and exchanged some pleasantries. I teased him for having missed my recent ordination and consecration in Mutare after a 'feigned illness.' Curiously, he attended the ACZ meeting in Masvingo in rude health. He took it all on the chin. We agreed to call a truce.

It was a long day. We bought mangoes by the roadside on the way back before stopping in the suburb of Mabelreign to pray with a family that was recently bereaved. They had asked Bishop Chad to stop by on the way back. As a passenger, I did not have much say in the matter. I bit my lips through the short service and drinks afterwards. I was glad to be home by evenfall for my skype calls and a gin and tonic.

Chapter Twenty-Nine

THE NEXT DAY I WAS BACK on British Airways, bound for London to join other newly ordained bishops on the Bishops' Course at Canterbury Cathedral. For the next two weeks, about twenty recently ordained bishops were in residence led ably by Ed Condry, erstwhile Bishop of Ramsgate. The Dean of Canterbury Cathedral and the Bishop of Jamaica assisted him. In my group were Bishops Chad Gandiya (Harare), Brighton Malasa (Upper Shire, Malawi), Cleopas Lunga (Matabeleland) among others.

The group was lively especially the very friendly and delightfully irreverent Bishop Moses Deng Bol of Wau diocese, South Sudan. One morning, he appeared in my room, unannounced, half dressed. He asked me for body lotion, as his had run out! I gave him the last tube of Nivea Cream in my toiletry bag and watched in horror as he helped himself to my cologne and toothpaste.

The giant Bishop Edmund Dawson Amoah from Ghana was much visible. He hated the endless supply of broccoli served at all meals. He referred to the vegetable as 'flowers' and advised, jovially, that if his wife ever cooked that for him at home, then he may be responsible for domestic violence. During a sombre discussion of challenging scenarios in the diocese, the question of how to deal with recalcitrant priests and church wardens was posed to all participants.

After some thought, Bishop Deng's response was that he would reach for his AK47 rifle and shoot the 'trouble-makers.' This sent a chill through everyone as it highlighted vividly the realities and choices that different bishops faced in their jurisdictions. There was silence when I explained my theory that the best committee in any diocese should comprise two people, the Bishop and one absent member.

One afternoon, after tea, Bishop Deng looked at Bishop Malasa and said, "Brighton, you have incredibly soft skin, like a woman. Do you do any work?" There was so much laughter around the hall, the Course Administrators had to call on the holy lord bishops to turn the volume down as there were worshippers in the Cathedral. The highlight of the trip was a visit to Lambeth Palace where the then Archbishop of Canterbury, Rowan Williams, hosted us for the day.

The Archbishop served us excellent refreshments. He led prayers and gave an uplifting homily before seeing us off, back to Canterbury. The Dean also served us delicious food on our return. The Bishop of Jamaica's daily addresses were thought-provoking while Ed Condry's and the Bishop of Peshawar's practical tips and guidelines on being an effective bishop were invaluable. After the course, I joined Tinao and left for Paris for the weekend.

Before returning to Mutare, I spent time in London as a guest of one of our biggest supporters, Canon Mark Nicholl, vicar of St. Mary's Parish, Rotherhithe. I celebrated and preached at High Mass. I also spent time with Bishop Christopher Chessun before he took up his appointment as the Bishop of Southwark. I gave a series of fundraising talks in the City. Towards the end of the tour, I had a wide-ranging interview on Hard Talk, on the BBC. and took part in a panel discussion on topical church issues including women bishops, homosexuality and the place of gay marriage in the Church.

The issues concerning the troubles in the diocese of Manicaland and Harare were discussed extensively. This gave me the opportunity to extend coverage of my fundraising effort on behalf of the diocese. I managed to raise enough funds to pay clergy arrears in stipends, purchase a small car for the bishop and pay rent for the bishop's accommodation. I rented a two-bed-roomed townhouse downtown Mutare, near the museum. Prior to that, I had rented rooms at La Rochelle, near Penhalonga, Leopard Rock in the Vumba and the White Horse Inn. I was tired of living in cramped hotel rooms.

In Mutare, my offices were now furnished with furniture that I had shipped when LTB moved from 30 Upper Grosvenor to 58 Grosvenor. Pictures from my Cambridge University graduation and Westcott House days adorned the walls. Half my theology library was artfully arranged on bookcases around the old LTB boardroom table. Next to my desk was a large fridge-freezer loaded with cold beers, vodka and soft drinks. My P.A.'s office was next door. She shared the office with her daughter, Farirai (Farie), the diocesan projects coordinator. Through the entrance door was a staircase leading to the basement which had the bishop's bathroom, ablution facilities and a small smoking room.

Overlooking the back garden was the Vicar General's office and some spare rooms for visitors. There was also a large prayer room that doubled up as a dining facility or meeting room. The upper floor had the main boardroom, diocesan and education secretaries' offices, a large kitchen and a full bathroom. I would park my car under the huge mango tree near the front gate where a pair of barn owls roosted. Wild monkeys would play hide and seek in the trees when they were not being fed on the veranda outside my office. Sometimes they would taunt the vine snake that lived in the bottle brush tree in the front garden outside my bay window. This was the 'command headquarters' for the diocese, my new home.

In the evenings, Martin Nyaundi, my friend from the liquor company which I once served as a board member, African Distillers, would come to the office for a drink on the veranda. He was one of the Trustees and a member of the Standing Committee. We would discuss church affairs and review our strategy. Martin has a beautiful wife, Isabella, possessed of beauty, discretion and courage. Their family comprised three daughters and two sons, the elder of which succeeded in doing nothing or 'this and that,' much to his father's chagrin. They looked after a niece and three nephews, orphans, adopted by the family. Often, Isabella invited me to join them at dinner. They were a delightful family to be with. They all had a rare gift for friendship and hospitality.

Martin and I played golf at Hillside Club on Thursday afternoons. Our golf matches were rarely competitive. They were a welcome break from the pressure of work and an opportunity to share a beer and ideas away from the workplace. Martin was President of the Golf Club, so we enjoyed special privileges whenever we played or just met for a meal or drinks. I selected a sixteen-year old, emaciated boy, Robbie Chinhoyi, to be my caddy. He was polite but not shy to tell me what I had done wrong whenever I hit a bad shot.

Robbie was an orphan. He had dropped out of school because he could not pay the fees. We agreed that he would enroll at a local college to finish his O-levels. I would pay his school fees in lieu of caddy fees. Robbie worked hard at his studies. When he passed his O-levels, I bought him a set of golf clubs and paid for his membership at the golf club. He was a naturally talented golfer destined to be the next club champion. Within three years, he turned professional. I often watch him compete on the international circuit. He has never forgotten his roots and has threatened to buy me a set of clubs on several occasions.

On Mondays I visited my parents or spent a quiet day at my house in Harare. Tuesday through Friday I would be at my desk in meetings with people from the diocese and beyond. Thursdays I celebrated the Mass for staff and townsfolk who worked downtown. Once a month, we would have Benediction after work on Thursdays. The Roman Catholic Bishop of Mutare, after hearing how our monstrance had been broken by my predecessor, donated his own so that we could use it at our Benediction services. Friday afternoons I would visit patients at the various medical establishments in and around Mutare. Saturdays were taken up with preparations for Sunday services, especially Confirmation, in the parishes round the diocese.

Initially, I wrote my sermons in English, translated them into Shona with the help of Fr. Hannan's Shona Dictionary, then I would memorize them before delivery. It was hard work. I also relied on Canon Nyazika and Fr. Chigwanda with translation of theological concepts and Biblical texts into proper, colloquial, contemporary Shona. There had been whispers on the mealie patch that the new Bishop spoke Shona with an English accent.

The children often found my accent funny or intriguing and sometimes burst into laughter when I struggled to articulate certain Shona words. This was always a bone of contention with my Mum who found this embarrassing. She felt I could do more to improve my Shona vocabulary. The point was not lost on me. Eventually, I learnt how to read my sermons to myself in English while I delivered them in Shona simultaneously. It was a lonesome and gruelling task which became easier with practice as time passed.

I soon established a routine of confirmation services or 'Big Sundays' where I would visit congregations from five or six neighbouring parishes gathered at one central parish and celebrate the Mass. I would meet the flock for lunch and a question-and-answer session. I encouraged questions about the diocese and its future and endeavoured to answer all the questions. The heart-breaking thing was that we could only gather out in the open and the elements sometimes were unfavourable. Gusting winds, rain or biting cold were conditions we had to contend with often. This was disheartening. To make matters worse, the police were always on hand to disrupt our worship and declare our gatherings illegal. Many of our priests were often arrested. We had to engage lawyers to have them released on bail. We did not always have the funds to challenge the oppressive system, but we soldiered on.

At St. Barnabas Parish, Chipinge, a group of 'war vets' disrupted a service just before my sermon. They sang war songs, 'chimurenga songs' and hurled personal insults at me as I stood at the altar before a bewildered and confused congregation. Wisps of incense smoke made graceful volutes in the air behind the altar. I was aware that something within me, the essential spirit within me, willed emphatically not to retreat, but to press on with the service.

Suddenly I lost my cool. I divested myself of my mitre, cope and other vestments. At my most frumious, I launched myself at their leader who was moving and shouting menacingly. I decussated my arms firmly on his neck. Nobody saw this coming, not least from the Bishop. The gang fled in shock. I continued to hold their leader in a headlock. The intruders met their comeuppance as the congregation sprang to life and chased the marauding savages, including the police, far from the church. We regrouped and carried on with the service. Word went around the diocese like wildfire. The Bishop was now seen in a new light, different from some of his more docile, maybe irenic predecessors.

Many different versions of the incident were reported in the press. All of them got the message that we would fight back with violence if need be. The struggle, from then on, assumed a new twist. It got more personal and vicious. I received at least two death-threats almost every week. I comforted myself and those around me by reminding them that if whoever were issuing threats really meant to do serious harm, they would get on with it without warning. Death threats come from cowards, I often told them. I had to show a strong face to my troops. I often wondered what God made of all this.

In my sober and lucid, lonely moments in my room at night, fear, anxiety and uncertainty challenged my faith in God. Pain, evil, fear and suffering now confronted me and pushed me hard to question my relationship with God and my belief in Him and His being, in a way I had never experienced before. C.S. Lewis's 'The problem of Pain,' became real, not just academic. I was now living it. One thing was clear to me, this pain and suffering was beyond logic. Was there, however, an ultimate, point to this pain and suffering from the perspective of my belief in and understanding of God?

As I agonized, a perfectly cromulent way to pass time, I felt and sensed that the more I witnessed and experienced suffering, the more I found God more believable, somehow. I could not quite fathom it but there was a glimmer of hope that ran through all these experiences and increasingly, rather than dwell on the dimensions of pain and suffering and its origins, I focused on this palpable hope as the fulcrum of my message to the flock throughout the diocese. This proved to be an excellent fillip and rallying call for persecuted Anglicans in the dioceses of Manicaland and Harare.

I reminded myself, constantly, that in counterintuitive, if not schizophrenic theology, it may be considered desirable that some leaders in the church are flawed persons, indeed wicked sinners. God glorifies himself by selecting such persons as 'vessels' for His sovereignty. How could it be clearer that God's hand is guiding events than to witness a person who has never darkened the door of a church calling for greater public recognition of Christianity or religion? What may appear like hypocrisy, or at least deep irony, from the outside appears from within some perspectives as the surest evidence that God is in control. After all, the prophet Isaiah went so far as to honour Cyrus-no Israelite for sure-as a messiah:

"..only a pagan ruler who knows nothing of God of Israel and who was in fact just as happy to finance the building of pagan abominations as part of a general policy of restoring the local religious observances his predecessors had uprooted, can restore the righteous remnant to the Promised Land."

I saw the rending of the Church and Anglicanism in Zimbabwe as a pivotal moment in the evolution of Christianity in Zimbabwe and indeed, modernity. The rending of the church in 1896, after the murder of Bernard Mizeki, played at the back of my mind in so far as that event became a rallying point for the church and Christianity in Zimbabwe and beyond. Now, there was fear in us all. We were nervous, timid and suspicious of each other. In many ways, the church fathers were timid about asking tough questions about the origins of our troubles. They eschewed deep debate on it. The Provincial leadership was weak and clearly inept in the face of the challenge. They were consumed by their own personal agendas and power politics. More about that later. It was left to Bishop Chad in Harare and me in Manicaland, to figure out how to survive, rebuild the church and heal the wounds. We had to face and conquer fear. We could not cozen our way out of this situation.

In my sermons, I would boldly state that this suffering and senseless, evil persecution would end sooner rather than later. By faith in God, we accept that God will cause all things to work out for good. We were assured, therefore, of victory. I preached this message much to the amazement of those who heard me. On our way to a particularly difficult confirmation service at Holy Family, Nyatsanza, in the Honde Valley, Arthur Mutsonziwa, who was visiting with me, offering his moral support that weekend, asked me if I really believed, in my heart of hearts, in the message that I was preaching. Without hesitation, univocally, I answered in the affirmative. "That is why I am here with you today," he said softly as the car roared noisily up the Christmas Pass towards Nyanga.

I reminded Arthur of the old gem of wisdom that says that grapes must be crushed to make wine, diamonds form under pressure, olives must be pressed to release oil and seeds grow in darkness. Whenever we feel crushed, under pressure, pressed or in darkness, we are in a powerful place of transformation. We must have faith in God and trust the process. This was a time of reckoning, a time to be sifted like wheat or pass-through fire, like a kiln testing the potter's handiwork. In life, we are all tested. This is how we grow. Our old habits and ways of thinking had been shaken up, our priorities and lifestyles challenged. I assured him of my confidence that we would come through the crisis as better people.

As we approached the Parish Church at Holy Family, in the beautiful, scenic Honde Valley, a few hundred metres after turning off due west at the Nyatsanza Shopping Centre, there were disturbing signs of trouble ahead. Three trucks laden with armed police details in full riot gear and dogs, blocked the road. Behind the police line were groups of Mothers' Union Members in full-throated song, pushing fearlessly towards the amassed show of force. Suddenly, teargas was unleashed on the worshippers scattering them in all directions. They screamed their heads off as maniacal police details wielding batons went in full pursuit of the defenseless worshippers. I jumped out of the car with Arthur hot on my heels. I was clad in my purple cassock and must have cut a mythical figure as I shouted at the police to cease and desist. Arthur also shouted that he was the people's lawyer. Their rights were being violated.

A voice shouted that the Bishop had arrived and needed to be protected from the vicious police details. Mothers' Union members, villagers and other well-wishers massed menacingly and fearlessly around the police. The police were heavily outnumbered but armed to the teeth. The situation was ugly. Ironically, it was played out in the idyllic setting of a peaceful patch at the bottom of the Mtarazi Falls at the foothills of the majestic Nyanga mountains. I approached the head of the police unit and negotiated that he withdraws his men. The worshippers would be allowed to go into their church. I would go to Ruda Police Station, 5 kilometres away, to talk to the provincial police head who had authorised the police action. Eventually, we settled for that.

Arthur and I spent the next four hours in a clammy little room at Ruda police station being interviewed and cross-examined by the provincial chief of police, a bewhiskered choleric monster who clearly had the requisite scienter for persecuting innocent worshippers. The police evidently had no basic understanding of the issues at stake. They were just following 'orders from above,' they claimed repeatedly. We re-emerged from police custody with a caution and orders not to go back to the church. As we left the police station, Arthur vomited violently on the veranda. The entire contents of his stomach comprising generous helpings of alcohol from the night before, hurriedly consumed oatmeal and black coffee ingested before we left my apartment, issued out in an impressive gush onto the doorstep into the member-in-Charge's office. The day's stress was taking its toll.

Curiously, I recalled, at that point that Arthur had previously told me that he had been forced to read John Donne's sonnets in front of a group of children when he was young. This had given him metrophobia to the extent that he could hardly look at greeting card poetry without getting sweaty palms and a dry mouth. His mouth showed no signs of dryness now.

Clearly, this was to the chagrin of police details who were in obvious discomfort as they moved to clear the offensive mess from their doorstep. There must have been a divine sign somewhere in all this. On our way back, we stopped near the church. I could not have expressed my own feelings better than my friend Arthur did. The worshippers gathered and sang as I gave words of encouragement after narrating our sojourn at the cop shop, including Arthur's contribution, much to their delight. I then pronounced the blessing and dismissal as they sang a recessional hymn. We abandoned our planned confirmation service.

When we got back to Mutare, Martin Nyaundi invited us to join him for drinks and dinner at the Mutare Club. The drinks were welcome after the challenges of the day, the heat, dust and the police. As we tucked into our dinner, an anxious headwaiter, Peter, the man who had comforted me on the morning of my ordination, rushed to our table and whisked our plates away. "They are laced with poison," he explained with obvious discomfort. One of the waiters, a fanatical follower of the renegade bishop, relying on his ability to dissemble, had been planted by the disgraced faction "to poison and eliminate the new bishop." The matter had been reported to the police who classified it as a 'domestic quarrel' and declined to prosecute the idiot. Martin, in his capacity as Club Chairman, dismissed the waiter. I felt a twinge of masochistic satisfaction as if I had walked across flaming coals and survived. Peter apologized profusely.

We decided to go to the Vumba and check ourselves into the Leopard Rock Hotel for the night. Just after crossing the railway line, going up the first rise on the Vumba Hills, a huge, majestic black mamba, clearly hurt, was trying to cross the road to the safety of some bushes on the other side. I decided to jump out of the car and find a long stick to toss the choleric creature over the road, away from traffic. The nervous snake, in obvious self-defense mode, raised his head as I approached. At that moment, a mad motorist drove speedily and smashed the hapless creature as his car sped down towards the city, a smirk plastered on his face. I hurled the dead snake into the bushes on the other side of the road and clambered into my car. I was gutted. The snake meant no harm. He was in his habitat going about his business. That senseless act summed up my day.

While I sat at the window and gazed into the distance from my room above the casino at Leopard Rock, the phone rang. An exasperated voice informed me that during the day, two more death threats against me had been received by the office staff. Unofficial whispers from our contacts in the state security system had sent word to say that the situation was deteriorating fast. If possible, could I slip out of the country in the next few hours. A car had been sent to collect me. The enemy knew where I was. Could I leave everything except the few bare essentials in my room with a 'do not disturb' sign on the door, climb through a designated back window overlooking the car park where someone would meet me with further instructions.

I clutched my prayer book and pectoral cross as I lay on the backseat of the car. We drove for a seemingly interminable time before the driver asked me if I was 'O.K.' and if I wanted a drink. I was too upset to answer. A lot of planning had obviously gone into all this. I cleared customs at a small but friendly airfield. Two hours later, I was waiting to board a flight to London from a busy regional airport. It had been a day to remember.

At Lambeth Palace, two days later, Archbishop Rowan, other bishops and clergy listened to Chad and I relate our most recent experiences. We narrated, in detail, how the unholy duo of Kunonga and Jakazi had discombobulated the Anglican community in Zimbabwe. "These are real bastards we are dealing with," pronounced one erstwhile African diocesan Bishop. I spent time alone with the Archbishop. He had a gift of listening sympathetically without being patronizing. I felt at home in his presence. He was extremely well-informed and determined to work with us to resolve this situation.

In all this, Archbishop Rowan never lost his sense of humour. He teased me gently about having left the City of London for martyrdom. We laughed heartily before joining others for prayers and more discussions. As I left, I asked him if he would visit my diocese soon, ergo, I would welcome martyrdom in the wake of his visit. With a glint of human kindness in his eye and an unusually avuncular smile, he pressed hard on my shoulder, handed me a small icon of Christ's crucifixion and assured me that he would give my request serious thought and consideration.

Rowan is clearly in a class of his own. An aura of holiness, simplicity and an incredibly perceptive, brilliant yet humble mind behind a welcoming shy visage accompanied by a genuinely gentle smile which belies univocally forthright views expressed when the situation demands. His presence was felt in every corner of the room. He simply captured my imagination and reassured me that I had made the right decisions. Suddenly there was some meaning to my life and endeavours in my ministry as a diocesan Bishop. My epiphany had happened again in a different guise. The scales had just dropped off my eyes. I left Lambeth Palace with a spring in my step as I headed towards Mayfair's Boudin Blanc. It had become our favourite watering hole and eatery.

The following week was hectic. I decided to upscale my fund-raising campaign for the diocese of Manicaland. I spoke about the church, politics and the role of government to enthusiastic audiences at the historic and iconic St. Mary-le-Bow on Cheapside, Busbridge Church (St. John the Baptist) in Godalming, St. Mary the Virgin, Rotherham, St. John the Divine, Kennington, St. Mary the Virgin, Cardington, Beds. and the Royal Masonic Trust, Great Queen Street. Later that week, I took time off and had lunch with the erstwhile principal of Westcott House, now Bishop, Martin Seeley, in Cambridge. I went up to the House of the Resurrection at Mirfield and spent three days in retreat. As always, stimulating discussions and prayers in a familiar, friendly, numinous environment did a lot to re-charge my batteries. The walks to the village gym, the odd game of golf and a shared glass of whisky in my room were an acceptable and welcome part of the exercise.

Later, in Basingstoke, I would drive Tinao to the train station every morning before rushing back to clean the house, wash the car, do the daily shopping for the evening meal before running chores like laundry or dry cleaning. I would collect her from the station about seven every evening then settled down to drinks, dinner and sometimes, television, depending on what was on. Weekends we would often go away. Cambridge, Winchester and Bath were our favourite getaway to places. Occasionally we would find ourselves back in Paris enjoying cheese fondue in the quartier Latin or some other small eatery just off Champs Elysée.

Towards the end of my three-week tour, I booked myself in for my annual medical with my GP on Harley Street. He pronounced me to be in rude health apart from, "A couple of worrisome readings which need to be looked at and monitored closely." He suggested that I see a specialist. After my visit to the specialist and further tests, my GP told me that the two doctors who had seen me could not agree on whether I had a medical condition to worry about or not. That evening I talked to my brother, Steve, at Trinity Medical Centre in Minot, North Dakota. Steve advised me to visit him for further and more thorough tests at Trinity.

Later that week I was in the long queues at Minneapolis Airport in Minnesota, changing planes to get to Minot, North Dakota. In Minot, Steve met me at the airport and drove me home where the family awaited with a huge meal and champagne on ice. We had a feast then repaired to Steve's local watering hole, 'Paradiso,' for drinks. I spent the next couple of days familiarising myself with 'The magic City,' especially the medical facilities and the church. My father had, from time to time, assisted the parish priest, Revd. Mary Johnson and her predecessors, preaching or taking services at All Saints Church, downtown Minot. Later in the week, I was subjected to a battery of tests including being rendered unconscious while samples were extracted from my innards. After several blood tests, I felt like a pin cushion. It was stressful.

Waiting for the results was the toughest part. Over the weekend, we went fishing on the Missouri river and came back with a respectable catch of assorted local fish. On the Sunday, I was invited to baptize my surgeon's little daughter. I also preached at the main service. On the Monday afternoon, as I sat by the piano in the living room, Steve walked in and announced, rather nonchalantly that, "Cancerous cells had been detected in one sample." He suggested that this be removed sooner rather than later, although there was no immediate urgency. The treatment was scheduled for September, three months later. Meanwhile, I was free to return to my diocese.

I felt lost and lonely. Suddenly life took a different meaning. I tried to be brave and read up about my condition. It was not extremely helpful. Steve took it personally and avoided discussing it with me. 'We will knock the living daylights out of that cancer,' said my sister-in-law, Felistas. She worked at Trinity as a doctor in internal medicine. Steve's friends, Thompson Kamba and his wife,

Ellen, both doctors at Trinity as well, did their best to counsel and make me feel at ease without trivializing my condition. After extensive interviews with Dr. Hedgepeth, the resident urologist surgeon and Dr. Kevin Morris, the Radiologist, I opted for radiation treatment rather than surgery. The treatment would be over nine consecutive weeks.

Tinao met me at Heathrow and drove me home to a hearty, ambrosial meal. We spent the week visiting the Roman baths and the cathedral in Bath before flying to Milan then onto Rome for a few days. As we sat enjoying a long lunch at Agrippa's, I realised, much to my horror, when it was time to settle the bill, that my wallet had been stolen from my jacket inner pocket. I had all my credit and debit cards, ID cards, driver's licence and about two hundred Euros in cash. We searched frantically around the restaurant, the hotel and shops that we had visited earlier before going to report the matter to the police. We were assured of follow-up investigations and warned that, "Romanian gypsies were about; they were responsible for many cases of pickpocketing." It was a case of locking the door after the horse had bolted. That put a dampener on our trip. Despite the incident and the inconvenience, it caused, we enjoyed ourselves, as usual. Eventually, we returned home to Basingstoke much relaxed and much in love.

Chapter Thirty

I MADE A VERY LOW-KEY return to my 'valorous troops' in Manicaland. Shortly thereafter, I was embroiled in the ongoing wrangling in the diocese, the Church and beyond. In my absence, more members of our congregations had been arrested for daring to worship in their churches. I spent time visiting people in police stations or prison. I was heartbroken as I watched them processed through the courts and given fines for daring to be near their churches and being a threat to armed police. The situation in both Harare and Manicaland dioceses was getting out of hand. Our people were increasingly less scared of the police and other state agents. Rather than sit on their laurels and catastrophize their situation, they had now decided to take the fight to the enemy.

I supported them fully. My view was that we could not simply pray our plight away. The faithful were not being sequacious. They now agreed with me that we all had to be more proactive and pray for God's guidance and protection in our endeavours to restore sanity in our church and rebuild our diocesan properties for the good of all Christians in Manicaland and beyond. We had to play our part actively so that God's will would be effected. We were not, suddenly, of the view that the end justified the means, but, after careful thought and assessment of our strategy, we decided to be more flexible about the means than we previously thought. Futilitarians were not welcome among us. This was not a viable option.

Soon it was time to attend the annual provincial episcopal meeting in Lusaka. This would be my first as a bishop. I met up with fellow Zimbabwean bishops, Chad Gandiya, Godfrey Tawonezvi, Ishmael Mukuwanda and Cleopas Lunga at the check-in desk at Harare international Airport, for our Emirates flight to Lusaka on a Thursday morning. Reports that we would elect the new archbishop were untrue since there were two vacant Sees in the province, Northern and Central Malawi. All Sees in the Province must be occupied by a bishop before an archbishop can be elected. As we passed through immigration, an officer took my passport away and asked me to follow him.

I was led into a back office where I was informed that I was to be detained and taken to court for attempting to travel on a fake document, my usual passport. I had travelled to at least ten countries on this passport. I had been in and out of Zimbabwe several times using the same document. It was now ruled to be a forged, fake travel document. The other bishops tried their best to reason with the hoard of security men who had now gathered round me, but they were ordered to stay away and proceed to the lounge or face arrest. They watched helplessly as I was handcuffed and frog-marched out of the airport to the police station and holding cells.

At the police station, I was divested of my jacket, belt, wrist-watch, glasses, shoes, pectoral cross and episcopal ring before I was interrogated for about two hours. The interrogation centred on how I obtained my passport. It was issued in London, as confirmed by the Zimbabwe Embassy records. Fortunately, the records and paper trail supported my case. This, however, made no difference to the police. They kept changing tack, trying to find something to charge me with. When all failed, I was informed that the senior officer who could authorize my release could not be located. I was to stay in the cells until he was available.

I was shoved into a tiny cell with a stinking, filthy hole in the floor for a lavatory. In one corner, a dirty, bloodied old blanket on the floor harboured fleas waiting to feast on my flesh and blood. It was now getting dark outside. I stood on the rim of the feces-plastered toilet hole and leaned towards the tiny windows with broken glass to try and get some fresh air, only to be greeted by mosquitoes headed into the cell to feast on my helpless body. I kicked the flea-ridden blanket away from me, sat on the floor and prayed The Lord's Prayer and the Hail Mary. I broke into tears as I peeked through the broken window at the desolate, rubbish-littered police car park.

I could not make sense of what was happening to me. I prayed to God to make me understand it all, but I knew better than to expect a sudden answer via a big voice coming from the sky. I sat in the dark, smelly, filthy cell and listened to thoughts racing through my mind as I struggled to breathe. My thoughts drifted and wondered in the funky whiff, as I reminisced about all the things I had done in the past; how God had worked through my life and how it came to pass that I was in prison. I tried to recall the specifics that brought me to prison and wondered what I could have done to avoid it. Had the zeal for the Lord consumed me? In my heart of hearts, I knew that I could have never been at peace within myself if I had not stood for the truth. I felt God's presence in my funky cell. He was there with me, for me. What a contradiction!

One would think it easy for God to remove all this in a mere wave of His hand. I never imagined, nor did anyone else, I bet, that my special call would end up in prison. Was this part of the mission? On my knees, I asked God, in a vale of tears, for forgiveness for my impatience, weaknesses and frustrations. I prayed for my eyes to be opened so that I could see God's significance and work in this mess, rescue or no rescue. What I needed was wisdom and insight rather than allow my mind to play tricks on me because of my predicament. I needed to be able to open the eyes of my heart to perceive His love and witness an array of angels protecting me as events unfolded by His grace.

It was going to be a long night. At about midnight, I was startled by a soft knock at the door. I instinctively jumped and stood with my back to the wall. I was ready to attack any intruder who meant harm. A boyish voice softly advised me to be brave and to stand away from the door as it was about to open. "I have been made aware of your fighting skills," the voice said. "Please do not attack me when I open the door. I am here to help you." As if he had read my mind. The door opened slowly. One of the youthful security details from the airport motioned to me to follow him to the main hall where a large fire roared in a fireplace. This was a welcome change from my freezing, smelly, flea-ridden cell. I was dumbfounded.

Two grumpy policemen sat quietly in the hall. After a brief silence, one of them explained that they knew I was innocent. What they were doing was wrong. They were Christians and could not live with what they were doing. My arrest, they explained, was the denouement of Kunonga's and Jakazi's machinations and their bid to disrupt the Bishops' meeting in Lusaka. The least they could do, as junior police officers, was to let me out of the cell and sit by the fire till the early hours of the morning. "We trust you Bishop. You can call your driver to take you to your house but be back here at five in the morning so we can lock you up again," said one of the officers. I declined the offer. Sentience, I guess. I had heard many stories of accidents happening as prisoners tried to 'escape.' I sat quietly on a bench and gazed pensively into the glowing fireplace.

At about four in the morning, the front door swung open and a fat police officer carrying a rifle and three dead rabbits burst into the main hall. It turned out this was one of the senior officers. He had been out on the perimeter of the airport hunting for rabbits and gallinaceous fowl, mainly guinea fowl and quail that roamed the bush near the runway. On seeing me, the choleric pederast monster shouted, "What's the prisoner doing in here? Lock the bastard up now." That was the end of my short sojourn in the luxury of the main hall in the untidy police station. I was shoved back into my cell, my own cold space, complete with hungry mosquitoes, lice and fleas and a feces-decorated toilet hole. Alone at last and still alive. It was a strange feeling but somehow, I was relieved to be back in my little cell. I was now quite inured to my prison life and the tough conditions even just after some hours. I felt safe that way, strangely.

At about ten the following morning, I was ushered out of my cell and escorted by two burly police details, barefoot, to the ablution facilities at the domestic terminal. I managed to wash my hands and face, relieve myself and look at myself in the mirror before I was escorted back to my cell. In the main hall of the police station, I spotted my driver, Roderick, in tears, carrying a flask of coffee and sandwiches. He asked the officer on duty if he could approach me and hand over the food that he had brought for me. His request was denied on the grounds that he could poison me.

I instructed Roderick to give the food to the two moronic thugs who had escorted me to the domestic terminal. I watched them gobble up my sandwiches in undeniably simian fashion before loudly gulping my coffee without fear of poison. I retreated to the now familiar, my very own safe space, my cell. At about three in the afternoon, I was escorted out to the main hall again, then informed that I was to be taken to the magistrates' courts at Rotten Row, but I had to provide my own transport. I wasted no time in calling Roderick. Shortly thereafter, I sat between two police details with clear signs of schadenfreude plastered on their faces, on the back seat of my Landcruiser. We headed to the appropriately named Rotten Row magistrates' courts.

My lawyer, Innocent Chagonda of Atherstone and Cook, was waiting for us at the entrance to the courtroom. I was led to the Chief Magistrate's office. Straightaway, I recognized him. It was a relief to see a familiar face in the mess and confusion of the chaotic magistrates' courts which felt like shuffling during a zombie horde from 'The Walking Dead.' Silently, I wondered how the collective acid exhalations of the masses who gather round the courtrooms daily has affected the legal community that works in that environment.

After listening to the police story and my lawyer's account of events, the Senior prosecutor, Mr. Kumire, asked to see a copy of my passport before handing it to the Chief Magistrate. "Why do you think this is a fake passport?" inquired the magistrate, who was clearly puzzled. As the police stuttered through an incredibly infantile response, the magistrate asked me to step out of the room for a minute. I obeyed without hesitation.

When the door to the magistrate's office eventually opened, the two police officers looked like lost sheep as they evacuated the office. They walked past me like they had never seen me before. Innocent told me I was free to go but my passport had to remain with the police. On the way out, he advised me to go to the Ministry of Home Affairs and apply for a new passport without delay. I did this the following day and received a brand-new passport two days later. I went home to ponder my ordeal and read messages of support from the House of Bishops. My brother Bishops had decided to postpone the meeting in Lusaka to the end of June, three weeks later, in Harare. Once in the comfort of my home, I wasted no time in tucking into the cook's ambrosial concoctions which clearly towered above anything I had consumed in the recent past, accompanied by generous helpings of blushful, beaded claret.

Three weeks later, we held the episcopal synod in Harare. At that meeting, I was elected Dean of the Province, a position I held for the next three years. We discussed the difficult situation in the dioceses of Harare and Manicaland and the upcoming elections for the bishops of the two vacant Sees of Northern and Central Malawi. A couple of weeks later, I was in Malawi to attend the consecration of Francis Kaulanda as the new Bishop of Central Malawi. We later convened to elect Fanuel Magangani as the Bishop-elect of Northern Malawi, pending his confirmation which would happen a month later. Once all the Sees were filled, we would then elect an Archbishop for our Province of Central Africa from among the fourteen bishops of the Province.

After Francis Kaulanda's ordination and consecration as Bishop of Lake Malawi at St. Peter's Cathedral, on the shores of Lake Malawi, we drove back to Lilongwe at dusk. It was a bumpy four-hour drive. We were taken to a dimly lit, almost derelict house, where we were supposed to put up for the night. I refused to check into the dingy hotel. After an uncomfortable exchange with one of the local bishops, we were taken to a better lodge where we put up for the night.

During dinner I remarked that the bishop who preached at the ordination service that morning, sounded like one of those motor-mouthed autodidacts that one finds on old tourist attractions like Roman ruins, Zimbabwe ruins and the like. The joke went up like a lead balloon. One could have cut through the pregnant, deafening silence that ensued, with a blunt knife. The rehearsed lines of his sermon seemed to have been imagined in moments of exhaustion, following convulsions. They were discordant notes in a harmony of sombre madness, comical and ridiculous. I meant what I said without malice. The words just came out of my mouth. The sermon was undeniably bunkum. It had been a long day.

In Mutare, I had to make sure that I prepared well for my upcoming medical absence. I briefed the Standing Committee, Trustees and Chapter, then embarked on a punishing round of parish visits. Most of them included confirmation and the occasional baptism. I also had a visit from my friends from Cambridge, Adam Boulter, his smart wife, Beth and their intelligent son, Joseph. Adam preached and assisted me at Mass at parishes round the diocese. It was delightful to have them supporting me. In July and August alone, I confirmed six hundred candidates, four hundred of them at one service. Four churches in the chapelry gathered at St. Thomas in Marange, on the edge of the diamond fields. It was back-breaking work but satisfying. This was one of the few services that the police utterly failed to disrupt. The renegade Jakazi priest could only gaze in horror and wonder at the large number of ardent Christians professing their faith in God as members of the CPCA.

Before my departure, I paid a visit to the Provincial Police Commissioner to protest at continuing and deteriorating relations between the police and members of our church. Despite having a prior appointment, I was kept waiting for almost an hour before I was ushered into a dark boardroom with a row of police officers seated on one side. I introduced myself then launched into a tirade against police brutality and the unfair treatment our members were subjected to. This happened despite court rulings that urged the two warring factions to share church properties and worship at different times. When I finally stopped, the Chief of Police said, "We have our orders. We will follow them. Your case is at the Supreme Court and we will wait for the judgement before we change our behaviour. May I remind you sir that he who laughs last will laugh the loudest. Good day sir."

At that point I was escorted out of the boardroom onto the street. After my recent ordeal with the police at the airport, I was quite relieved to get out of the police building. The poor personal hygiene that characterized the atmosphere in the building, especially the boardroom, was overpowering. The rundown state of the police headquarters, sadly, reminded me of that horrible saying by Ian Smith about Africans in charge: "..they will walk on raw sewage until they believe it is normal and infrastructure will collapse..." It could not have taken much to clean up the place and work in decent surroundings. As Orwell's dictum goes, in times of deceit, telling the truth is revolutionary.

As I was preparing to leave for Minot, I received summons to do jury duty at the high court in Kingston-upon-Thames, near London. I could not get out of this one despite trying hard. I was assured the case would not go beyond three days but alas, a week later, I was still reporting for duty at Kingston Crown Court. At the end of the week, I asked to see the judge and explained to her that I had to leave for urgent medical treatment. Luckily, she agreed for me to be released from jury duty at that time, much to the annoyance of the legal teams. "My Lord Bishop," she said elegantly. "We thank you for having made the effort and wish you well in your treatment. You may take leave of this court," she said with a little bow and a sweet smile. What a beautiful judge, I thought to myself as I left the courtroom for Heathrow Airport.

I spent the next ten weeks in Minot, North Dakota. I stayed with Steve and his family. I doubled as sous-cook, child minder and driver. Treatment was Monday to Friday, generally at eight in the morning. It lasted three painless minutes per session. A team comprising three nurses and a technician would treat me with competence and compassion in a jovial atmosphere. We became good friends by the end of the nine weeks of treatment. After treatment each day, I would drive back to the house and clean up after breakfast, play a few tunes on the piano or the guitar, have a skype call with the diocesan office, read my daily office before going to collect my delightful nephew, Ishe, from school and take him for his music lessons or dance classes.

I wrote my weekly 'Letter from Minot,' detailing my activities and treatment, by the bay window with a lovely view of the hills, parts of farmland and affluent western suburbs of the Magic City. I would also prepare sermons or prayers for the Sunday service at All Saints Episcopal Church where Rev. Mary Johnson, was the Vicar. Over time, I talked the team who treated me into attending services, especially when I preached.

Friday nights we would go out to Paradiso with Steve and Thompson Kamba. Saturdays were reserved for fishing just south of Garrison Dam. Walleye, northern pike, perch and bass were in abundance. From time to time, we would go to Fargo, where we would eat at the Tru Blu Social Club and attend church services at Gethsemane Cathedral or St. Stephen's Episcopal Church. On one occasion, we attended a service by the erstwhile Presiding Bishop, Catherine Jafferts-Schori, who I had met and dined with previously, in Harare.

Mother Mary at All Saints gave me my own key to the Church so I could use the church for my daily office. This was an opportunity for me to spend time in meditative and contemplative prayer. I sought to understand my illness and prayed for healing. It was also a time to pray for my diocese and everything we were trying to achieve. I prayed for success in our efforts to regain our properties and rebuild our schools and hospitals. I experienced periods of euphoria and sometimes I went through patches of doubt and feeling helpless. Overall, however, I found prayers to be uplifting and morale- boosting.

I prayed for my own spiritual growth as I said my office at least twice daily. It was a joy to pray with Mother Mary. Sometimes we read and studied the Bible together. Praying with the family, especially at All Saints on Sundays was always a treat. The congregation was as warm and welcoming as they had been to Dad, according to his recollection. He had also baptised Ishe at the same church. I enjoyed my role as Mother Mary's assistant, which was sanctioned by Bishop Michael G. Smith of North Dakota. I still enjoy and look forward to my frequent visits to All Saints.

After ten weeks in Minot, it was time to say good-bye to my family and friends. The team at the hospital gave me a native American patchwork healing quilt and a cornucopia of cards and presents. I gave them chocolates and flowers and left them in stitches as I imitated their accents and little phrases during treatment. It is always special whenever I call in to greet them and thank them, once again, for an excellent job. I was cured of my ailment completely. I have fond memories of the whole community that I interacted with in Minot. I am sure the family misses a driver, cook, fisherman, babysitter, musician, preacher and 'Man Friday' in the house.

Tinao and I often share memories of the Magic City. On one visit, she took it all in her stride as I drove her round the great metropolis and showed her some of the flesh spots. We went fishing one day and came home with a small catch. None of it was attributable to Tinao.

I returned to Minot to help when Steve was taken ill and had to spend time in hospital in Minneapolis. I drove the children through snowstorms from Minneapolis to Minot, a hair-raising seven-hour ordeal. I could hear the children praying in the back of the car as I struggled to keep the car on the road. Eventually, we made it home. We welcomed Steve and Felly home a few days later. The visit would not have been complete, of course, without a visit to All Saints, where I gave an impromptu homily. At Trinity Cancer Centre we were greeted with loud cheers and screams. We repaired to Paradiso, for drinks with friends in the established manner.

On my way to London from Minot, I had a stop-over in Washington D.C. as a guest of Joe Wambia and his delightful family. Joe had just married a stunning Japanese lady and had two children about six and three. It was great to be back in my old neighbourhoods and stomping grounds. I looked up and met with many friends including Clarence Haynes, Joel Maweni, Barbra Wilson, James Wise, Paula Hanson and some others. From Washington I joined Tinao in Basingstoke for Christmas.

On Christmas Eve, Tinao cooked one of her elaborate, ambrosial meals before we went for the midnight service at St. Michael's Church, downtown Basingstoke. After the service we walked briskly in the driving rain and made our way back to the house where we sat by the fire dunking sippets in warm cognac as we enjoyed the Christmas spirit. We spent Boxing Day shopping for food, wine and household goods at Costco and other shops in Reading. I was never any good at shopping, but I quite enjoyed this trip. It was not entirely to do with the extensive amounts of discounted claret and champagnes. A new computer, gas and electric range, a double door fridge freezer and seafood, especially crab cakes, were also in the mix. Pushing the huge trolleys behind Tinao was an exercise in patience.

Chapter Thirty

OUR ANNUAL RETREAT, which we held jointly with the Diocese of Harare, was once again disrupted by the police. The police asked us to leave as the school, according to them, belonged to Kunonga and his church. Chad Gandiya and I spent the day arguing with the police at the Marondera Police HQ on Ruzawi Road. Meanwhile, riot police in armoured cars were dispatched to remove our priests from Peterhouse Girls High School, where we normally held our retreat. I had invited my training incumbent, Canon Derek Winterburn, to conduct the retreat for us. This was a huge embarrassment for us.

We hastily secured accommodation at the Belvedere Teachers' College in Harare, at short notice, for a shortened retreat. It was impossible to hold a totally silent retreat at this noisy venue, but Derek did an excellent job of calming us all down and conducting the retreat superbly. He appeared unfazed by all the police disruption and preached about reconciliation, faith and prayer. We left inspired and rejuvenated. We carried the message back to Manicaland.

Derek stayed with me for a week. On the Sunday, he accompanied me to two services in the Marange chapelry. After the service, the priest, Fr. Mukome, a diminutive thanks giver, announced that the congregation was grateful and touched by Derek's visit and sermon. They had organized a present for him to take back to England. Derek watched in disbelief as a billy goat with a ribbon around its neck was led up the aisle by school children and presented to a clearly amused Derek who smiled gently, thanked them profusely. He donated his bleating gift to the Bishop. The tethered goat sat in the back of the car as we drove to Mutare.

On the way back to Harare, we stopped at my parents' house for lunch. Derek's goat was led to a pen where other donated goats and sheep were being fed and watered. The goat looked relieved to be among more agreeable creatures and goatly surroundings. I am sure Derek was happy not to have to escort a goat to the British Airways check-in counter at the Harare International Airport.

One of my favourite pastoral undertakings, apart from my homilies at the Thursday Mass, Benediction, talking to students, youth groups and blessing infants, was to visit the sick in all the medical facilities in the diocese. When word spread that the Bishop, unlike some of his predecessors, visited the sick, requests for such visits rose exponentially. I did what I could. After a short while, however, the requests diminished and indeed, almost vanished. One day the Vicar General explained this phenomenon to me: Every time I visited or anointed the sick, they would recover very quickly then die suddenly shortly thereafter. Word from the mealie patch was that the Bishop's prayers were so powerful that God wanted the person prayed for to be with Him before they had a chance to sin again! My lardy-dardy Aunt Miriam died only three hours after I had anointed her, as did one of my senior priests.

On a balance of probabilities, I am sure patients increasingly decided to try their luck without the divine intervention that came on the heels of the Bishop's prayer visits and anointing. Amazingly, however, I still receive, admittedly not doorbusters, requests for visits and anointing of the sick. I always preferred funerals to weddings: the former tended to be more to the point than the latter. I tried my best to avoid officiating at either one of them except in the case of clergy deaths or marriages. Counselling of priests in distress and confusion and hearing confession were unavoidable but I never looked forward to them. I found this part of my vocation stressful, draining and taxing yet humbling and spiritually nourishing.

In one of his sermons, Lord Rowan Williams of Oystermouth, the erstwhile Archbishop of Canterbury explained that when a bishop visits a parish, stumbles his way through an interview, sits with a priest in trouble, he is 'the good news' for those he serves. However, the real and only 'good news' is Jesus Christ. Importantly, the bishop cannot do those things 'in his own strength.' This message was a constant mantra and personal reminder in my episcopal ministry.

Archbishop Rowan's message was a constant reminder that the Bishop is to be a shepherd, a prophet, a priest, a person of understanding and learning, a good disciplinarian and teacher, business-like in administration, alive to current affairs and social responsibilities. That said, I think that it is unreasonable to expect bishops to be endowed with all these excellences and that there must be among them, as among other people, the clergy and laity, diversities of gifts to be exercised under the control of one Spirit.

Almost every week, as Bishop, I was, like any other bishop, expected to preach somewhere in the diocese and sometimes beyond, to celebrate the Mass, confirm and sometimes baptize candidates, attend meetings and committees. At regular seasons there would be ordination candidates around me. I would teach them, send them out ordained and commissioned. Frequently I would institute a new incumbent. It was a mix of pursuits requiring cerebral, intuitive, emotional and instinctive approaches.

Daily, I would have correspondence and interviews, people seeking ordination or wanting to join the diocese or just change their work, people with all sorts of joys and troubles. I found life as bishop exacting. It is a life with manifest dangers and temptations. In all this, I found and had to make sure that my quiet time, period of study and prayer life had a place of privilege. My day off, every Monday, I tried to keep and was known to be kept. Mondays were not merely for personal relaxation, but I considered it to be a sacred duty to God, family and work. Most Mondays if in Harare, I shared lunch and drinks with Bishop Chad Gandiya. I looked forward to spending time in my music room, my private atelier with a beautifully cluttered warren of musical instruments, art pieces, karate memorabilia and ephemera.

In national affairs, as bishop, in common with other church leaders, I had to choose the words of my public utterances and the time for delivering them, very carefully. Instances of fearlessness in this respect are well documented, historically, with innumerable examples of brave words and actions of bishops in connection with injustice, prejudice and oppression. Our case was unique in that apart from internal divisions, the state was also involved visibly in our dispute. Authorities used state apparatus to aid one group to the detriment of the other. I felt that in any case, come what may, the Bishop must be a focal point of unity. This was not easy.

I criticized the police in the media when they forcibly removed villagers from areas in my diocese where diamonds were suspected to occur. I was determined to give the authorities tsuris on this. When pressure in the media failed to yield the intended result, I led villagers and defied serried ranks of riot police as we stood in front of bulldozers that were set to demolish houses, driving people out of their homes without providing alternative accommodation or compensation in any form. We were arrested, sometimes assaulted and forcibly removed and taken to police holding centres.

This did not endear me to the provincial and national authorities who saw me as a thorn in their sides. In time, my efforts paid off as a resettlement programme eventually materialized and compensation offered for destroyed homes and communal facilities such as roads, schools, churches, clinics and other infrastructure. In my stand against injustice in this respect, I managed to unite all people, not just Anglicans. I led a resistance movement against injustice. I even earned the respect of the local, waggish police force and prison wardens for standing up to government greed, oppression and callous acts of unprovoked aggression against ordinary people in my diocese.

One area that occupied me much was the appalling living conditions of refugees at Tongogara Camp, near the Tanganda Tea Estates. The camp houses refugees from as far as the Congo, Somalia, South Sudan, Ethiopia, Eritrea, Syria, South Africa, Burundi, Kenya, Mozambique and Rwanda. The inhabitants are not allowed to find work outside of the camp, nor leave the camp after dark. They live in shacks with only communal and filthy ablution facilities. They can grow vegetables in little gardens around their shacks and sell their produce to each other.

Whenever I approached the Ministry of Labour and Social Welfare in Mutare to discuss how to improve the lot of the inmates, the corpulent officer-in-charge always seemed to be more anxious to identify reasons to take offence rather than provide friendly, constructive service: the 'refugees' had not proved themselves to be genuine refugees, they could be common criminals seeking refuge from punishment in their countries, they could be spies or maybe terrorists, he droned with a practiced brusquerie.

As a result, the refugees, by and large, innocent folk, women, men and children fleeing political oppression, intersectionality, marginalization and economic hardships in their countries of origin, still subsist in appalling conditions lacking access to basic necessities such as soap, sanitary pads, cooking and edible oils and salt among other items, at this sprawling prison-like facility in the arid and remote Middle-Sabi scrubland in the Chipangayi area of Chipinge District, near Birchenough Bridge. From time to time, the UNHCR visits the camp but there has been no visible positive impact resulting from their visits.

With the help of the C.R. fathers, Fr. Nicolas Stebbing especially, we raised funds to build a small church where Anglican refugees would worship. The building doubled up as a classroom and school for the inhabitants. Father Nicolas and I took turns to celebrate Mass at the church after I dedicated it. I also confirmed adults and young people at the church. Sometimes the refugees would join the congregation at our church in Chipinge. The choir, led by a Congolese music teacher and women folk mostly, danced and sang beautifully in Kituba and Lingala at our services. Their singing and swaying during and after services created an arresting and unforgettable effect.

One hot day, we held the service under a huge tree. As though stirred by furious pokers, the sun appeared from behind sparse clouds and shorn like a kiln-hole. It darted a light almost white hot, burning our faces. A hot, brown dust rose from the footpaths, scorching the seared trees. The yellowed grass was now a deep brown colour. Temperatures like that of a foundry hung over the camp and surrounding scrubland.

Despite their miserable living conditions and years of isolation, the refugees were always cheerful, well-dressed and quite modish in appearance and manner. I would always greet and thank them in French, which they appreciated. By the time I left the diocese, we had managed to send five children from Tongogara Camp to secondary school at St. David's Bonda and St. Augustine's Penhalonga. At the time of writing, I believe there are about twenty thousand refugees at the camp. The government has now established a primary and secondary school for them.

In August 2010 I was in Kampala to participate in The All-Africa Bishops Conference organised by The Council of Anglican Provinces of Africa (C.A.P.A). This was hot on the heels of another conference on rural development in Embu, Kenya. The subject, in Kampala, was "Securing Our Future: Unlocking our Potential." The Conference was hosted by Archbishops Henry Orombi of Uganda and Ian Earnest, of Mauritius. The Archbishop of Canterbury, Rowan Williams, delivered the Keynote Address and sermon.

We were hosted to dinner by President Yoweri Museveni at the impressive Presidential Palace. There were several excellent speeches and outstanding Bible Study sessions from African theologians and physicians. The conference had a lively and robust debate about homosexuality, women bishops and the split these issues were causing in the Anglican Communion. The dimensions of intolerance, ignorance and oppressive tendencies expressed by some bishops was overwhelmingly shocking. They read out prepared speeches which were simply works of unparalleled stupidity.

I took the opportunity at tea-time, one afternoon, to update the Archbishop of Canterbury on the situation in my diocese and Harare diocese as well. I suggested, once again, that on his upcoming visit to Malawi and Zambia, he could stopover in Zimbabwe to visit the persecuted and displaced Anglicans in Harare and Manicaland dioceses. This would be a morale-booster for the Church in Zimbabwe and would be an opportunity to confront President Robert Mugabe and his cohorts about the ongoing persecution of Anglicans in Zimbabwe. Soon we were discussing the logistics of such a visit with the Bishops of Botswana, Harare and the Archbishop's staff. The Archbishop's dream visit was fast becoming a reality. For me, the said visit was the best thing to come out of the conference. It made up for all the minor inconveniences of the whole event.

A short three months later, Zimbabwe's Anglicans were set to receive the Spiritual Leader of the Anglican Communion. The Government had been informed through the president's Office, Foreign Affairs and Home Affairs. On hearing of the Archbishop's impending visit, the renegade clergymen, Nolbert Kunonga and his minion in Mutare, Elson Jakazi, organised a demonstration to meet the Archbishop at the airport on his arrival into the country. Alert to the plans of the evil men, we agreed with the Archbishop's idea of coming by road from Malawi.

So it was that Bishop Christopher and I, accompanied by a hired minibus full of Anglicans from the two affected dioceses, left Harare at two in the morning, drove in darkness for three hours, 215 kms, to Motoko's Nyamapanda border post, the north-eastern gateway into Zimbabwe, to meet the Archbishop. The situation was tense. Christopher and I prayed in the car at the empty border post, parked near the immigration offices and waited for daybreak.

As it was getting light, a thick-set man approached our car as two police patrol cars rolled up and parked just behind our cars. I got out and greeted the stranger, who turned out to be an officer from the Ministry of Foreign Affairs. The man knew who we were and why we were there. He informed us, much to our relief, shock and utter amazement, that he was here to assist us welcome the Archbishop and his entourage. The police cars were part of a police escort assigned to protect us for the duration of the Archbishop's stay in the country. They already knew that we would go to my house in Highlands for breakfast before taking the Archbishop to his accommodation in Mt. Pleasant. We had arranged this to throw any of Kunonga's people off the trail. How the security services discovered our secret plans is still a mystery to me. Very unnerving in many ways. Meanwhile, Kunonga's people were gathered at Harare International Airport waiting to demonstrate against the visiting Archbishop.

As the sun crept up the sky, we saw purple cassock-clad figures leave the Mozambique side and wander into 'no-man's land' towards the Zimbabwe post. As they came closer, I recognised the beaming face of the agreeable, affable Bishop James Tengatenga leading Archbishops Williams and Chama, their staff and a few more bishops in tow. As soon as they cleared immigration and customs formalities, Bishop Tengatenga announced loudly that his duty was done. He had delivered the Archbishop of Canterbury into my care, and he was making his way back to Lilongwe, 345 miles away.

There was relief and laughter all-round as we briefed the Archbishop before piling into our cars. We were escorted by wailing police cars and outriders speeding across the countryside to an unsuspecting sleepy suburb of Highlands in Harare. I rode with the

Archbishop. We talked about the political and church situation in Zimbabwe. He was extremely well informed and asked after the current status of other churches, especially the Roman Catholic Church. He knew of bishop Francis Markall S.J., a former Jesuit, Roman Catholic bishop of Harare, whose work he admired.

At the house, 5 Rietfontein Close, the Archbishop and his entourage set about refreshing themselves and settling down to a cooked breakfast at tables scattered round the garden, the gazebo and the main dining room. After breakfast, the Archbishop led us through morning prayers before walking round the house and amusing us all by splaying at the piano in the entrance hall. Revd. Joanna Udall played more tunefully on the grand piano in the main lounge. We applauded Joanna's and the Archbishop's musical efforts and shared light moments before setting off for Mt. Pleasant, where the Archbishop and some of his staff were to be housed in a private house near bishop Chad's house This was arranged by the Harare diocese.

As I left the Archbishop's room after leaving his suitcase and packages, he summoned me back into his room and with a stern voice said to me, "You should not say anything about this, it is your present from me." With a smile, he handed me a huge portrait of himself, that a Malawian 'artist' had kindly donated to him. It could pass for his portrait after a few drinks. I could not hold back the tears as I laughed loudly and walked to my car carrying the gift, much to everyone's amusement. I had to look for a suitable place to display my present. I had an idea at the back of my mind.

That afternoon, the Archbishop's convoy, with a police escort, snaked its way from Mt. Pleasant, through downtown Harare, past the occupied Cathedral of St. Mary's and All Saints, heading west to the Glamis Stadium where thousands of Anglicans had gathered to attend Mass celebrated by the Archbishop. As we entered the dressing rooms, more police had gathered to remove demonstrators who had now found out our plan, late in the day. The invaders tried to disrupt our service, in vain. There was much rejoicing, singing and praise-worship as the huge congregation, estimated at about twenty thousand, broke into song and dance as the fifteen bishops in attendance and the rest of the clergy processed into the huge arena.

It was a long service with a passionate sermon from the Archbishop. He exhorted us all to stay strong as we fought the good fight. We were set on a battlefield and we must fight courageously, he urged. This was vintage Rowan, at his best. We should not dodge the blows or retreat, but keep our eyes on Christ, our King and Leader and persevere like he did, thus fulfilling God's command and our salvation. "To be Christian," he explained, "is to share in Christ's endurance. We needed the courage of endurance, trusting that in God's time what we long for will be given, even if not as we anticipate."

This was a riveting, edifying sermon. We were energized. We then 'wailed' and snaked out of the Arena, behind the police escort, exhausted. It had been a long day. Back at the Archbishop's residence, we met to consider what our next steps would be. We still awaited news from the president's office to inform us what time we were expected to meet with the president. The Archbishop decided that we should leave for Manicaland early in the morning and wait to hear from the president's office while the Archbishop and his entourage visited displaced congregations in Manicaland. This was a brave and wonderful decision for the diocese of Manicaland.

I sent word to my diocese to organize people and to prepare for the Archbishop's visit. I decided that we would stop in Rusape to visit the displaced congregation at St. Matthias in Vengere, then stop for a ground-breaking service at a site on Christmas Pass where we intended to build our St. Paul's Cathedral. From St. Paul's, we would go to the Botanical Gardens where the Archbishop would address Anglicans gathered from all over the diocese and beyond. We would stop to pray outside our St. John's Cathedral before gathering at my office for breakfast. After breakfast we would go to St. Augustine's Mission to see the C.R. Fathers' old monastery, the iconic church and the Convent of the CZR Sisters. I prayed that we could accomplish all this according to plan. By now, I had be-friended our police escort. I provided them meals and refreshments, especially cream-doughnuts which they devoured in large amounts, at an incredible rate.

Our convoy left for Manicaland at half past five, the next morning. Two hours later, we were driving through cheering crowds in Rusape as we headed for the Town Hall in Vengere Township, where our St. Matthias congregation met for their services. The Archbishop was visibly touched by the warm welcome of the people of Rusape. He was shown, from a distance, the Parish church which had been taken over and converted into a nursery school by Jakazi's followers. Once again, the Archbishop gave his message of hope, faith and endurance before blessing the congregation. As we left, the lugubrious Parish Priest, Fr. Mushipe, presented the Archbishop with a small pestle and mortar with the words, 'Your Grace, this is a reminder that we will crush our enemies like we crush grain using these tools.' The Archbishop's message clearly had not quite hit the spot!

Soon we were back on the highway, speeding on the pre-cleared road towards Mutare. At Christmas Pass, we stopped briefly for the ground-breaking and blessing of the gathered faithful who then piled into vehicles and drove in our convoy to the crowded Botanical Gardens which was a sea of Mothers' Union white and blue uniforms.

The gathered faithful erupted into song as the bishops led the Archbishop to the prepared raised platform and podium. The number of bishops had increased since Archbishops Thabo Makgoba of Cape Town and Valentino of Tanzania had joined us. After opening prayers led by the Bishop of Manicaland, the bishops were introduced. The Archbishop of Canterbury moved to the podium where he delivered his amazingly simple but effective message of faith, hope and endurance. As we left the Botanical Gardens, we stopped briefly as the Archbishop greeted my parents and said a prayer as he laid hands on Dad. The man's sensitivity and generosity never ceased to amaze me.

The traffic and life in Mutare came to a standstill as our convoy, which had now swollen to at least two hundred vehicles, left the Botanical Gardens and drove through the City Centre to St. John's Cathedral. We gathered to pray outside the locked Church. All the Bishops walked with me to the main entrance. I knocked on the locked doors three times with my crozier before praying as we stood in a circle. The crowd erupted into song and dance as they followed us to the bishop's office, a quarter of a mile from the Cathedral, up Herbert Chitepo Road.

After breakfast, the Archbishop and I emerged from my office to a heaving mass of MU and other Christians in full song. Without hesitation, much to the delight of the crowd, the Archbishop did a jig and danced with the worshippers as we worked our way to the waiting cars. Soon we were on our way. We drove through the centre of Mutare towards Christmas Pass and St. Augustine's, Penhalonga, fifteen kilometres away in the mountains. When we arrived at the main gates, the guard refused to open the gate. He was under orders from Jakazi's somnolent priest, Mr. Maunze, to deny us entry. However, the police and our friend from the Foreign Office who met us at the border, pushed their way through the gate and let a bench of bishops, about fifteen in all, march behind Archbishop Rowan. We walked four hundred metres up the hill to the church, next to the Convent.

I snatched a placard from a bewildered, little man as we walked past the pathetic motley crew of demonstrators. He had the look of a one-legged man at an arse-kicking party. The rest of the demonstrating idiots decided to abandon their placards and joined our procession. We gathered to pray and posed for photographs in front of the locked church. The Archbishop and I then went on a tour of the Convent. We prayed with the Nuns before re-joining the rest of the crowd outside the church. As we left, I whispered in Sister

Anna-Maria's ear that I had a present for them. I wanted it hung in a prominent place in the Convent Chapel. Archbishop Rowan's portrait from Malawi now graces that place.

As soon as we got back to the church, we were informed that the president's Office had just sent word that the president would meet us at his offices in about three hours. We made the journey back to Harare in the quickest time ever, just over two and half hours. We went straight to State House where all the bishops, a sea of purple, were ushered into the anteroom to meet His Excellency, President Robert Gabriel Mugabe and his attendants.

As soon as the introductions were over, the Archbishop leaned towards the president and at his most imperious said, 'I do not like what you are doing to my people. This needs to stop immediately.' The president was visibly taken aback. He was clearly lost for words. The Archbishop handed him a dossier of crimes against Anglicans in the diocese of Harare and Manicaland that we had compiled. The president made guttural noises as he cleared his throat. He was in obvious awe of the stern-looking Archbishop and his bishops around him.

The president handed the report to his attendants and demanded to hear from them what the position was, on the ground. The president's men could only mumble and choke on words of denial. Their account of the relationship of the government and the Anglican dioceses of Harare and Manicaland amounted to an abusage, simplistic, ahistorical and glaringly wrong. The Archbishop pressed home his advantage as he demanded answers and an immediate cessation of the persecution of Anglicans by the police who always cited 'orders from above.'

The meeting, scheduled to last thirty minutes, went on for over two hours. The Archbishop, having extracted promises of the cessation of police brutality and an investigation of the cases cited in our dossier of human rights violations, tactfully eased the pressure on the visibly shaken but now a little more comfortable octogenarian President. The relieved ruler gave us a history of the relationship between his government and the British government from the time of the Lancaster House talks, independence and the aftermath. He was amazingly lucid and polite. He offered us cream tea and scones which we enjoyed. He then suddenly asked the Bishop of Harare why he thought Kunonga was acting on his orders. Bishop Chad answered that these claims came from Kunonga himself.

The Archbishop explained that Kunonga and Jakazi were not Anglican bishops. They were renegade, Svengali thugs who had since been expelled from the Anglican Church. He then introduced the five Anglican bishops in Zimbabwe. At the end of the meeting, the president stood and sheepishly asked for the Bishops to pray for him. We stood round him and prayed as the Archbishop laid hands on him and blessed the president and his staff. This was an amazingly emotional, touching and special moment. The president hung on to the Archbishop's cassock as he walked us to the porchway. As I walked past him, the president said, "I heard you are now the bishop of Manicaland. Please come and see me. Don't forget to pray for me." I fought back tears as I walked to our waiting car with Bishop Trevor Mwamba, Archbishops Thabo and Valentino and drove behind the Archbishop's car and police escort to Mt. Pleasant for a debrief.

When we got to Mt. Pleasant, we were informed that the Prime Minister, Morgan Tsvangirayi, was expecting us. We stopped for a wee break then took off to the Prime Minister's house in Avonlea. It was a brief but cheerful courtesy call on an obviously elated Prime Minister who promised to assist us in our struggle. We then rushed to Bishop Chad's house where invited guests, about one hundred Anglicans, waited patiently at neatly set tables around the swimming pool. The buffet dinner was sumptuous. There were speeches by the Archbishop of Cape Town and Archbishop Rowan. Bishop William Mchombo of Eastern Zambia, ever the amiable jollier, gave a lively vote of thanks laced with funny anecdotes that left us in stitches.

We saw the Archbishop of Canterbury off at Harare International Airport the next morning. As Archbishop Rowan gave me a firm bear hug, he expressed satisfaction at the turn of events then, ever the shy gentleman, bowed to the British High Commissioner before walking up the stairs end waving good-bye when he got to the top, before disappearing into the plane. Outside, I approached our police escort and asked them to escort me to the house. They were amused but obliged. They 'knew' that treats awaited them. After munching doughnuts washed down with cold beers and a dollop of cash as a tip for a job well done, the merry policemen drove away quietly.

A few days after the Archbishop's visit, I got a call from the erstwhile Chief Justice, Godfrey Chidyausiku, to meet him for a drink. I asked him to come to my house in the evening, as we had done in the past, so he could have his favourite Macallan Inspiration and eat grilled prawns in hot sauce. As we discussed over drinks, Godfrey informed me that the president had asked him to tell me to be patient with him and not make noise in the press. Our case with Kunonga and Jakazi would be heard by The Supreme Court and we must expect an agreeable result.

This was no ben trovato occurrence. True to his word, the diocese of Harare won their case as did our diocese, against the two renegade former bishops. We took back control of our church buildings, offices, schools, hospitals and other investments. There was much rejoicing in our establishments as we prepared to cleanse and re-dedicate all previously occupied and desecrated buildings, especially the Cathedrals in Mutare and Harare. The Archbishop of Canterbury's visit, especially his tour of displaced congregations, speeches and tactful meeting with the president made all the difference in our struggle; it was catalytic in the achievement of victory for us and the Anglican Communion as a whole.

The whole saga in the Anglican Church in Harare and Manicaland showed clearly that Christianity's eschatological hope of God's

Kingdom on earth, a dominant theme in New Testament theology, does not allow any easy accommodation between the Church, the community called to bear witness to the reign of God and political powers. St. Augustine (The city of God) recognized , with sensitivity, contrary to the breakaway faction we were at war with and their puritanical fundamentalist allies, that even if there were two cities or kingdoms, a 'fallen' worldly one and a perfect heavenly one, human beings are, nevertheless citizens of both. Christians are to approach the world with a loving worldliness, born out of a recognition of the world's abundant goodness and blessings as opposed to simply hunkering down in the church. Earthly institutions have a real claim on us, ergo, we would best be served by accepting that we are dual citizens. The same complications of national dual citizenship apply to spiritual dual citizenship. Archbishop Rowan Williams' message encapsuled this observation eloquently.

The sound of the Manicaland Anglicans celebrating victory while marching triumphantly along the centre of Mutare towards St. John's Cathedral was deafening. This was evidence of formative 'creative destruction' at work. The marchers were joined by ten cope and mitre-clad bishops at the Mutare Club. The Diocesan Bishop, Julius Makoni, was flanked by Church wardens bringing up the rear of the procession. The crowd roared and cheered as I processed towards my Cathedra, blessed it then blessed the congregation. I sprinkled holy water on the congregation to the sound of the Magnificat.... "My Soul doth bless the Lord and my Spirit has rejoiced in God my Saviour...."

This was the service of cleansing and re-dedication. In turn, the Bishops cleansed and blessed the Church, the Altar, the baptismal font, the pulpit, the side chapels, crucifix and other icons, vestments, vessels and cruets. The sweet scent of burning incense hung above the worshippers pierced by sounds and rhythms of praise and worship. It was a long, emotional but gratifying service. The Bishop of Lichfield, Michael Ipgrave, preached an erudite sermon about reconciliation and rebuilding the diocese, with a rutilant, smiling face. The sermon was laced with amusing, clever logogriphs. All the Bishops, in turn, gave messages of solidarity and support from their Sees.

The next big cleansing service was at the iconic Church at St. Augustine's Mission. The students sang as they welcomed the bishops who, led by Bishop James Tengatenga, filed into the Church which was redolent of incense, to the sound of ululating Nuns and a Choir in full throated voice in the famous gallery above the main entrance. The Bishops took turns to cleanse the High Altar, sections of the church, the icons, vessels, vestments, pulpit, baptismal font and the side chapels. I led the celebration of the Solemn High Mass followed by Benediction. The Bishops took turns to say words of encouragement, reconciliation and stressed the value of education to the appreciative students. They had been traumatised by the violence and disruption of the previous years, at the hands of Jakazi and his followers.

Back in Mutare, the ever-generous Nyaundi family hosted all the Bishops to a welcome, near-liquid dinner of roast pork with all the trimmings, grilled fish, wines on tap and the iconic stinking bishop (blue cheese) served on matzos with an amazingly good Mukuyu Tawny port to wash down a superb meal. It was quite a sight, a bench of bishops scrooching around and feasting on an undeniably mature monastic cheese, stinking bishop.

Cleansing ceremonies were carried out in all affected churches throughout the diocese amid much rejoicing. It was then time to call a diocesan synod where I would outline the roadmap, next steps and the way forward. The synod was an opportune time to reassign my priests, carry out a selection conference for new ordinands destined for Bishop Gaul College in Harare, The Trans-figuration in South Africa and Westcott House in Cambridge. The synod was successful. My plans regarding rebuilding the diocese, building new churches and restoring old ones that had been destroyed when we were in exile, re-staffing and expanding our diocesan hospitals, clinics and schools were all passed unanimously. Competent people were elected to the various diocesan committees much to my relief.

At the end of the synod, I announced my vicar General, Dean, Archdeacons and Canons, including three lay-Canons. I installed the Canons in their seats in the Cathedral in a colourful ceremony. Bishop Joe Seoka of Pretoria was the preacher. We had a service to ordain six deacons the following day. Fr. Nicolas Stebbing C.R. preached at that service.

The synod marked the beginning of a new era of re-building the diocese. Unfortunately, since the old enemy now had evident characteristics of a dead parrot and was therefore no longer a threat, there was now a worrying tendency for people to pettifog, jostle for positions, or being distracted by other pursuits that were not always helpful in achieving our desired goals. Ironically, even without a significant divertissement from us, our enemy had provided us with a rallying point: the church, despite the troubles, had grown in numbers. This was an amazingly counter-intuitive, intriguing phenomenon, especially since some Anglicans had left to join other denominations at some point.

A huge problem that I had to solve was how to deal with those faithful members of our church, the laity, who had been misled into following the renegade faction and in some cases, had been tricked into persecuting their colleagues who had remained loyal and true to Anglicanism. Furthermore, would we receive the renegade clergy back into our fold after all the deep rage, violence and animus that they had unleashed on our church members fervently. Surely, they were able to know better than the laity. How would we treat them as a Church? Forgive and forget, punish them or send them for remedial training in Anglicanism then welcome back those deemed suitable, by some criteria, at the end of the process? This was a nasty conundrum, an unappreciated, unforeseen and real consequence of victory. It put all our Christian values to the test in an uncomfortable and mentally excruciating way. There was no room for tergiversation nor nice nellyism in handling this matter.

This was a matter for the Province to resolve and set the pace. As a Church, we needed to set a common policy that would be applied by all dioceses consistently now and in the future. In the event, the Province decided that the CPCA should accept all the laity who had been misled and had followed the renegade faction. The procedure was that all those re-joining the CPCA would have to renounce their faction publicly and ask for forgiveness and re-admission in an open congregation. Re-admission would not be unreasonably denied. After re-admission, there would be no further action taken against the returning members.

In the case of clergy, since they were supposed to be leaders who should know better but consciously decided to mislead their congregations, persecute CPCA members and deliberately violate the Canons of the CPCA, their re-admission would be a protracted affair. First, they would have to re-join and be re-admitted as ordinary members of the laity. They would then have to be ordinary members of the congregation for at least three years, show contrition, humility and genuine repentance.

If they wished to be members of the clergy again, they would have to go through a Selection Conference. If successful, they would have to attend Bishop Gaul College for at least a year. They would be re-trained, with a special focus on Anglicanism. The Provincial Bishops produced this blueprint after much debate, some of it quite robust. Enforcing it, however, would be at the discretion of the diocesan bishop. The process was therefore executed with variations and inconsistently in the affected dioceses of Harare, Manicaland and Masvingo.

In Manicaland, we welcomed back hundreds of Anglicans. It was not always easy to get previous warring groups to work together. There was always an underlying feeling of revenge and retribution. I had to send a circular to all Anglicans in my diocese reminding them that hostilities were now over, reconciliation was now the order of the day. We just had to find a way to work together for the good of the Church, our diocese and the Anglican Communion as a whole. We were mindful that the Worldwide Anglican Communion had supported us morally and materially when we were in exile. One way to show our gratitude and appreciation was by making our situation a shining example of co-operation and post-conflict unity.

There was a clear divide among both the clergy and laity. It was well and good for the Provincial leadership, most of whom had no direct involvement in the conflict, to set out parameters and the modus operandi for conflict resolution. It was another thing living with the realities of the struggle, the personal relationships, loss, hatred and pain that had been endured by those who remained steadfast in the CPCA. How should they treat the same people, both clergy and laity, who had caused them so much pain and suffering. This was not a straight-forward matter.

My job was cut out for me: I had to bring an end to the toxic, destructive atmosphere and build in its place, something desirable. This would be the key focus of my leadership and Ministry at this time. I had to find a relationship-centred, as opposed to a context-centred solution to achieve my goal. I had to try and achieve an agreement and solution to problems that had created this situation in the first place. These problems were not always clear as various interested parties and vested interests had hijacked and co-opted the situation to suit their own agendas, complicating the matter beyond recognition. It therefore made sense to promote constructive change processes inclusive of but not limited to immediate solutions.

My solution had to go beyond conflict resolution to reach a conflict transformation perspective concerned with responding to symptoms and engaging the systems within which relationships are embedded. I adopted a mid to long range horizon. The people had endured suffering for a long time. My strategy was a dynamic ebb: conflict de-escalation to pursue constructive change and flow, conflict escalation to pursue constructive change. Addressing all personal, relational, structural and cultural aspects and dimensions of conflict would eventually reduce violence and make way to increase justice. The change that I envisioned would be at the level of immediate issues and the broader patterns of interaction. It entailed creative responses and solutions.

I prayed, agonized and spent many long hours, sometimes till the early hours of the morning, to craft a solution. Sometimes I just followed my gut instincts. It is easier now, as I look back, to write a rationalized analysis of how I acted, not to claim it is the most luculent account! It is certainly easier to write about it, ex post, than it was to act out at the time, faced with real people and making life-changing decisions on the spot. My first three years as Diocesan Bishop were marked by leading a church in exile. I was now well into my fifth year and in the rebuilding phase.

The crisis in our C.P.C.A was our 'Noah moment.' It forced us to realize that we had to find our way to the Ark of the ties that unite us, our common purpose, mutual love and respect, a common belonging. Noah's story is about God offering a path out of destruction. It goes further to show regeneration of human society, forgiving each other and restoring relationships. This was a time for us to shun the culture of indifference in a society where heart breaking poverty co-exists with inconceivable wealth, which was at the root of our crisis. The leaders were making lemonade out of the lemon of godly silence. We needed antibodies to the virus of indifference if the crises were not to recur in future. This was a time for those on the margins of our church society to find fresh hope as they rediscovered their souls. That would be the light during our tribulation as a diocese.

I could tell that I was now getting tired. The strain was taking its toll on me. I took leave and went on a mini sabbatical. Tinao and I spent time in South Africa, Key Biscayne, West Palm Beach, Jupiter, Florida, Washington D.C. and Charlottesville Va., U.S.A,

France, Italy and the U.K. The break was good and refreshing, some of my energy was restored to me, but I remained restless and irritable. That restlessness had now returned and had a grip on me with vengeance.

On my return to work, I attended yet another Bishops' workshop organized by Trinity Parish, Wall Street, in Kumasi, Ghana. I could tell that my enthusiasm was diminishing. I left the workshop with a couple of days to go. I was bored. I could not concentrate on the discussions which I found quite infantile and irrelevant. The chauvinistic and bigoted way that some male bishops treated the two female Bishops, Swaziland and False Bay, was most appalling. They were ignored and were never invited to celebrate Mass. On the one occasion one of them participated at the Altar during Mass, several bishops did not take Holy Communion. This was unbecoming and upsetting. I made my views known, much to the chagrin of the workshop sponsors and my own archbishop who was more bent on scrounging for funds from the sponsors. There was much froideur when I pointed out these shortcomings to my colleagues on the bench.

The differences between career clergymen and someone in my position, with broader experience of the world and a business background were quite pronounced. There was a Kenyan bishop, James Ochiel, who shared a business background and outlook with me. He too was unpopular. We became good friends. The tension on the bench, especially whenever I expressed my views robustly, was palpable. The rising temperature in the alembic of their subdued vituperation was unmistakable. However, I enjoyed dinner with the Ashanti King, the Asantehene, Otumfuo Osei Tutu 11, in his palace one evening.

This was followed by a quick visit to Accra. Martin Nyaundi accompanied me. We visited my friends, George Prah, Afare Donkor and their families. We visited the Bishop of Accra, who had become a friend at the workshop (as did the seemingly stolid Bishop Jacque Boston of Guinea, who celebrated a memorable High Church Eucharist Service one morning). It was good to see all the new buildings, roads and developments which made Accra a more modern City than it was during my last visit, six years earlier.

I was soon back in Mutare, back to my Episcopal duties and routine. It was back to meetings, confirmation services, preaching, presiding at the Eucharist, benediction and other services, pastoral visits to schools, hospitals and orphanages. One Good Friday I preached at six different churches. I particularly enjoyed my interactions with students at St. David's Bonda, St. Mary Magdalene, Nyanga, St. Augustine's, Penhalonga, St. Faith's, Rusape and St. Anne's, Goto. I enjoyed the question-and-answer sessions especially. At St. Matthias Tsonzo, I played the saxophone to the mesmerized students. They gave me a present, an iPad with jazz music already loaded on it! My eyes watered up, but I did not cry.

The students at Bonda were the best behaved and most attentive. They enjoyed solving puzzles that I threw at them, sang beautifully and always crowded round my car pretending to hold me prisoner, much to the amusement of my driver, Mr. Chasinda. I would always promise to pray for them when they wrote their exams. I also promised to visit them 'as soon as possible' before they dispersed. This left a frustrated Chasinda, my driver, muttering under his breath. I just sat in the back of the little old, battered Noah Toyota vehicle that was my official car. I waved fondly at the screaming students as they ran behind my car all the way to the main gate.

Preparations were soon underway for yet another diocesan synod, that biennial event. By now my staff were adept at organizing these events. It was a good synod. Progress was reported from all corners of the diocese. Peace at last! I felt that somehow my message had now permeated down to the grassroots. We were all making efforts to pull together as we rebuilt our diocese. I was now more relaxed than I had been in the past. During the closing remarks, I felt I would just more than hint that I felt I had played my part and needed to take a break from overseeing the diocese.

The words just came out of my mouth as the confused delegates gazed at me in horror. I announced that this would be my last synod as the Diocesan Bishop. I would go on sabbatical and not return. I had no dates in mind but would keep the diocese informed. There was silence, then muted mutterings followed by loud exhortations for me to rethink and reconsider my decision. I promised to consider their pleas.

When I got home, Tinao greeted me with her usual smile. She guessed what had happened. She asked me why I looked so happy with myself. We sat in the garden of our little apartment and drank a large amount of champagne before settling down to a delicious meal of spaghetti with porcini mushrooms and Chateau Figeac to wash it down. We drained the wine with gustatory ecstasy akin to the reverent zest of a wine-taster savouring some rare vintage. The next morning, we drove to my parents' house. Dad almost jumped out his wheelchair when I told him my news. He was delighted. This is the best time to leave, when they still love you, he whispered. His brown eyes lit up; they had a boyish twinkle as they danced eyeing the champagne that had started to flow.

Mum greeted me and listened to my news with a little furrow of anxiety between her brows. She was gutted. She felt that I could have done more. In any case, she pointed out, bishops in this part of the world never resign voluntarily. Traditionally, they must be chased out of office or just refuse to go. Examples were plenty. She rattled off some of them. As we left for Harare, I decided I would proceed to Lusaka, to inform Albert Chama, the Bishop of Northern Zambia and current Archbishop, of my plans.

The meeting in Lusaka was long but jovial. A medley of the ridiculous, splendidly ironical and hypocritical. The Archbishop, who always had the air of an ageing preacher who uses old stirring phrases without clear apprehension of their significance, had invited his favourite cat's-paws, Bishops William Mchombo and Ishmael Mukuwanda to join us. They all made half-hearted attempts to persuade me to reconsider my decision or delay my departure, but there was a simultaneous undercurrent of joy and relief at the withdrawal of a thorn in the obscurantist, orgulous Archbishop's side.

I was relieved just to distance myself from a group of men whose views have been said to be nebulated by envy, ignorance, corrupt agendas and a basic lack and appreciation of theology due to poor education. They exhibited what someone described as 'the deleterious effects of inadequate or the lack of ecclesiastical training'. At least, our parting was cordial, as remains our personal relationships.

The ecclesiological deficiencies in this Anglican Province of Narnia were horrendous. I believe, according to accounts from clergy still serving and those who have left for greener pastures, they are worse now, with simony rife. 'Fish rots from the head' is not an inappropriate aphorism in this case. Instead of trying to work out why a clown is a clown, I promised not to visit 'the circus' again. Is it the case that the leitmotifs of honour, honesty and personal guilt are rare concepts in the ecclesiology of this Anglican Province?

We were locked in a mutual embrace of fear and suspicion. Analyzing how the Province is run is like trying to look through an opaque window wearing dark sunglasses. It left me grateful for and appreciative of the doctrine of penal substitutionary atonement. To avoid needless engagement during the meeting, I often took to abient behaviour: gazed out the window, scratched my groin with a painful grin on my face or studied the ugly wall hangings in the untidy meeting room.

I spent the next three months going around the diocese reading out my valedictory address to my flock. I did my best to access that wellspring of charisma and charm as I bid them Adieu. The students at Bonda cried their eyes out as did many others wherever I went in the diocese. I announced my news at the ACZ meeting in Bulawayo and left the room to much applause and a standing ovation. The farewell service at the Cathedral in Mutare was a tearful event. I then realised how attached I had become to the diocese and just how much the privilege of being called to serve was and had been a huge honour. I had learnt a lot about the diocese, myself and my own ministry. I made many friends, upset some people but believe that I made a difference. Like the Roman statesman, Cincinnatus, it was time for me to return to the 'plough.'

The time that I had spent in exile, thanks to the monstrous beast who inhabited the RBZ Governor's office, bore similarities and parallels with the experiences that I endured together with my flock as we suffered persecution at the hands of the police, politicians and the factions led by manqué clerics, Kunonga and Jakazi. This was, for all of us, a time of testing. It was a period of critical scrutiny when things had to be sorted out, especially in my head. Things that are unimportant or simply do not matter in the scheme of things had to be clearly discriminated.

On this matter, it is facile and appealing to dismiss the break-away, Kunonga/Jakazi followers as 'a basket of deplorables' with homophobic, racial, sexist and tribalistic views as espoused by their leaders. Doubtlessly, people who hold these views exist in the group as they do in the wider church. However, even if such people comprised Kunonga and Jakazi's main base, I am reluctant just to dismiss them, given their sheer numbers, political clout and influence. Among these folks were decent citizens who genuinely felt that the Anglican Church in its present form, had let them down. They believed that the Church's hierarchy from the Provincial level, led by the Archbishop and his fellow Bishops, did not care about their spiritual welfare, their lives nor their future.

The Church was perceived as a rudderless vessel led by greedy, ambitious, narcissistic, uncaring Bishops and other leaders. Many people were desperate for change. They had a point. Their cause, however, was hijacked, diverted and misdirected for personal gain by two renegade bishops. The people were caught in a catch-22 situation that they had not foreseen. Political theology possibly plays a part for some of these citizens, but I am not convinced that theology was the question then or now, nor was it the answer for most of them.

What is clear to me is that this was a great opportunity to over-haul the leadership of the Anglican Province of Central Africa. The selection, vetting and appointment of bishops had been co-opted and riddled with corrupt practices especially simony (Acts 8:18). This led to the appointment of incompetent and unfit people onto the bench. The appointment of the two renegade bishops, Kunonga and Jakazi, the recent sacking of one bishop and frequent imprisonment of another, both on charges of abuse of office and corruption is testimony to this. This was the root of the ensuing havoc in the church. The problem persists, nurtured by entrenched self-interests on the part of the senior leadership, mostly on the bench. Fish rots from the head.

The displaced Anglicans' vision and desire to have their properties restored to them was unfairly characterized by the break-away group supported by the Government media as 'nostalgia.' However, as the word denotes, what the displaced Anglicans felt was a pain for their lost spiritual 'home,' (nostros=return home, algos=pain). This quintessential 'narrative of loss' is always associated with a 'program of recovery.' The experience of something lost, out of joint or broken is at the heartbeat of all social movements. Why else move, or fight for one's rights and in what direction does one move? Irredentist social movements explicitly aim at returning to a lost homeland.

Ironically, both sides in the dispute were striving to serve the same God. The same God who made us all in His image, the one who sustains all of us. We were, contrary to the doctrine of Christ, struggling for the same living space. Competition became, for us, the last word. It became a question of winning or losing, a zero-sum game. Instead of seeking reconciliation, we spent time attacking, defending and protecting people and buildings rather than focusing on helping the marginalized and most vulnerable members of our society. We forgot about being human in a way that acknowledges that we all belong in a neighbourhood with a shared context. As a church and a human community, we lost that essential aspect of life, understanding our dependence and interdependence as part of God's creation. We completely failed to see God's image in each other. In many ways, a tragic lesson for us all.

I am often asked how I coped with life and existence during these times. I can only sum it up by quoting from the Dalai Lama's philosophy that whenever we experience suffering, we realize that many others around us and in the world, also suffer. It helps to look at suffering from a wider perspective. This has the effect of reducing the pain and worry which is often beyond our control. This is not a denial of pain and suffering. That remains. Rather, it is a shift in perspective: it is a shift of focus from oneself towards others. It is a shift from self-pity and anguish to compassion.

When I realized, through my own suffering, the agony of others, persecuted Christians in Myanmar and other parts of the world, victims of genocide in Matabeleland soon after Zimbabwe's independence, persecuted and tortured political prisoners and innocent people before and after independence, then I realized I was not unique, nor alone. I eventually got to appreciate that when we unite our situation with that of others as opposed to contrasting our situation with that of others, we become part of a wider identity. This recognition of interconnectedness gives rise to empathy and compassion, which mitigates our own pain and agony.

According to St. Augustine, societies are unified by what they desire. There is a problem when the wants of a community are diverse and fragmented because any sense of goals and visions is lost. They cannot be owned as a unit, together. The Church is not united by any institutional framework but by the urgency and urge of the Holy Spirit enabling us to desire and want to experience the comfort of God's assured justice and compassion ruling on earth. When we recognize our desire and become aware of what we lack, we celebrate what we long for, with joyful anticipation.

My time in exile when I left NMB Bank was my 'COVID moment': It turned out to be a positive pause in my life. It was painful but positive as it rescued me from worldliness, what a friend referred to as mammon, an egotistic self-satisfaction. According to ancient wisdom, self-indulgent living brings sterility. I am sure that is why my heart and soul were forever restless. This was yet another epiphany for me: for the first time, I experienced limits, loneliness, excruciating pain and anguish. I could barely figure out who I really was. In retrospect, I appreciate that crisis in my life and in the Church that I oversaw in Manicaland, was a time of purification. It dawned on me that crisis brings one to a shaming of arrogance and leads one to trusting in God.

In all my 'COVID moments,' it has become clear to me what needs to change. It is the lack of true freedom; it is the 'idols' that we choose to serve, including the misguided ideologies we choose to live by and the relationships we have neglected. I have learnt that patience and a modicum of humour allows one to endure and create space for change to happen. Ignorance thus becomes an unwillingness to acquire new knowledge and see things differently, rather than the lack of it. Rowan Williams says that idolatry is ultimately not the worship of things so much as the worship of self. This is the reduction of God to the scale of one's wants and comfort. How apt.

Now I understand Faith in a way that I did not before my COVID moments and epiphanies. Faith, rather than giving me what I want, as I now know, tends to upend one's existence, to disrupt and leave things in the last place one expected them to be. Living by faith, then, one should expect to be surprised by where God leads us to and what He wants us to do. There may be new horizons one is being called to do, roles and vocations one never imagined one would be good at, ways of serving others that one never thought might be for oneself.

Lastly, there is hope. I am reminded of Curt Richter's famous experiment where he placed rats in a pool of water to test how long they can tread water. On average, they gave up and sunk about fifteen minutes later. Just before they gave up on exhaustion, the rats were pulled out, dried and rested for a few moments before being returned to the water for another round. On the second round, the rats continued swimming for about sixty hours. The researchers concluded that the rats now believed that they would eventually be rescued and saved. They therefore pushed their physical limits far beyond what they thought was previously possible.

If hope can make exhausted rats swim so long, what could belief in oneself, one's abilities, with God's help, do for one, I often wonder to myself. I know what I am capable of. I now know why I am here. With His help, I will keep swimming!

Chapter Thirty-Two

IT HAS BEEN A LONG DAY, full of memories and highlights of and glimpses into my life and times. Tinao and I drive in silence past the clump of trees leading up to my parents' house in Makombe village, near Rusape. My stomach tenses up. I break into tears. Tinao and I embrace Mum. We all sob as we greet each other and exchange condolences. After a little while, Steve arrives. He joins us on the veranda. We sit and enjoy a quiet, amazingly peaceful sunset and sip sundowners as we talk about Dad.

I had spent a quiet moment praying next to Dad's lifeless body at the mortuary. He looked at peace. Serene, He cut a majestic figure, clad in his favourite gold-coloured Mass vestments. I put my pectoral cross around his neck and paid my last respects. Time stood still. The moment was eternal, ubiquitous, everywhere and everywhen. Strangely, this personal first encounter with caducity led to a pullulation of literary zeal in me. Need I say more? I can feel Dad smiling at this development, even though an empty space now rules where a solid oak tree once occupied in glorious majesty.

Dad passed on two months after I had vacated my post as the Bishop of Manicaland. Bishop Chad Gandiya was the Celebrant at the Requiem Mass. Bishop Bakare preached. Four thousand people took Communion. We buried Dad just behind his bedroom, where he died, on a spot he had chosen, in the shade. We celebrated his life with joy and sadness. I held hands with Tinao as Dad's coffin was lowered into the grave that my brothers had taken great care to prepare. Everything went well, almost: when it was time to eat lunch, we realized that while everyone was at the Requiem Mass at St. Columbus Church, some daring thieves broke into my parents' house and took off with a few items. Immediately noticeable was the cutlery. Dad had a sense of humour till the end. What a day!

His resting place is marked by a small plaque bearing his name. It rests at the centre of the 'peace garden' designed by my Sister-in-law, Eunah, in his honour. His wish was that his grandchildren should play ball games on his grave without fear of falling over a mound or concrete. His grandchildren wasted no time as they played ball games on 'Grandpa's lawn' as soon as the gravestone unveiling service was over. As I watch the children play ball on his grave, I often muse at the huge impact and influence Dad had on me and how this continues to shape and guide my life.

Just before I left Manicaland, I received offers and enquiries about my interest in a few consulting assignments. I had taken time off my episcopal duties to work on a few of these. In that respect, I found myself back in Washington, signing up once again, with the Bretton Woods Institutions, as a Senior Consultant on parastatal (credit) rehabilitation and reform. In my lucid moments, I spend time working on these assignments, which take me from place to place all over the world. Even more enjoyable is my work on various banking transactions which seem to be endless. I enjoy the creativity and meeting up with old colleagues in the banking sector especially in the U.K. and the U.S.A.

I probably sometimes take on too much work. I still spend long hours in meetings, on conference calls and negotiations. Since leaving Manicaland, I have restructured and sold an oil refinery, worked as an advisor for three Investment Funds and memorably, completed a debt-swap transaction that had been going on for over three years, among other transactions.

As I look back at my life and try to identify issues or experiences that have shaped my worldview, I am compelled to focus on a few salient 'lessons' that I consider to be significant. In all I did, I believed strongly that mediocrity plays no part in my life's pursuits. I chose 'In pursuit of Excellence' as the motif for NMB Bank, for that reason. I created a rebus for strength, innovation and savvy which included a lion, buffalo, eagle, snake and a dove carrying a sprig of acacia. Excellence or perfection, for me, expressed my refusal to accept or make excuses for outcomes being 'good enough,' as opposed to adamantinely striving for them at all costs. I learnt from my parents early in my life that most things can be improved if one puts in the effort to make the difference. Excellent outcomes can be improved into 'outstanding' ones. In addition, one is never too busy. If one truly cares, they make time. Since decisions are the key to success, time to think must be a priority.

In pursuit of excellence, one soon realizes that the goal of excellence works in harmony with an attitude of fairness. Treating all people with respect and fairness cannot be underestimated in the part it plays in reciprocal treatment and success. As a leader, I soon appreciated the value of empathy and accessibility. I learnt to accept that human beings make honest mistakes. These need not be punished, nor should culprits be harshly judged and shamed. I tried to avoid behaviour that would intimidate, cause anxiety, discourage honest communication or thwart innovation. I think this should be drummed into all bishops, especially in my old Province. I learnt to stop expecting loyalty from people who cannot give you basic honesty. Loyalty is a responsibility, whereas cheating is a choice. 'The best thing a human being can do is help another human being know more', is an adage that guided my life.

I found it helpful, always, to create an atmosphere that would attract the best staff and thus enable the pursuit of excellent quality of work, integrity, honesty and high ethical standards. Concomitant to the foregoing, I learnt the value of owning up to my own mistakes.

I think that this is crucial for one's credibility. Acknowledging one's mistakes, learning from them and moving on, set an example that mistakes need not be a death sentence. NMB staff from my era will testify to this. The key is to accept, without apology, that in certain situations you do not understand nor have an answer. After all, 'knowing what you don't know is more useful than being brilliant,' as the saying goes. It helps to remove ego from the equation. This served me well as I climbed the corporate, managerial ladder. Now I appreciate that understanding is deeper than knowledge. Many people got to know me, but few understood me. People do not always need advice. Sometimes all they need is a listening ear, a heart to understand them or just a hand to hold.

From being at the helm of a sprawling, vibrant, bellicose and financially distressed diocese as the Bishop, to steering an African-based, FTSE 500 financial conglomerate, I was confronted with diverse, difficult situations which needed brave and timeous decision-making. In the Church situation especially, I had to make 'life or death' decisions that could have far-reaching implications whose impact entailed potentially huge positive or negative outcomes. These included exposing information that could damage families and colleagues, firing or disciplining close or loyal employees for various reasons or misdemeanours or decisions involving benefits or remuneration. I have given examples of such occasions.

I quickly learnt that in different organizations, be it in the church or industry, indecision leads to unhelpful outcomes. It is counterproductive. At best it corrodes the morale of all those depending on the leader to resolve issues. The lesson here was to consult widely, wisely, timeously and have the courage to make and effect balanced decisions that one could stand by honestly and confidently.

The leadership role, as I experienced it, demands courage to operate in the face of opposition, danger or disruptive circumstances. This calls for a certain degree of calculated risk taking, 'banking by faith,' sometimes. It is not reasonable to expect success out of absolute fear of failure. From the prophet Isaiah (35:4), "Be strong, do not fear," to St. Paul's, "In hope, we were saved. Hope that is seen is not hope...." Being courageous entails optimism and like forgiveness, is an act of faith. Hope, like optimism, must be lived even as things get worse. Pragmatic optimism at the top permeates all levels of any organization through good and bad times. I made a conscious effort to avoid the tendency to yield to pessimism. This would only demotivate those around me. In all this, one must accept the leitmotif of the inevitability of change and loss. It was one that I experienced palpably as time passed. One must be bold, go against the grain if need be. If one does the same as everyone, one will get similar results. The saying, "Mimicking the herd invites regression to the mean," is apt.

My training in banking and finance helped me to focus and consciously, habitually, make the effort to allocate resources such as time and energy to study situations and seek to understand them before tackling them. This was helpful in running the diocese. In this endeavour, I found it relatively easy but still imperative, to communicate my priorities as often and as clearly as I could. I was pleasantly surprised when my priests informed me that this approach, in church affairs, was new to them, different and welcome. It was well received and implemented with success in many parishes in my diocese. In my experience, focus is a dimension of 'thoughtfulness.' Some of the errors we make in life are caused by losing focus, being distracted or just forgetting what we are trying to do

Devoting time and thought to issues gave me the opportunity to delve ever deeper into matters at hand. This enabled me to make better-informed decisions. My staff were always shocked and visibly pleasantly surprised when they found out how much I knew about their families, hobbies and clients. I devoted time to these seemingly banal tasks. This gave authenticity and credibility to my opinions. My staff gave me their trust and respect in return. This removed any need or temptation, on my part, to fudge or fake my stance on matters.

Growing up, I was naturally curious. I remember perusing Dad's liturgy notes, at a young age, to understand his sermons or so I thought. It was akin to exploring a cabinet of curiosities with compartments containing uncanny and startling mirabilia. In time, the same curiosity served me well as it drove me to meet a wide range of people, developing an extensive network of contacts in business, politics and the church. I travelled the world over, meeting people and exploring ideas. I then dared to venture out to be innovative in banking and finance. I also carried this curiosity and urge to innovate into the church, contributing to liturgical changes, updates and more inclusive, different forms of worship and appreciation of the scriptures. As the saying goes, 'Knowledge is an asset that compounds over time; those who keep learning, will keep rising.' The more one knows, the better one thinks. Better choices lead to great outcomes.

Finally, something I have been appallingly hopeless at: REST. Stop, reflect, rest and pray – the core values of Shabbat, written into stone as one of the Ten Commandments. Nobody functions well without rest, especially in the middle of crises. I certainly do not. Anybody who has had a sleepless night appreciates the need for rest to restore good mental and physical health. I confess to have been an offender at this: I like to be busy. I feel guilty if I am not. There is just so much to do. However, working constantly wears one down. Rest gives one the mental and spiritual energy to go on with a fresh mind. I have not given up trying. I still say my prayer office, twice daily. The doxology, whether I sing it, say or whisper it, lifts my spirits without fail. Ultimately, one needs to accept that no one is permanent. Life must move on.

As for my decision to train for the ordained ministry and serve as a priest and eventually accept the offer to serve as a diocesan Bishop, I simply followed my heart. I have had criticism, intrigue and suspicions cast on my motivation. Prominent politicians, colleagues, friends and others have asked me the big question, WHY? There is always an implied tone that I could have done better in politics or remained in full time finance and banking to make oodles of money. Some people whispered that I had either lost my mind or saw an opportunity to grubstake the Diocese much needed dollars in return for celestial favours!

All I can say is that unbelievable as it may be, I enjoy my ministry. I accepted the challenge and the privilege to serve, with gratitude. I tried to heal the malignant culture at the heart of the Anglican Church in Manicaland. The collapse in trust in the leadership of the church cannot be exaggerated. By God's grace, I was able to give hope to marginalized people, Christians and non-believers alike. I strove to carry God's people in my heart, at least. My time in exile was a period of regeneration and growth in many ways. It was like the new growth that ensues a severe pruning.

I always bear in mind that I never could have done what I did in my own strength. Ordination and being Bishop did not take away my humanity. I still misread people and situations. I made and still make decisions that have been judged to be too bold and sometimes not bold enough. I sometimes reached for procrastination and evasion. I was afraid of the burden that came with the privilege to serve as Bishop. However, I tried to deal with this by gratitude: I thank God that I was enabled to minister and continue to strive not to stand in His light. By my weaknesses, I have been able to point to something of His strength. By my inconstancy, I have been able to point to something of His faithfulness. All said and done, I was never and could never be 'The Good News.' All I can do is to keep silence in the face of The Mystery, so that 'The Good News' heard. I have Rowan Williams to thank for lucidity here.

Through the tough times and the good times, I have learnt to accept life as it is, without qualification, without feeling cheated or wronged. Some of the names I have mentioned remain so distasteful that I can never expect to hear them again without an involuntary shudder but I do not seek to revenge myself. I try to listen carefully and talk less while paying attention to what people say in words and body language. I try to take time to look at first impressions while making use of what I have learnt, as time passes.

Discretion is key in all I do. Rather than blow my own trumpet and give away what I have learnt about others, I prefer people to learn about my qualities from third parties. As far as possible, I try to detach myself from situations before they heat up. I strive to act rather than react and stay in control as much as I possibly can. I have also learnt to listen to my own common sense then getting on with the business of turning those theories into practice. Focusing on the best practice and committing to quality right from the start certainly helped me to start off on the right path and gave me a huge competitive edge in all my undertakings on this journey.

Through my journey's ups and downs, I have come to realize and accept that we do not exist for ourselves alone. We exist in a complex web of relationships with those near and dear to us, those who have influenced us for good and those whose influence may have been detrimental to, even abusive of our human dignity, those who are not dear to us and those we would love to flee from. This is a factor and risk of being human. This is one of the reasons why we give thanks for what is good while at the same time, we ask for forgiveness of our own failure to honour the dignity of others, seek reconciliation and healing. This translates into our quest for justice, equality, responsibility, and peace.

In my journey, I have been lucky to meet and interact with a kaleidoscope of people, apart from Mum and Dad, who have had more than a fleeting impact on who I am today. I am grateful to them all and pay credit to some of them now. They all taught me, "Never give up on things you really want." It is difficult to wait but worse to regret.

Memorable experiences of learning how to 'speak correctly,' coupled with an early encounter with Shakespeare's plays and English

Literature in general at the hands of the aristocratic, avuncular, Fr. Godfrey Pawson C.R., are hard to forget. He had been my father's College Principal at St. Peter's, Rosettenville. Thanks to him, I read Coleridge, Joseph Conrad, William Blake, Wilfrid Owen and Virginia Woolf, among others, at an early age. By the time I got to secondary school, I amazed my teachers just by rattling off and analyzing texts that some of them were unfamiliar with. They must have hated Fr. Pawson or held him responsible for nurturing a little intellectual monster! Fr. Keble Prosser C.R., hot on the heels of Fr. Pawson, was my first French teacher. He told me I had a voice better suited to the French language and encouraged me to keep learning the language.

Curiously, he was a Cambridge-trained historian who tricked me into loving his subject, especially European history, till it became an obsession. We just clicked. Like his fellow C.R. brothers, Keble spent a lot of time during school holidays with my family. They loved Mum's cooking. They helped in the kitchen, which earned them countless invitations to stay with us. Godfrey and Keble were both warm-hearted priests. They were excellent company, even for young people. I learnt a lot about etiquette, good manners, work ethic and study from these two special men. I often visited Godfrey Pawson's grave at Mirfield and felt privileged to assist at Keble Prosser's Requiem Mass.

As luck would have it, after a start with some monks for mentors, I went straight into the hands, tutelage and influence of four Jesuits who had an important influence on my early life. Fr. John Davies, the affable Englishman, strengthened my love of literature and European history mostly in his palladium, the Rector's Rooms. His love of music, especially baroque and classical, was infectious. I never recovered from his influence and direction.

He was a man of prayer. He taught me how to pray whether I was happy or distressed. We managed to share a meal in Mayfair and pray together in the Jesuit Church of the Immaculate Conception, Farm Street, London, before he died. John 'Toots' Davies remained a close friend of my family till his death. I received news of his passing when I got home from work one evening, in Washington D.C. I was gutted. I inherited John's vast collection of classical music. It now graces our entrance hall. A Rector's service plaque and college badge bearing his name were delivered to me by Fr. Brian Enright, who knew my relationship with John better than anyone else. The badge now takes pride of place on a bookshelf in my study.

Fr. Greg Croft, a brilliant, pawky physicist and horticulturalist, was a different kettle of fish. He was not everyone's cup of tea, thanks to his choleric disposition, which I found strangely endearing. He gave most people the fantods. To me, it was just a front. The man was painfully shy and just could not face ordinary people. On parents' days, he would noodle himself out of mingling with parents but still organized laboratory tours of note for all visitors. He was brilliant with students especially those who had a flair for his subjects, physics and gardening. I spent hours with him in the laboratory and in the garden, helping him graft roses and grow exotic plants.

Over the years, we became friends. We exchanged long letters from time to time. Greg adored my family. He introduced me to the wild world of the outbound adventures in the rugged Eastern Highlands of Zimbabwe. I remember him fondly. Despite his legendary bad temper, Greg never raised his voice at me despite occasionally making silly errors in my physics assignments. His fecundity of original ideas was simply amazing. He had an esemplastic, eclectic, deep and complex mind. He seemed to process everything he saw as potential fodder for use in his various tasks and undertakings as a priest and teacher. He had a synthetic, resourceful, practical sensibility, always about cobbling together the most disparate, miscellaneous ideas and things.

Fr. Brian Enright, who John Davies enviously referred to as the man in the grapefruit advert, cuts a skeletal and disarmingly handsome figure with a permanent smile and crystal blue eyes. He is the only boy from a family of six. His beautiful youngest sister, Clare, became a close friend when we were students. She still lives in Cambridge with her husband, Doug, and their children. Brian taught me Maths. He was the Prefect General and my Housemaster. Every morning I would serve at Mass in the small Middle House Chapel, next to the House library near the Prefects' bathroom. I would sneak into his rooms most evenings after prep for a cup of hot chocolate and a chat. Brian was never one to mince his words and would spell out issues in politics, religion or sport with clarity and awesome authority. He adored my father. He often talked about the vocation. His homilies were brief and to the point.

When I was ordained and consecrated as the Bishop of Manicaland, I appointed Brian an Honorary Canon of the diocese. I asked him to preach at the installation of all Canons that I had appointed. Brian, with a straight face, declined the offer with the words,' I hate preaching'. After I had preached at one College event, Brian, as a douceur after a robust chat, assumed the role of my Chaplain with the words, "I have worked around Bishops for a long time, I know how to handle them." He had been the Jesuit Fr. Socius at the Catholic Cathedral in Harare and had worked with and shared the Bishop's Palace with the late Archbishop Patrick Chakaipa. He does know how to 'handle' Bishops and direct them to remain focused, as I found out. Brian has been a little frail lately but has lost none of his wit and candour. His kind message of condolences and support when Dad died made my eyes water up.

Fr. Patrick Makaka, ever the self-appointed impresario at all school sporting events, was my Housemaster, Form Master and Geography teacher for a short time before he was whisked off to Ireland, then to London, for studies. He remains a good friend and trouble-shooter. Patrick is a great socialite, golfer, eye winker and keen fisherman. I used to dismiss his self-reported performance on the golf course as mythomania until 'Toots' told us a story of how Patrick belted the ball off the tee on the sixth, par five hole alongside Second Street extension at Royal Harare Golf Club, astray onto oncoming traffic.

His colleagues watched in horror as the ball bounced off the roof of a truck only to land about fifty yards behind the tee box. Patrick walked back to his ball nonchalantly, took out a rescue club and belted the ball again with a hefty smackeroo at least three hundred metres down the fairway, leaving only a short chip to the green. Patrick loves the good, happy life. However, his homilies, despite a divine salvific theme are labyrinthine, and menacing. He loves to pontificate and vaticinate, haranguing his congregants with apocalyptic language.

I nick-named him 'Fr. Eschatology' for the eschatological preoccupations embedded in most of his sermons. He has been a good sounding-board and helper especially when I was struggling to hold my life together, as a diocesan Bishop. He prayed for me and reminded me often, that God had always wanted me to be a Bishop as he predicted when, as my Housemaster, he had knelt and kissed a ring on my finger, where my episcopal ring now sits. He told me, then, that I would be a bishop one day! Patrick had the congregation at a funeral service in stitches as he introduced me as his favourite thin student who has now joined the ranks of 'expansive bishops' and is now as fat as all of them. In retaliation, I gave Patrick a clerical shirt from Barbiconi, that I knew to be a size too small. I told him, 'If you lose weight father, you may even wear that beautiful shirt to a dance.' He winced.

David Napier Hamilton descended from the Scottish peer, Lord Napier, a close friend of then Prime Minister, Lord Palmerston. He had a very unusual C.V. By no means a dilettante, David excelled at Eton before reading PPE and a D. Phil in political history at Oxford University. He then read for a master's degree in education at Harvard. He joined the British Navy and rose to the rank of Lt. Commander before he was assigned to the Naval School at Asmara, Ethiopia. David, an aristocrat, unrepentant royalist, never accused of haphephobia, immersed himself in the Ethiopian culture. He was close to the Emperor Haile Selassie and his family.

David made many friends in Ethiopia before he travelled to Rhodesia where he established a wine business. His sojourn there was short. He left in disgust at being unable to stomach the injustice of the oppressive regime based on racial discrimination and segregation. While in Rhodesia, David met my family and became a close member of the family. He adopted me as his godson in the process and so became my chief mentor. He returned to England where he worked as a taxi driver for a year before he was posted to work in the Governor's office in Barbados.

A few years and many friends later, David returned to London to head the Greater London Council team under Ken Livingstone. By all accounts, he excelled at his job but hated the 'working class environment.' He had a good working relationship with the left-wing leader, Ken Livingstone. The latter, apparently, was fiercely proud of his working-class origins but recognized David's polished, aristocratic conduct, poise, charm, professionalism and human touch. David was punctilious about the English language. His circle of friends included royalty, his contemporaries from Eton, especially, Conservative Peers and politicians, bankers, Bishops and Diplomats. I lived with David for many years in his palatial home, 109 Brixton Road, an unlikely address for such a stately residence at that time. Vintage cars, wine, exquisite cuisine and theatre were the order of the day. We travelled to France and stayed with his friends at Figeac, in the South of France and in Paris.

Though an Oxford man himself, David, understandably, preferred Cambridge. He visited me most weekends. His elder brother was a bishop in the Exeter diocese. In time, David left the GLC to take up a position as Private Secretary to his close friend, Princess Margaret. Sadly, he was destined for an early, shocking and gruesome death at the hands of a 'friend' shortly after taking up his appointment.

Never myopic in his outlook on life, he was on a mission to make me into a true, blue-blooded Englishman, from the day he adopted me. He spared no effort at this. He arranged for me to spend time at selected establishments including his aristocrat friends' country homes, to hosting lavish dinner parties where he would invite his friends, including Mara Lane, Roger Moore, Cecil Parkinson, Peter Brooke and Michael Heseltine, among others. In his will, David bequeathed a sum of money, pictures and books "..to Julius, to remember me by." I still have the urge to reach for the phone and call David when I am in trouble or upset. I remember David Napier Hamilton fondly, as does my family.

Arthur Morris Mutsonziwa, Alan Carvell, George Prah, Richard Archdeacon and Richard Small were friends, fellow travelers, that I met in my student days. There were other travelers, but I single these five out because they were close to me and invited me into their own lives, homes and families in an intimate and gracious way that impacted positively on my own life. Sadly, Arthur was destined for an early death. As I wrote this account, I learnt of Richard Small's sudden and unexpected death. The news was conveyed by his long-time Italian girlfriend, model, Angela Cerasella. Richard was not known to be knowingly underdressed at any time. We had lunch at Finos Wine Bar three weeks previously, on Ash Wednesday. He was in apparently fine fettle. I am eviscerated. Alan, George and I speak occasionally. We are soul mates. George and I share a birthday.

Professor John Charles Constable was an enigmatic figure who guided me and supervised my research for a Ph.D. in International Finance. Intellection was his hallmark though some of his colleagues regarded him with fear and envy. Some referred to him as 'awkward.' Initially, I found John to be cold and too English for my liking. He would tear through my research ideas like a sharp, hot filleting knife cuts through warm butter. For some reason, however, I never found him intimidating.

I quickly discovered that John really had a soft spot for me and

BON VIVANT BANKER-BISHOP **481**

wanted a friend. He clearly wanted me to fulfil my promise and achieve academic excellence. He was very much a Cambridge academic, possessed of formidable intelligence and wit but not much humour. After I beat him at squash, he decided that we should compete on the golf course. We had our tutorials during golf sessions at Biddenham or sometimes Woburn. He was extremely competitive. One day, after a round of golf, we drove to his house in silence. His wife, Liz, looked at a sullen faced John and with a smile said, 'I know who won.'

John taught me how to think. His father was a great thinker and had taught him how to think. His focus was general mental ability and the capacity to be creative, solve problems and find innovative mental solutions rather than memorize other people's thoughts expressed in books and articles. I benefited immensely from John's approach. It is not about the I.Q., qualifications or experience, John taught, but rather, the capacity and ability to think are the most significant factors in performance. His lectures were legendary. Every M.B.A candidate attended his Corporate Strategy lectures assiduously.

John abhorred pseudepigraphy which was rife as MBA students notoriously sought to enhance essays by claiming, falsely, to have read widely. I was privileged to have John as my Supervisor. I was delighted when he accepted to be a director of my bank, NMB. He said he was proud of me. This was a mutual-admiration club with zero tolerance for flimflam. John often recounted the story of Mr. Bristow, a plebeian Manager at NatWest, Wharley-End Branch, who frog-marched me out of his office after declining to lend me £20, on the grounds that I was a 'perpetual student.' Mr. Bristow died a week before he received my letter appointing him as my personal assistant at NMB bank.

After years of working closely with John, I inevitably became a member of his family. This was with a little help from his beautiful, kind wife, Liz. Liz still has a mile-wide smile that makes one's heart miss a beat and weakens the knees. Some kind person remarked that I somehow reminded him of John, in the methodical way that I approach my business dealings and conduct myself in the workplace. That is a touching compliment and tribute to my mentor, who donated half his library of Harvard management reports and books on Corporate Strategy to my own library. They occupy a long bookcase in the corridor outside my study.

When his health was failing and he could hardly speak, John, a confirmed atheist, said to me, 'Bishop, if you can talk to your boss and relieve me of this blooming stomach cancer which is excruciating, I promise to go to church every Sunday from now on.' I assured John of my prayers. He died the next day. I attended John's memorial service in Taunton. I hugged Liz as she greeted mourners at the door. It was a cheerful, touching service with pictures of John on the walls. The speeches were exceptionally good and engaging, just the way John would have planned it.

Michael Whelan is a shy, almost Trappist, American gentleman who sat at the end of the table taking notes at Executive meetings at the World Bank and I.F.C. He came to life and into his own when he gave seminars on report writing and project presentations. These later became mandatory in the Group. He emphasized clarity of thought, lucid presentations, focused and to the point. I particularly enjoyed following him as he dissected, grammatically, selected newspaper financial reports especially in the Financial Times and Washington Post. Michael would dismantle any writer's diction, highlight superfluous words, malapropisms and other inappropriate use of language prevalent in report writing.

I bumped into Michael one hot Friday afternoon in the lush gardens of the Nesbitt Castle in Bulawayo when I was at the helm of NMB Bank. He was in Zimbabwe on a World Bank assignment. There was no mistaking the soft-spoken, seemingly diffident, handsome figure with an unmistakable gait, thoughtfully admiring the foliage in the neat gardens. After a brief chat, Michael agreed to extend his stay and give his now-famous seminars on good writing to NMB staff. The tailored seminars were an instant hit with all participants. Michael's seminars became a staple, just like they were at the World Bank Group. NMB now has an established pattern of writing and presenting documents that became the envy of the financial sector in Zimbabwe and beyond. Commenting on my memorist abilities, Michael quipped nonchalantly, "I'm sure there's a word for that disorder."

I had not realized the profound impact that Michael's philosophy and approach to writing and presentations in general, his patented 'secrets,' had on me until I settled down to writing board reports, speeches and sermons. His clear, lucid, direct methods and approach permeated and remain in my being. This may not be always evident! I have always wondered what became of Michael. I always imagine him cheerfully holed up in a secluded environment, having fun writing books and reading avidly, pen in hand, editing every sentence. Despite all his clarity, no place for skimble-scamble in writing, Michael and I disagree on one subject, split infinitives. He tolerates them.

In business, family and personal life, Robert, Marquess of Salisbury, has been a close friend and confidante. Affectionately referred to, in my family, as 'Lord Harare,' Robert is an excellent listener. Truly bel-esprit, he is also humble and generous beyond words. He is blessed with a heart of gold. His equally kind, classy, gentle but formidable wife Hannah, and he looked after my family when times were not so easy for me. They accommodated me whenever I needed refuge from woes and pressures of the world and gave me sound advice when I had to make tough choices. No impedimenta were insurmountable to them.

I have been a constant guest at their excellent dinners in the aristocratic confines of his stately country home. Robert and I have had memorable, umami culinary excursions at the Gavroche and J. Sheeky's. We have enjoyed hearty, claret-fueled lunches at White's.

My waistline especially bears testimony to these efforts. On one such occasion, we were deep in conversation and were startled to find Algy Cluff, ever unctuous, sitting demurely at our table, helping himself to the claret. Without batting an eyelid, Algy joined in the conversation. It turned out to be an amazingly engaging afternoon.

Robert writes well. He is not exactly donnish, but there is more than a hint of a jazz-loving academic in the otherwise traditional, game-slaughtering, upper crust Englishman. I enjoy reading his reviews in the Spectator, formerly famously owned by Algy who served as Chairman for many years.

Missing from this gathering were two friends who have always been there for me, the charming, generous, brilliant banker who fed me on numerous occasions at his favourite club, Buck's, Brian Fitzpatrick, and the equally generous, brilliant, keen golfer, erroneously reported by a Sunday newspaper as 'almost reclusive,' Nick Roditi. These friends have had a huge, positive impact on my life and outlook. I owe them a huge debt of gratitude. It would take many chapters to detail the adventures that I have embarked on with these special men. I am proud and privileged to count them among my friends.

Malcolm Pryor, James Friedlander and Afare Donkor are business associates who, over time, became confidantes and family friends. 'The Spondulicks Club,' we were once known as. I am godfather to Jim's grandson, Zach, and remarkably close friends with Zach's Mum, Natasha. We had to suffer through Jim's bad jokes as he was the MC when Tinao and I got married. Since our days at the World Bank in Washington D.C., the four of us have co-invested in many enterprises including three financial institutions. Malcolm, Jim and Afare, successful entrepreneurs, nurtured my own entrepreneurial spirit and guided me to success.

From confabulating and sipping champagne with Malcolm and Clarence Haynes at Flutie's in Georgetown, dancing with friends at an impromptu party in Accra, playing golf at Royal Harare, negotiating with investors in Lagos, or sitting through Board meetings at NMB and CAL Bank, these friends/mentors were always a joy to be with.

We spent many hours doffing on houseboats and drank so much, we forgot to fish for our meals often. On one such occasion, we moored the boat and ventured ashore to a lakeside hotel, to find food after a procellous spell on the lake. After much shouting and arguing with the proprietor who pointed out that only hotel guests could be served, Afare let out a string of choice, colourful words, opprobrious epithets which included an insinuation of the dubious origins of the hulky proprietor. Mercifully, there was no donnybrook; instead, we were herded back to our tender-boat unceremoniously by the massive, brutal, muscular, Afrikaner man-beast.

We all took a scunner to him. The beast brandished a huge rifle menacingly, 'totis viribus.' He stomped behind us as he spat out vituperative, metathesised words to boot. His epizeuxis, damn, damn, damn, like a man trying to stop a stream of urine issuing out of his penis without his permission, rose to a frightening crescendo in a tirade incoherent to the point of lunacy. His badly dressed, gargantuan wife sat at the bar staring at us as she drew furiously on a smelly cigarette. She had lots of red lipstick which was applied with little reference to the shape of her mouth. The woman was blessed with a corvine nose and faience, blood-shot, mouse-like eyes.

The bilious, umbrageous giant was a true master of tmesis: expletives graced every other minatory word he spluttered. We were not inclined to argue. We took our leave of the choleric beast's property with unmistaken alacrity. We were quite prepared and preferred to face the fabled thalassic instrumentalities in the fading light, to dealing with the revenants stirring ashore. This was the nadir of an otherwise excellent, enjoyable cruise. We would slake our thirst elsewhere, another time. No intellection needed here, just a vinculum among our motley crew as we departed in deafening silence.

I never got the opportunity to spend much time with my god-father, the late Archbishop Desmond Tutu, but I had enough quality time with him from when he was a young priest to the time he retired from active ministry. Uncle Desmond was one of my father's friends from theological college. I enjoyed listening to four sides of stories about happenings when they were students at St. Peter's College. They came from Dad, Uncle Desmond, Arch Makhulu and Fr. Pawson, their College Principal.

An important lesson that Uncle Desmond engrained in me is tolerance, fair play and that there is no neutrality in fighting evil. I wrote about his theology in one of my dissertations when I was at Cambridge. I showed him what I thought of his Southern African Black Theology, he laughed uncontrollably. With tears in his eyes, hugging me, he told me that I had missed the important point which was that St. Augustine was never concerned about oppression despite his deep intellectual exposition of theological themes. "He never coined Ubuntu," he cackled. "Augustine's unclarity is brilliant, like his intellectual comrades," he said. "They give us flawless answers to questions we are not asking!"

Along with his friend and contemporary, Archbishop Walter Khotso Makhulu, Uncle Desmond has been a big pillar of support, especially in my ministry. 'Arch,' as we call Khotso, cuts a formidable figure that hides a very shy, yet forcefully intellectual character. Arch loves to show off his infectious love of language, his 'Sprachgefühl,' as the Germans call it. This inspired me immensely as he illuminates the nooks and crannies of several languages. I have had the joy of spending many hours with him. Having him marry Tinao and I was the icing on the cake.

On my father's birthday, Khotso sat with Dad sharing port on the veranda after dinner. I sneaked into his bedroom, dressed myself in his cope and mitre then jumped in from the darkness behind them, pretending to be an episcopal ghost. Dad was horrified that his banker son would embarrass him like this. Khotso was more sanguine: "God will punish you for this. You may even be ordained one day and wear a mitre because it suits you, even in darkness. I would hate to be your Bishop." This spoiled my fun. I divested myself of the ecclesiastical accoutrements and stumbled past a shocked Mum to return them to Khotso's room. We drank a lot of champagne and claret that evening. Arch remains a mentor, tutor, father and above all, a friend.

As for my theological grounding and outlook, I have found myself, over the years, drawn ever closer to Rowan Williams, erstwhile Archbishop of Canterbury, a neoteric St. Augustine/ Thomas Aquinas being. The time I spent with him driving for hours from the border post to Harare and from Harare to Mutare and back, opened my eyes to a warm, compassionate yet incisive way of approaching issues in my ministry. I enjoy reading his works and always look forward to that bear hug and genuinely welcoming, happy smile, whenever we meet. He is one of a few special friends who puts up with my warped humour. A true friend.

I will always cherish memories of Rowan outstretching his arms and belting out the Sursum Coda to auspicate his tour of Zimbabwe during Mass at Glamis Stadium in Harare. The huge congregation was truly uplifted and rivetted by the masterly, rich polysemy which was the basis of poetic ambiguity in his sermon heralding our return from exile. His brilliant essays on St. Augustine have given me much food for thought. Theodore Roosevelt's 1900 maxim, 'speak softly but carry a big stick,' is an apt description of Lord Williams of Oystermouth.

Despite her advanced age of 93, Mum continues to be a sentient wellspring of love and affection. Naturally, she misses Dad, her tag team partner in bringing us up. She continues to pamper me. In her eyes, I could never do wrong. I visit her often and sometimes I fall asleep while she repeats stories of my entrance into the world and my childhood. She loves Tinao and still adores my cooking. Tinao and I often take her parcels of cooked pork belly, stuffed fried chicken and lamb. We come home laden with creamy avocados from the huge tree in her vegetable garden. My sister Emmie still lives in Godalming, Surrey. Never knowingly otiose, she is forever knackered, as a result of work, social commitments and religious pursuits. We all had a scare when she tested positive for the dreaded COVID. COVID in a 93-year-old must be seen to be believed. Mum was quite poorly for a few days but happily, recovered to good health.

Dominic is still incorrigibly sesquipedalian, a redoubtable luminary in his field as a business consultant, largely incomprehensible but brilliant. He runs a thriving management consultancy downtown Harare. Nathaniel does a lot of work with the Bill Gates Foundation focusing on esoteric animal genetics and breeding programmes when he is not running his dairy enterprise. Steve, the baby, has since moved from Trinity Cancer Centre to ply his medical skills as a Partner at a more accessible Oncology facility in West Palm Beach, a place where we have had much fun, especially fishing off Jupiter Island with the famous lighthouse silhouetted against the Utiki beach bars, in the glorious sunset.

Memories of Felly, Tinao, Steve and I landing tuna, yellowtail, king mackerel and other fish while sharks circle the boat menacingly, are lasting. Also memorable is the special time we shared with Bishop James Tengatenga and his beautiful, charming wife, Josey. After James blessed Felly and Steve's new home in Ballen Isles, the gathering degenerated into three days of continuous carousing and mirth.

Our family is undeniably not diffident. As siblings, we meet often, corralled by our ever-voluble spouses and offspring. We love to party. We all miss Dad. We thank God and are grateful that Mum and Dad gave us a good start in life. They made sacrifices so that we could have good lives. I hope we did not disappoint.

The most enjoyable part of my life now is spending time with my wife, Tinao. Her smile never fails to tug at the heartstrings. She is of German-Zimbabwean heritage, a member of the 'sinistrality society,' an English solicitor, as she is always at pains to point out. She works in wealth-management and some tax advisory matters with respect to succession planning and offshore structures. Tinao is possessed of formidable intelligence, disarming beauty and a desirable disposition. Despite her German heritage, the spirit of persiflage and gracious repartee flows in her veins. While nature was not particularly sparing with its gifts to her physically, it was extravagant mentally in its generosity.

I eschewed co-habitation for a decade but eventually succumbed, thus ending an adventurous, episodic life of fleeting liaisons, consigning most of them into the realm of null and void "textlationships", at best. We are friends in love with each other first and foremost. We are married, have clients in common and share a love and passion for travel, good wine and French-Italian cuisine.

Our families have always been close. Sometimes I feel like we are in an arranged marriage, a feast for green eyes. We enjoy travelling together. We did our best to institute a 'family breeding programme,' to have children of our own and justify our existence on earth. However, after losing the first one prematurely, we were devastated. We then agreed that we had done our bit. We have since abandoned that programme. We are more than happy now to enjoy our time together, just us. It may sound weird but somehow, that is how we like it.

I try to describe our relationship without disparaging it or insulting it with the tawdry decoration of sentimentality. It is a delicate balance of dependence and independence, coolly critical but loving contact. At our first meeting, our eyes encountered, I recall. She looked at me with quiet attention for a moment, I imagined romantically, with obscure, deep-lying recognition. In my fever of amorous loneliness, I recognized my destiny. Our union seemed predestinate, yet quite fortuitous! Now, as a long-married couple, we fit rather neatly, like two close trees whose trunks have grown upwards together as a single shaft, mutually distorting but mutually supporting. Overall, sensible companions. We leave each other a certain freedom so we can enjoy our proximity.

We spent part of our honeymoon enjoying the wine and campestral vistas of Bordeaux. We visited and enjoyed gastronomical delights at the fine restaurants and vineyards in the St. Emilion, Pomerol, Medoc, Haut-Medoc and Grave regions. We took a trip down memory lane to the coastal city of Arcachon, where we feasted on seafood a go go, especially freshly harvested mussels and succulent brill. We love Italy and frequent Rome where we often visit our favourite restaurants. We love Washington D.C. but regard that as work, so we tend to spend our time chilling in Key Biscayne and Jupiter, which is our other home. We enjoy Jupiter, where we love to watch the common grackles, blue jays, starlings, great egrets, herons and other birdlife feed on the lawns and waterways at the bottom of the garden during our time off from shopping, sight-seeing, eating out, fishing or enjoying sundowners at Juno Beach.

Our shared love for culinary delights has made ours one of the most sybaritic tables I know. It has been referred to, by none other than Chef Mike Norrie, an omphalos in the cult of gastronomy, or something to that effect. We also love to eat at our favourite restaurants. One day, while feasting heartily on Cuban gastronomical delights, in foison, at the Copacabana Restaurant downtown Abacoa, near Jupiter, I suddenly felt the alarming discomfort of a fishbone embedded deep in my throat. I was devouring a whole, fried red snapper at the time.

Efforts to dislodge the offending item, including gulping down large amounts of mojitos and swallowing half a lime, were in vain. Tinao then had the presence of mind to threaten to thump me on the chest and back as a solution. At the thought, I heaved a hefty cough which dislodged and expelled two sharp fishbones from my throat. They both landed on her lap. Without batting an eyelid, she refocused on her well hung, perfectly saignant rib of beef. The speakers in the restaurant continued to belt out light, tripping, Chan Chan Cuban melodies, oblivious of my plight. After a round of post-prandial drinks, mostly Cuban rum, we packed the rest of our food and left the restaurant for home.

Increasing visits to Kyoto, in Palm Beach Gardens, have revealed many new favourites, Boucheron and café des Artistes, The Dive bar, Waterway Café and Carmine serving excellent international cuisine are the hot picks.

The U.K., however, has always been the heartfelt home where we have many friends. We do not manage to spend much time there in the less hibernal times or when the weather is good but enjoy our little 'hideout' in Kensington and the delightful Mayfair environs.

We still spend time on Lake Kariba where we have had memorable times including watching a stand-off between two young bull elephants and a pride of white lions deep in the forest on the shores of the lake. The elephants won. We have had excellent fishing trips on Kariba. The Matusadona hills draped in effulgent sunset colours are memorable. Overhead, we have watched the young moon, a curve of incandescent wire. The milky way, a vague hoop of light appearing to encircle the universe. From horizon to horizon, the sky was an unbroken spread of stars. We gazed in awe as a shooting star blazed across the sky and disappeared in the bush, on the far side of the lake. Planets stared, unwinking. The more unobtrusive of the constellations asserted their individuality. I pointed out to Tinao, Orion's foursquare shoulders and feet, his belt and sword, the Plough, the zigzag of Cassiopeia, the intimate Pleiades, all duly patterned on the night sky.

We have been fishing and guddling on the Missouri. In the icy winter of North Dakota, we have watched the wind churn up the lake's surface and droplets freeze into frazil. However, nothing beats Kariba. Victoria Falls has been an enjoyable destination, including hiring the Booze Cruise twice, once with family and then just the two of us. We enjoy being by ourselves, left to our own shenanigans.

Occasionally we meet friends for social events. We work from home in separate study and work areas at each end of a long corridor. A music room separates us.

I enjoy playing tunes for her on my guitar, now my vade mecum. This is despite her constant protestations that my verses, as I wax lyrical in my efforts to please my Regina with song, are hardly melic and sometimes border on lese majesty. To add to my collection of instruments, she bought me a beautiful Horner harmonica and a tenor saxophone for my birthday. I frequently blow blasts of corybantic or sentimental chords on it, much to her amazement. We meet in the bar or on the patio overlooking the swimming pool after work.

I often watch the Heiligenschein on the just sprinkled lawn as she walks across it in the setting sun, to stroke her favourite dog. Peace at last! The days of languishing in 'Chateau Bow wow' seem to be over. A quiet night in our tastefully emulous home watching a cooking programme or murder movie, something a lot of my friends' dread, is a welcome respite for us both after our hectic days when we hardly see each other. She has redecorated our house to transcend its less favourable, cottage core ancient location to magnify its beauty through classical restraint rather than ostentatious display. Between us, we have a wealth of experience in banking and finance spanning over fifty years.

Along the journey, I have had to deal with the undesirable consequences of success and a high profile. Baseless allegations, malicious innuendo, deliberate smear campaigns and brabble that are commonplace around high-profile beings have visited me also. Most, if not all of these have emanated from the Zimbabwean media. Curiously, they all coincide with landmark events and milestones in my life's journey. I have never bothered to dignify any of them with a response since they have been apocryphal and anonymous. This has given me an appreciation of the expression, 'fake news.' I conduct myself with decorum as well as maintain and guard

my honour and integrity with assiduity. In times of trial, I have remained firm in faith and stayed faithful to what matters.

Now in the throes of middle age, I look back with astonishment,
gratitude and wonder at how much I have enjoyed a healthy existence, a happy life despite a couple of poor choices and one
particularly ill-judged, dismal, dreadfully dysfunctional, mercifully
relatively short-lived relationship. It was a monumental matrimonial
fiasco: the person I could only be 10% of the time was wanted 100%
of the time. I found myself increasingly excited the further apart we
were physically. The flame of imagined love fanned by unrealistic,
delusional expectations was, expectedly, gradually reduced to an occasional smoldering warmth which could not even be mistaken for
mere lust. The result was a bitterness and rage which dethroned,
decisively, any lingering stirrings of decency in one towards the other.
It could not have been worse. Now I count my blessings as I savour
the benefits of life away from 'Chateau Bow Wow.'

In any case, historically speaking, nature has seemingly instilled
in me a specific affinity for my spouse. Choosing one's partner is
choosing one's future. Happiness comes from within, not from
people. If one is not happy single, one would not necessarily be
happy taken. We learn the hard way. Nan once told me, "A good
heart will always be happy." I discovered, however, that a good heart
is prone to being hurt badly because it expects good things from
others all the time.

Notwithstanding the nimiety of accolades that I have received
as a phenomenally endowed memorist with retentiveness so acute
that I am still able to recall details of events, phone numbers, names
and faces readily without reference or prompting, I have not tried
to gussy up my story. I have maintained a shard of truth throughout.
Despite this eidetic memory phenomenon, I have not tried to account for every bit of experience, encounter, gewgaw and kerchief
of my existence nor have I slyly elided sections of my life. For the
benefit of the reader, this is a memoir. I have therefore selected sa-

lient times and moments that mean much to me. In this exercise, my foibles aside, I have been reminded, oftentimes, of how esprits de l'escalier, particularly for a writer, seems to be a recurrent experience. I enjoy the vividness that in my mature age, I find in childhood memories.

Writing these memoirs has made me appreciate how powerful memory is. Hardships, life experiences, successes and failures, make up a life fully lived...my life. The factual part of my memories focused on details such as individuals, names, locations and events. There is, however, an abstract adjunct to this: how I felt when and why? What was my motivation? Is it a good memory or one I want to forget? Mercifully, my dearest memories are of those moments I spent with my parents, my spouse, siblings and much-loved friends.

I am surprised at how I continue to touch some lives. I always wanted to be in funemployment by now, but I am still enjoying my episcopal ministry away from the arms race of running a diocese. I enjoy banking assignments and consultancy engagements the world over. I shall forever cherish my role in setting off a cascade of salutary innovations and entrepreneurial endeavours in Zimbabwe's financial sector. I have played golf over many years. I enjoy playing at PGA, in West Palm Beach, among other courses. I was quite good at it once upon a time. I have often thought I can make a come-back and play seriously again one day. Time will tell.

Chapter Thirty-Three

I HAVE WRITTEN PARTS of this book in hotel rooms, on airplanes, a yacht, offices in London and Washington D.C. and Florida. Inspiration came in phases as that prefatory feeling of 'tickly well- being' gradually yielded it's secret, opened a window and the wind continues to blow in. I have relied on notes and diary entries from way back when. I write the closing lines, hopefully my facetiae, in the same study in the same house, overlooking the same garden, rottweiler kennels and birdbaths. Here, denizen flocks of colourful birds including tits, babblers, robins, crested grey and purple louries and wood hoopoes jink across the lawn.

The birds call out as if to express their joyance at the dawn of yet another glorious day as they head for the skillfully constructed bird tables nestled on erumpent patches of green on rich red soils. Occasionally, the resident miniature avian battleship, a sparrow hawk, darts across the lawn in the pursuit of lethality. I have witnessed him feasting on a turtle dove twice his size. Unlike our gardener, a master of pleonasm, prone to using a hundred words where ten will do, the birds evince no symptoms of anthophobia as they go about their business.

This is the space that has been my personal and private Athenaeum since I moved to Harare from London, to establish NMB Bank. In 2010, I was the guest of honour and gave the keynote address at the bank's rhapsodic vigesimal celebrations. This is the house whence I have sallied forth, with aplomb, on many missions, some mischief, naught and adventures. Since I discovered that 'vegetarian' and 'vegan' are ancient derogatory terms for idiots who could not hunt or fish, I now enjoy seafood prepared on a special woodstove at the back of the house. A 'runner' supplies us fish from Mozambique whenever we need it, otherwise we import stocks or carry it in our luggage, mostly from London. I have not eaten beef or chicken or any other animal meat products in over forty years.

My life is still unfolding. So far, I have not received a handsel for this stage of it. I look forward to the day that my peacherino co-viator, Tinao and I will tootle off and sublimate into the sunset to enjoy our life in retirement. Not entirely on the hedonic treadmill, I hasten to add, remembering our avocations, but in haimish environs. We need to move far away from the economic woes of Zimbabwe which constantly fill us with the mulligrubs as we stodge along through the mire and vicissitudes of existence marked by snaking fuel queues, unemployed folks begging on the streets, high inflation and pothole-filled roads. I have not heeded calls to join the political fray in any capacity. We watch and follow the fortunes of the post-Mugabe administration, 'The new dispensation,' with wonder and amazement at the dimensions and concatenation of incompetence, misrule and corruption.

I have heard folks call for and yearn for 'the good old days of colonial and even apartheid government' as they seek to survive and earn a crust in turbulent economic times. I do not take these calls at face value: these are not calls for the bondage and brutality of those days of colonization. They are pleas, shrill critiques of the failures of governments born out of liberation movements; 'cries of dereliction' coming from the crosses they bear. These are desperate attempts to raise a shaming mirror to those in power to do better than the oppressive regimes of the past.

It is a way of putting pressure on all our leaders to distinguish themselves from those dark days by delivering substantive liberation and true freedom to their people. This can be achieved by ensuring the rule of law, respecting human and property rights and desisting from corrupt practices. In their simplicity, these cries are a sophisticated combination of indictment, challenge and encouragement.

I am tempted but happy to temporize, for now, as I append my John Hancock to the script. I believe that an exercise in omphaloskepsis will buy no Cristal nor Dom Perignon for sundowners nor brioches for breakfast. Some future Easter eggs sit in their reserved baskets. Totients. Champers on ice beckons in the bar next door. I need a break from the post Brexit debates and the horribly sad news of the devastation caused by cyclones Idai, Anna and Batsirai in Manicaland and Sofala Province of Mozambique, the port of Beira in particular, not to mention the inferno that consumed the Notre Dame Cathedral in Paris recently and hurricane Ian poised and threatening to pounce on West Palm Beach and the whole U.S. South-Eastern Seabord.

We did catch a flight to bombinate over Africa on one of the last scheduled flights out of Southern Africa at the outset of the corona COVID-19 virus global pandemic in late March 2020. Our work, life and travel plans were savagely disrupted. We languished in lockdown in the U.K. We rented accommodation in Kensington, Richmond, West Byfleet and Gloucester Road for three months. We almost went berserk at times. It was sometimes so awful we even wished we were back in Zimbabwe despite all the tales of woe from there. We were rather grateful that the protests across the U.S.A following the brutal murder of an unarmed black man, George Floyd by police details in Minneapolis happened before we got there. They showed how woke black communities in general are.

On the bright side, this has been a time and opportunity for rest, prayer, reflection and soul-searching in our incredibly haimish abodes. The impact of the global COVID-19 pandemic and the consequent economic lockdown have been brutal on the poorest in our societies. The bluster and gasconade of fear mongers have added to the confusion. We have been vaccinated thrice against the virus, however, the Omicron COVID variant has taken the world by storm and thrives while the Delta variant remains stubbornly pervasive. Ironically, as the Russians, at Putin's command, invade the Ukraine, most countries worldwide have announced the end of all COVID restrictions. We gasp and exhale simultaneously.

The world-wide marches following George Floyd's murder, are a sad reminder to us all that justice waited for is justice denied, thus highlighting the need for us to recognize each other's humanity. The global outpouring of grief and anger about injustice and racial violence, however, shows us a world whose imagination may not have grown more selfish and individualistic despite reports to the contrary, in the media. The guilty verdict against the despicable former police detail was a welcome change, in the nature of things. It has been a time to discover who one's true friends are. More than anything, the pandemic has shown how quickly things can change if they must. Carpe diem.

At last count, I had read many books in lockdown and am still fascinated by the macaronic nature of the English language. I listened to, at least, thirty-six hours of music, in this period. Thanks to my friend, Patrick Smith, I have had the pleasure of playing a few rounds of golf at the majestic Buckinghamshire Golf Club. With masks handy, life goes on and time passes. This is the new way to live and work. It is an unexpected cultural shock. We embrace it and move on as encouraging vaccine news is announced daily as the virus takes its toll. Hopefully, Donald Trump will see the light and move on too! Signs are that he will go kicking and screaming. Eventually, he did! Sort of...

My life and my thinking keep evolving. I take the view that unless the buffalo tells it's own life story, it will only be heard from the hunters' perspective. Closure is not yet an option for me. I aspire to inspire before I expire. This stage may be regarded as an endpoint of a part of my life's journey, but it should be, for me, my friends, fans and readers, a springboard to new thoughts and a bridge to new conversations. We are faced with complexities such as the coronavirus pandemic, ever more subtle racism, climate change, corruption and polarisation in politics, the church and world economic constituencies.

There is much disorientation around us in these unusual times we live in. One of the symptoms of extreme hypothermia is the urge to remove all one's clothes, even in a blizzard. Panic is a truly faithless and fruitless response to the challenges confronting us. Faced with these evolving threats to our survival, I think that faith, persistent experimentation, humility, rethinking, doubt and curiosity may, among others, offer us hope.

While writing this final chapter, I heard the news of Queen Elizabeth II's death. This was followed by the passing of The Holy Father Emeritus, Pope Benedict XVI and Pele. We all knew that they would die at some point, but the news still came as a shock to us. Listening to glowing tributes and messages of condolence from all over the world, I wondered what my descendants would possibly wish I had done better for them. I have thought long and hard about the Apache saying that "We do not inherit land from our ancestors; we borrow it from our children." Not only our own children, but all children and their descendants will judge us from the future. I see my legacy not as some material articles, chattels, that I will leave behind when I exit this world. At the heart of it will be how I have lived my life and carried myself in my lifetime, my daily routine and practice, the example I set, as opposed to a bequest expressed in a written will or wishes.

My legacy will be grown in my wife, wider family, friendships, siblings, as a parent, banker, priest, bishop, a responsible citizen, a co-worker, entrepreneur, a responsible member of the human community mindful of the consequences of my actions on others now and on future generations. I am inspired by all those before me, who chose this path. They include my parents, Martin Luther King Junior, Desmond Tutu, Trevor Huddleston, Wangari Maathai, Greta Thunberg, Nelson Mandela, among others. Care for the environment and education for deprived youths, especially orphans, have been among my passion and will continue to be. I am always mindful of whose son I am. I refuse to be ordinary. I enjoy the serenity of travelling alone sometimes and strive to be humble yet confident.

It is irresponsible to assume that our children and their descendants will be able to reverse, easily, the cataclysmic events such as ecological devastation, the demise of sylvan communities in Africa, Asia and South America, species extinction, gravitational collapse, climate change, polar iceberg melts or the rampant spread of genetically engineered viruses that our generation has unleashed on our world and bequeathed to them and their descendants.

David Korten's concept of an 'ecological civilization,' one that 'secures material sufficiency and spiritual abundance for all in balance with the regenerative systems of a living Earth,' has appeal for me. The spectre described vividly by Olaf Stapledon in his prophetic, 1937 sci-fi novel, 'Starmaker,' looms real: by fiddling distractedly and not caring about the environment, we run the risk of becoming yet another lost civilization to be discovered in the rock strata by the geologists of tomorrow. Record warm summer temperatures across Europe and America and unusually low winter temperatures across Southern Africa may be a prelude to major climate change in future.

What I have written is an acceptance of my existence with ownership but no apologies. In the words of my favourite hymn at Compline, "Before the ending of the day, Creator of the world I pray..." It is now the end of the day. I sit on my bed, quietly, so as not to disturb Tinao. She purrs gently in her sleep. I lift my feet off the floor, turn off the bedside lamp and wish you good night.